"Congar's *True and False Reform in the Church*, although now six decades old, is perhaps even more relevant for the life of the church today than it was when he first penned it. This volume reflects the singular virtues of Congar, his fidelity to the Great Tradition, his generous ecumenical spirit, and his commitment to authentic ecclesial reform as a manifestation of the work of the Holy Spirit. This elegant yet precise translation by Paul Philibert makes widely accessible what is, perhaps, Congar's most important work."

— Richard R. Gaillardetz, PhD
Murray/Bacik Professor of Catholic Studies
The University of Toledo

"Yves Congar's book, first published in 1950, gave Roman Catholics permission to view the Protestant Reformers positively and to speak of Reform in their own church. Today, after fifty years of post-conciliar renewal and recent years of scandals and repression, this book still offers a theology of authenticity, holiness, and honesty in the church. Its pages hold insights on how the Christian community can pass beyond introverted structures to ecclesial forms of life and ministry."

— Thomas F. O'Meara, OP
Warren Professor Emeritus
University of Notre Dame

"I warmly welcome Paul Philibert's excellent translation of Yves Congar's *True and False Reform in the Church* (1950). The publication in English of one of the great Catholic books of the twentieth century will be of benefit to church leaders, theologians, philosophers, and to all who work for justice and reconciliation in the world. Renewed consideration of Congar's timeless principles for true reform should provide the Christian churches with new possibilities for regeneration at a critical moment in the history of Christianity. Essentially what Congar proposes in *True and False Reform in the Church* is a renewal of vision that would effect a fundamental transformation of the pastoral life of the church. This work should be essential reading in systematic, pastoral, moral, and historical theology modules at undergraduate and graduate levels. Paul Philibert and Liturgical Press are deserving of the highest praise for this timely publication."

— Gabriel Flynn
Mater Dei Institute, Dublin City University
Dublin, Ireland

"Vatican Council II, in the Decree on Ecumenism, proclaimed that Christ summons the church to perennial reformation, a task that demands learning and wisdom. To accomplish it we have no better guide than Congar's *True and False Reform in the Church*—the study that inspired the efforts of Vatican Council II for true reform. Paul Philibert's translation from the French is both fresh and faithful."

— Ladislas Orsy, SJ
Professor of Law at Georgetown University
Author of *Receiving the Council* (Liturgical Press, 2009)

Yves Congar, O.P.

TRUE AND FALSE REFORM IN THE CHURCH

Translated and
with an Introduction by
Paul Philibert, O.P.

A Michael Glazier Book

LITURGICAL PRESS
Collegeville, Minnesota

www.litpress.org

over the opening of the Second Vatican Council which he had convened. In his opening address at the council, he described its goals in terms highly evocative of Congar's description of authentic reform. Pope John called the council not to reform heresy, not to denounce errors, but to update the church's capacity to explain itself to the world and to revitalize ecclesial life at the periphery and to open the doors to ecumenical conversation. For us today, this book fills in the blanks of what we have been missing in receiving the council and its call to "true reform."

Congar's own life, however, is an incredible witness to the very principles that he lays down in this book. In 1954, in part because of Vatican reaction to this book, he was sent into exile from his home, his books, his colleagues, and his friends in Paris. He suffered genuine anguish because of the interruption of his intense theological work and because of the injury to his freedom and his reputation. Eventually, however, Congar was vindicated by Pope John. He was one of the first theologians to be appointed by the pope to the council's preparatory theological commission.

It remains to future historians to trace the exact influence of Congar's *True and False Reform* upon John in advancing the idea of a council. But it is already clear, as Avery Dulles put it, that "Congar's ecumenical ecclesiology permeates the Dogmatic Constitution on the Church, *Lumen Gentium*, and the Decree on Ecumenism, *Unitatis Redintegratio*."[5] Despite repeated suffering from Vatican measures against him, Congar always considered the church's well-being the important issue in his life. In one of the last interviews he gave, Congar remarked: "While for a time I was suspect and criticized in Rome, in the same way I became recognized as an important theologian who during the Council was active as an expert in five commissions and was subsequently for fifteen years a member of the International Theological Commission."[6] Much later, Pope John Paul II created him a cardinal some months before his death, in recognition of his contributions to the council.

What did not become integrated into the council's documents, however, is precisely what is found in this book. Its message is sorely needed for a church divided not only over the value of the council for the present and the future but also over the meaning of the church. As you will

[5] Flynn, op. cit., 28.
[6] From Frano Prcela, O.P., "Pioneer of Church Renewal: Yves Congar (1904–1995)," trans. Thomas O'Meara, *Wort und Antwort* 36:3 (1995), pp. 130–133.

Yves Congar, O.P.

TRUE AND FALSE REFORM IN THE CHURCH

Translated and
with an Introduction by
Paul Philibert, O.P.

A Michael Glazier Book

LITURGICAL PRESS
Collegeville, Minnesota

www.litpress.org

A Michael Glazier Book published by Liturgical Press

Cover design by David Manahan, OSB. Photo courtesy of PhotoSpin.com.

A translation of *Vraie et fausse réforme dans l'Église*, revised edition. © 1968 by Les Éditions du Cerf (Paris).

2	3	4	5	6	7	8	9

Library of Congress Cataloging-in-Publication Data

Congar, Yves, 1904–1995.
    [Vrai et fausse réforme dan l'Église. English]
    True and false reform in the church / Yves Congar ; translated and with an introduction by Paul Philibert. — Rev. ed.
      p. cm.
    "A Michael Glazier book."
    Includes indexes.
    ISBN 978-0-8146-5693-8 — ISBN 978-0-8146-8009-4 (e-book)
     1. Church renewal—Catholic Church.   I. Title.
 BX1746.C6313 2011
 262'.02—dc22

                                                    2010031330

Contents

PART TWO
Conditions for Authentic Reform Without Schism

PART THREE
The Reformation and Protestantism
[omitted in this translation]

CONCLUSION
Perspectives on the Attitude to Take toward
Concrete Reform Initiatives

Translator's Introduction

You are about to explore one of the transformative masterpieces of twentieth-century theology. Cardinal Avery Dulles once called Congar's *True and False Reform in the Church* "a great work [that lays] down principles for authentic Catholic reform."[1] Many others have pointed out its importance: Gabriel Flynn calls it "arguably Congar's most important and original contribution to Christian theology,"[2] while Jean-Pierre Jossua has said in several places that this is Congar's most personal and most powerful book.[3] It is also a book that is, in my view, more potent today than at the time of its original publication in 1950, when it was badly misunderstood. Not long after its publication, the Holy Office forbade its reprinting or translation into other languages; yet less than twenty years later most of its insights had found their way into the major documents of Vatican II. Congar himself once remarked, "If there is a theology of Congar, that is where it is to be found."[4] Following Vatican II, Congar released a second and revised edition of *True and False Reform* in 1968. It is that edition that has been translated here.

It is clear that Archbishop Angelo Roncalli (later to become Pope John XXIII) discovered and read *True and False Reform* during his years as papal nuncio in France. He asked in response to reading it, "A reform of the church: is such a thing really possible?" A decade later, he presided

---

[1] Avery Cardinal Dulles, "Preface," in Gabriel Flynn, ed., *Yves Congar: Theologian of the Church* (Louvain, Paris, and Dudley, MA: Peeters, 2005), p. 28.

[2] Flynn, op. cit., p. 9.

[3] Jean-Pierre Jossua, *Le Père Congar: La Théologie au service du people de Dieu* (Paris: Les Editions du Cerf, 1967), 30–31; also, Flynn, op. cit., p. 133, n. 113.

[4] Yves Congar, "Letter from Father Yves Congar, O.P.," trans. R. J. Zawilla, *Theology Digest* 32 (1985): p. 215; cited in Flynn, op. cit., p. 101.

over the opening of the Second Vatican Council which he had convened. In his opening address at the council, he described its goals in terms highly evocative of Congar's description of authentic reform. Pope John called the council not to reform heresy, not to denounce errors, but to update the church's capacity to explain itself to the world and to revitalize ecclesial life at the periphery and to open the doors to ecumenical conversation. For us today, this book fills in the blanks of what we have been missing in receiving the council and its call to "true reform."

Congar's own life, however, is an incredible witness to the very principles that he lays down in this book. In 1954, in part because of Vatican reaction to this book, he was sent into exile from his home, his books, his colleagues, and his friends in Paris. He suffered genuine anguish because of the interruption of his intense theological work and because of the injury to his freedom and his reputation. Eventually, however, Congar was vindicated by Pope John. He was one of the first theologians to be appointed by the pope to the council's preparatory theological commission.

It remains to future historians to trace the exact influence of Congar's *True and False Reform* upon John in advancing the idea of a council. But it is already clear, as Avery Dulles put it, that "Congar's ecumenical ecclesiology permeates the Dogmatic Constitution on the Church, *Lumen Gentium*, and the Decree on Ecumenism, *Unitatis Redintegratio*."[5] Despite repeated suffering from Vatican measures against him, Congar always considered the church's well-being the important issue in his life. In one of the last interviews he gave, Congar remarked: "While for a time I was suspect and criticized in Rome, in the same way I became recognized as an important theologian who during the Council was active as an expert in five commissions and was subsequently for fifteen years a member of the International Theological Commission."[6] Much later, Pope John Paul II created him a cardinal some months before his death, in recognition of his contributions to the council.

What did not become integrated into the council's documents, however, is precisely what is found in this book. Its message is sorely needed for a church divided not only over the value of the council for the present and the future but also over the meaning of the church. As you will

---

[5] Flynn, op. cit., 28.

[6] From Frano Prcela, O.P., "Pioneer of Church Renewal: Yves Congar (1904–1995)," trans. Thomas O'Meara, *Wort und Antwort* 36:3 (1995), pp. 130–133.

discover, Congar was at pains to clarify the equally necessary roles of the *center* (hierarchical leadership) and the *periphery* (local churches with their prophets, their people, and their pastoral geniuses). He draws upon an astonishing array of historical examples not only to clarify his meaning but also to demonstrate how the church dealt with specific challenges in the past. Church leaders will find here what Avery Dulles calls "the dialectic between structure and life in the church"; pastors will find a penetrating challenge to understand their ecclesial mission as essentially prophetic; and laity yearning for a church more in tune with their own experiences as Christians in the world will find both encouragement and light for their roles. Ecumenists will receive important direction from a theologian who believed that the catholicity of the church needs to be enriched by the cultural and theological genius of Greeks and Russians, Scandinavians and British, indeed, all the rich diversity of the various peoples of the earth.

It is remarkable, then, to discover that the vision, the theological principles, and the arguments for effective catholicity and unity that suffuse Congar's writing from half a century ago ring so true to the cultural and pastoral situation of today. In many ways, despite changed circumstances, the restlessness of the early twenty-first century Roman Catholic Church mirrors the ferment that Congar described in the church's yearning for renewal following the Second World War in Europe. A great many ordinary Catholics feel that they are not understood or being listened to, priests are facing the problem of a gap between parish life and the spiritual hungers of an increasingly disaffected laity, bishops are facing painful administrative choices in the light of a shortage of ordained pastors, and the Catholic Church as a whole is sliding further away from the innovative and creative elements of the scientific, cultural, and artistic evolution of a globally mediated world.

Maintenance or mission—nostalgia or *aggiornamento*? This question immediately becomes ideologically charged today with the competitive ambitions of traditionalists and progressives. In just such a world, Congar's book is an apology, among other things, for daring to believe in God's promise: "See, I am making all things new" (Rev 21:5). Many Catholics who want to remain Catholic are waiting for just such a deep and authoritative theological analysis of their church in a state of cultural transformation.

In 1950 when Congar wrote the first edition of this book, as now, the tension between the Roman Curia and the renewal initiatives of the prophetic voices in the church was not only palpable but painful. Congar paints the picture of this tension in careful detail. His analysis of the complementary roles of the "center" and the "periphery" contributes lucid insight into what we are experiencing today. Further, his clear defense of the role of the center, the apostolic authority of the Holy See and its responsibility to govern the church for the sake of the church's unity, is fulsome and articulate. This principle was evidently important to him.

However, Congar likewise describes the periphery as having an equally important complementary function of bringing the church's preaching and witness into every culture, adjusting the life and practices of the church to the human dynamics of linguistically, culturally, and historically diverse nations and devising initiatives to bridge the gap between what is familiar and what is urgently needed.

In the service of this understanding of the church, Congar describes what he calls two levels or kinds of "fidelity." While apostolicity means for him that the church will never depart from the deposit of faith that it received from Christ and the apostles, it also means that the apostolic witness simply must come alive in new cultures and that the church is obliged to explain itself in the languages and sensibilities of those cultures. The church will never abandon or distort the divine gift of revealed truth, but in order to express it in a new age the church must be conversant with and articulate in the habits and perspectives of that newness. To cling to formulas that have become outdated and dry for the sake of preserving the past is a kind of fidelity, perhaps. But Congar calls this "flat" or superficial fidelity. It is incapable of entering realistically into dialogue with the very areas of culture that the church has the duty to evangelize.

A full and genuine fidelity requires both a thorough grounding in the sources of the faith and their changing expression through history as well as the courage to address the same faith in terms that can be not only understood but also embraced by our contemporaries. This sort of fidelity requires commitment and resourcefulness. It makes demands upon believers and is far more difficult for the individual to live than a passive acquiescence to what is familiar in the religious world. Here, as so often elsewhere, Congar articulates experiences familiar to us that are elusive to describe, and by naming them he provides a critical analysis that can break through the impasse of hardened ideological opposition.

One of the richest contributions of *True and False Reform* is its profile of the prophetic principle in the church and of those called to be prophets to their age. Prophets are usually found on the periphery and have the burden of challenging the complacency of the center. At the heart of his understanding of prophecy is his conviction that God's word has the power to address the present world. He personally understood the radical nature of the prophet's gift of himself/herself to the demands of that message and the graced instinct that informs it. More than once he was personally crushed by its demands. Yet he is also demanding in insisting that prophets are never dispensed from holding the unity of the church as the Body of Christ and its concrete social communion at the very center of their field of vision. His profile of the traits of genuine prophets, contrasted with other voices that proved not to be authentic, offers both encouragement and critical guidance for those who struggle today to find a way to make themselves heard for the sake of a living church.

I need to explain why the third part of this work has not been included here. Congar himself noted (as you will see in his "Preface to the Second Edition") that in 1967, burdened by bad health and by incessant demands for his collaboration in international conferences and symposia on the council, he was unable to redo his long essay on Protestantism. While the first two parts of *True and False Reform* remain pertinent and necessary, the third part required considerable revision, both because of the extraordinary changes brought about by the documents of the council and because of new books on ecumenism and the work of the bilateral ecumenical commissions. Congar himself noted that, in the light of those influences, he would have written a much more positive assessment of Protestantism than he had done in 1950. An additional reason for not including the third part has to do with the realities of publishing. This already large book would be even larger (and more expensive) with part 3. With the publisher's advice, I decided the best solution is this abridged edition of the work, presenting what is most valid and important for our present pastoral situation.

I am indebted to the members of the Congar Study Group of the Catholic Theological Society of America for inviting me to undertake this translation. They had already attempted a translation of parts of the book, and I have profited from partial drafts of various sections of the book done by Catherine Clifford, Susan Brown, and Joseph Mueller, as well as from the encouragement of other members of the group, especially Mark Ginter. I owe an immense debt of gratitude to Myriam Frebet who, as a native French speaker and someone familiar with the currents in French Catholicism in the post–World War II period, was able to advise me and correct my errors in translation. Her contribution to this project has been inestimable.

With the consent of the editors at Liturgical Press, I have decided to maintain Congar's format for his huge scholarly apparatus. Obviously, the immense richness of this text depends upon the thousands of references to be found in the notes. I have translated into English the majority of Latin and German citations, both in the text and in the notes. I hope this heavy scholarly resource, which will be of genuine value to scholars, will not put off general readers, who should find in the text tremendously rewarding insights for their practical Christian life.

I wish to express my gratitude to the Collegeville Institute at Saint John's University in Minnesota for a year as resident scholar at the institute (2008–2009), where the major portion of this translation work was done. I equally owe gratitude to my provincial, Very Rev. Martin J. Gleeson, O.P., and to my Dominican confreres for giving me the time and freedom to undertake such a time-consuming project. In addition, I wish to thank Liturgical Press, especially Hans Christoffersen, editorial director, for his encouragement in bringing this work to press and Mary Stommes, managing editor, for her careful and invaluable assistance in preparing the manuscript for publication. If this translation helps reinsert Congar's wise and courageous witness into the stream of current Catholic thought and theology, the effort will have been worthwhile.

Paul Philibert, O.P.

Preface to the Second Edition (1967)

This is a second "revised and corrected" edition of a book first published in November 1950. In many ways the first book is dated, not only because of the scholarly resources which it used but also because of the ecclesial and theological climate it evoked and, in a deeper sense, because of the way its concerns were raised. In all these respects the current situation (1967) is not that of the years between 1947 and 1950. With regard to scholarly references, the difficulties are not too serious; they can always be brought up-to-date, and I have tried my best to do that. Differences still remain, however, with respect to the climate within the church today and in the way the central question has been posed.

Between 1947, when the book was first written, and 1950 the church—especially in France—sought to respond pastorally to the actual situation in which it found itself. But some initiatives worried Rome. Pius XII, a great pope, was not fundamentally opposed to change, but he wanted strict control over any change and even wanted all initiatives for change to be his alone. Further, although he put in motion certain reforms within the Catholic Church (e.g., in exegesis and liturgy), he was much more reserved about areas in which Catholics might find themselves in contact with non-Catholics. Finally, with regard to theology, he not only was anxious to retain strict control but also was upset about certain methods that theological research was employing. His encyclical *Humani Generis* is dated August 12, 1950.

I may be wrong, but it seems to me that in 1947–1950 I was doing my theological and pastoral research within the framework and on the basis of traditional church practice. Of course, I wanted to *adapt* my work to the new situations brought to light by pastoral research and experience.

1

But I never questioned the church or its authority. The basic issue was that of adaptations in the apostolate, and the papacy willingly acknowledged the soundness of this principle.[1]

For me, the distinction adopted by Emmanuel Mounier (and, in substance, also by Jacques Maritain) between "Christianity" and the "Christian world" provided an effective intellectual framework within which these hopes for renewal could be acknowledged and dealt with. It was a question of liberating the Gospel from more or less outmoded sociological, pastoral, and liturgical forms so as to give it the best possible chance of success in a world calling for new forms, new expressions, and new structures.

In a few short weeks John XXIII created a new climate in the church, and then came the council.[2] This most significant breakthrough came from on high. All of a sudden, forces for renewal which had scarcely had room to breathe found ways to be expressed. The cautious suggestions for reform mentioned in my text of 1950[3] have been surpassed by far. What is happening right now, insofar as it is positive, is certainly in line with what I had intended, yet it goes a great deal further, well beyond what one could have hoped for in 1950. Liturgical reform is still in full swing, parish and pastoral councils (with lay participation) are being formed, and there is a restoration of what one could call the conciliar life of the church (the Synod of Bishops, episcopal conferences, diocesan synods, etc.). Further, research in the area of religious studies is being

---

[1] Note, for example, these statements of Pius XII, characteristic of a program of adaptation: "The mystical Body of Christ, following the example of the physical members which comprise it, does not live and act in the abstract, outside the constantly changing conditions of time and place. It is not, and can never be, separated from the world which surrounds it. It is always of its century; it goes forward with it day by day, hour by hour, continually adapting its ways of doing things and its attitudes to those of the society in the midst of which it must act" (Pius XII, "Speech at the Anagni Seminary," April 29, 1949, in *Discorsi e Radiomessaggi* XI, p. 50; and R. Rouquette in *Études*, April 1951, p. 68).

[2] I had wondered if John XXIII had ever read *Vraie et fausse réforme*. I got the answer one day from a missionary who willingly told me the following story: In 1952, while he was visiting Archbishop Roncalli at the nunciature in Paris, he found him in the midst of reading this book, in the margins of which he had been writing in pencil (this copy still exists somewhere, no doubt). Archbishop Roncalli said to his visitor, "A reform of the church, is such a thing possible?"

[3] I had intentionally refrained from proposing or even suggesting a concrete program of reforms so as to remain on the level of a theological study (rooted in history) about the nature and conditions of a genuine reform *within* the church.

officially encouraged, as well as research about and the first steps toward a new program for the formation of the clergy, etc. On the whole, despite some unfortunate exceptions, theologians now enjoy the freedom that they need for their research and writing. But more than anything, two great changes already characterize the climate within the church and will continue to do so more and more: an ecclesiology based on the "People of God" and ecumenism.

But I have not yet finished pointing out the consequences of the ecclesiological initiatives of Vatican II. The council transcended a purely "hierarchy-centered" ecclesiology and it denounced legalism (without, of course, proposing ignorance of law!). It gave primacy to an ontology of grace rooted in the sacraments, and primacy as well to baptism with respect to all other roles in the church as a society of persons. The council adopted an apostolic, rather than a primarily ritual, understanding of the priesthood, giving full value to the place of the Word and to catechesis; and it recognized charisms and the variety of ministries in the church, etc.

As for ecumenism, it has become or is on the way to becoming a dimension that touches the church's entire life, even its internal concerns.[4] This change of perspective will entail reinterpretation, opening and broadening out our thinking to a degree that we cannot at present measure. But this link between ecumenism and the spirit of renewal, which I perceived and emphasized from the beginning, is equally apparent now from the other side; renewal is not only required by ecumenism as a sort of prelude, but renewal is also nourished by ecumenism.

Just as the ecclesial climate is new today, so also is our way of posing questions. We now proceed more by addition and deepening than by substituting new data for traditional sources. Our questions are still questions about adaptation, but they have become more radical, not only because they are more difficult, more rigorous, and more urgent, but also because they are posed today in a way that touches the very roots of the church and its faith.

Although we functioned in 1947–1950 on the basis of and within the framework of a solid Catholic structure, today we are intellectually and culturally torn out of a Catholic framework, perhaps even out of a religious framework, and thrown into a world which, by its vitality and its

---

[4] The address of his holiness Paul VI, at the opening of the Synod of Bishops, September 29, 1967, is particularly significant in this regard.

innovation, imposes *its* problems upon us. The study of the history of ecclesiological doctrines which I pursued for thirteen or fourteen years made me realize that one's sense of the church depends, in a decisive way, upon one's sense of the world and of the relationship one sees between church and world.

Here we have the problematic relation between the "two powers" and their characteristic confrontation, which has in large part determined the prevailing concept of "church" as authority and power. The temporal power had to become fully "lay," and the church had to acknowledge that lay character fully for the church to be able to understand itself and define itself purely as "church." Thank heavens, the Catholic Church didn't define itself until Vatican II, after all the often violent confrontations between it and temporal society had been more or less put to rest. Furthermore, in defining itself, the church benefited from a retrieval of rich biblical sources as they reemerged formally and frankly for the first time since the Middle Ages. In the end, the church has adopted a new way of understanding the temporal order in keeping with the real situation of the world.[5]

There is no longer really a question of "two powers." Certain questions are still posed in those terms, but they are decidedly of little and perhaps narrow concern when one considers what "the temporal" represents today for the consciousness of Christians. At issue now is the question of how to grasp the world and its history in their full dimensions, their full significance, with all their dynamism and all their problems. Temporality has to do with the determination of Christians to exercise their responsibilities in building up the world with a view toward the kingdom of God.

You don't need to go as far as inferring that an interest in the world represents a betrayal of the faith (as did Maritain in *The Peasant of the Garonne*) in order to recognize that our period in history can be characterized by a genuine discovery of the world by Christians. This discovery is accompanied by a shock of awareness, grasped often only in general terms, that Christians have new responsibilities for the world. In making

---

[5] On this point, see G. Martelet, "L'Eglise et le temporel: Vers une nouvelle conception," in *L'Eglise de Vatican II*, published under the direction of G. Barauna (*Unam Sanctam* 51b), 1966; also Y. M.-J. Congar, "Eglise et monde dans la perspective de Vatican II," in *L'Eglise dans le monde de ce temps* (*Unam Sanctam* 65b), 1967. See also the lecture by B. Lambert, given on June 7, 1967, at the Exposition in Montreal (*Doc. Catholique*, 1967, col. 1401–1455).

such a transition, what pertains to the world may feel as though it has an importance, an immediacy and a relevance that outweigh the claims of the faith and the affairs of the church. While wanting to remain faithful Christians, we nonetheless find that the world, not the church, sets the agenda. The world poses challenging questions with respect to the faith's claims and goals.

These questions are those that were fundamentally brought up already in the eighteenth century, but they arise today among a greater number of persons and with more intense feeling. For all practical purposes the facts of science, of technology, and of a purely rational and humanistic social organization remove the God-question from the horizon for whole segments of the population today, without any need for discussion. Everywhere we find ourselves tempted not only to leave behind claims that feel too objective and naive but also to give up the ground of ontological claims about religious truths and spiritual realities in order to lead everything back to the one question of the meaning and fulfillment of humanity.

From that perspective it is no longer simply a matter of adapting Catholicism and the church to a modern society born outside the cultural influence of Catholicism. We also need to rethink and reformulate what we mean by Christian reality, in response to the claim that now nothing else exists but a world where human beings are the center and master of everything. Today's problems are radical in a different way. The difference between the situation of 1947–1950 and that of 1967–1968 is expressed rather well by the difference between the titles given by the journal *Esprit* to its August–September 1946 issue (*Monde chrétien, Monde moderne—Christian World, Modern World*) and its October 1967 issue (*Nouveau Monde et Parole de Dieu—The New World and God's Word*). The issues raised, even by Christians, go a lot further than previously, and so more is required to provide answers.

These issues require that the council's *aggiornamento* not stop with adaptations inside the church but go further to insist on the church's complete return to the Gospel, and to its finding a new way of being, of speaking, and of commitment *which correspond to the Gospel's wholehearted service to the world*. The *pastoral* aspect of *aggiornamento* has to go that far. Today that is what must be done to reach people, because they are no longer waiting in some neutral, empty space where the clerical church can find them. Rather, they are involved full time and energetically in the activities of this world. We have to meet them there in the name of Jesus Christ.

Sometimes people imprudently call everything into question without sufficient background and without submitting their ideas to critical reflection or taking stock of the implications and consequences. I would not describe the current situation with the same optimism that I had used to describe the reformist thrust of the immediate postwar period. This is not because I have become pessimistic but because certain approaches and even certain situations today are troubling. I am still confident about the final outcome but also conscious that for some, on certain points, we are now in a critical moment. I would have to rewrite certain parts of the book differently today to take all this into account.

So, then, why this new edition? Is it still worth reading?

If I didn't think that it was still useful, I wouldn't have republished it. In that case, this book would have had value only as testimony to the past. But for me it represents something more, despite its limitations and its imperfections. First of all, it expresses a certain mentality, a way of approaching the reality of the church. Furthermore, it is an attempt to study that reality *theologically* in one of the dimensions of its *history* or of its real *life*. This requires a method, which I will have to explain, that integrates history and theological reflection. Finally, this book concerns an area of *theology*: that is why, to the extent that this theological method succeeds, it achieves something of permanent value. The dynamics governing reform in the church and the conditions for a reform without schism uncovered here seem to me to deal with the question at a "formal" enough level to remain applicable at the present time, even though it is different from the less difficult situation of 1947–1950.

Nevertheless, some updating and some corrections were required. I have not been able to alter things to the point of writing a new book. That would have been necessary if I wanted to deal with the new postconciliar situation as such. Sadly, that was a practical impossibility for me. I have only been able to amplify certain suggestions that I made in the 1950 text, to nuance certain expressions, and to correct things that might be misunderstood. However, even the censors from the years 1950–1954 acknowledged that a statement from one section that might have displeased them was completed, balanced, explained, or rectified three or four lines later. I removed the 18 pages of appendix 3, "The

Mindset of the Right and Integral Catholicism." This constitutes on my part neither a change of heart nor a retraction; it is just a fraternal gesture inspired by my desire to contribute to the peace and mutual understanding among the Catholics of France, something much to be desired.

I have felt the greatest hesitation about the third part of the book.* On the one hand, I think that any theological examination of the conditions for authentic reform needs to be adequately treated. Further, on the basis of substantial documentation, I offer considerations which still have value in my view. Yet from another perspective, many things in those 180 pages no longer satisfy me because they correspond neither to the level of dialogue reached today by the ecumenical movement nor to the ecclesiological awareness of postconciliar Catholicism.

While my portrayal of Protestant positions is not false, it is incomplete. It is not sufficiently sympathetic. Some statements are contrasted at the level of opposition between confessional statements, while these signify in Protestantism a positive content much richer than just words.[6] There is even a hint of polemic in the third part. Polemic, however, if it is accurate, loyal, and irenic, can be a form of dialogue. That is how these pages are meant to be read: they articulate genuine questions that have to be put to the Protestant Reformation. I have, nevertheless, nuanced here several stereotypical expressions. Nowadays ecumenical work, and thus Protestant thought to the extent that it has profited from ecumenism, would permit the addition of some further, more positive comments to my presentation. For example, I would speak more positively about the meaning of the church, about the role of the ecclesial community in the reading of the Bible, about Karl Barth's current views, etc. But, in fact, I was unable to rewrite all that . . .

Likewise today I would present somewhat differently certain Catholic views opposed to those of Protestantism, not so as to reject those which I had held before but in order to expand upon and nuance certain points. The ecclesiology that is implicit in this third part is not sufficiently expressive of *Lumen Gentium*'s teaching on the People of God, a people gifted in its entirety with spiritual charisms. In this way too my book shows the years that have passed since the date of its first publication.

Nonetheless, with these present revisions, I think that this new edition will still be useful. People have often requested its reprinting since the

---

* As noted in the translator's introduction, the third part is omitted from this translation.

[6] One example would be what I say about the Word of God in Protestantism.

first edition was sold out! That is my justification for this present edition, which has received due approval from competent authorities, for which I am genuinely grateful.

Y. C.
Strasbourg
Christmas 1967

Foreword

Theologians have only studied the *structure* of the church, so to speak, not its actual *life*. Naturally, the church has a structure deriving from its constitutive elements, but with this structure it *lives*, and the faithful within it live in unity. The church is not just a framework, however, not just a mechanism or an institution; it is a communion. Within it there is a unity which no removal of parts can destroy; the constitutive elements of the church themselves assure us of that. However, there is also the unity made up of living persons. This unity calls their attitudes into question, and its effectiveness can be made or broken by those attitudes. This is the reality of communion. For this reason we can't really know the church unless, over and above the institution and its structure, we study the nature of this communion, its conditions, its implications, and the ways in which it can be injured.

In such a study the investigation of actual instances of reform is necessary because, as we shall see, reform represents an ongoing feature in the life of the church as well as a critical moment for the Catholic communion. I am considering reform here from the perspective of the theologian, the ecclesiologist. Don't look in this book for a reform *program* but only for a study of the place of the phenomenon of reform in the life of the church, of the factors which eventually make reform necessary, and of the conditions under which reform can develop without undermining Catholic communion. Theologians could only give up studying the reality of "reforms" if they were first to abandon investigating the life of the church theologically.

In fact, Catholic theology has devoted little study to the life of the church. It would be easy to show the reasons for that historically. Chapter 2 of my *Lay People in the Church* offers a sketch of the reasons. Further, schism and heresy have been defined only in terms of the elements of unity or of orthodoxy which they lack, that is, from the point of view of the accepted orthodoxy (the *quo*, as scholasticism might put it). We have scarcely sought to characterize them in themselves, by means of their contents, their origins, their variants, or by means of their attitude (the *quod*, one would say, using scholastic terminology). In general, Catholic theology has given little consideration to Christian realities *as experienced by religious subjects*. It has considered the church as an institution with an objective existence—and it certainly is that. But theology has given little consideration to the church as an assembly of faithful people and a community with a life that springs from their activity.

Once again, while theology has considered the church according to its unchangeable essence, it has given little consideration to it as something existing in time. Neither the social interaction of religious subjects nor the conditions of their temporal existence has held much interest for theologians, who have left these topics either to canonists or to spiritual writers, to apologists or to historians. Among theologians of stature who have addressed this particular domain, one is hard pressed to think of anyone but Möhler[1] and Newman, two great minds who were precisely the ones to introduce into theology a consideration both of the religious subject and of historical development. However, the development of my work will show, I think, that the classical theology of the great masters, including first of all St. Thomas Aquinas to whom I owe the foundations of my own thinking, is far from useless for this present interest.

It is indispensable to have such guides, for the area is quite difficult. This is not only because the direction has not been clearly laid out but also because there are so many obstacles along the way. It is always tricky to develop a theology about life. The pitfalls are twofold. The first, which need not be fatal, is due to the fact that it has to deal with cases that are "individual instances," with which, as such, the science of theology would not normally be concerned. In this case, we can grasp some sufficiently representative facts and consider them rather "formally," so as to discover invariables of behavior which might have value as practical norms. The second pitfall, however, could be more perilous. It concerns not only the methodology but also the objects of this kind of theology. In fact, a lot of attempts to create a theology about life have been disappointing. The church itself, by which I mean primarily the teaching church, has felt this dissatisfaction and has expressed it fairly clearly.

---

[1] The titles of great books are often significant. Möhler did not write a treatise on the "unity *of* the church" but an essay on "unity *in* the church."

The two great minds which I mentioned above, although truly Catholic and worthy of our serious attention, both raised many questions. Some critics went so far as to label them "forerunners of Modernism." Even though the injustice of such an insinuation is clear, the fact that the allegation could be made says something significant.

Modernism, by breaking out of the framework of Catholicism, made clear the danger of any reflection on life that is not based upon a pre-existing, well-established theology treating the church's structure. Furthermore, in the case of Modernism, there was something quite different than a mere weakness in theological foundations; there was a perversion, a genuine breaking down of foundations. This at least shows us the direction from which dangers could come. I have indeed learned from that example and will attempt to ground my theology of communion upon a theology of unity, and my study of the character of "reforms" upon a solidly framed ecclesiology. This dogmatic base will, I hope, give balance to the present study in yet another respect.

Putting forward a theology of the *life* of the church, that is, of the church in so far as it is also made up of human beings, risks so focusing upon the church in its human framework, according to the relativity and contingency of its historical dimensions, that its reality as a supernatural mystery might seem diminished. But in fact this mystery must shine through everywhere within what is human, so that the eternal and divine structure of the church can be felt as everywhere present. I hope my treatment has not failed to emphasize this conviction about the importance of mystery.

The Methodology of This Study

These remarks about the object and the character of my work make clear the kind of methodology needed here. A classical theological method would suffice for a study of the church in its structural aspects and simply as an institution, taking a two-step approach involving as full an awareness as possible of the "revealed facts," and as rich and as rigorous as possible an elaboration of those "facts." However, in order to study the church according to its life as a communion, the insights of history as well as those of experience must be integrated along with insights from doctrinal sources.

My work remains theological, but its object, taken from the *life* of the church, makes it necessary to add to the bare theology of the church a consideration of present and historical facts which are also *loci* for theology—*sources* for theological reflection. The classical theology of the church will still be in evidence, although I cannot be asked to say or to defend everything, since that would require the compilation of a whole formal treatise. Nor can I be asked to say or to defend everything in detail about the *facts* to which I refer. I can only choose among them the ones that are most significant and provide documentation that allows a judgment to be made about whether my claims are proven and my interpretation correct.

By employing such a method in theology, there is sometimes a risk of giving the impression that the perspective is too personal: interesting, perhaps, but reflecting the ideas of only one person. However, all theological work represents an element of personal elaboration, unless it has lost contact with personal reflection and become a mere rubric, something akin to the liturgical calendar or the regulations at the post office. But here the link between theological doctrine and the experiences of the church's life is being made through the reflective operations of one person. It is impossible to achieve the same degree or the same kind of objectivity here as in a thesis of classical theology about the Trinity or about Christology. Furthermore, what is involved here is only an *essay*: a genre less dogmatically complete but perhaps fully as necessary as the classic treatises. This is why I employ the first person rather often. This is fitting for ideas that have a solid basis but are the product of an inquiring mind rather than the doctrine of a church or of a school in possession of the truth.

Reassurance about my objectivity will be found, on the one hand, in the quality of the ecclesiology on the basis of which the work is done (and of this, theologians will be the judges) and, on the other hand, in the quality of the historical documentation (and judgment about this falls naturally to historians). At the risk of weighing down the book and having it appear a bit pedantic, I have included a rather large number of footnotes so as to show that my work can claim, as a sort of reassurance, the support of a great number of thinkers as well as the support of the shared experience and agreement I have found in many places. This is a way of remedying the shortcomings of a highly personal thought experiment.

Perhaps others will be dissatisfied with this study because of its subject matter. With the exception of part 3, this book was written in 1946, in that atmosphere of pastoral renewal which the introduction calls to mind. I have wondered myself about the appropriateness of treating such a topic. Might there be a risk, in doing so, of encouraging excesses in the movement of reform, of supporting a kind of discontent or lack of confidence in the church, in its structures or in its hierarchy?

It strikes me, however, that my solidly based conclusions are anything but disloyal. I think that theologians, without going beyond the realm of their competence, need to enlighten priests and faithful on this point as well as on others, that it quite reasonably pertains to theologians to study a fact which is as constant in the life of the church as is the fact of "reform," just as it pertains to historians or sociologists to study the fact of "revolution" in the history of societies.[2]

Sometimes people are frightened by the word "reform" because, unfortunately, history has associated this term with revolutions as such. A sort of curse seems to hang over the word. Admittedly the term is a bit vague and can designate equally well either the simple determination to go back to following one's principles (in this sense, we ought to reform ourselves daily) or the great upheavals that destroy more than they create. We are well aware that there are *inauthentic* reforms. But, all things considered, reform refers only to what is normal and even ordinary. I will make good on this claim when I give a precise explanation of exactly what is involved.

Further, if the question is a delicate one, can't we treat it with delicacy, with seriousness and respect, coherent with a view of the church which is constructive and traditional? Since the question is certainly a real one, can we afford to leave it to those who would treat it superficially and without nuance, in order to avoid bringing up what some may consider an inopportune topic? Is it not better to enlighten those who are concerned about it, to indicate the appropriate constraints, to show them that the church is even greater, more beautiful, and more worthy of their trust and their love when it undertakes its own renewal than when it is imagined to reside in an illusory and artificial heaven of immutability and perfection? "The truth must be told," wrote St. Augustine, "especially when a problem makes it more urgent to tell the truth. Those who can understand, do so. By refraining from telling the truth for fear of harming those who cannot understand, not only do we obscure the truth, but we deliver into error those who might grasp the truth and who could avoid error in that way . . ."[3]

---

[2] This is what Paul Perrier, for example, tried to do in his "Révolution," part of a *Grammaire de l'Histoire*.

[3] "Dicatur ergo verum, maxime ubi aliqua questio ut dicatur impellit; et capiant qui possunt; ne forte cum tacetur propter eos qui capere non possunt, non solum veritate fraudentur, verum etiam falsitate capiantur, qui verum capere, quo caveatur falsitas, possunt . . ." (*De dono perseverantiae*, ch. XVI, n. 40 [PL 45:1017]).

However, we want to keep our distance here from whatever is unhelpful or dangerous. We want to avoid causing or creating bad will. It is best to avoid, even when tempted, a journalistic or media-focused tone. This is why I wanted, first of all, to give a scholarly tone to this study, so that by its literary genre it would belong to the science of theology, not to the popular media. Next, after it was written, I submitted my text to several censors, among whom were a prelate and a bishop. I hereby thank them for the comments which they were kind enough to offer; I took advantage of them. On one important point I modified my language on the basis of their observations, thus correcting, over and above the words, a category of my thought. I published four pieces from the first version,[4] attracting in this way either new critical comments or encouragements, both of which were equally profitable. Finally, I imposed on myself a delay of three years, at the end of which I reviewed the entire text of 1946. I completed it and brought it up to date with works which had not appeared at the time of the initial writing.[5] Most of the time my amplified and reworked reflections, the richer documentation, and later critical exchanges have confirmed my initial positions. Criticism is not always negative; it plays a necessary testing role, as much by confirming as by invalidating positions called into question. It must always be exercised, and exercised freely.

After having been submitted to the judgment of friendly critics, then put to the test of a complete revision, this book is now available for the consideration of all those who want to read it. But above all, and in the spirit of its second part, it is submitted to the judgment of the holy church. I am confident the church will understand that this is not a book of negative criticism but of love and trust—above all, of total love for and absolute trust in the truth. Truth, which each friar preacher has been called to serve with all his might, truth alone can captivate the mind, while at the same time saturating and stimulating it.

---

[4] "Péché et sainteté dans l'Église," in *La Vie intellectuelle*, November 1947, 6–40 ; "Conditions d'un vrai renouvellement," in *Je bâtirai mon Église* = *Jeunesse de l'Église* 8 (1948): 151–164 — "Pourquoi le peuple de Dieu doit-il sans cesse se réformer?" in *Irénikon* (1948): 365–394 — "Culpabilité et responsabilité collectives," in *La Vie intellectuelle*, March–April 1950.

[5] In June and July of 1948, I published the *Esprit* article on *Christianisme et Monde moderne*, etc., before the work of Ida Görres and Papini, *Essor ou déclin de l'Église*, appeared.

The truth can only be served, here as elsewhere, by absolute and total sincerity. By absolute sincerity, I mean without any tinge of subtlety, hidden agendas, or timidity; by total sincerity, I mean honoring the full extent of the truth, according to all its aspects, and thus arriving—not by some artificial addition of "prudence" but by facing facts—at a respect for all that needs to be respected. This spirit of respect for the truth is proud and humble at the same time, a respect which belongs to those who stand up for themselves, yet who are aware of their dependency as servants of the truth. They submit themselves to the accepted order, since order is only another name for the truth.

That is why there is nothing said by *implication* in this book, but only what is loyal, what can be held loyally and understood by any upright and informed person. Cleverness of thought and of style only deceive those who are not worthy of the simple truth, because they are not looking for it in an unconditional manner. By contrast, a completely confident forthrightness is the only attitude conceivable among the children of God who have been given the liberty of Christ (Gal 4:31) and who celebrate forever a passover of sincerity and truth (1 Cor 5:8).

The Plan of the Book

The plan of my book is simple. Between an introduction describing the actual reforms we find in progress today and a conclusion, there are two main parts (to which I decided to add a third*): (1) Why and in what sense does the church unceasingly reform itself? (2) Under what conditions can a reform be authentic and be carried out without schism? (3) The Reformation and Protestantism. I eventually added the appendices to deal with some further developments that seemed to be required, in order to deal in depth with one or another problem raised in the book.

I had not anticipated the third part in the 1946 version. Several of the questions which are treated there were, however, touched upon briefly, particularly in part 2 under the First Condition. But could one treat the theological problem of "reform" without raising the question of the Protestant Reformation, and could one raise that question without being obliged to treat it in a sufficiently thorough manner? I soon found myself involved in substantial new work, begun in my thinking a long time ago. No doubt the present book has thus become notably more weighty.

---

* Omitted in this translation.

However, the subject required that this topic be addressed, and many points touched upon in the preceding chapters can be found better explained and substantiated in part 3. The laity, or even priests, who have no particular interest either in Protestantism or in certain technical theological questions can just skim over this third part and proceed directly from part 2 to the conclusion. The detailed analytical tables will assist them in finding their way around.

May the present work, with all its imperfections, serve the church which is itself the servant of the Lord—although it is also something more as well, since, in truth, it bears the names of Spouse and of Body of Christ. I dedicate this work to my brothers in the priesthood, as a testimony to my ardent and affectionate sympathy for them and to a sincere feeling of profound fraternity in the service of Christ and of his Body. Had he been still living, I would have dedicated this book to his Eminence, Cardinal Suhard—had he deigned to accept it.

Fr. Yves M.-J. Congar
Le Saulchoir

COMMENTS ABOUT VOCABULARY: Especially in the third part of this book [not included in this translation], the words *reform* and *reformation* are used, sometimes with, sometimes without an initial capital. Capitals are used when it is a question of the historical fact of the Protestant reforms of the seventeenth century, except when the adjective "Protestant" is added ("the Protestant reformers"). This is a bit like the way one simply says "the Revolution" to designate the revolution of 1789. This way of employing terms clearly does not prejudice our judgment, which is rather well explained and substantiated in the third part.

Also in the third part, "word of God" is written sometimes with, sometimes without capitals. It will be seen that this way of doing things is required by an appreciation of the ambiguity of that concept which can refer either to an act of God or to an ecclesial reality (biblical text and preaching).

Sometimes the word "reformism" is used. This is admittedly not very elegant, and it risks suggesting the idea of a systematic exaggeration in the direction of "reforms." I understand by it a tendency toward reform, and not so much the movement itself toward reform or the ensemble of activities which reform entails as what precedes these things and provides their context. Reformism thus understood is therefore ambivalent; it could be simply an openness to problems and a desire for improvement or a taste for stirring things up, for criticism, and for novelty. The word, as I have made use of it, does not necessarily imply that latter kind of excess.

Introduction (1950)

I. The Church Is Constantly Reforming Itself

The church has always tried to reform itself. At least since the end of the classical period, when the first great councils, the writings of the Fathers, and the development of a fixed liturgy more or less defined the church's nature, its history has been marked by periods of reform. This fact has struck all the historians, both Catholic and Protestant, who have studied the papacy and the church.[1] Sometimes the reform movement

[1] Here are some examples: J. Haller, *Papsttum und Kirchenreform* . . . (Berlin, 1903), p. 11: "The need for church reform . . . extended over many centuries, and is perhaps as old as the church itself . . ."

F. Mourret, writing in *Apologétique* (Paris, 1937), p. 693: "It is a fact that the church has never ceased to work at reforming itself. All of its saints were, in their own way, reformers. To limit myself to those whose reform activity was evident: St. Benedict called his contemporaries, who were too lax or too attached to external concerns, back to a spirit of prayer; St. Bruno awakened a spirit of recollection for a century that was too restless; the life of St. Francis of Assisi was a preaching of disinterestedness addressed to religious who had lost their primitive fervor; and the life of St. Vincent de Paul, in the midst of a century filled with egoism and worldliness, was a lesson in charity and self-sacrifice.

"Similarly, each council (maybe we could say each papal encyclical) was a work of reform. There were nineteen general or ecumenical councils, convoked to remedy abuses in the universal church, and an incalculable number of national, provincial and diocesan councils. All had as their purpose to reform abuses that had crept into dogma, morality and discipline. In reality, the Catholic Church is in a perpetual state of reform, that is, a perpetual state of trying to restore beliefs and morals to their original purity."

J. Lortz, *Die Reformation als religiöses Anliegen heute* (Trier, 1948), p. 212: "Reform within the church is a never-ending theme of the history of the church." Also, J. Guiraud,

has been the result of religious orders correcting their own failings or returning to a more exact expression of their original inspiration, often with an energy that reinvigorated Christendom as well (cf. St. Benedict of Aniane, Cluny, St. Bernard).[2] At other times the popes undertook a general reform of abuses or addressed moments of crisis (Gregory VII, Innocent III). In lending their energies to reform movements, the popes likewise took the occasion to extend and strengthen papal authority. Sometimes an evangelical spirit, an apostolic "yeast," developed, touching people's hearts, as was the case throughout the twelfth century, finding expression in the mendicant orders of St. Dominic and St. Francis. At other times it was church councils which addressed themselves to needed reforms.

Gregory VII used annual councils in Rome as a tool in his program of reform. As Hauck has noted, with the Lateran Council of 1215, a new type of council comes on the scene.[3] These new councils are councils for Christendom which for four centuries will be concerned with church reform. As Msgr. Durand, the bishop of Mende, makes explicit at the Council of Vienne, this is reform "in the head and in the members." After the failure to bring about serious reform in the fourteenth and fifteenth centuries, followed by the shock of the Protestant Reformation (which

---

Histoire partiale, histoire vraie, 14th ed. (Paris, 1912), vol. II, ch. 13, pp. 288f. Msgr. Keppler, *Ueber wahre und falsche Reform*, 1903, p. 24 (trans. in French by C. Bègue, *Vraie et fausse réforme: Discours de S. G. Msgr. Keppler . . ., 1 Dec. 1902* [Fribourg en Suisse, 1903], p. 24).

   [2] Until their decline at the end of the 18th century, then their restoration in the 19th, reform was a persistent activity of all the religious orders. *Reformatio* is assigned by Jean of Limoges (mid-13th century) as a regular activity of an abbot with respect to his monks, without the word meaning exclusively a purely interior or moral reform (J. Leclerq, "Un opuscule inédit de Jean de Limoges sur l'exemption," *Analecta S. Ord. Cisterc.*, III [1947], pp. 147–154). Jacques de Vitry, an author from the beginning of the 13th century, gave church reform as a characteristic of the Western church by contrast with the Eastern church: "*Singulis autem diebus status occidentalis ecclesiae reformabatur in melius, et illuminabantur per verbum Domini, qui sederant in tenebris et in umbra mortis*" (*Historia occidentalis*, ch. 11 [Douai, 1597], p. 294).

   [3] A. Hauck, "Die Rezeption und Umbildung der algemeinen Synode im Mittelalter," in *Histor. Vierteljahrschrift* X (1907), pp. 465–482. *Reformatio* was indicated as one of the objectives of the councils in almost all of the bulls convoking them. At the end of the 15th and the beginning of the 16th centuries, priests prayed during the sermon that God would come and reform his church: cf. ritual books of Chartres and Autun, cited by P.-M. Gy, *La Maison-Dieu* 30 (1952), p. 131. The link between councils and reform has been brought up often. It is there already in the 5th century. Documentation on this point is so abundant that it could fill up a whole chapter.

covered up the significant Catholic reform initiatives at the beginning of the sixteenth century), the Council of Trent finally achieved a long-awaited reform of the church (at least a partial one). Everybody knows what followed that. (With Vatican II, we are living through a new moment of church reform flowing from that council's initiative and its spirit.)

These are only a few instances in the long history of reforms. I could never completely enumerate the countless partial reforms, reformist texts, or the historical studies dedicated to reform movements in the church.[4] Nonetheless, I can still allude to the many different activities which, without being called reformist, nonetheless actually represented a movement toward reform in the life of the church.

In effect, every active movement within the church represents a movement beyond what went before it and takes its force from a new inquiry into the sources and the enduring energies of the church's life. In that way, every active movement has a certain quality of reform. This is as true of the contemporary period as of any other, perhaps even truer today. That is why I wrote in 1937:

> The church is constantly reforming itself; it can really live only by doing so, and the intensity of its effort to reform itself measures at any given moment the health of its muscle tone (*tonus vital*). Don't be fooled: Pius X's initiative, which found its formula in his motto *Instaurare omnia in Christo* (Renew all things in Christ), an initiative diminished somewhat by the war, but not extinguished, is a true movement of reform. It led to a whole series of subsequent initiatives: the liturgical movement, the missionary initiative begun by Benedict XV and developed under the encouragement of Pius XI, the reform movement brought about by Catholic Action, the participation of the laity in the apostolate of the bishops, and most particularly to the superb realization of Catholic Action expressed by Young Christian Workers. It led as well to the internal renewal of contemporary Catholic theology through a more serious contact of theologians with the sources, a less total ignorance of the Oriental tradition, a more

---

[4] I had begun a bibliography on this topic for my own use, but I quickly got submerged in it and gave up finishing it. E. Brown, *Fasciculus rerum expendetendarum et fugiendarum. Sive tomus secundus Scriptorum veterum . . . qui Ecclesiae Romanae errores et abusus detegunt et damnant necessitatemque Reformationis urgent* (London, 1690), has published here a number of reformist writings (in the 1st volume, especially the texts of the period of the councils of Constance and of Basel; in the 2nd volume, pp. 794–800, see the list of authors who wrote in favor of reform in the Catholic Church, given in alphabetical order with a brief indication of their works and their dates).

living contemplation of the mysteries, a deliberate turning away from the narrow perspectives of the popular theology of the Counter-Reformation. This became as well a movement of reform producing a quiet assurance about the value of theological work both as interpretation of and a response to the world, signifying a return to intellectual initiatives and to a freedom of thought to which Catholics give evidence in history, philosophy, sociology, culture, and the arts (think, for example, of the work of Maritain) . . .[5]

II. Contemporary Self-Criticism and Reformism (Especially in France)

This interpretation of the chain of reform initiatives, which I wrote back in 1937, took on new meaning and even some urgency quite suddenly toward the end of the Second World War (1939–1945) and in the immediate postwar period. This new situation, which had matured only gradually, became suddenly apparent. After a period of time when free expression in the church had not been possible, a complex of ideas and feelings came to expression with both freedom and solidarity. I will analyze the causes of this explosion of reform initiatives later. For the moment, I want to make note here of some of its characteristic manifestations.

Almost all these initiatives date from 1946, in the form of literary manifestations. As such, they are easier to grasp and to acknowledge than some others, but it would be a mistake to believe that the spirit of reform was limited only to these manifestations or that these following initiatives were the most decisive examples. Some of the writings that I will make note of here produced a certain notoriety within their different contexts but did not play a significant role in the life of Catholicism, whereas others were more significant. All of them, however, are indications of a state or spirit of reform.

The first ones to speak up were perhaps the most eager but not necessarily the most reflective. The book of Aloys Masson, attractive because of his passion for evangelization, was nonetheless rather superficial.[6] He blamed the church for getting involved in politics, but at the same time he wanted the church to be involved in a way other than the one it had chosen. Beginning with an article by M. Dupouey, followed by another by Emmanuel Mounier, *Esprit* opened up an inquiry that we will examine

---

[5] *Chrétiens désunis* (Paris: Ed. du Cerf, 1937), pp. 339–340.
[6] Aloys Masson, *Pour une Eglise* (Geneva, 1945).

further on.[7] Dupouey was critical of the externals of the church, its socio-logical condition, its excessive "prudence," and the advanced age of its leaders as well as the mediocrity and the impotence to which Christians seemed to resign themselves within the church. This outburst was im-mature and much influenced by the experience of the moment, where Communists presented themselves as the leaders for the immediate future. Certainly during those years more than one sincere young Chris-tian asked himself if it might not be a good idea to introduce a bit of Marxist virus into the church so as to avoid the complete dissipation of the church's evangelizing yeast.[8] The dimension of illusion evident in such an idea only points out the tragedy of how deeply the problem was felt.

Mounier was more serious. He had a talent for linking captivating anecdotes with somewhat dubious formulas. He expressed the problem of the faith in the context of an anguished Christianity in such a way that he focused upon, not Christianity itself, but the "Christian world." He himself represented the interests of a group more specifically committed to Christian life and Christian theology than the journal *Esprit*. With this group, called the Youth of the Church (*Jeunesse de l'Eglise*), he felt great sympathy and solidarity.

This group came together and made itself known in Lyons beginning in 1942. It had two goals that were linked together: first, to emphasize the importance of Christian community in the church and, second, to investigate how Christians and the church can collaborate with the new social order that was in the process of being formed. In that way, the group "Youth of the Church" placed itself simultaneously on the course of breaking away from the past as well as of renewing its serious com-mitment—the predicament of a large number of generous Christians who found themselves faced with new and difficult problems. The pub-lications of "Youth of the Church" found an audience because of the loyalty with which they undertook a difficult examination of conscience for Christians faced with the need to both break out and yet renew com-mitment all at once.

We are getting close to discussing problems that are properly ecclesial ones. In 1946 both laity and clergy spoke up. They didn't speak exactly

---

[7] M. Dupouey, "L'Eglise va-t-elle émigrer?" *Esprit* (May 1946), pp. 703–716; fol-lowed by E. Mounier, "L'agonie du christianisme?" pp. 717–730.

[8] See several texts like that collected by L. Barjon, "Quand les chrétiens s'accusent," *Esprit* (May 1946), pp. 214–220.

the same language nor in exactly the same tone, but there was a deep and impressive harmony joining their complaints and their voices. The voice of the laity had a tone of complaint. They complained about the preaching they heard,[9] the liturgies they attended, the place given to the proletariat (their place) in the church,[10] and the outdated, inept, ineffective, and purely "bourgeois" style of so many of the forms in which parish ministry was being exercised. I won't go into more detail here, since later on I will give actual examples of the reformist initiatives of the decisive years 1945–1947.

The exposé of *Esprit* on "The Modern World and the Christian World," which appeared in the August–September 1946 issue, contained several contributions that were both interesting and moving. There were some articles that seemed to see only the weaknesses of the church. However, the essential function of self-criticism is assuredly not praise and flattery. On the whole, as I will point out further along, this critique was healthy and was linked to positive results. The articles made clear that the pastoral activities of the church no longer had much meaning for the majority of people, especially the more radical and dynamic among them. You might say that this is because people are more easily inclined to be carnal than spiritual; but it was also because people, both priests and lay faithful, received the things of Christ in forms inherited from an honorable but culturally obsolete past, in acts and formulas that were scarcely more than rituals, lacking the power to invite others to life or to express their life.

[9] About *Témoignages sur la spiritualité moderne* by Dr. Jouvenroux (Paris, 1946), P. d'Ouince wrote: "A suggestive and irritating booklet." I find it more suggestive than irritating—it's talking about real problems. See this same author's "Lettre d'un Catéchumène," *La Vie Intellectuelle* (Jan. 1948), pp. 32–36.

The question of religious education is at present intensely focused upon the use of the catechism. Cf. an article signed C.H., "Will my child lose his faith in the catechism?" in *Témoignage chrétien* (Nov. 12, 1948), and also several articles by Abbé Rétif, who has just published a book on the question (cf. below, 1st part, ch. 3, n. 34). Pius XII echoed this disquiet in his address to the International Catechetical Congress of Oct. 14, 1950 (*Doc. Catholique*, 1950, col. 1413–1414). This question of the catechism is a most serious issue, since the great majority of children still learn about the church through it. It is amazing that, given the seriousness of the question, the majority of the faithful are hardly interested. But we have heard the heartfelt cry of Canon J. Colomb, *Plaie ouverte au flanc de l'Eglise* (Paris, 1954). Since then the catechetical renewal has become one of the liveliest chapters in the renewal of the church. It is currently in full swing.

[10] This was the theme of "Lettre d'un Communautaire à son curé," published by M. M. Barbu in *Communauté* (1 and 15 July 1946).

The clergy will never speak completely in the same voice as the laity. That's the way it ought to be. Not that the clergy are vowed to expressing themselves only in a sacral, conventional, hollow, or unreal jargon, which is not the way any truly thinking person expresses what he really feels. But their consciousness of the responsibilities of the priesthood imposes upon the clergy a certain measure, a reserve, a concern not to wound anyone, and a need to take account of everything and everyone—all concerns that the laity don't feel quite the same way. It is not possible for a pastor of souls to be as radical as a layman in his options and in his criticism.

Nonetheless, a self-conscious critique has been very much alive in the last ten years among the clergy, and on the whole it touches upon the same complaints as those of the laity. I pointed out already in a summary way what those are, but I will give more detail about the exact sense of what they mean later on. The congress of the *Union des Oeuvres* at Easter 1946 in Besançon, on the theme "Parish: Christendom as Community and Mission," was the occasion to express and to examine collectively the pastoral dimensions of these problems. In the atmosphere of joy, enthusiasm, and fraternity created by this congress, the French clergy took on the role of apostolic deputies of the local churches. Further, the many bishops present did better than create an impossible night of the fourth of August [an abandonment of invested privileges, as in 1789 during the French Revolution]: they opened their ears to the demands being made, taking an active part in a collective examination of conscience and in a search for something better. One of them said to the chronicler of *Etudes*, "It feels like we are at the beginning of a great revolution."[11] This attitude of welcome and active attention, without which a reform spirit would have risked becoming either sterile or producing harmful results, resulted a year later in the startling publication of the historic letter of Cardinal Suhard, "*Essor ou déclin de l'Eglise*—Rise or Fall of the Church."

In those unusually fruitful years, there was not a conference, a retreat, or a conversation between priests and seminarians that did not take up in one way or another the same questions that were on the mind of every minister of the Gospel seeking to achieve a real and efficacious pastoral ministry, namely, a real, less artificial preaching; catechetics more apt to prepare Christians for real life; less routine and mechanical liturgy, one

---

[11] Cf. the chronicle of P. R. Rouquette in *Etudes* (May 1946), p. 257.

which really expresses the living worship of the community; forms of parish life that are less legalistic, more dynamic, truer to the real needs of the people, etc.

A spirit of reform in the liturgy was not something new. We could even say that the first of all modern reform movements is the liturgical movement and doubtless this is not by sheer chance.[12] If an organized liturgical movement was slow to take shape in France, nonetheless from its beginnings the French Center for Liturgical Ministry (Centre de Pastorale Liturgique—1943) not only was interested in a more communal and more intelligent celebration of liturgical rites but was also linked to the movement of retrieving the theological sources—the Bible and the Fathers—and to the renewal of preaching and catechetics. Indeed, it was tied in to the renewal of all forms of parish pastoral life, which are the objectives of apostolic renewal today. You can easily find indications of these pastoral hopes in the publications of the liturgical movement and in the chronicles of Père Doncoeur.[13]

More than all the other points noted above, the liturgy raises questions for the supreme authority in the church, doubtless because it is so tightly linked to questions of doctrine and to the structure of the church itself. We are not surprised, then, to see the Holy See intervene and itself take the initiative for liturgical reforms. Clearly, certain instances of liturgical renewal have come from Roman initiatives. The new translation of the Psalter (1945) was introduced in Rome as an act of "reform." You can see that as a first step in a reform which will include the reform of the Breviary in both its texts and its structure, and which will include sooner or later a reform of the celebration of certain sacramental rites, perhaps even a vernacular translation of the first part of the Mass. From here on, this liturgical reform is a movement on its way to further development.

Different proposals for the reform of the Breviary have been put forward by those in the hierarchy or by specialists in the liturgy.[14] A docu-

---

[12] G. Söhngen, "Der theologische Sinn der liturgischen Erneuerung," *Catholica*, V (1936), pp. 147–171, has convincingly laid out the reform aspect of the liturgical movement. He even thinks that a Catholic reformation, as opposed to the Protestant Reformation, is characterized first of all by a reform in worship. [This idea received a striking confirmation when Vatican II began its work with liturgical reform, undertaken through its beautiful constitution, *Sacrosanctum Concilium*.]

[13] See, in particular, "Etapes décisives de l'effort liturgique contemporain," *Etudes* (Nov. 1948), pp. 200–210.

[14] Cardinal J.-B. Nasalli Rocca di Cornegliano, *De Breviario Romano et Kalendario ejusdem Breviarii reformando* (Pro manuscript, 1946, 3rd edition)—French trans. in *Paroisse et liturgie* XXIX (1947), pp. 30–42. See the bibliography on this question in

ment like the Holy See's constitution *Sacramentum Ordinis* demonstrates a desire for historical and liturgical authenticity, which is the very soul of a spirit of reform in such matters. In his encyclical *Mediator Dei*, the Holy Father made a distinction between the divine and the human elements of the liturgy, and showed how the human elements, characterized by a certain relativity, must undergo modifications according to the needs of the times.

There would be many other examples of reforms to mention, if I were to try to be complete. But let me point out, at least, one area of considerable importance, namely, institutes of religious life (especially of women). There we find also a search for adaptation and authenticity expressed in a variety of areas of practical application.[15]

Nonetheless, how could this presentation of the present spirit of reform, limited here to certain examples cited in print and outlined in a dry documentary and bibliographical fashion, give to someone who has not experienced it a feeling of the reality? I want to evoke the immense goodwill, mixed with a certain anxiety, which for years now has led to an exercise of self-criticism of a new kind in the church (particularly in France), with an eye to revising, adapting, and purifying everything that could limit or impede the work of the Gospel. It will be better to give an account of the character, the causes, and the practical applications of this spirit of reform. But first I should note that similar problems and currents exist also in other countries. Unfortunately, here I need to limit myself to written examples, which are not always either the most important or the most significant.

The book of Papini that appeared in 1946 brought up fundamentally similar questions.[16] At first glance, he leaves the impression of superficial

---

Les Questions liturg. et paroiss. XXX (1949), pp. 23–24. Also add A. Bugnini, "Per una reforma liturgica generale," *Ephemerides Liturgicae* 63 (1949), pp. 406–430. For the liturgical reforms of Pius XII, see *Ephem. Theol. Lovanienses* (1955), p. 311.

[15] You can find descriptions of these initiatives in *La Vie Spirituelle* and the *Supplément*: cf. in particular *Le Supplément* of May 1948 on adaptations for feminine religious life. Observe also that the Congress of Religious in Rome, Nov. 1950, unfolded under the banner of reform; its title was "*Statuum perfectionis presentibus temporibus atque adjunctis accomodata renovatio*," a title reused (as to its substance, at least) by the decree of Vatican II *Perfectae Caritatis*. See also the addresses of Cardinal Piazza in opening the congress, that of Pius XII (Dec. 8, 1950), and that of Cardinal Micara (Nov. 12, 1950), all to be found in *Doc. Catholique*, 1950, col. 1699, 1676–1677, and 1698.

[16] G. Papini, *Lettere agli uomini del Papa Celestino Sesto* (Florence, 1946)—French trans.: *Lettres aux hommes du pape Célestin VI*, trans. J. Bertrond (Paris, 1948).

gossip about a serious problem, but he does express with literary talent what a lot of the faithful think without always saying enough about it.

Germany, a country noted for spawning serious critical ideas, is the source of the clearest examples of a reformist spirit outside of France. Writings of this kind have been so numerous there that an outside observer, H. Hermelink, was able to compile a list of titles of no less than fifty bibliographical entries.[17] He clearly went beyond the area in which I'm interested, finding in general publications evidence of a spirit of openness, and mixing with the self-criticism coming from the faithful other texts that are often equivocal or even unacceptable, coming from the Catholic Reform Movement (*Reformkatholizismus*) and published previously by G. Mensching and H. Mulert. On the other hand, Hermelink left out some writings that are interesting for our concern here.[18] Further, publishing in 1940, he obviously did not have access to the postwar publications.

Among those, the most important is doubtless the "Letter on the Church" of Ida Görres.[19] This article was certainly anything but scandalous: it explained why, "despite everything," a Catholic loves the church with a love linked to profound religious attachment. This text, however, gave expression to a feeling which had been growing for a long time and which, as in France, expressed the feeling of disproportion between what one hopes for from the church, namely, the Gospel, and what one finds in the concrete experience of approaching the church. Other examples might be given similar to her article. However, these suffice for the moment. Perhaps I should mention a more recent article, published in Austria, "Christian Honesty": a statement pleading for freedom of discussion in the church and for honesty in this exchange.[20]

---

[17] "Innerkirchliche Reformbewegungen im deutschen Katholizismus," *Theologische Rundschau*, new series 12 (1940), pp. 189–235.

[18] For example: P. Simon, *Das Menschliche in der Kirche Christi* (Freiburg im Br., 1936)—French trans.: *L'humain dans l'Eglise du Christ* (Mulhouse, 1950); H. Wirtz, *Ein Laie sucht den Priester* (Frankfurt, 1940); and in Switzerland, P. Winder and F. von Streng, *Laienwünsche-Priesterwünsche* (*Priesterwünsche an die Akademiker, Laienwünsche an die Priester*) (Lucerne, 1937). It would be easy to expand the bibliography on these topics.

[19] "Briefe über die Kirche," in *Frankfurter Hefte* (Nov. 1946), pp. 715–733. A partial translation in French: "Malgré cela, je reste catholique," *La Vie Intellectuelle* (Feb. 1947), pp. 26–35. Görres also published *Die leibhaftige Kirche: Gespräch unter Laien*. H. J. Schultz edited two volumes collecting contributions from various authors: *Kritik an der Kirche* and *Frömmigkeit in einer weltlichen Welt* (Stuttgart, 1959). And others . . .

[20] F. Jantsch, "Christliche Anständigkeit," *Gloria Dei* 3 (1948–1949), pp. 1–6—partial French trans.: "Pour la libre discussion dans l'Eglise," *La Vie Intellectuelle* (Feb. 1949),

III. The Church Today:
How Did Self-Criticism Become Suspect?

This kind of self-criticism is something rather new in the church these days; at least it has not been going on for a very long time. The Middle Ages had a freedom in such matters that the modern period has not known. St. Bernard's ability to speak frankly to the pope might have been explained by his particular circumstances if we did not also have similar texts by St. Colomba, St. Catherine of Siena, St. Bridget, and others . . . The reformist treatises published by bishops, monks, and theologians articulated criticisms straightforwardly, such that E. Brown has been able to edit a number of them as polemical material against the Roman Catholic Church (see above, note 4).

On the tympanum of our cathedrals, as in the paintings of Fra Angelico, you can find monks, bishops, and even popes being ushered into hell by grimacing devils; Dante put his contemporaries, Pope Nicholas III, Pope Boniface VIII, and Pope Clement V, in his *Inferno*. True, he had ideological and political motives for doing so, but the critique remains unsubtle. Such facts are sufficiently numerous and well enough known that I don't have to insist.

However, in that sociologically "healthier" period, a freely expressed critique of individual persons was nonetheless expressed with respect for the ecclesial institution and its functions. Those times did not have any more "morality" than ours perhaps, but they did seem to have a greater "code of honor," a healthy and solid public spirit, to use the helpful distinction made by M. G. Thibon following Prudhon. It would be a problem if criticizing persons undermined respect for their administrative function and for the institution itself. However, historians of the church, and particularly historians treating the origins of the Reformation, have shed light on this question.[21] It is a fact that the church has long maintained the point of view, perfectly healthy in itself, that the criticism of persons and of things within the church does not entail either loathing or loss of faith. As L. M. Febvre has pointed out with respect to

---

pp. 126–131. In addition, there are many writings that have appeared since, laying claim to freedom of speech and opinion in the church: K. Rahner and E. B. Roegele in *Wort und Warheit* (Jan. 1953), pp. 5–10; *Doc. Catholique* (1954), col. 799–803; E. Guerrero in *Razon y Fe* (1960), pp. 45–64, and (1961), pp. 365–382, etc. The idea is mirrored in John XXIII's address to the press of June 6, 1962, and in Vatican II (*Lumen Gentium*, no. 37; *Ad Gentes*, no. 28; *Apostolicam Actuositatem*, no. 37).

[21] See in particular Denifle-Weiss, *Luther und das Luthertum*, vol. 2 (Mainz, 1909), pp. 60f., 65f.

Rabelais, it is an anachronism to attribute to people living before the modern period attitudes uncharacteristic of their own time.

Since those days the Reformation has come on the scene, as well as revolutionary liberals, the spirit of the Enlightenment philosophers, Voltaire, rationalism and its modern progeny, Marxist atheism, Nazism, and similar expressions as well . . . As an undercurrent of its radical doctrinal attack upon the church, the Reformation developed a widespread critique of things Catholic, from monastic life to the priesthood and, above all, the papacy. This was a merciless critique which lacked scrupulous concern for the truth. Some of these themes, sadly, are still strong within Protestant consciousness and create complexes which constitute the most serious psychological obstacle to mutual understanding. Modern rationalism's attack upon all positive religion and, practically speaking, upon the Catholic Church has also expressed itself in a relentless critique of persons and things inside the church. It has mercilessly exploited all the scandals and all the frauds that we should have ourselves renounced long ago and, to tell the truth, should never have tolerated. The sarcasm of Voltaire did as much to fashion contemporary unbelief as the philosophy of Spinoza . . .

Surrounding all of that there is a great characteristic tendency in the modern world to move from an objective to a subjective world, from a world of order, hierarchy, and tradition to a world of personal consciousness and individual thought. Those who lived in the Middle Ages and those who lived in the *Ancien Régime*—Péguy claims in his *L'Argent* that it's the same thing—those who had a "code of honor" according to Thibon's meaning, lived with respect for classes, hierarchical functions, authority, and superiors. The leader, the priest, and the religious were respected then by reason of their capacity as leaders, priests, or religious, and by reason of their function, their state in life. Instead of urging respect for persons because of the dignity of their rank or their function, the modern world tends to respect functions only if the persons who exercise them have credibility because of their individual qualities. So today people do not respect a leader simply because he is a priest or religious but only to the degree that he is personally good and helpful. To the degree that this tendency toward a completely individualistic "sincerity" has won out, the common good (*esprit public*) has become shipwrecked. Morality has remained an issue, but not very brilliant; "honor" is on a downhill slide.

With respect to criticizing the weaknesses and faults of the church, all of this brought about new conditions and a new context. On the one hand, being critical, which formerly one could do freely, in good conscience, "in-house," without diminishing respect for the essentials, became a terrible weapon and the source of attacks that can no longer be controlled or even faced with the candor of previous times. A spirit of loyalty for the church, which did not impede criticism in the past, now demands that one be careful not to create an occasion to betray the church or to give comfort to the enemy. Even when a Catholic, informed by a sufficient historical perspective, might be inclined to utter the same criticisms that an unbeliever would, he or she is held back by the fear that their word might be distorted and used against the church.

The church has seen what a sincere self-critical statement can do to help its unscrupulous adversaries. At the time of the Reformation, there were already people in the church who thought that it was not fitting to aid Protestant polemics by publicly disavowing the faults of the popes or of other churchmen. Contarini replied that the best way to blunt the attacks of the Protestants was to reform the Curia. With other reformers who had the same tendency as he (Sadolet, Pole, Carafa, and a good number of other prelates), he wrote a memorandum which he gave to Paul III (1537). However, this memorandum, given by one indiscreet person to other indiscreet persons, was printed and disseminated. Luther made use of it to attack Rome, thus seeming to justify those who held for silence about problems in the church and spoiling for quite a long time any possibility of exercising ecclesial self-criticism.[22]

---

[22] Luther, *Ratschlag eines Ausschusses etlicher Kardinäle: Papst Paulo III auf seinem Befehl geschrieben und überantwortet, mit Luthers Vorrede* (edit. Weimar), pp. 191–308; cf. text on pp. 284f. For a treatment of this episode, see L. Pastor, *Geschichte der Päpste*, vol. 5, pp. 126f.; and H. Grisar, *Luthers Kampfbilder*, fasc. 3 (Freiburg im Breisgau, 1923), pp. 57f.

Luther even used the beautiful and humble text of Hadrian VI giving instructions to Chieregati, the nuncio at Nuremburg (cf. Pastor, vol. 4, 2nd part, pp. 93f.). He used it again, with a certain discretion, in his *Vermahnung an die Geistlichen* of 1540 (Weimar, XXX, 2, p. 354); but he ridiculed it in his *Vorrede, Nachwort und Marginalglossen zu Legatio Adriani* of 1538 (Weimar, L, pp. 355–363). Luther even edited and glossed the bull by which Paul IV adjourned the council (Weimar, L, pp. 92f.).

Because the Curia feared another use of such well-intentioned documents, access to the papers of the Council of Trent (originally intended for public inspection by Pius IV) was forbidden by Pius V, who limited publication only to the decrees of the council: cf. H. Jedin, *Das Konzil von Trient: Ein Ueberblick über die Erforschung seiner Geschichte* (Rome, 1948). Here is another symptom of this state of affairs: after the Council of Trent, the episcopal authority had a watercolor painted of the church of Santa Maria di Spelonca (Arquata), "*cum sint in inferno depicti Papa, Cardinales et*

Erasmus paid attention; in 1522 he wrote to Pope Hadrian VI, a Dutch-man like himself, that if he had spoken somewhat freely, it was the tranquility of those times that allowed him to do so.[23] However, in 1526 he complained that all that had been spoiled by the Protestant quarrel, and that papal authority had become stronger and weighed more heavily on the church since Luther (and Erasmus himself) had claimed the right to express themselves freely.[24]

Following this tragic period when everything was called into question, criticized, and disparaged, the Catholic hierarchy viewed Catholics join-ing in criticism of the faults and weaknesses of the church with pain and displeasure. St. Thomas Aquinas had claimed certain criteria in the law (based on apocryphal sources) that required stricter guarantees for any testimony or accusation against a minister of the Roman Church, citing this consideration: "Condemning one of these ministers would bring prejudice against the dignity and the authority of the Church in the opinion of others, constituting so grave an inconvenience that the Church might tolerate the evil actions of a single minister, unless the fault he performs is so public and so evident that grave scandal would result."[25]

Evidently these considerations still inspire the attitude of pastors re-sponsible for the life of the church. In their view too much attention to failures in the church risks destroying more than building up the church. This is not the moment, they think, to add our voice to the voices of those who bitterly attack the church.[26] Moreover, the hierarchy itself has been very sparing in any statements that risk discrediting sacred authority by condemning or disavowing faults (see below, page 76). The system of powerful central authority which has prevailed in the church since the sixteenth century has, in its way, tended to interpret every critique as

---

religiosi, quae res vero sapit Lutheranismum—with a pope, cardinals and religious, who delighted in Lutheranism, shown in hell." Cf. G. Fabiani, "Sinodi e Visite pastorali ad Ascoli dopo il concilio di Trento," *Rivista di Storia della Chiesa in Italia* 6 (1952), pp. 264–280; p. 280, n. 80.

[23] Cf. A. Renaudet, *Etudes érasmiennes* (Paris, 1939), p. 203.

[24] Ibid., pp. 261, 284, n. 4. Erasmus couldn't forgive Luther for having abused the true cause of the Gospel by his use of violence: ibid., p. 352.

[25] *Summa Theologiae*, 2a-2ae, q. 70, a. 2, ad 3. See Stephen Kuttner, "*Cardinalis*: The History of a Canonical Concept," *Traditio* (1945), pp. 190–192, 202–214, for a treatment of this *Constitutum Sylvestri* (Mirbt, *Quellen zur Geschichte des Papsttums*, no. 193) and of the group of apocryphal documents that constitute the "Symmachian Aprochry-phals."

[26] Similar to the position of Protestants in *Positions protestantes* (Paris, 1946), p. 15.

arising from a spirit of opposition and even from a dubious orthodoxy.[27] A simplistic apologetics has often thought that it was necessary to defend *everything*. This attitude has defended the sanctity and the perfection of the church using ideas that are not always correct and which can only be maintained, if the truth be told, by refusing to see things as they actually are.

Self-criticism is nonetheless still necessary. Every spiritual organization that is really alive must encourage genuine critique. A school of thought that ignores this rule would condemn itself to nothing more than mere survival. Ida Görres correctly observes that the impossibility of speaking critically under Nazism was a cause of its weakness. Further, the pressures of life are such that they will eventually become expressed despite everything. They will find expression but, unfortunately, that does not substitute for what should have happened in a well-ordered world.

The terrible attacks that the church has undergone in the modern period are, in part, a response to a regime of conformity that was too mistrustful of any new thinking—thinking in tension not with the great Catholic tradition so much as in tension with the received ideas of a narrow milieu that had lost touch with the currents of living thought. Papini correctly noted: "The stone with which we strike ourselves on the breast is one that our accusers won't be able to throw at us." There is an element of necessary criticism which, far from being opposed to the church, has to exist as a requisite element of the church's life.

How can Christians live out the absolute sincerity that the Gospel imposes on them if they aren't able, within the limits of respect for what needs to be respected, to speak about what is most precious to them, the community of the church? St. Thomas More alluded to this in explaining his own freedom of expression: "Do we need to keep a respectful silence even in the face of abuse? Must we call every criticism of the evils brought about by human malice a novelty, an absurdity, or an impertinence? Let's stop calling ourselves Christians, if we have to keep still about what Christ taught us. Almost all the precepts of Jesus condemn present behavior more than all of my criticisms."[28]

---

[27] The history of the First Vatican Council provides a perfect example of this. Any criticism, and even the simple discussion of certain points, was resented by Pius IX and his circle as an outrage to the dignity of the Holy See. See, for example, *Le Concile du Vatican d'après des documents inédits* (Paris, 1919), pp. 196f., 239–240, 244–245, 296–299.

[28] Cited in E. Dermenghem, "Erasme et Thomas More contre Machiavel," *Le Roseau d'Or*—Chroniques 2 (Paris, 1926), p. 235.

We need to note, however, that even though they use the same words, saying materially almost exactly the same thing, there are two kinds of criticism that are very different. One is evil or destructive; the other, good and constructive, that is, edifying in the true sense of the word. The church does not like someone who risks destroying more than building up, even using good form. A number of attitudes expressed by the hierarchy that are above all pastoral in perspective can be explained by this concern.[29]

We may be impressed by the forceful statements of violent figures who appear on the scene of history. Their power, even brutality, might appear appealing. But once such persons have turned everything upside down, they disappear from the stage of history, leaving to others, who are meeker and less glorious, the job of putting things back together again . . . The church operates with greater seriousness and weighs its words carefully because it takes its responsibilities more seriously. The church is guided not just by the light of an experience of the present moment or of one single aspect of reality but by the light of its experience of centuries and of the whole spectrum of life.

There are two distinct types of criticism, just as there are two very different ways of using punishment in education. You can punish out of anger, carried away by impatience and even by a feeling of resentment or getting even. But you can also punish out of love so as to help others to arrive at their real good. Similarly, you can criticize without love or respect in a spirit of disparagement and hatred; but you can also criticize out of love, with seriousness and respect. The church can accept criticism of the latter kind. Abbé Godin and Abbé Daniel made that kind of critique in their book *Is France a Mission Land?—France, pays de mission?* Clearly there is always some risk involved. Others can use our words to disparage the church in a completely different spirit from what we intended. As we saw, this is what Luther did. I know some secular anti-Catholics who literally devoured the book of Godin and Daniel in order to find

---

[29] In this respect we might consider the following rule, formulated at the 8th Ecumenical Council, as the expression of the attitude of the Catholic Church: "Si synodus universalis fuerit congregata, et facta fuerit etiam de sancta Romanorum Ecclesia quamvis ambiguitas et controversia, oportet venerabiliter et cum convenienti reverentia de proposita s[u]scitari et solutionem accipere, aut proficere, aut profectum facere, non tamen audacter sententiam dicere contra summos senioris Romae pontifices." 11th rule and 13th canon: cf. Mansi, XVI, 174 and 406, cited by Hefele-Leclerq, *Histoire des Conciles*, vol. 1, A, p. 74.

ammunition to express their antagonism against the church. Anyone who is candid and loyal, using only the light of truthfulness, is vulnerable in this way. Blessed is the weakness of the one whose defense is Truth itself!

In one of his addresses Pius XII said this: "We know that our words and our intentions risk being falsely interpreted and distorted for the sake of political propaganda. But the possibility for such erroneous or mean-spirited misinterpretations cannot make us stop speaking up."[30] Pius XII further said this as well, coming closer to the point that interests me here:

> The free expression of one's opinion is the prerogative of every human society where people, responsible for their personal and social conduct, are intimately committed to the community to which they belong. . . . In the eyes of Christians, repressing the expression of opinion or forcing it into silence is an attack upon the natural rights of persons, a violation of the world order that God has established. . . . We want to add another word concerning public opinion inside the church itself (naturally with respect to matters open to discussion). This may astonish those who don't really know the church or who only think they know it. The church is a living body, and it would lack an element of its life if the free expression of opinion was lacking—a lack for which both pastors and faithful would be blamed.[31]

Citing the letters of Pope Celestine VI, treated by Papini (and representing the German reform movement referred to above), P. A. Koch recently wondered about the conditions which would assure that criticism within the church could be good and fruitful.[32] He settled upon the following points that one could easily expand upon: love of the church; genuine and frank courage, which would inspire straightforward criticism in the manner of St. Paul disagreeing with St. Peter at Antioch face-to-face (Gal 2) instead of covert detractions; justice and exactitude: refusing loose generalizations, avoiding careless or unilateral judgments; prudence and humility.

---

[30] Allocution to the Sacred College, Christmas 1946 (*Doc. Catholique*, Jan. 5, 1947, col. 3).

[31] Address to the international congress of the Catholic Press in Rome, published in the French edition of *Osservatore Romano*, Feb. 18, 1950, and reprinted in *Doc. Catholique*, Mar. 12, 1950, cols. 322 and 327.

[32] "Kritik an die Kirche," *Stimmen der Zeit* (Dec. 1947), pp. 169–184.

Koch adds that, in response, the church ought to show itself open to criticism and to offer to those who are critical a calm response, shorn of the sort of agitation that excites suspicion. Koch also notes (p. 183) that the impossibility of any criticism was one of the fatal weaknesses of the Nazi regime. Finally, the church should acknowledge justified criticism in a spirit of realism.

IV. Four Traits of Contemporary Self-Criticism

The examples of criticisms of the church made by Christians given here ought to be classified as good critiques. I don't mean that everything said in them is perfect. Human frailty exists in each one of us along with spiritual integrity—the two tendencies are sometimes mixed or even alternated. Sometimes one clearly prevails over the other. In the writings of those like Mensching or H. Mulert, the bad tendency is so great that it spoils the element of truth in what they say.[33] By contrast, in the celebrated examination of conscience of Cardinal Manning (which I translated in *Masses ouvrières*, March 1951, pp. 20–44) and in the book of Godin and Daniel, the criticism is completely pure. Between these two types, there is a whole range of pluses and minuses, judged differently according to who it is who makes the judgment.

In France, however, there is a sort of consensus about what makes for a loving and respectful self-criticism. This self-criticism has had both blunt and subtle voices. Nonetheless, there is a certain homogeneity, a kind of generalized approach that is represented in this criticism. That is why I am going to try to point out the causes and the points of interest of the present movement of critique or reform, after describing it in some detail.

1. Catholic self-criticism is frank, sometimes even harsh. It does not arise from a lack of confidence or from a lack of love for the church but, on the contrary, from a deep attachment and from a desire to be able to trust, despite the disappointment of someone who loves and who expects a great deal from the church. If certain proposals for reform have given some people the impression of being revolutionary, it should be recog-

---

[33] *Der Katholizismus: Sein Stirb und Werde*, ed. G. Mensching (Leipzig, 1937); *Der Katholizismus der Zukunft: Aufbau und kritische Abwehr*, ed. H. Mulert (Leipzig, 1940). These two publications were put on the Index by the decrees of Jan. 22, 1938, and of May 7–16, 1941, respectively.

nized that these revolutionaries act in a spirit of fidelity to the church. Péguy gave us the model of this kind of fidelity and offered the justification for wanting to reform the church he loved.

These feelings are sometimes so strong that they produce an *outcry*, but at the root of such vehemence there is neither revolt nor bitterness. Rather, there is a very deep attachment, encouraged by the rediscovery of the church in the spirit of the 1930s. It is a fact, perhaps unexpected but nonetheless real, that the self-criticism of the years 1945–1950 have no relationship to Modernism, no link to this or that pamphlet coming from the Modernist revolt or from *Action française*.

This self-criticism would not have been possible without this kind of openness and energy or without the victory over Modernism. As always, of course, pressing problems have continued to prompt new research, some of which is troubling the Roman authorities (cf. the encyclical *Humani Generis* of Aug. 12, 1950). I wonder if there is actually anything more than a common historical context that links the research of specialists and the reform movement under analysis here. If anyone comes up with some coincidence between a current problem and some question that was raised by Modernism, with some defense of a previously condemned proposal (or one called into question at least), the matter can be problematic—even fatal. For example, proposals for liturgical renewal risked being compared to the articles of Pistoia that were censured in 1794.[34] There exists a kind of "raw material" for reform movements, just like there is "raw material" for political life. There can be various combinations of these elements, but the political spirit is very different from the spirit of true reform.

A crisis or an uneasiness lies at the root of present-day reform, but it is not a crisis of loyalty. I really mean "at the root," because it is not out of the question that the crisis, which I will soon analyze in detail, might have become a crisis of loyalty for one or another protagonist if their deeply felt, sincere, and worthy demands had not been listened to at all. It cannot be denied that certain critics have experienced—do now experience—a feeling of uneasiness, a malaise. They have felt that their pure, necessary, justified demands have been insufficiently taken into consideration or even treated with a prejudice of suspicion. They have felt that

[34] R. Pilkington, "La Liturgia nel sinodo Ricciano di Pistoia (1786)," *Ephemer. Liturg.* 43 (1929), pp. 410–424. Pilkington correctly notes that the proposals for liturgical reform of Pistoia were not condemned as "haeretica, falsa," but only censured as "temeraria et probato mori injuriosa."

their leaders don't recognize the urgency of problems as seriously as they do and that, despite the exhausting effort they devote to their proposals, they are in danger of failing, either because their urgency is recognized too late or because, in the end, the principle is called into question.

They think that too often considerations of "tradition"—meaning official support for received ways of acting or speaking—practically smother considerations about the most authentic sorts of improvements or the most urgent pastoral adaptations . . . Sometimes, listening to complaints about this sort of thing concerning matters I took seriously, I have reflected on those first years of the sixteenth century, when so many people felt that the situation of the church was extremely serious, that matters could be resolved if only people did the right thing, but that time was running out and unfortunately the hierarchy didn't seem to appreciate the urgency. The key difference—much to our advantage—is that the church today possesses a purity of spirit, resources, and pastors as well as a commitment to its apostolic mission that the beginning of the sixteenth century lacked. Vatican II has clearly proven that.

2. A second trait of contemporary self-criticism in the church is the serious nature of its foundations. Not only does it draw upon a real awareness of the apostolic situation of the church (as I will show) but it has antecedents or intellectual precedents of unquestionable importance. There would not be the present wave of reform without a clear and correct judgment about apostolic needs. Neither would this reform have come about (or, at least, not with the same quality) without the theological and liturgical renewal, whose first initiatives came from Leo XIII and St. Pius X.

This wave of reform, likewise, arises from a renewal of the very meaning of the church—above all within the last quarter century. The liturgical movement, with its spirit of reform, would not have become what it is without being preceded and then nurtured by the scientific research of its scholars. It never stops finding support in serious research. Likewise, the present movement, which is essentially apostolic or pastoral, owes much to a renewal of ideas about the church, and it never stops making reference to ecclesiology—for which pastoral life is the natural prolongation or application.

3. Among considerations about reform, there is one that represents a third characteristic trait. It is a fact, in the currents under discussion, that the role of the laity is considerable. Many of the writings referred to

above are the works of laypeople. This fact points to a new awareness by the laity that they are the church and that they have a responsibility, in a certain sense, to create the church. They discuss questions about the church because they feel responsible for the church.

How could we fail to recognize in this new situation the influence of Catholic Action and of the appeal of the Holy Father for the laity to do their part, under the direction of the hierarchy, in the church's apostolic mission to the world? Catholic Action was the great preparation of the movement under consideration. This will become even clearer further on.

Until now, priests and, above all, laypeople were simply expected to reform themselves. (A pastor would not have allowed a mere parishioner to tell him off—and he was right.) The bishop hears the advice of his priests, but at the diocesan synod the bishop alone remains the final arbiter and the only legislator. This way of doing things is part of the structure of the church, which is hierarchical. Nonetheless, a study of the history of the church indicates that its genius created in the past structures for communal or collegial decisions. In my *Lay People in the Church* I give examples. The *Pontifical*, in the introduction to the ordination of priests, remarks that the captain and the passengers are all in the same boat; they ought to have the same idea about a question that calls them both to understand the common life. Although the church is structured hierarchically, it leads its life in the ranks of the faithful as well. All the faithful are responsible for the whole body of the church in some way, especially when circumstances become critical. This justifies the fact that today neither priests nor laity can excuse themselves from paying attention to the problems of the church.

4. Among the conditions that can further seriousness and depth in ecclesial self-criticism, I must mention the practice of return to the sources—what we call today *ressourcement*.[35] Later we will see how an

---

[35] The word *ressourcement* comes from Péguy, and its first use can be dated precisely. In the *Cahiers de la Quinzaine* (Mar. 1, 1904) he had the idea but not yet the word: see the text in *Oeuvres complètes*, vol. 12, pp. 186–192. However, in *Argent* (con't.), the 9th notebook in the 14th series (Apr. 22, 1913—*Oeuvr. compl.*, vol. 14, p. 218), he wrote: "Nothing is as anxiously [*sic*] beautiful as the sight of a people who lift themselves up again through an interior movement, a return to the sources (*ressourcement*) of their ancient pride, by means of a new release of the instincts of their race."

For Péguy this meant going back to the sources of life—to a new release of energies. Péguy envisaged "an invincible Christendom renewing itself from the ground up"

examination of sources or principles of church life is demanded by the nature of the present reform movement. We will see it as one of the conditions—the fourth in my list—by which reform can come about without schism. *Ressourcement* is thus extremely important.

"The time is surely coming, says the Lord God, when I will send a famine on the land; not a famine of bread, or a thirst for water, but of hearing the words of the Lord" (Amos 8:11). The prophet speaks of a punishment, a withdrawal of God's Word. Today we are living out this text as a kind of blessing, because God has sent us, along with a hunger for his Word, an abundance of nourishment.

This is not the place to go into detail about the renewal of studies in the Bible, the Fathers, and the liturgy, which represent a kind of underground foundation that feeds the felt need to return to the sources. Once again, as we will see better further along, contemporary ecclesial self-criticism or the spirit of reform is accompanied by a return to the sources of theological and pastoral thinking within the living rivers of a Catholic tradition rediscovered in its deepest expressions.

V. The Reasons for Today's Self-Criticism: A Passion for Authenticity

Among the general causes for the reformist self-criticism of today, some are linked to current attitudes and others are more specific.

As for current attitudes, I necessarily point to a taste for sincerity. Here is an extremely rich personal quality that might have certain superficial (even faulty) manifestations but some profound ones as well. To mis-

---

(*Clio*, p. 170). The word *ressourcement* has been used (and I use it here) to express the idea of a return or going back to the sources. In this sense, the expression is old and even classic. Erasmus spoke of *"ex fontibus praedicare Christum"*; Lacordaire in 1828 wrote to Lorain: "Strength is found at the sources, and I want to go there to see . . ."; St. Pius X proclaimed the need to *"redire ad fontes*—go back to the sources"; M. Blondel spoke of the necessity of going back to the great authors themselves, who are often betrayed by formulas considered "traditional" but that are really recent (Testin, *La semaine sociale de Bordeaux*, Paris, 1910, pp. 67–68). Pius XII, in *Humani Generis* (Aug. 12, 1950), after opposing a return to sources which might neglect the living teaching of the magisterium, goes on to say, "Theologians ceaselessly ought to go back to the sources of divine revelation . . . By studying the sources, the sacred sciences keep growing fresher, while speculation that neglects to go all the way back to the study of the deposit of revealed faith becomes sterile, as experience shows us" (*AAS* 42 [1950], p. 568).

understand this is to misunderstand one of the fundamental characteristics of contemporary people (and the kind of humanity that they have
to bring to Christ). The superficial or faulty aspect of modern sincerity
is a tendency to attack whatever presents itself as sacred and to rob it of
its halo. It can even seem that attacking the sacred gives someone the
status of an adult, and sometimes in the view of the young, all authority
and all conventions are a priori suspect of betrayal or corruption.

By contrast, heretics seem to have a kind of prestige, identifying them
as superior persons.[36] To be avant-garde or nonconformist becomes a
value in itself. But as Emmanuel Mounier has rightly noted,[37] there is a
conformism and a professional pride in the attitude of the avant-garde,
to the effect that the attitude of the Young Turk eventually destroys itself.
Here as elsewhere, only the truth is really liberating. Being at the forefront doesn't make any sense or have any value in itself. The only thing
that really counts is to be true. That is the solid foundation and the best
part of this taste for sincerity.

Our age certainly goes further than others in demanding truth in actions and attitudes. Clearly, previous generations did not have difficulty
in adopting the habits and customs that tradition had laid down before
their time and without their assent, although our contemporaries do feel
that reluctance. Let me make note of a few superficial and inoffensive
examples . . . It was evident that priests in the postwar period of 1945
had personal ideas about how to celebrate the Mass (within certain
objective limitations), concerning what to say out loud, for example.[38]
They didn't do this lightly but out of concern for being faithful to the
meaning of things. We also saw priests introduce individual adaptations
in their clerical dress. Though a humble detail, this is not insignificant.
If someone feels a personal reaction he is not going to fall in completely

---

[36] Today, "the word heresy no longer means that one is wrong, but rather that one
has a perceptive and courageous heart. By contrast, the term orthodoxy takes on a
pejorative meaning" (Chesterton, cited by G. Marcel, *Du refus à l'invocation*, p. 238).

[37] *Témoignage chrétien* (Feb. 25, 1949); cf. *Feu la Chrétienté* (Paris, 1950), pp. 122f., 233f.

[38] For example: To say out loud the final doxology of the Canon of the Mass—"*Per
ipsum . . .*"—gives to the *Amen* of the faithful the sense of solemnity that it had at the
time of St. Justin; gives meaning back to the gesture of offering at the Offertory, etc.

Note from 1968 edition: All that had been written in 1950. Clearly we have gone
far beyond those suggestions and new initiatives have surpassed those of 18 years
ago . . .

with all the impersonal details of the rubrics; because objective truth, *the rights of which are not called into question here*, does not say everything about the authenticity of the gesture *of some particular person*.

What we find here is a present-day taste for authentic gestures, and one of the effects of this tendency is one of the great themes of the modern world—the discovery of the subject. This is not a complete "discovery," of course, because only those who don't know St. Augustine or St. Thomas Aquinas would imagine that they had been inattentive to the person as "subject." This point also has to be connected to one I made before, namely, that the church does not build itself up only from on high but also from below. Of course, in a real sense, the church exists antecedently to the faithful and is not created by them. But from another point of view, it is indeed also created by the faithful; the church only achieves its full living reality from human activity. So as I will show, that is precisely the area where the church needs reform activity, where the point of view of the subject comes into play, inspired by the taste for sincerity and by reasonable and worthwhile demands for reform.

We can admit, by the way, that the events of recent years have played their part in the growth of reform tendencies. The war and its consequences have been a tragic lesson for those paying attention. A great number of priests and active laity became more or less deeply involved in the resistance, all of them engaged in at least material disobedience. There is a qualitative difference between someone who has never disobeyed—never broken a rule—and those who felt they had to break through a wall holding them back from what was officially forbidden. When people have once broken the law, they have entered another world. We know that the domain of the good does not end on the frontiers of what is considered legal (materially speaking) but that it extends (and sometimes even begins) beyond those frontiers.

It is possible that the special and specific conditions caused by the war played some small role—I believe that this is the case. Wars speed up historical change. All kinds of traditional considerations that would not have been called into question so soon were suddenly questioned or denounced. During a war, many things count for so little; people are brought to hang on to only the essentials in lots of cases. Many instances of authority that made sense during a time of peace collapse during wartime; and when they collapse, they reveal where true values lie. In wartime there is an intermingling of people, a raising of questions, and an exchange of ideas that bring about more change in two years than in a half century of peace. In sum, with a shakeup of everything, whatever is precarious falls down more quickly. People are looking for true values and for the most effective structures.

In 1945, added to all that, people, a certain number at least, felt the attraction or the weight of a prerevolutionary situation and became aware of the call to structural reforms that the Catholic hierarchy itself proposed for society. So why not within the church too? the laity came to say.

Only concrete or specific causes were really decisive. In France everything came down to the realistic evaluation of the true apostolic or pastoral situation of the church. This evaluation took into account two stages. From 1925 to 1940, within the context of Catholic Action, this period was the springtime of a new spirit, and it introduced the practice of a new method of pastoral inquiry. From their "guys" and their "gals," priests heard questions that came from the pastoral environment (the milieu); they came into deeper contact with the objections, the problems, the readings, the distractions, the real state of the pastoral environment from which their formation, their clerical dignity, and their cultural functions had set them apart. This created a strong impetus.

Think of the circles of Young Christian Workers' study groups, the gatherings of Eagle Scouts (*Routiers*). Despite being disrupted by the mobilization of 1939, the war, captivity, exodus, the problem of surviving, the resistance, and the rest, it became apparent to me that the consciousness and the situation of the masses were far different than I would have believed. I remember the summary account made by priests right after Easter 1940; I remember the experience of the captivity—and I remember this testimony expressed in 1944 by a marvelous young Christian worker militant taken by the Gestapo from his work as a Christian in Berlin: "I thought I knew the masses. In fact, I didn't know them at all. The situation is far more serious than we ever imagined."

Is France a Mission Land? (the book of Godin and Daniel) appeared in 1943. The event of its publication is well known—it belongs to history. Once again, by insisting on the simple truth, someone pronounced words that others needed to hear. Only after his death was Abbé Godin's book fully accepted in the church. The man and his work were truly providential and prophetic. We have been guided by his message ever since: the apostolic and missionary face of the church has been strengthened and even transformed. Very quickly, Godin's work led to a new awareness of the situation of the world and to a new rapport between the church and the world. Here, in a few lines, is the situation:

The world is settling into religious indifference. The proportion of Christians may be reassuring (?) in some areas, but it is negligible in others. In proletarian circles which have taken on the character of a sociological milieu, a practicing faith is practically nonexistent. By way of example, here are two samples of what's going on. One comes from an observer inside the milieu of the proletariat: "We continue practicing the received traditions, without wondering if it wouldn't be more useful today to know if all this energy and all this time produce pastoral success, and if a fundamental change would not perhaps be indispensable."[39] And, by contrast, here is what someone says from outside the church: "Without a program of readjustment, of which it appears incapable, the Catholic Church seems to be on the way to collapse. As of now, it has the support of only a small fraction of society that might call itself Christian."[40]

In order to undertake the evangelization of a world which is becoming pagan or was never Christian, the church always carries within itself the deposit of faith, the sacraments, the seal and the assistance of the Holy Spirit. (We should note, however, that the pagan world of antiquity was religious, whereas the present-day world seeks to extinguish every religious need.) Many things in the church, however, are not actually sensitive to the work of evangelization. Certain forms of worship, the inappropriate use of excessively analytic and abstract formulas for catechesis, the bourgeois structure and weak community links of parish life (at least in the majority of France), the clerical attitude of the priests, and practices and expectations that belong to an idea of "Christendom" that is for practical purposes anachronistic make the assimilation of new members coming from a new and different world effectively impossible. The accumulation of venerable old pieces of furniture in its cultural baggage creates an impossibility for the church to make sense "to the barbarians," according to the famous ironic remark of Ozanam.

Even a good number of the faithful think that there are lots of things to adapt in the church: simplify its liturgy, attune its preaching to the real needs of people, reconsider and enliven the institutional forms of our pastoral organizations. As for the crisis of priestly vocations, one reason seems to be the feeling among young people sometimes that many

[39] P. Schulte, *Le prêtre d'aujourd'hui*, 2nd ed. (Mulhouse, 1941), p. 279.
[40] R. Kanters, *Essai sur l'avenir de la religion* (Paris, 1946), p. 42. This book, although one-sided in its criticism and not constructive in spirit, could still help serious readers to reflect on the pastoral situation.

present forms of ministry are poorly adapted to the conditions for ministry today, to say nothing of their attraction to the evangelical ideal in its absolute purity. Vocations are more abundant for a dedicated life that is frankly missionary or contemplative. Further, vocations seem to succeed in the line of an apostolate or a religious life in the world under conditions which require a continual re-creation of an evangelical life and which permit direct, Christian, sincere contact with people and their needs and anxieties.

So the distinction proposed by Jacques Maritain and Emmanuel Mounier some time ago between "Christianity" and the "Christian world" today means something more than a mere literary formula for those aware of the true pastoral problems of today. The Christian world is a necessity, a true appreciation of reality which simply must be translated into social experience. There is a link between reformist self-criticism and a certain "revolutionary" attitude (that is both healthy and normal). There is a revolutionary attitude that arises from the recognition that we need to change the shape of the "world," to judge that certain forms are outdated and to choose to substitute others. But, as you see, these ideas of the "outdated" or of "change" do not bear upon Christianity in itself or upon its dogmas and its hierarchical structure. What is called into question, frankly, are certain forms, practices, or habits of historical Catholicism—more exactly, of Catholics, of a certain Catholic world, and of certain historical-social realities of Catholicism.

VI. Applying These Insights: The Need to Adapt or Revise

So we have begun seriously to describe precisely the present dynamics of reform. Two of them give an orientation to all the others, namely, the wish for authentic self-expression and the need to adapt or revise some of our ways of acting.

The wish for authentic self-expression means just what it sounds like. This has always been a requirement of genuine Christian character, but it is now an irrepressible need in the light of modern sincerity—especially with respect to worship, which is our relation to God.

People want an altar that is really an altar, not a flower stand or a pedestal for statues. They want a Paschal Vigil or a Pentecost Vigil that is really a vigil, not a ceremony expeditiously celebrated in the morning to get it out of the way. People want a Mass that is genuinely the praise and the self-offering of a community united in faith, not just a ritual that goes its own way page after page as people, who may or may not follow the Mass, watch.[41] Here's the point: too many things have become "rituals" for us, that is, "things" that exist in themselves, ready-made. We are preoccupied to carry out the ceremony, meet the conditions for validity, but without being concerned whether these rituals are the actions of real living persons.

As Abbé Michonneau has well observed, people don't live by rites, and our parishes fail to attract people because "our Christianity looks like a ritualism that doesn't change anything in the lives of those who practice it."[42] In our beautiful and holy Catholic liturgy, as it is too often celebrated, there are many things that have lost their original meaning and have become a mere ritual vestige of an action that, at its origin, did express a genuine initiative of some person or some community.

Today there is a compelling call for true gestures carried out in such a way as to really be the gestures of living persons and to really express what they are meant to express. (We need to direct and guide this tendency, but who, in the name of the Lord, would dare to suppress it?) Look at this example: When the faithful of Abbé D., gathered for Mass in a worker's apartment at M., arrived at the *Confiteor*, they stopped and said to one of the participants, "You got into an argument and a fight with so and so. Go ask him for forgiveness." The person in question left the group to go ask for forgiveness, while the little assembly waited for him to return before continuing with the Mass. Everyone will recognize that this way of celebrating the Eucharist would be impossible in other circumstances. But who could fail to see the *truth* of the gesture. You could only object to it by misunderstanding the Gospel itself, as it is here applied both in spirit and according to the letter (Matt 5:23).

What I have said here about ritual gestures is likewise true in the area of doctrine, taking differences into account. Although doctrine is not

---

[41] Cf. text of J. Rivière writing to Alain Fournier at Easter, 1907: "The Mass this morning—terribly deformed, lacking grandeur or feeling—disgusted me. Everything was ugly, and I felt that no one understood anything" (*Correspondance*, III, p. 93).

The meaning of the present liturgical movement is expressed very well by P. Doncoeur in his "Chroniques" in *Etudes*; cf. in particular, "Etapes décisives de l'effort liturgique contemporain," *Etudes* (Nov. 1948), pp. 200–210. — On one particular point (the authenticity of *things* used in the liturgy), see also A.-M. Roguet, "Plaidoyer pour la vérité des choses," *La Maison-Dieu* 20 (1949), pp. 117–126. Finally, let us note that the two motives for reform that my analysis of 1950 highlighted are exactly those invoked by Pius XII in favor of liturgical reform. (Cf. as to the Paschal Vigil, F. Antonelli, *Osservatore Romano* (Mar. 4, 1951) — see *Doc. Catholique*, 1951, col. 341–342; and in Vatican II, the Constit. *Sacrosanctum Concilium*, no. 21, 62, 88.

[42] *Paroisse, Communauté missionnaire* (Paris, 1946), p. 258.

abstract or irrelevant in itself, it is less than it should be with respect to its impact on our lives, with respect to the way we ought to present it to others so that it doesn't just remain a truth *in itself*, but a truth with living roots in the minds of real persons, able to enrich them in the way they actually live. Further, with respect to the way the church becomes a sociological reality, all these forms are like the visible surface of the church through which people see and touch it. But they are always in danger of existing in themselves like rituals, cut off from the living heart of the Gospel and so representing merely a sociological crust without the capacity to transmit the sap that makes the Christian vine live.

What is actually at stake in this consideration is the truth about the very reality of being Christian—the truth about the religious relation of the human person with God. So it is completely different from a matter of taste or from an itch to call into question received customs. In this way, you can see that we are dealing with a reform of religion, not just a reformist attitude with respect to ecclesiastical matters. Christianity, when it is true to itself, requires a relentless obligation to pay attention to religious reform.

The taste for authentic gestures is also a taste for the authenticity of Christian reality. Christianity has lived for a long time. It is overloaded with all kinds of contributions from the history it has passed through and affected by all kinds of human circumstances. It's not that we condemn things that we should rather try to understand and explain historically. But the real point is this: there are things which come from history that it would be foolish to try to absolutize by making them identical with Christianity. Human and historical forms, developed throughout history, are linked to Christianity without pertaining to its essential reality.[43]

Once again, in one way or another, I come back to the distinction between "Christianity" and the "Christian world," between the church and the Catholic milieu. Granted, we shouldn't spurn any of the historical elements of our ecclesial life, but we cannot reproach our epoch for its hunger to rediscover, as far as possible, pure evangelical attitudes and the authenticity of Christian teaching—and this in all domains. In

---

[43] E. Mounier, "L'agonie du Christianisme," *Esprit* (May 1946), p. 724: "Just as in decorating our churches we should not add anything, but rather greatly reduce gold and plaster ornaments; so also in order to break through the wall of misunderstandings which suffocate the Christian message, we should not invent some new kind of magic, but rather rediscover Christianity itself, allowing the word of God to express its penetrating purity."

the area of thought, people want to taste the flavor of Christian teachings in their specificity and their purity (*ressourcement*) rather than a philosophical or apologetic syncretism.

Today's spontaneous current of reform has to be understood in this sense. However, this penchant (which is that of a whole generation) has unquestionably been reinforced by the situation of believers in the contemporary world. Modern rationalism has developed in a terrible way what I might call the critique of sublime motives. It accuses everything that has a reputation for nobility and disinterestedness of having secret, egotistic, or sensual motivations. In carrying out this merciless critique, rationalism makes use of formidable techniques. Marxism proposes to find within the great ideas of justice, religion, family, Fatherland, or property the mask for selfish personal or collective interests, and to discover a cynical hypocrisy in everything we hold sublime, including—in the first place—religion.

Psychoanalysis invites this generation to discover sexual motives underneath all our noble ideals, including (and in the first place) mysticism. Believers, who already possess the taste for the sincerity and authenticity that belongs to their age, have been driven further to seek absolute purity of intention in all their behaviors. They know that people cannot any longer put things over on them and so, in order to show religion in a worthy way to their contemporaries, religion must be seriously critiqued and stripped of everything in it that is in conflict with human interests of class or politics.

This kind of criticism has to be far reaching, because things are so closely linked together that you can't call one point into question without raising many others. For a world willing to accept the Gospel only when it is presented by a church of irreproachable purity, it is no longer possible to support dubious routines, comfortably installed in the bed that the "centuries of faith" has made for the church. To use the expression of Père Beirnaert, we need "a Christianity that makes an impact."[44] For him there is only one honest means of making such an impact (but it is efficacious): to be truly oneself, drawing as purely as possible upon the original spirit of the church.

One of the fruits of the merciless criticism that Christians have undergone is the discovery of the interconnection between spiritual things and

[44] L. Beirnaert, "Pour un christianisme de choc," *Construire* (3rd series), 1941, pp. 5–22. There are valuable ideas of the same sort in M. de la Bedoyère, *Le christianisme sur la place publique*—Christianity in the Market Place (Brussels, 1947).

the material world. Having learned this, they have undertaken for themselves a form of self-criticism. We are now suspicious of the link between an apostolic-evangelical fervor and the external conditions of life. You can discover this truth through theological reflection based on the study of history. Think of the work where Père Chenu has shown how evangelical reform could only have succeeded in Christendom if the structures of society themselves were called into question by a new return to the Gospel as its source.[45] You can find the same truth by looking at spiritual experience in the history of the church. An evangelical thought world or an evangelical heart presupposes evangelization right in the midst of the human situation. The history of the church and the history of the saints show us that these things are linked, and that it is truly difficult to think in an evangelical way when one carries the weight of triumphalism, prestige, certainty, and power. This leads us to understand that there is a strong link, indeed a passage, that leads from the wish for truth to the authenticity of Christian gestures—going all the way to the revision (reform) of certain forms of concrete ecclesial existence (see below, and chap. 2, first part).

This was, you recall, the immediate conclusion of the evaluation of the apostolic situation in France. I won't go back over the analysis I made above. Let's just remember the experience of many of the faithful who are among the most fervent Catholics: they realize that they won't find the Gospel outside the church, and they don't want to leave the church. Nonetheless, they judge that with respect to their own lives, as well as to the effectiveness of apostolic outreach, certain forms of concrete pastoral action are inadequate for these times because they hide or disguise the Gospel rather than express it.

A young woman doing religious missionary work in the world recently said, "In the name of the pagan environments in which we find ourselves living, we want our religious living to give people a simpler image of Christ that is easier for them to decipher."[46] This is an often-repeated fact. For many people today the external forms of the church have become a barrier that screens out not only the Gospel and God but also the mystery of the church itself.

---

[45] "Réformes de structure en chrétienté," *Economie et Humanisme* (1946), pp. 85–98, reprinted in the collection *Inspiration religieuse et structures temporelles* (Paris, 1948), pp. 261–281.

[46] Cf. *Le Supplément de la Vie Spirituelle* (May 1948), p. 116.

Many would receive the faith fairly easily if it were offered to them in the form that it receives from its sources (the Bible and early tradition). But they have trouble recognizing the Gospel beneath the historical baggage that hides its living reality and that seems foreign to it.[47] Because of this, it is often from outside or in a roundabout way that we discover the functional values of the Gospel in the church itself.[48] In the same way, we discover new forms of faith expression and worship; they are re-discovered—reinvented—by going back to the sources and remaining rooted in them. These are facts, and we can only misunderstand their meaning if we bypass one of the clearest directions given by the Holy Spirit to the present time.

From another perspective, when we have understood better the mystery of the church, we can be more understanding and clearer about the outdated structures and the delays that we mentioned earlier. This leads us to appreciate more fully the church's transcendence. The call for needed adaptations takes on a new urgency, an urgency motivated by fervent faith and an impatience for apostolic outreach.

I have already noted that many of our contemporaries are returning to a Christianity rooted in its sources. They stumble over the difficulties that the church poses for them, but they know that outside of this church, both historically and dogmatically, they cannot find the Gospel. What turns them off is not Christianity but the Christian world which contains so many non-Christian elements within its structures, inspired by a paternalistic quest for influence—even power, a bourgeois attachment to money, etc.[49] If only we could remake the human face of the church and help it appear more like the church of Christ!

---

[47] Cf. J. Guitton, *Difficultés de croire* (Paris, 1948), pp. 12f.

[48] Some references on this point: E. Mounier in *Esprit* (Aug.–Sept. 1946), pp. 214–215; J. Guitton, "Les sources de l'incroyance intellectuelle dans la France contemporaine," *Lumen Vitae* 2 (1947), p. 614, note; M.-I. Montuclard, "L'Eglise et les valeurs," *Jeunesse de l'Eglise*, cahier 5, p. 41; J. Folliet, in *Présence de l'Eglise: Les chrétiens au Carrefour* (Lyon, 1949), pp. 72f. (these are really remarkable pages); P. Duployé in *Cahiers Sainte-Jeanne* (July 1949), p. 203.

[49] These complaints, already clear for a thinker like Proudhon, have become commonplace today. See, e.g., the compilation of texts collected in *Jeunesse de l'Eglise*, cahier 8 ("Je bâtirai mon Eglise," May 1948). Cf. M.-I. Montuclard, *Rebâtir le temple: Deuxième lettre aux impatients*, p. 948: The author examines the difference between Christianity and the Christian environment—the structures and the face that history has imposed on the church. He sees in them one of the causes for de-Christianization.

Finally, certain changes in ecclesial life and "structures" appear to be needed.[50] By this I mean changes in the style of catechesis and preaching, therefore also in the formation of the clergy, in the external forms of worship, in the public face of parishes, and in the way in which the church presents itself publicly (sometimes scandalous, outdated pomposity). All this needs to be done in the light of and under the inspiration of a return to the sources: the Bible, ancient Christianity, the spirit of the liturgy, and major documents of the magisterium.

These observations, which will teach most of our readers nothing new, need to be made more precise by articulating how their spirit is expressed in the current reform of structures.

In the majority of reforms that the church has known, it was a question essentially of reasserting established rules that were fixed in decrees or canons. Some reforms, however, were accomplished or at least advocated in the name of a return to sources higher than church canons, canons whose holiness was not in question but that needed to be transcended by the stimulus for reform.

Such was the case with the evangelical or apostolic movement that ran throughout the whole of the twelfth century; it became expressed finally in the work of St. Francis and St. Dominic. At the beginning of the sixteenth century this was the case of the reform vision of John Colet,

---

[50] Those who use this rather vague expression, "structures," don't always bother to define what they mean. However, there seems to be a consensus about the following: (i) The question is not about the [essential] structure of the church (dogma, sacraments, hierarchy). No one is calling this essential structure into question. Rather, using my distinction between structure and life, the need for [structural] change has to do with issues about life. (ii) However, within the essential structure of the church, the church's life borrows forms, some of which are adaptable, while others have a certain stability. For example, the eloquence of some preacher is an ephemeral expression of doctrine, but the way the catechism is written, or the style and organizational structure of parishes, or even the manner of celebrating High Mass—these are more stable forms of ecclesial life. Such things do not belong to the essential structure of the church. They are historically introduced as expressions of its life, and so they have only a relative value. They are what we mean when we speak in the plural about "ecclesial structures."

I see a sort of verification of my definition in J. Folliet's article "Qu'est-ce qu'une réforme de structure," in *Chronique sociale de France* (1946), pp. 23–42. For Folliet, a social structure is "the permanent and organized element of a social reality, in the measure that this reality appears to be humanly constructed and submitted to the human will." Cf. J. Caryl and V. Portier, *La mission des laïcs dans l'Eglise* (Lyon, 1949), p. 54: "A structure is a social reality that is organized through human intervention . . ."

Lefèvre d'Etaples, Cardinal Ximenes, Erasmus, and others of less importance who have been studied by M. A. Renaudet. This is also the case without any doubt with respect to the current spirit of reform. It's not a question of reforming abuses—there are hardly any to reform. It is rather a question of renewing structures. That's a bigger job than simply re-insisting upon canonical practices.[51] It demands going much further back, all the way to the sources. What is in question is not just tracing an inappropriate form back to its original source but inventing new forms that go beyond the given patterns of action, based on the deep tradition of an always living church under the stewardship of the magisterium.

We've had the tendency, when challenged by reform initiatives, to say, "Reform yourselves, reform your own life, and everything will be okay." It is above all those who represent God who need to hear this! In 1900–1905, for example, A.-M. Weiss took this message to heart in the face of the German reform movement, of which the *Reform-Katholizismus* represented the outside extreme.[52] That was a moment when great anxiety upset the church from the inside, even calling its very principles into question; while, on the contrary, society enjoyed at least an apparent calm. The present reform spirit benefits from serious preparations, one of which surely was the strengthening of the doctrinal tradition of the church in its response to Modernism.[53] However, the state of the world and of people's hearts, plus the very nature of the conditions required for evangelization in the modern world, are extremely serious questions touching upon what one might call the structures or the forms of expression of the church. It is not outside or against the tradition of the church that the movement wants to find a solution, but in the very depths of the tradition itself.

These are the areas of application, the traits, and the status of the current reform movement at present.

---

[51] More important, [this reform spirit] goes beyond being a mere reinforcement of prohibitions or censures. As E. Mounier has written: "You can refute, condemn or wipe out an error or a heresy. But you can't refute a dramatic situation; and Christianity, while peaceful on the surface, is confronted today with the most challenging drama that it has ever encountered" ("L'agonie du christianisme," *Esprit* [May 1946], p. 730).

[52] See below: 1st part, ch. 2, n. 81.

[53] Cf. J. Guitton, *art. cit.* in *Lumen Vitae*, p. 626: "There is a huge difference between the intellectual generosity of 1947 and the ambiguity of Modernism in 1907. [In Modernism,] protestations of fidelity disguised profound disbelief. Now, the inverse is the case, and sometimes excessive statements becloud a full fidelity. The examination of the church's 'faults' or of its 'delays' are accompanied by a feeling for the concrete reality of the church and of its mysterious nature that is more alive than ever before."

PART ONE

Why and How Does the Church Reform Itself?

Chapter 1

The Church's Holiness and Our Failures

I. The Point of View of Antiquity and That of the Present with Respect to the Problem of Evil in the Church

People do not look at the problem of evil in the church today exactly as the Fathers did. If the church of the Fathers is the same church as our own, nonetheless, their way of thinking about it was different from ours. These differences need to be explained with reference to the history of doctrines about the church. From my point of view, the perspective of the Fathers can be characterized by the following traits:

1. The patristic tradition had a very mystical idea of the church. It saw the church as above all a descent to earth of heavenly realities, a movement of humanity and of the world into the "spiritual" quality of the kingdom of God and the body of Christ. These are realities whose true condition is heavenly. So the church appeared in this way as a mystery of holiness, a body brought to life by the *Pneuma* or Spirit of God. The church was therefore a body, a visible body constituted by sacraments celebrated by the hierarchical priesthood.

The characteristic proper to patristic ecclesiology that is at once both attractive and perplexing for us is this: the church is seen as fundamentally mystical, as a divine reality. At the same time patristic ecclesiology does not neatly distinguish the external and social aspect of the church from the interior and mystical aspect. What we call "internal forum" and "external forum" were not really distinguished.

We can find a great number of examples of this, touching different areas. For example, there was not always a clear distinction, such as we would make today, between a spiritual person and one having competence and power. Further, sin, even when completely personal, had the aspect of separating the person not only from God but also from the church. Therefore reconciliation had to be public. From this we can see that, to the degree that communion with God and with the church were blended into the same perspective, the problem of the status of sinners became an important ecclesiological problem. The problem of evil in the church was seen first of all as the problem of sin.

2. Even after the end of the patristic age, the ancient world was characterized by the predominance of an objective perspective and, correlatively, by a rather weak feeling for the importance of the subject. By contrast, the modern world is characterized down to its roots by the discovery of the point of view of the subject. In antiquity, in the Middle Ages, and still under the Ancien Régime, the spiritual point of view is that of the time before 1793.[1] It pertains to an objective world, a world which was perhaps not morally so much better than our own but which had "codes of honor" that controlled respect for groups, tradition, hierarchical functions, and the authority of classes and superior states of life.

I already spoke above about the idea of "modern sincerity." That idea is linked to the discovery of the subject and to an immense interest in subjectivity. While in the ancient world the way in which someone did something or discovered something was hardly worthy of mention, since the essential was the thing itself, in the modern world, the way in which things are done is what interests us. St. Thomas or Albert the Great might have written, in the spirit of Aristotle: "It matters little by whom and how something has been said; what counts, is to know if it is true or false"; whereas modern people might say: "It doesn't matter much if something is true or false; what is important is the manner, the tone, the

---

[1] I say 1793 and not 1789 in order to point to an important event, namely, the execution of King Louis XVI, rather than the seizing of the Bastille. I think that there is something deeply important in the use in sociology of the psychoanalytic idea of the murder of the father. That applies in this case to the murder of the king, which symbolizes the elimination of all authority, including (most of all) God's authority. Cf. J. Lacroix, "Paternité et Démocratie," *Esprit* (May 1947), pp. 748–755. Even before the psychoanalysts and the sociologists, the supporters of the monarchy understood this. See, for example, H. Delassus, *Le problème de l'heure présente* (Paris, 1906), vol. I, pp. 12f.

process followed, that is to say, to know by whom and how it has been done."

This modern attitude easily falls into subjectivism, into a sort of mystique of sincerity which is not justifiable, because it can lead to genuine crimes against humanity. But today's climate is constituted by these realities. You can understand then how our contemporaries raise questions about ecclesiastical ministry that hardly interested the ancients at all. They were not concerned about questions treating the condition of the faithful as religious subjects or about the relation between ministers and the faithful.

3. There is another difference to note. In ancient times the church impressed the faithful as the most excellent of realities. By comparison with the pagan world, its excellence was stunning. Under the regime of Christendom, which was a symbiosis of faith and the temporal order under the guidance of the church, all real social good and human progress harmonized perfectly with the church, existing only in and through the church. For this reason, the question of evil in the church was seen then only from the viewpoint and within the context of the church, so seen exclusively in terms of sin.

In the modern secularized world, things are different. The secular world operates outside the influence of the church, even sometimes in opposition to the church. It is a human world that is not exclusively material, but also spiritual, moral, and sometimes even religious in its own way. It can even happen that this human spiritual world aspires to guarantee people the fulfillment of their destiny by excluding the church. In any case, moral and spiritual values have developed outside the church. Humanity has taken its own path, made its own discoveries, conquered new frontiers and new forms of existence. Humanity has discovered new ideas, found new methods for doing things—all without the church—even when in fact it was building upon values originally derived from Christianity. Humanity has even had its heroes, its holy laypersons, and all of this has simply increased the new demands and the new objections with respect to Christians.[2] This situation is a matter of importance. The problem of evil in the church has widened and is now framed in completely new terms.

In antiquity, the world was stable and the ideal was to continue a tradition. The church was required to be faithful to itself and it hardly

---

[2] See M. de la Bédoyère, *Le christianisme sur la place publique* (Brussels, 1947).

felt any need to pursue new human initiatives.[3] By contrast, we have entered a world of perpetual change, marked by an evolution of events that the world interprets as progress.[4] We have acquired a sense of history that is something other than, and more than, simply knowledge of past events; there is a feeling of progress in the world, of development in human affairs. No longer is the church the framework for the whole of social life; no longer does the church carry the world within itself like a pregnant mother. From now on the world stands before the church as an adult reality, ready to call the church to account. It no longer suffices for the church to verify its fidelity to its own tradition. The church now must face up to questions and criticisms with respect to its relationship to the world, to social values, to progress, and to social developments.

Because of all that, our contemporaries think about the problem of evil in the church in a way that is different from previous ages and in broader terms. Previous ages considered evil essentially in terms of sin and thought about it in theological terms where, in such terms, it sometimes led to serious practical difficulties. But they did not let it bother them too much, in fact. Their confidence in the stability of sacred realities kept them from worrying too deeply about human behavior.

In a sense, our contemporaries are more easily scandalized by personal failings. A bad priest now discredits the church much more than would have been the case in previous times. People often fall away from religious practice because of some fault of an individual representative of the church. Furthermore, today the idea of good order is more demanding than it was before. We said above that modern "sincerity," especially in France, can fixate upon almost any issue, but still with sincerity and depth. Those who live their commitment honestly and completely are met with respect. But those who appear to be superficial or insincere are judged severely, especially if their actions are characterized by pretensions to grandeur or prestige. A great number of churchmen are blamed for not genuinely believing in the so-called sublime realities by which they live at the expense of the credulous faithful. People are turned off by anything that strikes them as pure ritual traditionalism without real personal investment. Clearly, a part of the scandal that the church excites is aggravated by considerations of this kind. (The analysis given here is for the sake of understanding these things, without attempting to judge them.)

---

[3] In this respect, as in several others, perhaps the modern world began at the shift from the 12th to the 13th century.

[4] Cf. Paul Hazard, *La crise de la conscience européenne*, vol. 3 (Paris, 1935).

Above all, however, our contemporaries are now familiar with a new field for scandal, namely, the posture of the church with respect to the historical progress in which the world is caught up. People are more scandalized today by the church's lack of understanding, its narrowness, and by its slowness to act, than by the sins and faults of its individual members. (Once again, my point here is to analyze the facts, not to judge them.)

"Becoming" means opening the mind to new dimensions of reality; failing or refusing to do that constitutes a new kind of moral category—a historical fault—a sin against the truth that reality has this dimension of becoming. Further, this is a collective failure, a historical-social failure of responsibility. (I return to this topic at the end of this work in a special appendix.)

It is not necessary to refer to Marxism here. These ideas are so much in the intellectual atmosphere today that you find them everywhere. Nonetheless, of course, in this intellectual climate, Marxist ideas do play a role.

Influenced by these ideas, our point of view for evaluating human acts has changed. The thing that counts now is *results*, while the *intention* (interior and subjective right judgment) has become secondary.[5] In a recent study undertaken by *La Vie Spirituelle* on holiness, one of the outcomes was to highlight an idea of holiness widely accepted, especially by the laity, that is in some ways troubling: the saint is someone useful to his or her neighbor and who succeeds in helping out others in human misfortune.[6] Those qualities have sign value, of course, and do create a sort of atmosphere.

Once again, people complain of the church's slowness to adapt and to "understand," its narrowness and its excessive rigidity in considering the "subject" (that discovery of the modern world which allows the contributions of persons, their discovery of new forms, new values, and new possibilities to come into play).

You can add this as well: the criticism of the church becomes livelier to the degree that specifically ecclesiastical elements grow in dimension. The church of the Fathers, which lasted in the West until the eleventh century for the purposes of the present discussion, was regarded above

---

[5] See the rather telling article of J. Dumazedier, "Libération par le Marxisme," *Jeunesse de l'Eglise*, cahier 7, pp. 37–63.

[6] The results were published in *La Vie Spirituelle* (Feb. 1946). I oversimplify here. There were a lot of very good and very evangelical elements in the responses to the questionnaire.

all as a heavenly reality, participating in the heavenly mysteries, as St. Cyprian put it.[7] It was regarded above all according to its mystical aspect. So true was this, that the Fathers and the first scholastics thought they had treated the church sufficiently by discussing Christ, the sacraments, and the communion of the faithful. They did not develop an ecclesiology properly so called or, if you will, a theory about the ecclesial apparatus in itself.

After the eleventh century, and especially after the end of the thirteenth century, a reflection upon the church itself and especially its powers took on considerable scope and continued growing down to the sixteenth century, and then with renewed energy even down to our time. Is this simply a simultaneous development, or was there a relation of cause and effect? It seems to me that the criticisms of the church, as well as the need for reform, are concomitant with the growth of ecclesiastical structures or of what I just called the ecclesial "apparatus."[7a]

Here is another fact that confirms rather well what was just observed. The great Christian communions outside the Catholic Church have been largely spared from the criticisms that have fallen upon the Catholic Church. The Protestants glory in the fact that the countries where the Reformation flourished have not experienced the anticlericalism that thrives in Catholic countries. They say that this is because clericalism has been rampant in Catholic lands.[8] There is some truth in this.

People criticize a church more severely when it vaunts the claims of its powers—some would say its pretensions. One day I will show how this is the basis for the well-known "anti-Roman complex," which began to lessen significantly only in non-Catholic countries. What gives such an edge to the question of the church's faults are its "pretensions." The accusations that people make against the church would not be so serious if they were made against some other institution. They are troubling, however, when the church as a society and as an institutional apparatus claims for itself the quality of holiness, the prerogative of infallibility, and calls people to obey, to have confidence in its actions, and to revere it.[9]

---

[7] Cyprian, *De unitate Ecclesiae catholicae*, 6: "sacramentis caelestibus cohaerentium."

[7a] G. B. Ladner has shown that until the 11th century, the verb "reform" was applied to the Christian faithful who needed to be "re-formed" to the image of Christ; the theme is applied to the church itself beginning in the 11th century (*The Idea of Reform: Its Impact on Christian Thought and Action* [Cambridge, MA, 1956]).

[8] See, for example, F. Hoffet, *L'impérialisme protestant* (Paris, 1948).

[9] Dom Vonier understood this, and he opened his meditation in *L'Esprit et L'Epouse* (*Unam Sanctam* 16 [Paris: Cerf, 1947]) with this theme.

From that perspective, you can understand some of the present-day attitudes with respect to the failures that people see in the church: its sins, limitations, and historical mistakes.

I have just expressed, then, for all practical purposes the themes of the Protestants and of a good number of secular critics, perhaps especially those who still find the church interesting despite everything. Their scandal is increased by the fact that this same church, that makes such exalted claims for itself, fails to recognize its mistakes, refuses to acknowledge its failures, and to be humble. In truth, this idea feeds itself on a theology of the church that is Protestant and that allows Protestants to denounce what they called "the faults of the churches" with a sort of religious delight. In the third part of this work I will attempt to identify the theological positions that underlie this attitude.*

This question of the "failures of the churches" and, in particular, their "historical faults" that brought about the sad divisions of the Christian people is a question of the highest importance for the ecumenical movement. A humble confession of faults appears to be a condition for a dialogue between the Christian communions.[10] In fact, Catholics *do* recognize the "historical failures" that they committed in the great tragedies of the "Eastern Schism" and the Reformation. We will see later on that this avowal of failure does not date only from the present moment. However, this awareness is nonetheless clearer in our day because of our more exact knowledge of history and because of the grace of the Holy Spirit moving so many hearts toward the work of unity that the Spirit is preparing.

But on this point, as on others touching ecumenical dialogue, it quickly becomes clear that the least formula, if it is not going to be meaningless, will have ramifications for the whole spectrum of dogma and particularly the whole spectrum of ecclesiology. The same words do not always mean the same thing, because each side interprets them within its own frame of reference. So it is necessary to make very precise what we mean by the expression "faults of the churches" and to identify the *idea* of the church that is implicit for each side, hidden beneath the affirmations that it makes.

Catholics have become more sensitive to the weaknesses of their church. Confronted with attacks against their church, Catholics want to

---

* As noted above, part 3 is not included in this translation.

[10] Otto Urbach (a Catholic) has written something along these lines in *Zum Gespräch zwischen die Konfessionen* (Munich, 1939), p. 49. Cf. Möhler, cited below, n. 61.

be on irreproachable ground; they don't want to have to defend the indefensible. They, like others, belong to their century and carry within themselves its taste for sincerity, further heightened by its concern for historical objectivity. Further, they have learned the lessons of history. They think that serious self-criticism done in a timely fashion would have effectively stripped adversaries of their strongest weapons. They want to separate the eternal and living essence of Catholicism from all the baggage that the church has accumulated through the centuries—the waste, the excesses, and the dead skin, so to speak. They want this all the more because they have acquired a renewed and expanded awareness of their Christian responsibility, of the urgency for a perfectly pure apostolic witness, a witness that is not vulnerable to attack in the midst of a re-paganized world (re-paganized, some would say, "because of our failures").

Further, we have seen in recent years a growing number of "examinations of conscience" that lack, in truth, the full seriousness of persons genuinely struck by the solemn nature of penitence. In the introduction, I made reference to the principal literary examples of the self-criticism of the years 1945–1946. Let me note, in ending this section, how relevant all that is to my present purpose. Authentic gestures, adaptation of forms —these were the two principal themes of this reformist self-critique. A lack of genuineness in commitments, slowness to respond, and narrowness of spirit with respect to what historical development requires or demands: these are the areas where modern people are particularly sensitive concerning the weaknesses of the church. We will return to these two points again in order to demonstrate that in theology they are precisely the themes to which a reform spirit is linked. At the moment, however, it is important to affirm theologically that it is possible to address the faults or defects of the church and, above all, to make clear their theological dimensions. To do that, I first of all take up an exploration of the church's tradition.

II. The Teachings of the Bible, the Fathers, and the Magisterium

As to the teaching of the Bible and the Fathers, I can only claim to provide here a summary sketch. Each of these topics would require research and development going well beyond the limits of the present treatment. I will make do with furnishing some direction that hopefully touches upon the essential elements of the question.

1. *Holy Scripture*

A) *The People of God under the Old Law*: A fact of great significance, which Protestant writers especially have underlined, is that Israel is a sinful people, incessantly falling into infidelity, repeatedly destined for punishment, even death, because of their faithlessness. But they are also ceaselessly forgiven and lifted up again by the grace of God. From the beginning, Adam had been a sinner, condemned and forgiven. In the desert, then under Joshua and the Judges (i.e., during the whole time when Israel left Egypt, walked toward its inheritance, and finally entered into possession of the Promised Land), Israel never stopped falling, never stopped being condemned and chastised for its infidelity, never stopped crying out to God, who sent help to Israel and saved it. Here are a people incessantly destined for death and then saved from death. This people, in the framework of its history, proclaim the central mystery of the death and resurrection of Jesus Christ. The themes of punishment joined to mercy, of judgment from which a small number escape, and finally of the remnant—these are the themes of the history of Israel.

Sometimes the fidelity of God's people can be found only in one single heart. At the moment of the golden calf, it was the heart of Moses; at the time of the discouraging story of scouts sent into the Promised Land while the people murmured against God, it was the hearts of Caleb and Joshua (Num 13–14). Confronted by the prophets of Baal, under Ahab and Jezebel, it was the heart of Elijah (1 Kgs 18–19), who was at the end of his strength and courage.

The leaders of the people—kings and priests—are themselves sinners. Only the word and the fidelity of God do not fail. Sometimes God seizes upon a man and makes him a prophet, someone to speak for God, who speaks a word *from God* and thus becomes, in the midst of a faithless people, a sort of link to God. Israel really continues to exist only through these interventions from God.

B) *Under the New and Definitive Law*: The kingdom of God that Jesus came to announce will embrace nothing but the pure and the purified,[11] nothing that is not robed in a wedding garment. However, the church only represents the earthly phase of the kingdom, a period of proclamation, of preparation, and of germination (the "firstfruits"). The parables of the kingdom that are applied to this preparatory phase show us the

---

[11] 1 Cor 6:9, 10; 15:50; Gal 5:21; Eph 5:5; Rev 22:15; etc.

church including both good and bad fish,[12] both weeds and wheat,[13] both well-dressed guests and others without a wedding garment . . .[14]

I don't have to belabor this theme of the *Ecclesia mixta* (a church with mixed elements) that is so abundantly evoked by the Fathers, especially by St. Augustine. The church in its earthly phase is a community of sinners and not just of saints. Sin can indeed separate a person from Christ and also in some way from the church. But sin does not take away one's membership in the church—a fact that presupposes the distinction, already made in passing and treated again further on, between the frame or structure of the church and the church's life.

No member of the church completely escapes from sin—with the exception, as we shall see, of the Mother of God. Even the apostles were sinners. It is remarkable that in all the episodes where Jesus promises or gives to Peter what we cannot avoid calling his primacy, we find a sign of the personal weaknesses of Simon Peter.[15] Clearly, Peter seems to have become another person after Pentecost. In a general way, the apostles appear to us as charismatic personalities habitually moved by the Spirit of God. But limitations and weaknesses remain in them (cf. Gal 2:11f., etc.). Even more clearly, evil continues to exist in the community of believers. Let me try to elucidate this fact. What general indications can we find about this matter in the apostolic letters?

First of all, there are evidently numerous allusions to personal sins along with exhortations to lead a pure life. Some sins imply a social disorder requiring exclusion from ecclesial communion (1 Cor 5). Next, there is mention of more or less serious abuses leading to the formation of cliques (1 Cor 1:10f.; 11:18f.; cf. Jude 12f.), jealousies, and disputes (1 Cor 3:3). Here again the most serious cases may lead to exclusion (Titus 3:10). Third, the gravest of sins is false teaching or false practices. Almost all the epistles make reference to this problem. Sometimes it is a case of the Judaizers (Gal; cf. Phil 3:2), sometimes the case of a pseudo-philosophy or of a syncretistic gnosis (Eph; Col 2:8; etc.), sometimes pointless observances (Col 2:16-23).

But above all, the apostles, to the degree they move along in their career and reflect on what will occur when they have left the scene, find

---

[12] Matt 13:47.

[13] Matt 3:12; Luke 3:17.

[14] Matt 22:10-11.

[15] Matt 16:17-19, 22-23; Luke 22:32, 34; John 21:15-17, evidently linked to Peter's threefold denial; cf. Mark 14:37.

themselves warning of an "increase of the perils." It is not only in the Pastoral Epistles (1 Tim 1:3-4; 6:2b f.; 2 Tim 2:14; 4:1-8; Titus 3:9-11) or in the non-Pauline letters (2 Pet 2:1f.; 1 John 2:18f.; 4:1-6; 2 John 7; Jude 17f.; Rev) that we find such warnings. They are likewise found in the captivity epistles (Eph 4), in Paul's great letters (Rom 16:17-18), and even in Acts.

Nothing is more significant in this respect than St. Paul's exhortation to the elders at Miletus (Acts 20:28-31) at the moment when he was leaving them for Jerusalem, aware that he was facing troubles from which he might not come out alive. Here is a form of direct witness from Luke (this text is part of the *"Wir-Stücke"*—the *we* passages), and the impressive cross-references with many Pauline texts guarantees its authenticity. We find here an expression of the great preoccupation of the apostles about the churches. They were led to imagine the moment when they would no longer be present, and they address the threat of false doctrine and divisions.

One fact seems really remarkable to me and has great meaning for ecclesiology. Faced with these risks of doctrinal error, St. Paul appeals to the apostolicity of doctrine, that is to say, to the tradition, the received teaching (Rom 16:17-18), to the apostolicity of ministry, since ministers exist precisely to avoid succumbing to the winds of false teaching (Eph 4). Timothy and Titus, the *episcopoi* of Miletus, by the authority and the grace of the laying on of hands, have the pastoral charge to watch over the purity of doctrine. Paul counts on those who exercise the charge of *episcopè* [overseer] to assure the purity of his churches when he will no longer be around. In this respect, the witness of Clement of Rome (XLIV) on apostolic succession in the *episcopè* is fully in accord with the accounts of the Scriptures. He describes, after the fact, precisely what the Acts and the Pastoral Epistles express as their ecclesial vision and their intention.

In the letters to the churches in chapter 2 of the Book of Revelation, the "Angel" of each church probably designates both the community and the pastor who, charged with the *episcopè*, watch over the communion of faith and love in which the congregation (*Ecclesia*) must live.[16]

---

[16] According to W.-H. Brownlee, "The Priestly Character of the Church in the Apocalypse," *New Testament Studies* 5 (1959), pp. 224–225: the angel of the church is at one and the same time the bishop and the community itself. On the idea of the angel of the church interpreted as designating the bishop who incarnates, personifies, and symbolizes the unity of the community, cf. commentaries on the text, and also J. Colson, "Aux origènes de l'épiscopat," *La Vie Spirituelle, Supplement* (Aug. 1949), pp. 149f.

These letters are made up of both praise and encouragements as well as reproaches. Only the churches of Smyrna and Philadelphia are not reproached.

Against the other churches, these complaints are lodged: to have abandoned their first love and their original fervor (Ephesus), to keep in their midst people attached to the doctrine of the Nicolaitans or those too indulgent about eating food sacrificed to idols or practicing fornication (Pergamum), to allow a false prophetess to seduce the faithful (Thyatira), to be a bit lax (Sardis), to be lukewarm and proud of their riches (Laodicea).

All those things represent weaknesses affecting the behavior of the members of the community and eventually their pastors. The community is collectively responsible for those who make it up, both faithful and leaders. In sum, what is criticized or praised (with the promise of fitting recompense) is both the personal and the collective behavior of the members of the churches. When these members behave more or less well, the churches are affected in their way of living.

However, it seems here, as in the pastoral letters, that there is a fundamental reality of the church that is not compromised by the disorderly behavior of its members.[17] The sinner who defiles himself does not turn the church into a sinful church. Fundamentally, to the degree that people sin, they place themselves outside the church. If their sin concerns the domain of the Christian life, sinners become less alive, but they still remain within the framework of the church's saving grace. If their sin has to do with constituent elements of the church as an institution, then sinners withdraw from the framework of the church, which however is not itself harmed by the sinner's error.

In speaking of heretics who deny some aspect of the mystery of the incarnation (cf. John 5:22; 4:2-3; 2 John 7), St. John writes: "They went out from us, but they did not belong to us; for if they had belonged to us, they would have remained with us" (1 John 2:18-19). Before the

---

[17] Consider this interesting note by Cl. Chevasse, *The Bride of Christ* (London, 1940), p. 95: In the Old Testament, in Hosea and Ezekiel, the same woman is both unworthy and graced, both unfaithful and capable of conversion. In Revelation, there are two women—the courtesan who is hopelessly fallen, and the pure, holy and eternally young spouse. Of course, this refers to the heavenly Jerusalem; but John and the entire tradition of antiquity conceive of the church on earth as a beginning of the church in heaven.

troublemakers were expelled from the church, they had been in its midst as a sort of trial and temptation, something necessary to allow for the discernment of true believers and thus, in a certain way, necessary for the purity of the faithful people (1 Cor 11:19).

Second Thessalonians 2:3f. is a troubling text which the Reformers frequently applied polemically against the papacy[18]: "Let no one deceive you in any way; for that day will not come unless the rebellion comes first and the lawless one is revealed, the one destined for destruction. He opposes and exalts himself above every so-called god or object of worship, *so that he takes his seat in the temple of God*, declaring himself to be God."[19]

Can we draw from this text the idea that the mystery of iniquity exists within the temple, that is to say, within the church? (The true temple according to the New Testament is the Body of Christ, that is, the church.)[20] This appears exegetically debatable. The "lawless one" [or "man of sin"] is a Semitic expression like "son of perdition" and likewise an apocalyptic figure drawn from the Book of Daniel,[21] where it refers to Antiochus Epiphanius, the type of the enemy of God, who went so far as to violate God's temple. The Lord makes allusion to this in his eschatological discourses (Mark 13:14; Matt 24:15). St. Paul only uses the classic terms of the Jewish tradition to designate the Antichrist. Even in this perspective, it can be said that evil comes from outside, not from within the church. Antiochus Epiphanius made war on the saints . . . There is then, in the text of St. Paul, mention of the Antichrist-type, of which Antiochus Epiphanius had been a figure, having gone so far as to profane the temple. There is not, however, an affirmation about the fact that the mystery of iniquity might be found within the church itself, a spiritual temple under messianic rule.

---

[18] Luther, for example, in *Wider Hans Wurst* (1541), cited by Münchmeyer, *Das Dogma von der sichtbaren . . .*, p. 29; *Von der Wiedertaufe* (1528) and *Commentary on Galatians* (1535), cited ibid., p. 30; *Ad libros . . . Catharini . . . Responsio* (1521) [Weimar, VII: 742]. See also H. Grisar and Fr. Heege, *Luther-Studien: Luthers Kampfbilder* (Freiburg, 1921). For Calvin, for example, cf. *L'Epître à Sadolet* (ed. Je sers, p. 71).

[19] Cf. 1 Tim 4:1; 2 Tim 3:1.

[20] The view of H.-M. Feret, "Le temple du Dieu vivant," in *Prêtre et apôtre* (Dec. 15, 1947), col. 182–183.

[21] Cf. Dan 7; 9:27; and especially 11:31, 36–37.

I think that the apostolic church presents itself, from the point of view of the fidelity and the evil that can reside within it in continuity with Israel, in one way, and in very different circumstances, in another way.

In the old dispensation, the relationship between Israel and God was that of a covenant.[22] God would abandon Israel when Israel turned away from him. We see these formulas again and again: "If you observe my law . . . I will be for you your God . . ." There is nothing like this in the New Testament touching upon the church. Rather, there are firm and unconditional promises: "I will build my church, and the gates of Hades will not prevail against it" (Matt 16:18). "I am with you until the end of time" (Matt 28:20; cf. John 16:33). "The Father will give you another Paraclete to be with you always" (John 14:16). "He will teach you all things; he will guide you into the truth" (John 14:26; 16:13). "As my Father has sent me, so I send you. Receive the Holy Spirit" (John 20:21, 23), etc.

Under the old dispensation, Christ was yet to come and the Spirit only appeared in transitory ways. This old regime is essentially *prophetic*. The new and definitive dispensation, after which there will be no other that can be more perfect, is characterized by the fact that Christ has come. The fully sufficient cause for communion with God has been introduced into the world, given to the world in a definitive way. It is no longer only a question of announcing this communion, of serving it from afar, but of applying it and serving it as fully present and active.

Parallel to the entry of God's son into the world by his incarnation there is the entry of the Holy Spirit by his mission (Pentecost). The Holy Spirit also is truly *given*—as "firstfruits" in a manner still imperfect but nonetheless real. The terms in which the New Testament describes the relation of the Holy Spirit to the church are borrowed not so much from the metaphor of "breath," that is, of a passing inspiration, but rather from that of indwelling, from the fact of "filling up" the church.[23] The governance of the church is no longer *prophetic* but *apostolic*.

The church is the continuation of Israel—it is the new and genuine Israel, the true people of God. But this quality of being the people of God

---

[22] I believe that the word *diatèkè*, usually translated as "arrangement" [*disposition* in French] as the most suitable meaning, signifies "covenant" more particularly in the Old Testament, and "testament" more particularly in the New Testament. This is what Erasmus thought also.

[23] H. B. Swete, *The Holy Spirit in the New Testament*, pp. 328–389. These same considerations are further developed in my part 3 [not included in this translation].

which sufficed to define Israel adequately does not suffice to define the church. The church is not only the people of God that has finally received and recognized its Messiah. It has also received from on high a new dispensation or covenant with the substance of the Word and the substance of the living bread. The status of the church is not the same as that of the ancient Israel because the final realities, those after which there will be no more, are present and active within her. The church, like Israel, subsists by the fidelity of God with respect to his purpose of pouring out his grace. However, throughout the time of Israel, this purpose *was on the way toward* its realization; in the church, however, *it has come to completion* through an apostolic ministry that applies and, in some way, distributes what was accomplished in Jesus Christ in one single stroke. The church is the reality of a mysterious happening that has come to its plenitude: it is the Body of Christ, the Spouse of Christ. We can easily see that, by the fact that it is "people of God," it is composed of fallible members. However, in its reality as Body and Spouse of Christ, as living temple of the Holy Spirit, it receives the capacity to be "the pillar and bulwark of the truth" (1 Tim 3:15).

Basically, the theological tradition resolves the question of evil in the church (and my treatment goes in the same direction) by placing it entirely in this line of thinking. I am about to lay out the ideas.

2. *The Fathers: Their Theology Is Essentially "Symbolic"*

On this point, the patristic tradition, as more generally ecclesiology itself, is expressed according to two modes or two plans of analysis. We need to consider both of them if we want to grasp patristic thinking fully. There is first a mode of explanations based upon biblical figures and then, second, a mode of propositions elaborated on the basis of the life of the church.

Two great symbols are employed: first, that of the moon and, second, that of women chosen from a life of impurity and then introduced into the order of holiness.

The theme of the moon has been studied by Hugo Rahner.[24] Leaving aside other complexities, it will suffice here to show the application of

---

[24] " 'Mysterium lunae': Ein Beitrag zur Kirchentheologie der Väterzeit," *Zeitschrift für katholische Theologie* 63 (1939), pp. 311–349, 428–442; 64 (1940), pp. 61–80, 121–131, reprinted in *Symbole der Kirche: Die Ekklesiologie der Väter* (Salzburg, 1964). *Idem, Greichische Mythen in christlicher Deutung* (Zurich, 1945), pp. 139, 200f.

this theme to our topic. This speculation, at once strange and fascinating, has its point of departure in biblical texts like those where the sun is shown going forth like a spouse from its nuptial couch (Ps 19:5); where the sun and the moon are placed in relationship one with the other as in this text: "*Orietur justitia, donec auferatur luna*—May righteousness flourish . . . until the moon is no more" (Ps 72:7); or even this text: "*Per diem sol non uret te, neque luna per noctem*—The sun shall not strike you by day, nor the moon by night" (Ps 121:6), etc.

The Fathers liked to underline the fact that the moon symbolizes by its periodic changes the mutability characteristic of the historic condition of the church, showing alternating weakness and renewal. They also developed the following theme: the star of life is the sun, but during the night, when it is hidden, it lends its brightness to the moon. When the sun appears and rises in the sky, the moon decreases even to the point of disappearing and becoming lost in the light of the sun. Likewise, the moon, by the submission that it offers in its nuptial encounter with the sun, becomes the mother of things living on the earth, and it brings forth during the night the life-giving dew. In the same way, the church—by dying for Christ in the self-giving submission that it offers everyday visibly on earth in the obscurity of its union with Christ—receives the power to communicate the spiritual life, to become the source of the baptismal waters, and the channel of the dew of grace. And this, *donec auferatur luna*—until the moon is no more. There is a daily and constant self-giving of the church, which will become total at the end of time, when the church will bring forth its fruit through the resurrection of the flesh.

For our purposes, the interesting idea here is that the church receives all of its brightness from the sun, Christ, its Spouse. By itself, the church is obscure: it has a twofold aspect, one shining and pure because illuminated by Christ, and the other obscurity. As Augustine says, either it includes both the spiritual and the carnal or, without power or beauty of its own, it owes all of its power to the Sun—who is Christ.[25] St. Augustine is attached to the idea that the church, like the individual soul, is ugly and sinful in itself. At the point at which it confesses its sins, it begins to become beautiful through the action of the one who is himself true Beauty.[26] In this way, the church finds the source of its beauty in feeling

---

[25] *Ennarrationes in Psalmis*, n. 3 (PL 36:132).

[26] *Ennar. in Ps. 103, Sermo 1*, n. 4 (PL 37:1338). Let me cite this text that is so characteristic of Augustine, where the word "reformer" is found (which pleases the Protestants): "Vis ei placere? Non potes quamdiu deformis es. Quis facies ut pulchra

and confessing its need to be purified.[27] Each of the faithful and the church itself can say, "I am holy," because they receive their holiness from their Head, of whose body they are members. All their beauty and all their holiness come to them through the grace of this Head.[28]

If we understand the theme of the moon in this way, we can see how close it is to the theme of the women caught in impurity and purified. In both cases the themes have a spousal quality which goes to the very heart of our topic.

The Bible gives us a number of examples of women living in impurity who are chosen and purified after being called. The story of these women has been given an ecclesiological interpretation by Origen, who founds a whole tradition of typological exegesis of this kind.[28a]

There is Rahab, the prostitute of Jericho, who took in and saved the scouts of Israel and merited, because of that, to be saved herself from the anathema and then to be justified.[29] She is a figure of the church that, like her, has been drawn out of paganism and idolatrous impurity. Or there is the case of the daughter of the Philistines, also idolatrous and likewise *meretrix*—a harlot, whom Samson took for his spouse.[30] There is Thamar, whose story is so strange for our way of thinking.[31] There is the "spouse of fornication," whom Hosea is ordered by God to take as his wife.[32] Finally, there is Mary Magdalene, the very type of the sinful woman, who is chosen, loved, and pardoned, and who becomes the most

---

sis? Prius tibi displiceat deformitas tua, et tunc ab illo ipso cui vis placere pulchra, mereberis pulchritudinem. Ipse enim *reformator* tuus qui fuit formator tuus" (The same One is your *Reformer* who once formed you).

[27] *Ennar. in Ps. 69*, n. 6 (PL 36:871).

[28] *Ennar. in Ps. 85*, n. 4 (PL 37:1084); *Sermo 138*, n. 6 (PL 38:766). Cf. also Origen, *Homily 2 on the Song of Songs* (PG 13:50): "Apart from the bridegroom, the spouse is not beautiful; she becomes beautiful when she is united to the Word of God, when she is very near to the Word"; cf. Theodoret, *On the Song of Songs* (PG 81:133, 177, 201), cited in *La Vie Spirituelle* (May 1949), p. 538.

[28a] Cf. H. Urs von Balthasar, *Geist und Feuer: Eine Sammlung von Origenes Texten* (Salzburg, 1938), p. 221: "Hure und Heilige." See likewise H. de Lubac, *Méditation sur l'Eglise*, pp. 82f.

[29] Josh 2; cf. Heb 11:32; Jas 2:25. Jean Daniélou, "Rahab, figure de l'Eglise," *Irénikon* 22 (1949), pp. 26–45. See especially the texts of Origen (p. 33) and of Gregory of Elvirus (pp. 41–42). To the texts cited by Daniélou, you should add *Opus imperf. in Mat.*, hom. 1 and hom. 49 (PG 56: 618 and 909).

[30] Judg 14. Cf. St. Augustine, I, n. 2 (PL 38:1640).

[31] Gen 38. Cf. *Opus imperf. in Mat.*, homily 1 (PG 56:614).

[32] Cf. St. Jerome, on Hosea, ch. 1 (PL 25:823); Jerome collects different examples of harlots from the Bible and connects them to the church.

faithful of souls. She is a figure of the church, says St. Ambrose,[33] for the church has been able to take Mary Magdalene as a symbol for herself— for Mary has the outward likeness of a sinful woman, as Christ took upon himself the outward likeness of a sinful man.[34]

Finally, the idea that comes to light through these symbols, and to which St. Augustine often returns, is only one aspect of the theology of the church as Spouse of Christ. This church, which arises out of Israel which was so often unfaithful, or which comes from idolatrous Gentiles given over to so many impurities—this church Jesus Christ chose for his spouse even while it was still a prostitute. He loved it and mercifully took it to himself while it was still impure. But it is now purified by faith and baptism—the theme here touches the text of Ephesians 5:26—it is made his spouse, a virginal spouse, and now, it has become virginal by faith.[35] What we draw out of these symbols, then, is the idea that the church has been chosen in its sinfulness, but in making Jesus Christ its spouse, it has been purified and is now virginal in its faith.

There are also texts using literal and no longer symbolic expressions that help us to clarify these ideas. There are first of all texts that point out the effect of sin. For Hermas, the Spirit who lives within the faithful is saddened by their sins, sins which can even bring about their losing

---

[33] *In Lucam*, 6, n. 13f. (PL 15:1671f.). Cf. Severus of Antioch: M. Brière, "Les Homiliae cathedrales de Sévère d'Antioche," *Patrologie orient.*, IV, 80, and XXVI, 367.

[34] Ambrose, op. cit., n. 21, col. 1674. This same idea is taken up by Paulinus of Nola, Letter 23, n. 33 (PL 61:278). One cannot argue from this text, as does Damasus Winzen ("Büssende Kirche," *Catholica* [1932], p. 127), that Ambrose accused the church of being sinful.

[35] Here are some characteristic texts: "Meretricem [Christus] invenit [Ecclesiam] virginem fecit. Quia meretrix fuit, non debet negare, ne obliviscatur misericordiam liberantis. Quomodo non erat meretrix quando post idola et daemonia fornicabitur? Fornicatio cordis in omnibus fuit, in paucis carnis, in omnibus cordis. Et venit, et virginem fecit: ecclesiam virginem fecit. In fide virgo est . . ." (*Tractatus I de Symbolo* in *Tractatus et semones inediti*, ed. G. Morin [Munich, 1917], p. 6; cf. also Sermo 213, n. 7 (PL 38:1063); Sermo 364, n. 2 (38:1640); cf. *Ennar. in Ps. 44*, n. 26 (PL 36:510), and Cl. Chevasse, *The Bride of Christ*, pp. 149–150. Cf. Philo of Karpasia, *Commentary on the Song of Songs*, cited by Welsersheimb in *Zeitschrift für Katholische Theologie* (1948), pp. 38–39; St. John Chrysostom, *Quales ducendae uxores*, III, 2 (PG 51:227–228); in *Mat. Hom.* 3, 4 (PG 57:35): Christ assumed the church (human nature) as impure and prostituted, "quemadmodum hi fornicarias duxere mulieres [examples given from the Old Testament], ita Deus naturam fornicatam copulavit sibi: id quod olim prophetae circa synagogam factum esse dixerunt. Sed illa quidem conjugi suo ingrata fuit, Ecclesia vero a patriis malis semel liberata, in sponsi amplexu permansit." Same theme in *De capto Eutropio* (PG 52:402). We can only regret that these themes that are fundamental for the Fathers no longer play any role in the modern theology of the church.

the Spirit's presence. But the Spirit remains forever in the church, which remains forever holy because of this.[35a] And then, St. Ambrose: If the church is made up of good and evil persons, it has sinners within it, yet it remains itself holy and immaculate;[36] the sin does not affect the church in itself, but only in us.[37] However, because its members are sinners, the church weeps tears of penitence.[38] It does not claim to be without weakness, but it confesses its wounds and desires to be healed; the church says of itself, as did the woman of the Gospel: "If only I can touch his garment, I shall be healed," and the church prays along with Jeremiah, "Heal me, Lord, and I will be healed . . ."[39]

Basically the line of thinking used by the Fathers is the following: the church itself is holy, but her members are sinful. However, we can apply to the soul what is true of the church, and to the church what is true of the soul. The church is spouse, the soul is spouse; the soul needs to be forgiven, the church needs to be forgiven.

This last point, touched upon by St. Ambrose, will be used often by St. Augustine. The church, like Peter (who is a symbol of the church), is both strong and weak,[40] following the Lord during his passion but then denying him. Augustine freely insists on this point: Like the individual soul, the church, called out of sin, ceases to be ugly and sinful at the point at which it confesses its iniquity: "The moment that you confess [your sin], you begin to become beautiful through him who is Beauty itself."[41] The earthly church, says St. Augustine, is only holy and beautiful by the

---

[35a] See *Mand.* V, 1, 2, 3; X, 2, 1, 3; 3, 1, 2.

[36] As to "holy": In *Hexaemeron*, III, 2, 3, and 5 (cited by Battifol, *Le catholicisme de saint Augustin*, p. 122, from whom I borrow several of the following texts of St. Ambrose). "*Ex maculatis immaculata*," see *In Lucam*, I, 17 (Battifol, p. 122).

[37] "*Non in se, sed in nobis vulneratur Ecclesia. Caveamus igitur ne lapsus noster vulnus Ecclesiae fiat*" (*De virginitate*, 48 [Battifol, p. 123]).

[38] "*Ecclesia et aquam habet, et lacrimas habet, aquam baptismatis, lacrimas poenitentiae*" (Battifol, p. 122).

[39] *De Poenitentia*, bk. I, ch. 7, n. 31 (PL 16:476); cf. ch. 15, n. 81, col. 490, where Ambrose says that the whole church bears the "onus of sinner," showing penitence by its tears, its prayer and its grief. This whole treatise, directed against Novatian and the party of pastoral severity, claims that the church is a church of sinners and that the sacraments are given for the use of sinners, etc.

[40] *Sermo 295*, n. 3 (PL 38:1350), but this text has the character of referring to biblical figures and symbolic applications.

[41] *Ennar. in Ps. 103, Sermo 1*, n. 4 (PL 37:1338). Because the church has first confessed its need for healing, it can now affirm its holiness: *Ennar. in Ps. 69*, n. 6 (PL 36:871); cf. St. Hilary, *Tract. in Ps. 125*, "*ubi peccati confessio est, ibi et justificatio a Deo est*" (PL 9:690); St. Ambrose, *In Ps. 118, Sermo 18*.

beauty and the holiness that come to it from its Head, by grace (see n. 28 above); it only lives and subsists through the pardon it receives from God.[42] For if the church is holy in itself, because of its members it has reason to say each day, "Forgive us our trespasses."[43] By confessing its sins, it is purified from them, and in saying this prayer incessantly the church becomes *sine macula et ruga*—without stain or wrinkle.[44]

This process of purification, as well as the full incorporation of human beings into their Head and the perfect wedding of the church to its spouse, will only come about at the end of earthly existence. Like the full justification of each one of us,[45] the complete purity of the church is eschatological.[46] This is a theme on which St. Bernard insists, by bringing Augustine's ideas together with Origen's typology from the Song of Songs and applying it to each individual faithful and to the church. The church is not yet arrived at the condition in which it will no longer know either spot or wrinkle. It will only have that condition when, with the final resurrection, it finally becomes fully spiritual.[46a]

This condition, however, is not uniquely eschatological. For someone like St. Ambrose or St. Augustine, the *sine macula et ruga* is a quality which is constantly being realized by the action of penance and the sacraments, where the Holy Spirit is operating. The prayers of the ancient sacramentaries ask for a progressive realization of this purification as far as this is possible upon earth.[47] But both for the liturgy and for the

---

[42] *Enchir.*, 64 (PL 40:262), "per hanc [remissionem] stat Ecclesia quae in terris est, per hanc non perit quod perierat et inventum est" (*Luc.*, XV, 24).

[43] "Ubicumque autem in libris commemoravi Ecclesiam non habentem maculam aut rugam, non sic accipiendum est quasi jam sit, sed quae praeparatur ut sit, quando apparebit etiam gloriosa. Nunc enim propter quasdam ignorantias et infirmitates membrorum suorum habet unde quotidie dicat: Dimitte nos debita nostra . . ." (*Retract.*, bk. 2, ch. 18 [PL 32:637–638] and bk. 1, ch. 7, n. 5 [col. 593]). Cf. also *De continentia*, n. 25 (PL 40:366); *In Evang. Joan.*, tract. 57 and 124, n. 5 (PL 35:1796 and 1973); *Sermo 181*, n. 7 (38:982). Cf. St. Bernard, *Sermo 3*, in *Festo omnium Sanctorum*, n. 2 (PL 183:469); St. Thomas Aquinas, *Summa Theol.*, III, q. 8, art. 3, ad 2; etc.

[44] *Sermo 181*, n. 7 (PL 38:982). Here we find the idea of the forgiveness of sins by praying the Our Father.

[45] Cf., e.g., *Sermo 144*, n. 6 (PL 38:790).

[46] Refer to the texts cited in n. 43 above.

[46a] Cf. *In Dom. Ia post Oct. Epiph. Sermo* 1, 3; 2, 2 (PL 183:155D–156A, and 159); *In omn. Sanct.*, 3, 2 (469); *De diversis Serm.* 33, 8 (182:994); *In Cant.*, 25 and 38, 5 (183:900 and 977); *Epist.* 113, 2 and 126, 6 (182:257 and 275C).

[47] Cf. *Missale Bergomense* (Solemnes edition, 1900, p. 50); *Libellus orationum gothicohispanus* (*Thomasii opera*, ed. Blanchini, pp. 27, 62, 81); Mozarabic Liturgy, *Liber ordinum* (ed. Férotin, pp. 268, 286); *Liber sacrament.* (ed. Férotin, p. 944). See texts cited

Fathers, as for Scripture itself, the perfect realization of the purity and sanctity of the church comes only in heaven.

Some critical clarifications, which have a properly ecclesiological value, came about in the West following the Donatist crisis. We know that the Donatists insisted that the holiness and efficacy of the means of grace depended upon the personal purity of the ministers. Optatus of Miletus is the first to show how the sacraments are holy in themselves, not because of those who celebrate them,[48] and that the holiness of the church comes from the sacraments and is not limited by the condition of persons.[49] But it is above all St. Augustine who was the providential teacher here. He elaborated an ecclesiology in which the acts of the Christian minister had a sort of objective and stable consistency, independent of the dignity and personal sanctity of the minister. The church is made up of sinners and of just persons, and sinners are found even among its sacred ministers. This fact has been announced to us by the Lord himself, so we shouldn't be scandalized. But the sacraments retain their value, even when they are administered by unworthy ministers. "The baptism of Christ, consecrated with the very words of the Gospel, is holy even when performed by the most vile adulterers, for the intrinsic sanctity of baptism cannot fail and the power of God acts within it. . . ."[50] "When Peter baptizes, it is Christ who baptizes; when Judas baptizes, it is Christ who baptizes. . . ."[51]

Even when these technical clarifications, introduced by St. Augustine, are not known to the other Fathers, they still follow this teaching, in particular, St. John Chrysostom, according to whom bad priests take nothing away from the holiness of the priesthood.[52] In this way the tradition of

---

in G. Manz, *Ausdrucksformen der lateinischen Liturgiesprache bis ins 11 Jahr.* (Beuron, 1941), p. 285.

[48] Optatus, *De schism. Donatist.*, bk. V, ch. 4 (PL 11:1053).

[49] Ibid., bk. 2, ch. 1, col. 941: "Ecclesia una est, cujus sanctitas de sacramentis colligitur, non de superbia personarum ponderatur . . ."

[50] *De bapt. contra Donat.*, bk. 3, n. 15 (PL 43:144).

[51] *In Joan.*, tract. V, n. 18 (PL 35:1423); tract. VI, n. 7, col. 1428; *De bapt. contra Donat.*, bk. 3, n. 10; bk. 4, n. 4; bk. 5, n. 19; *Contra Crescent.*, IV, 20, etc. Cf. *Sermo de ordinatione episcopi*, n. 11 (ed. G. Morin, *S. Aurelii Augustini Tract. sive Sermones inediti* [Munich, 1917], p. 154): "Why are they separated from us, they who are our brothers? Let them tell us why. Were the bishops evil? But they were seated on their legitimate throne; they governed in the name of Christ . . ."

[52] *De sacerdotio*, III, 10 (PG 48:646–647); *In Tit.* (62:672); cf.: "When you see an unworthy priest, don't attack the priesthood. You shouldn't blame the thing, but rather

the church has become fixed with precision from this classical period on. A galaxy of saints and geniuses (whom we do not call "Fathers" in vain) providentially define the principles on which the church had lived and must continue to live. From that source we have drawn an idea of the church already included in the notions of the church as house and temple of God, as spouse and body of Christ, which are fundamentally biblical ideas—the idea of an objective holiness *of the ecclesial institution itself,* independent of the holiness of the persons who live within it. The error of the Donatists had consisted precisely in seeing sanctity as only personal. But in response, the Catholic doctors showed that there is an incorruptible sanctity which comes to the church from its faith,[53] from the sacraments,[54] and from the hierarchical powers of the priesthood (see n. 52). We come back once again (and not for the last time) to the distinction between the structure of the church and its life.

3. *The Teaching of the Magisterium and of Theologians*

Declarations by the hierarchy concerning the faults of the church are rather rare. What I said earlier about the situation created by criticisms of the church in the modern period explains in part why. However, there are a certain number of statements about this where a rather precise position was taken that has not varied. In a word, occasionally the church can clearly admit the faults of persons, even in the hierarchy, but it refuses to impute defects to the church as such.

In the sixteenth century the explosion of Luther's protests punctured an abscess of discontent which had been ripening for a long time. Compelled to admit the urgent necessity of a serious reform in the church, official declarations about reform from the highest sources multiplied.

----

the one who uses badly something in itself beautiful. For if Judas was a traitor, that calls for the condemnation not of the apostles but of Judas' own life. It is not a grievance against the priesthood, but a sin on his own conscience . . ." (*Vidi Dominum*, hom. IV, nn. 4 and 5 [PG 56:126]), cited by C. Journet, *L'Eglise du Verbe incarné,* vol. I, p. 125, a passage that cites other texts of Chrysostom and Augustine. Cf. A. Moulard, *S. Jean Chrysostome* (Paris, 1949), p. 119; cf. St. Leo, *Epist. 105,* 3 (PL 54:1000).

[53] In addition to the texts of Augustine just cited, see St. Leo, *Epist. 80,* ch. 1 (PL 54:913).

[54] Optatus, *De schism. Donat.,* bk. 2, ch. 1 (PL 11:941); see n. 49 above. St. Augustine, *De bapt.,* VII, 9, 13 (PL 43:162–163).

Hadrian VI,[55] a reforming pope too soon removed from the superhuman task that he had courageously undertaken, wrote as follows to Chieregati, his envoy to the Diet of Ratisbon:

> You should say that we freely recognize that God has permitted this persecution of the church because of people's sins, and particularly because of the sins of priests and prelates . . . Holy Scripture teaches us throughout [the Bible] that the faults of the people have their source in the faults of the clergy. That is why the Lord, when he desired to purify the ills of the city of Jerusalem, went first to the Temple . . . We know that for years many abominations have been committed even by the Holy See—abusing holy things, breaking commandments, in such a way that everything became scandalous . . . All of us, prelates and ecclesiastics, we have become turned away from the path of justice.[56]

Some years later, at the Council of Trent that was convoked to strengthen the church in its faith and to reform its life, the highest prelates—Cardinal Pole at the very beginning of the council and Cardinal Lorraine at the end—solemnly proclaimed a *mea culpa*—"through our fault." If the salt loses its savor, Cardinal Pole reminded the council, it is good for nothing but to be trodden underfoot—and he added this profound thought: "If we do not recognize that, then it is vain for us to go into the Council, vain to invoke the Holy Spirit, who enters the soul of people first of all 'to convict the world in regard to sin and righteousness and condemnation' (Jn 18:8). To the degree that the Spirit has not accused us to ourselves, we are still unable to say that the Spirit has come inside us; and he will not come inside us, if we refuse to pay attention to our sins."

Cardinal Lorraine, for his part, told the council: "You have the right to ask us the cause of such a tempest. Brother bishops, whom shall we accuse? . . . It is because of us that this tempest was born, my Fathers . . . 'Let the judgment begin with the household of God' (1 Pet 4:17); 'Let those who carry the vessels of the Lord purify themselves' (Is 52:11)."[57]

---

[55] Hadrian VI, *Instructiones au nonce Chieregati* (1522), cited in L. Pastor, *Geschichte der Päpste*, vol. 4, 2, pp. 93f. (French trans., vol. 9, pp. 103f.). On Luther's usage of this humble and beautiful text, see my introduction, n. 22.

[56] Admonition to the legates to the second session of the Council of Trent (Jan. 7, 1546), in *Concilii Tridentini Actorum*, vol. 4, first part (Freiburg-im-Breisgau, 1914), pp. 550–551.

[57] Speech given Nov. 23, 1562, in *Conc. Trid. Act.*, vol. 9 (Freiburg, 1924), pp. 163–164.

In 1537 a commission of cardinals and bishops, addressing a memo-randum to Paul III on the reform of the church—particularly *in capite* (in its leadership)—likewise proclaimed in terms taken from Scripture: "It is by us that the name of Christ has been blasphemed among the nations."[58]

With great frankness some of the highest churchmen (Cardinal Pole and Cardinal Lorraine both came close to being elected pope) recognized their responsibility and their faults as churchmen and as leaders of the people of God. But nowhere did they talk about the corruption of the church itself. The tradition of St. Ambrose, St. John Chrysostom, and St. Augustine continued here: priests are poor humans and sometimes at fault, but the priesthood itself is holy.

Following this same line, Bossuet explained that the church may always be exempt from error but not always free of vice.[59] Cardinal de Noailles replied to Zinzendorf in 1721: "You attribute to this church, which is the spouse of Jesus Christ and is always pure and holy in itself, the failures of its ministers. The church laments these faults, it punishes them, but the church itself is not guilty of them . . . Condemn as much as you want the bad conduct of the bishops, the cardinals, and even the pope when their actions do not correspond to the holiness of their role. But respect the church, which gave them holy rules and which itself is guided by the Spirit of holiness and truth . . ."[60] It was this same tradition that Möhler continued, that theologian of great value whose remarkable sense of the church so many times moderated certain excessive tendencies. He wrote:

> We have to acknowledge meeting bishops and priests who trample underfoot their most sacred duties and who have let the heavenly fire become extinguished at their hands. Several have even quenched the smoldering reed by their misrule. Catholics don't have to dread confessing such things, in fact they have never dreaded it. How can we deny the deep decadence of the priesthood, when the very exis-

---

[58] *Consilium delectorum cardinalium et aliorum praelatorum de emendenda Ecclesia*, 1537. Text found in Mirbt, *Quellen zur Geschichte des Papsttums*, n. 427, and see Pastor, *Gesch. der Päpste*, vol. 5, pp. 117f.—another text that Luther mocked (cf. n. 22 in the introduction here).

[59] Cf., e.g., *Instruction pastorale sur les Promesses de l'Eglise*, art. 7.

[60] Text found in A. Salomon, *La Catholicité du monde chrétien d'après la correspondence inédite du comte Louis de Zinzendorf avec le cardinal de Noailles et les évêques appellants, 1719–1728* (Paris, 1929), pp. 21–22.

tence of Protestantism is undeniable proof of it? . . . So, Protestants, learn to measure the magnitude of the abuses for which you blame us by the magnitude of your own mistakes. Here is the ground on which the two churches will one day meet and shake hands. In the felt awareness of our common failure, we ought to cry out to one another: "We have all failed. Only the church cannot fail. We have all sinned. But the Church alone is pure and without spot."[61]

Official statements of this sort have become weaker and less striking in the contemporary period, perhaps, at least until Vatican II. Still they used the same ideas: people, even churchmen, are subject to all kinds of weakness; but the church, divinely instituted and assisted, is itself without fault. Listen to Leo XIII: "The church historian will underline the divine origin of the church more clearly by hiding nothing about the trials that the faults of its children and sometimes even of its ministers have imposed upon this spouse of Christ."[62]

Listen to Pius XI, speaking particularly about the faults for which our separated brethren can blame us and because of which, perhaps, they try to justify their secession. With respect to the Reformation, the pope spoke of "the deadly decadence, the dissoluteness and the corruption of the human milieu that, here below, is mixed in with the divine element —the negligence, the laziness of the friends of goodness, the miserable audacity of the wicked, the bad example from on high and the willing imitation by the people, the return to paganism in public and private behavior that unleashed in the 16th century the terrible tempest in Europe of the Reformation, which would snatch so many people from the heart of Europe . . ."[63] And with regard to the Orthodox, Pius XI said: "The separated Orthodox need in this respect to abandon their old prejudices so as to seek to know the true life of the Church, not to impute to the Roman Church the faults of private persons, faults that the Church condemns and which it will bring itself to correct. The Latins, for their part . . ."[64]

---

[61] *Symbolique*, no. 37 (trans. Lachat, vol. 2, pp. 33–34).

[62] Letter to the bishops and clergy of France, Sept. 8, 1899 (*Acta Leonis XIII*, Desclée, vol. 7, p. 295). Cf. a similar but more timid statement in Benedict XV, Encyclical *In praeclara*, Apr. 30, 1921, on the occasion of the centenary of Dante (AAS 13 [1921], p. 214).

[63] Homily for Pentecost 1922 (AAS, 1922), p. 345.

[64] Encyclical, *Ecclesiam Dei*, Nov. 12, 1923 (AAS, 1923), p. 580.

Using a declaration of more general application, Pius XI went on: "The divine mission of the church, which is carried out by humans and has to be carried out by human persons, can become painfully overshadowed by an all too human humanity that, at times, sprouts and comes back again and again, like the weeds within the wheat of the kingdom of God." [65]

Finally, the firm ecclesiological teaching of Pius XII contributes clarifications in which the tradition of the Fathers can be found: "We find in the church a need to denounce human weakness. This comes from the tendency toward evil from which each of its members suffers, even the highest. But the church itself is holy in its sacraments, in its faith, in its laws, and in the spiritual gifts by which it ceaselessly engenders saints . . ." [66]

The preoccupation with ecumenism has evidently favored, just as it has called for, an avowal of the faults within the drama of Christian divisions. Let me mention in this respect the collective letter of the bishops of Holland on the occasion of the Conference of Amsterdam of July 31, 1948. [66a] But it is the Second Vatican Council that gives us the most authentic teaching. Its Constitution on the Church, *Lumen Gentium*, shows the church coming forth from God, but committed to human history as it moves laboriously to its culmination:

> Christ [was] . . . "holy, innocent and undefiled" (see Hb 7:26) [and] knew nothing of sin (see 2 Cor 5:21), but came only to expiate the sins of the people (see Hb 2:17) . . . The church, however, clasping sinners to its bosom, at once holy and always in need of purification, follows constantly the path of penance and renewal." (LG 8) [66b]

> [The church] enters into human history . . . Advancing through trials and tribulations, the church is strengthened by God's grace,

---

[65] Encyclical, *Mit brennender Sorge*, Mar. 14, 1937 (AAS, 1943).

[66] Encyclical, *Mystici corporis*, June 29, 1943 (AAS, 1943), p. 225 (ed. Bonne Presse in French). Cf. the discourse of Pius XII (then Cardinal Pacelli) at the Eucharistic Congress of Budapest, May 25, 1938 (*Doc. Cathol.*, 1938, col. 717).

[66a] See *La Vie intellectuelle* (Nov. 1948), p. 44, and the first edition of this work, pp. 623–624.

[66b] Cf. LG 48: "For the church on earth is endowed already with a sanctity that is true though imperfect. However, until the arrival of the new heavens and the new earth in which justice dwells (see 2 Pet 3:13) the pilgrim church, in its sacraments and institutions, which belong to this present age, carries the mark of the world which will pass . . ."

promised to it by the Lord so that it may not waver, through the weakness of the flesh, from perfect fidelity, but remains the worthy bride of the Lord, ceaselessly renewing itself through the action of the Holy Spirit until, through the cross, it may arrive at that light which knows no setting. (LG 9)

By the power of the Holy Spirit the church is the faithful spouse of the Lord and will never fail to be a sign of salvation in the world; but it is by no means unaware that down through the centuries there have been among its members, both clerical and lay, some who are disloyal to the Spirit of God. Today as well, the church is not blind to the discrepancy between the message it proclaims and the human weakness of those to whom the Gospel has been entrusted. Whatever is history's judgment on these shortcomings, we cannot ignore them and we must combat them assiduously, lest they hinder the spread of the gospel. (GS 43)[66c]

"The church" does not content itself only in exhorting its members to purify and renew themselves.[66d] The church applies the same obligation to itself, not only in words[66e] but also in actions. The Second Vatican Council was a reform council, both by its own actions as well as by the initiatives which it unleashed in the entire body of the church, even at the highest levels.

There is then, with respect to our problem, a position that can be considered traditional: the position of the Fathers of the Church, of the magisterium, or of the pastors in charge. It is the tradition which, in one way or another, we find in the writings of recent theologians. Each one has nuances proper to his or her theological orientation and according to the perspective taken in their works, but they have all repeated in some way the distinction between the weaknesses of Christians and the purity of the church itself. This is expressed more historically and

---

[66c] Cf. the Decree on Ecumenism, UR 4: "As a result, the radiance of the church's face shines less brightly in the eyes of our separated sisters and brothers and of the world at large, and the growth of God's kingdom is retarded. All Catholics must therefore aim at Christian perfection . . . that . . . the church . . . may daily be more purified and renewed." As to admission of historical failings, cf. ibid., UR 3; GS 36 (Galileo!); Declaration on Religious Freedom, DH 12.

[66d] LG 15 and see preceding note.

[66e] Decree on Ecumenism, UR 6: "Christ summons the church, as she goes her pilgrim way, to that continual reformation of which she always has need, insofar as she is a human institution here on earth."

psychologically in the work of Newman, more apologetically in that of P. Pinard; it is precise and theological in the work of Charles Journet. But it is always the same position which is basically held and expressed: the church is not without sinners in its midst, and thus there is evil within it, but the church itself remains without sin (see excursus below, p. 114).

Let me add that, with the exception of Newman, the problem of evil is thought about only in terms of sin, not in terms of delays, lack of comprehension of the culture, or narrowness, which are the principal objections raised by our contemporaries. But as we will see, the principles for explaining evil in the church are the same for the two positions. By the way, the breadth of the word *peccatum* (sin) in ancient and medieval Latin embraced both of these positions.[67]

We need to try to understand an expression according to its meaning in the Catholic tradition. For, in the terms that we have summarized here, we find a solution, but one that needs to be explained in order to be real, authentic, and useful. Otherwise it can seem simplistic, glib, and too cheap. Nothing puts off a contemporary thinker more than a simplistic apologetic explanation. Let's put aside apologetics, then, as a subsidiary consideration, and stay on the level of a theology of the church. There we will try to shed some light on the question.

III. Principles for a Solution:
Several Meanings of the Word "Church"

God Alone Is Infallible

One principle dominates the whole question of the fallible character of the church. I borrow the formula for it from St. Thomas Aquinas. In asking whether angels can sin, the Common Doctor answers:

> The angel and any other spiritual creature can sin, if we consider them according to their own nature. If any creature has the privilege of being sinless, it draws this quality not from its own natural condition, but from grace. Here is the reason why: to sin is to deviate from the rectitude that an act should have. This definition of "sin" applies to the natural order as well as to art or to morality. However, to be

---

[67] Cf. St. Thomas Aquinas, *Comm. in Phys.*, bk. 2, ch. 8, lect. 14 (Aristotle, 199a:33); and the *Summa Theol.*, Ia IIae, q. 21, a. 2, for examples of how in both profane and classical diction *peccata naturae*, *peccata artis*, and *peccatum* meant defect or failure. Cf. n. 68 below.

incapable of deviating from rectitude, there is only one act whose directive power would be the very energy of the agent who performs it. In cutting a piece [of something], if the rule for the operation is the craftsman's hand, then the result will always be correct. But if someone has to follow a model—a pattern determined elsewhere— then the cut is sometimes correct, sometimes not. Now only the divine will is the rule of its own acts, having nothing above it to give it order in guiding it towards its goal. By contrast, the will of any creature only finds rectitude in its acts to the degree that it is regulated by the divine will, from which it receives its ultimate goal. This is a bit like the will of an inferior who should regulate his (or her) will according to the will of the superior—the soldier, for example, with respect to his chief. That is why sin as such is impossible only in the divine will . . ."[68]

So metaphysics shows us how God alone is infallible. All created reality, on the other hand, can fail to achieve what it ought to be or to do. If the church is holy and infallible in itself, that is only insofar as it is *from God*; it is so according to the aspect that it comes *from God*, and to the degree that it is *of God*.

This simple metaphysical analysis coheres remarkably with the fundamental affirmation of the Bible on the topic of holiness. In the Scriptures, especially in the Old Testament, what comes from God and belongs to God is holy, and thus it is withdrawn from the condition of common things.[69] In the New Testament, under the regime of the Messiah who has come, the dimension of transcendence will be made complete in a dimension of immanence, due to the gift and communication of the Holy Spirit (the *Spirit* is himself communication: 2 Cor 13:13). The holiness of the church and of its faithful always derives from what there is within them that comes *from God*. This holiness consists in a state of greater interiority. There is a real communication of God's holiness to the church and to the faithful.

In fact, the ancient church was aware of itself as an organism of spiritual life communicated from on high.[70] Whatever the date was when the

---

[68] *Summa Theol.*, Ia, q. 63, art. 1, c. For the meaning of "sin" in this text, look at n. 67 just above.

[69] P. Delehaye, *Sanctus: Essai sur le culte des saints dans l'antiquité* (Paris, 1927), pp. 1–57.

[70] F. Kattenbusch, "Der Quellort der Kirchenidee," in *Festgabe Adolf Harnack* (Tubingen, 1921), pp. 143–172.

church gave itself the predicate of "holy," this is the first title by which it characterized itself.[71] It truly is the holy church. The title of this chapter is not misleading.

But this holy church is also the church of our limitations and our failures. We see in a general way how that can be. The church, to the degree that it is *from God*, is holy, whereas to the degree that it is from us, it is subject to our limitations and our failures. This, in substance, is what the tradition said. The difficulty is to see how the same church can be at one and the same time holy and sinful, to distinguish exactly what is from God and what is from us, to see clearly what we mean when we speak about "the church itself." Either the church is sinful, as the Protestants and sometimes the Fathers chose to say,[71a] or the church is without sin, as Catholic theologians and frequently the Fathers as well preferred to say. Basically, the opposition (and the misunderstanding, if there is one) comes from imprecise language, doesn't it? The same word, church, has several meanings, and it will help us to distinguish between them. To a colleague of the Chamber who interrupted one of his presentations by ironically saying *Distinguo . . .* , Bishop d'Hulst answered: *To distinguish* —that is still the only way that we have found to avoid confusion . . .

Two Aspects of the Church: Institution and Community

The distinction between two aspects of the church—the church as institution and the church as community—is important and helpful for this question (and for others as well).[71b]

The church is made up of believers, and the most common definition of it found in the patristic tradition and theology is *congregatio fidelium*. However, it is *from* the church that we receive the faith. The church is made up of the baptized, and in this definition "faithful" means "baptized." Yet the church gives us baptism: "Go therefore and make disciples

---

[71] Cf. F. Kattenbusch, *Das Apostolische Symbol* (Leipzig, 1894 and 1900); H.B. Swete, *The Holy Catholic Church* (London, 1915), pp. 24f.; P. Nautin, *Je crois à l'Esprit-Saint dans la sainte Eglise pour la Résurrection de la chair* (*Unam Sanctam* 17, Paris, 1947).

[71a] So in the Carolingian period, Alcuin to Charlemagne in June 799 (*Monumenta Germ. Hist. Epist.*, IV, 288, 14); or Charlemagne to Angilbert (PL 88:909B).

[71b] I have used and explained this distinction (which shouldn't be thought of as a dichotomy) in my *Lay People in the Church*, trans. Donald Attwater (Westminster, MD: Newman Press, 1959), revised edition with addenda published in 1965: see ch. 6, esp. pp. 278f. See how H. de Lubac treats this in distinguishing between *Ecclesia congregans* and *Ecclesia congregata*: *Méditation sur l'Eglise*, p. 78. These are clearly different aspects of the same reality.

of all the nations, baptizing them in the name of the Father and of the Son and of the Holy Spirit, and teaching them to obey everything that I have commanded you" (Matt 28:19-20; cf. Mark 16:15-16). There is a sense then in which the church is made up of its members, and another in which the church makes its members and is anterior to them. The sense by which the church is a community made up by its members is more accessible to us because it corresponds to our experience. It is the other aspect above all that needs explaining. We should pay careful attention to it. The church is in this way anterior to its state as a community in two ways.

a) In the first way, by reason of the incarnation, the church exists *in Christ* before its foundation *by Christ*. This existence of the church in Christ is twofold: first, in God's plan, by the election and predestination that God makes of men and women by means of grace to be conformed to the image of his Son (Rom 8:29-30); second, at the moment when the incarnation takes place. At that point, effectively, according to the whole patristic tradition interpreting Scripture, the Son of God espoused human nature and became truly united to it. From then on, in a way that is not easy to explain but that is truly real, he contains human nature within himself in its entirety. This is why the messianic acts by which he returns to his Father through death, the tomb, the resurrection, and the ascension—his "journey to his Father"—are truly done for our sake and, in a certain way, are already done by us. An abundance of Pauline texts comes to mind for this point.

Looking at this twofold existence of the church in Christ, we might speak of a reality of the church *as mystery*, anterior to its reality as *congregatio (collectio) fidelium*.

b) The church anticipates itself in yet another way, namely, *as institution*. This signifies the reality of the church by which it *precedes* its own members not only in Christ but also in its own existence in this world, according to which it engenders the faithful and, as the spouse of Jesus Christ, becomes our mother. How can that be?

It precedes us by faith, by the sacraments of the faith, and by the exercise of the apostolic authority received from Christ (cf. Matt 28:19). Before existing as a community of the faithful, the church exists as an institution. That is, it exists first as that ensemble of means by which Christ willed to animate and unite the faithful. These means, which build and structure the church, are: the deposit of faith (and principally the revelation of the Holy Trinity); the sacraments of the faith, instituted by Jesus

Christ, as the means for being united to the mystery of his passage to the Father; and, finally, the ministries or apostolic powers. These are the elements, we discover, that can generate and form communities to be the church—as we see in Acts[72] and in, for example, Tertullian.[73] This is a constant tradition which modern ecclesiology has maintained, even as it contributes certain clarifications.[74]

In another sense that is very real, we can say that Jesus did not found the church, for, as people of God and community, the church existed already in Israel. What Jesus did that was decisive was to institute the people of God as a new covenant. How did he do that? He did so by introducing the church, through his very person, into the heavenly world (church as mystery), by revealing to it the true faith (in the Holy Trinity), and by instituting the sacraments of the new covenant in his blood, establishing the apostolic powers (derived from his own) according to the threefold function of prophecy (or magisterium—corresponding to the true faith), priesthood (corresponding to the sacraments), and royal authority.

Jesus gave efficacy to all of that as a new covenant in his blood through his death. When he had done all of that, the church had its structure, its skeleton. Something like the dry bones brought back together in the prophecy of Ezekiel, the church now only has to wait for the living force, the breath of life, that the Spirit of Pentecost will give to it. Then it will engender peoples by the Word and the apostolic sacraments: *quae virgo est sacramentis mater est populis*—virginal in its sacraments, the [church] is the mother of the peoples.[75] Chaste in its faith and its sacramental life, the church engenders and becomes a people; it becomes the people of God according to the new covenant in the faith of Christ, the sacraments of Christ, and the ministry of Christ.

The church exists according to a second aspect, that of a community that creates the members that compose it. It is in this particular sense

---

[72] "They devoted themselves to the apostles' teaching and fellowship, to the breaking of the bread and the prayers" (Acts 2:42).

[73] In places where he lists the elements that the local communities ought to receive from the apostolic churches "*ut Ecclesiae fiant*" (*Praescr.* 20, 5; 36).

[74] Two examples: first, the classic analysis of the elements of ecclesiastical communion through communion with the faith, the sacraments, and a unique community life. Second, the text of the encyclical *Mystici corporis* (see n. 66).

[75] St. Ambrose, *De virginibus*, bk. 1, ch. 6, n. 31 (PL 16:197). There is a widespread patristic (especially liturgical) usage of the word *populus, populi* which refers in this context to the material increase of the church within humanity through baptism.

that Pius XII said, speaking of the laity: "They above all ought to have an always clearer awareness not only that they *belong* to the church, but that they *are* the church, that is, the community of the faithful on earth led by their common head, the Pope, and by the bishops in communion with him. They are the church . . ."[76]

We can note that according to these two ways in which the church exists (as mystery and as institution) before being a community of the faithful, its existence has something both very real and also something virtual at the same time. Predestination, the espousal of human nature, the inclusion of human beings within Christ, on the one hand; the deposit of the faith, the sacraments, and the apostolic powers, on the other hand—what could be more real? However, all of that still needs to be made actual precisely by way of bearing fruit in the community of the faithful. Finally, when all of that is accomplished and brought to its fullness, the church will be the *true* temple, the *true* spouse, and the integral Body of Christ—the *whole* Christ.

With respect to this reality of the work of God bearing fruit in the lives of human persons, everything else is only a *sacrament*, in the patristic sense of the word so happily highlighted by Henri de Lubac in his *Corpus Mysticum*. Eschatologically, when everything shall have come to pass—predestination, the mystery of espousal and of the faith, and the sacraments—there will be nothing other than *church-communion*. To see only this aspect of interiority and communion, as many extreme Augustinians have done throughout history, is to practice a kind of *theology of glory* . . . For the church to recognize itself as first an *institution* is to acknowledge its true state as an earthly church as well as its role as the *servant* of the Lord, of whom she is destined to be eternally the *spouse*.

In the light of this first distinction between the church as a community made up by the faithful and the church as a mystery and institution that precedes its members and brings them to birth, we can distinguish several senses of the word "church." It's not a matter of dividing the church into several parts. It is the same church that is the people of God destined to a historical existence and that is also a divine institution as the universal sacrament of salvation. The point is to distinguish different aspects in this unique and complex reality. These distinctions permit us to speak of the church in different ways, attributing different qualities to her and referring them to the church with the proper analytical discernment.

---

[76] Allocution of Feb. 20, 1946; cf. *Documentation Catholique*, 1946, col. 176.

Four Meanings of the Word "Church"

1. We can understand the church as the elements of the institution itself, that is, those things that correspond to the new covenant given by Christ to the people of God. In this way, the church refers to the saving grace acquired in Christ and destined to be communicated to people; the deposit of faith; the sacraments; and the apostolic powers of priesthood, magisterium, and governance, derived from Christ's own powers. On the whole, Vatican I spoke of the church in this sense at the beginning of its constitution *Pastor aeternus*,[77] comparing it to the house of the living God, that is, to a place established by God where the faithful can be united by the bonds of a common faith and a common charity.

The Middle Ages said the same thing on the basis of patristic texts: *Ecclesia constituitur per fidem et fidei sacramenta* (the church is constituted through faith and the sacraments of faith).[78] In this way, the church is considered in its formal and constitutive principles which come from God and are God's gifts. We might speak of an *Ecclesia de Trinitate* (a church coming from the Trinity) in the way in which I wrote about it in *Chrétiens désunis*.

2. Using the same point of reference, we might speak next of an *Ecclesia ex hominibus*—a church made up of human beings. In this way, the meaning of church would be the people, adhering by faith to the salvation that flows from Jesus Christ and adhering to the means of salvation instituted by him, who fill up the house of God and form the community of the faithful. *Congregatio fidelium* is the most common formula for the church in the Fathers and the theological tradition.[79] In this way, we designate as church no longer the formal principles coming from God but the material principle representing the people—no longer the institution but the people or community who form its membership. In this sense, *we* are the church.

This is the meaning of *ecclesia* (church) principally[80] used in Holy Scripture and which signifies in an exact way the congregation or the convoked assembly. This doesn't mean that the biblical idea of church

[77] Denzinger, n. 1821.

[78] For St. Thomas, see my *Esquisses du mystère de l'Eglise*, pp. 35 and 85.

[79] Cf. my *Esquisses*, p. 69; and also A. Darquennes, *De Juridische Structuur van de Kerk volgens Sint Thomas van Aquino* (Louvain, 1949).

[80] I say "principally" because the meaning of the word *ecclesia* has sometimes evolved beyond its original sense under the pressure of the reality that it points to, as e.g., in Acts 8:1; 1 Cor 15:9, where it signifies, in addition to its immediate meaning, something stable, much like an institution.

should be sought only in a semantic analysis of the word *ecclesia* and in the passages where that word is found. We have already pointed out that the idea of church is fully present in 1 Peter, where, however, the word *ecclesia* is not found even once.

3. The people who make up the church don't all take the same part or play the same role. Yet they are all the faithful and they have all received faith, grace, and salvation. But among them there are those who are not only the faithful, but who are also bearers to some degree of one or the other of those energies (powers) instituted by God that in their entirety constitute the church in the first sense of the word and represent the church's formal principles. In this third sense, the word "church" designates the hierarchy, that group of the faithful who have been called and ordained so as to exercise hierarchical functions. We talk about the church very frequently in this sense. This is the meaning when someone says, with respect to a point of doctrine or discipline: "The church has not yet decided about this matter . . ."[81]

Note also that this third sense cannot be understood without referring to the powers of priesthood or magisterium. However, what is referred to are not the powers *in themselves*, but rather certain members of the church, insofar as they bear and exercise these powers. By reason of this, they merit in a special way the title *churchmen*. This third sense comes about through a conjunction of the first and second meanings: a churchman is a person who does the acts of the church itself, "hierarchical acts," which he performs *in persona Ecclesiae*—in the name of the church. On the other hand, such a person is never completely identified with the church itself. Even when persons perform in the name of the church, they remain themselves—and that can be seen in what they do.

4. Finally, we can designate the church in a fourth and final sense, not by referring to its pure formal principles alone (that come from God as a gift), nor by referring to the humanity that sociologically makes up the people of God, but rather by the conjunction of the two—uniting the divine formal principle with the human material principle. In this sense, the church is the divine-human reality that is born of this union.

---

[81] For example: "They obey what the church commands. They say 'church' here like they would say 'the government'—as if they were not part of it themselves" (Monsignor Chevrot, "Pour une prédication évangélique," *Congrès des Oeuvres de Bordeaux, 1947*, p. 74). In my *Lay People in the Church*, op. cit., p. 48 and notes, I have given numerous examples of this reduction of the word "church" to mean exclusively the hierarchy.

Here the word "church" takes on its full meaning and designates synthetically the concrete church in its totality. It is a church made up of human persons, but according to the degree that these persons have received Christ and accepted to live by a new principle of being, of organization and action. This is the Body of Christ. This is humanity, insofar as it exists by a new existence in Christ within the church, thanks to the energies and to the realities instituted by him for that purpose. As I showed already in *Chrétiens désunis*, the *Ecclesia de Trinitate* and the *Ecclesia ex hominibus* join together and become one in the *Ecclesia in Christo*, the Church of the Word Incarnate, the Body of Christ. This meaning includes all the other meanings and synthesizes them. This is the meaning when we say simply "the church," or "the treatise on the church," etc.[81a]

Additional Remarks on This Theme

Before applying and reaping the fruit of these distinctions, let me make two remarks in which I will highlight a certain benefit for ecclesiology from the preceding exposé.

1. I have already briefly[82] expressed the characteristic norm for the action of God and of the church, which I called the dialectic between what is *given* and what is *done* with it. The church is the result of the synergy of a gratuitous divine gift that is pure in itself and a human activity that is characterized by human freedom, limitations, and natural fallibility. This fact determines two types of holiness for the church, well known to theologians and to those who do apologetics. There is the *objective sanctity* in the church that comes from God's gifts, and it gives the church its life and its structure. And there is the *holiness of the members*, the touching, precarious but magnificent fruit of the cooperation of human freedom with God's gifts. This is a fruit that God desires to reap and enjoy after having sown it and brought it to maturity.

The *communion of saints* is in the area of the *sancta* (holy things)—the objective gifts of God. There is also the *communion of saints* at the level

---

[81a] G. J. Adriaansen, "Ik geloof in de heilige Kerk" in *Bijdragen* 11 (1950), pp. 51–75. Adriaansen thinks that we have placed the formal and the material principle of the church too close one to the other: he prefers the way *Mystici corporis* compares them to the two natures in the hypostatic union. For my part, I see no fundamental difficulty with either formulation.

[82] *Chrétiens désunis*, 1937, p. 86, n. 2, pp. 119, 130; *Esquisses*, pp. 26, 30, etc. (text from 1937).

of the *sancti*—living saints whom the church does not hesitate to celebrate, along with the mysteries and the sacraments of the Savior, for they
are the members of Christ.[83]

But while it is clear that the gifts of God and the *sancta* are pure, being
the source of sanctification for the rest, the *sancti* are mixed up with
impurity, needing always to be redeemed and sanctified. (The Virgin
Mary alone represents a special case, for she is something other and more
than merely the first among the saints. In God's plan, she is found on
the side of the Cause of salvation himself [Christ], introducing him into
the world by her title of Mother of the Savior. That is why Mary is also
the "eschatological icon of the church," as Louis Bouyer called her and
as the conciliar constitution *Lumen Gentium* 8 presents her.)

2. The great scholastic theologians, commenting on the Creed, raised
a problem concerning the wording of the ninth article: *Credo . . . in
sanctam ecclesiam*. How, they ask, can the Creed speak not only of believing *that there is a church* but also of believing *in the church*, when the
movement of faith in (*credere in*) can only have God as its object—and
also, how can one call the church "holy"?

Calvin, who knew the traditional nuances of the two expressions,
preferred to say: "I believe the holy church," rather than, "I believe in
the holy church."[84] The Catholic doctors replied by linking the article on
the church to the article on the Holy Spirit and giving it this meaning:
"I believe in the Holy Spirit sanctifying and uniting the church."[85]
Rediscovering the trinitarian meaning and structure of the Creed, they
showed how everything spoken of at the end of the *Credo* ought to be
attributed to the Holy Spirit as his proper effects.[86] The Holy Spirit is the
agent of every return to God.

Here is how St. Albert the Great expressed it:

> Considering that the Holy Spirit is given and sent in order to sanctify
> creatures, and that this holiness, even if it fails sometimes in indi-
> vidual persons, never fails in the church—we can say "*sanctam eccle-
> siam*." Since every article of the faith is founded upon divine and
> eternal truth (for the creature is useless and does not possess an

---

[83] For this question, cf. Swete, *The Holy Catholic Church*, op. cit., pp. 259f.

[84] *Institutes of the Christian Religion*, ch. 4 (vol. 2, p. 120).

[85] Cf. *Chrétiens désunis*, p. 69, and especially St. Thomas, *In Sent.*, III, d. 25, q. 1, art.
2, ad 5; *Summa Theol.* IIaIIae, q. 1, art. 9, ad 5.

[86] St. Thomas, *Compendium theol.*, 147.

enduring truth), the present article should be brought back to the personal action of the Holy Spirit, that is, to "I believe in the Holy Spirit"; not only in the Spirit himself, as the preceding article says, but: "I believe in the Holy Spirit as to his proper action, which is to sanctify the church through his own holiness that he pours out in the sacraments, through the virtues and the gifts, and finally through the miracles and graces *gratis datae* (freely given)" . . . that the Holy Spirit gives in order to manifest the holiness of the church.[87]

There is no better way to link the holiness of the church to God and to the divine action attributed to the Holy Spirit. By that fact, the root of the holiness of the church is shown to be hidden in God with Christ and the Holy Spirit. There is a visible holiness, seen in the works that demonstrate a sort of proof of holiness. But the essential holiness of the church, deeper than the works of its members, characterizes its very existence. That holiness can only be affirmed by faith in the Holy Spirit, whose proper activity this is. We see something of the holiness of the church in the *sancti* as well as in the *sancta* (the divine gifts) by way of the effects that they produce. But as to the radical and deep holiness of the church as mystery, as institution, and even as people of God, the church believes in that by believing in the Holy Spirit who sanctifies it. Further, even historically, *Holy Spirit* and *Holy Church* appear to be linked in the Creed.[88]

In general, then, such is the classic theology of the meanings of the word "church."

IV. Application of These Principles: Holiness and Failure in Light of the Different Meanings of Church

In Its Formal Principles (Given by God) the Church Is Infallible

In the first sense, *church* is the institution coming from God, representing the totality of principles established by Jesus Christ to make humanity his body. To repeat, these principles are essentially the faith (the revealed doctrine) and the sacraments of the faith, then the apostolic powers derived from the sovereign energies of Christ as king, priest, and prophet (related to the faith and the sacraments). Further, there are

---

[87] *De sacrificio missae*, II, ch. 9, art. 9 (Borgnet, 38, 64–65).
[88] Cf. P. Nautin, op. cit., *supra*, especially p. 61.

the "charisms," the gifts of grace, and finally the gracious plan of God conceived in divine wisdom and made manifest in the divine word.

We are dealing here, then, with gifts and promises from God that, flowing from God, participate in divine infallibility. Of course, these gifts are given to human beings and sometimes, as is the case with the doctrine communicated by the prophets and apostles, the gifts have been made through the mediation of other human beings.

But here I am not considering the *personal* reception or *personal* use that persons make of these gifts. Rather, I am looking at the gifts in themselves, such as they are in coming forth from the hand of God and as they exist by his goodness. In this respect, even if gifts are given or communicated through the mediation of a human being, the infallibility of God remains in place with respect to his gifts, because the human intermediary has a purely instrumental role here. The instrumental cause, says the philosopher [Aristotle], is the paradoxical means that allows a result greater than what pertains to the power of the agent. The agent is the cause of something which it does not itself have according to its own power, because the energy at work comes from on high. This is what happens to creatures if God extends his goodness to the point of using them to produce his own divine work.

Considered in this way according to its constituent principles (not only such as they exist *in God*, but as they are *given* and exist *within the church* as its formal principles), the church is impeccable, infallible, and virginal, with the impeccability and the virginity of God himself and of Jesus Christ. The faith of the church cannot deviate, and its sacraments, insofar as Christ is in them, are saving and effective (the meaning of the expression *ex opere operato*). Likewise, with respect to these things in themselves, there is no question of limitation, aging, or being out of touch. I hold, then, that with respect to its essential principles, the church is incapable of failure and has no need to reform itself.

However, that need for reform arises with respect to the use or the abuse that humans may make of its principles, as we will see further on. In this way we define precisely where a wrong turn, an insufficiency, and so a need for reform can happen in the church. This cannot be on the level of constitutive principles themselves, that is, with respect to doctrine or the sacraments or the powers relative to them. For these things are the part that God plays in the church—God laying the foundation, in a certain way. Human beings can turn aside from them or be inadequate to exercise them properly, but the principles themselves are incorruptible, not only in God, but also *in the church* to whom God has given them. These things are irreformable. This is where the Protestants take leave of the Catholic tradition (still held also by the Orientals). In the third part [not included in this translation], I will show how and why.

In this first sense, then, the church is seen as flowing forth from God, taking its identity from God, and united to God as to its principle. The church is truly a spouse, and this is what Dom Vonier describes in his book *L'Esprit et l'Epouse*. The church is united to Christ and, by reason of this indissoluble union, it is pure. God alone cannot sin. God alone is infallible simply in being himself, in needing to follow no other rule than himself. For only the One who is everything that he is and cannot be otherwise has no rule outside himself. The church is free of failures and mistakes only to the degree that it is joined and united to God, insofar as it is his spouse, even to the point of becoming one flesh with Jesus Christ.

I cannot here elaborate a whole theology of the church according to the theme of spouse. However, this idea is central for the present problem, and we will come back to it at every step of our analysis. But following what has just been said, we can, in passing, make note of an idea which is important for the problem of the status of a reform in the church (and to which I will return later in the third part).

Möhler strongly insisted[89] that the church is not founded upon a text or upon a letter exterior to itself, even if that should be the letter of the Holy Scriptures; but the church is founded through a gift of the Holy Spirit as a living reality which has its law within itself. In this way the church follows an interior and living law, which includes the Scriptures, through the Spirit who lives within it. The church is given its own norm, then, from within and does not have to submit to any exterior law formulated in a text. — Such an idea is acceptable only on the condition of seeing the church in its aspect of spouse united to the Holy Spirit and to Christ. The church's quality of *holiness* follows precisely its quality as spouse, and follows the same conditions just noted.

In this sense by which we first consider the church, it is holy, with an objective sanctity that it cannot lose (because of the gift and the promise of God). This holiness does not depend upon persons in the church but depends upon its formal, constitutive principles. As House of God, the church is holy independently of those who live within it. It is holy in its

---

[89] Cf. above all *L'Unité dans l'Eglise*, nos. 7, 8, 14, 63, and 68 and appendix 3. Cf. below p. 216.

faith, in its sacraments, and in the apostolic powers derived from the powers of Christ relative to the faith and the sacraments. It is objectively holy and cannot lose this holiness, inherent in the gifts that it receives from God.

This does not mean any inappropriate glorification of the ecclesiastical institution. On the contrary, this is the way in which the sovereignty of God's action within the church is expressed. "*Hoc ad excellentiam Christi pertinet*" (this belongs to the excellence of Christ), as St. Thomas put it.[90] So there exists in the church an order of holiness and of worship that flows from the priesthood of Jesus Christ and that has its own proper consistency, going beyond the fickleness of persons and independent of the precarious and changeable dispositions of human beings. There is a principle and a criterion of truth that exists in the episcopal charism, and in a singular way in the charism of the Holy See. So there exists in the church a holiness and a truth that are in a way institutional and that precede and dominate the personal life of the church's members. This is the church's grandeur and its "juridical" role, de facto and de jure, in order to render its institutions stable and independent of fluctuations due to time and culture.

As a People Made Up of Human Beings, the Church Is Fallible

In the second sense of the word "church," it means the Christian people, the assembly of the faithful. The church is made up of its members. Here we are taking account not of God's gifts considered in themselves in all their purity, insofar as they flow forth from God and have been given to the church and remain in the church through the action of God. Rather, we are looking here at the use that human beings make of these gifts—humans with all their freedom, their weakness, their instability, and their essential fallibility. This is the doorway through which sin and various other weaknesses penetrate into the church. This is the "material cause" of the church, the human beings who make up the people of God who are vulnerable to these weaknesses,.

It will be good to look separately at sins properly so-called, on the one hand, and at historical faults brought about through narrow-mindedness and slowness to respond, on the other hand (about which we have already spoken and which we will treat again in an appendix).

---

[90] *Summa Theol.*, III, q. 82, art. 5, c.

a) *The area of sins properly so-called.* "If we say that we have no sin, we deceive ourselves, and the truth is not in us" (1 John 1:8). We are all sinners. However, it is not useless to make a distinction here.

Looking at the faithful individually, they are all, at one moment or another and in one way or another, sinners. Looking at the community that they form, this community as such is holy, for the Holy Spirit who was given to the church at Pentecost has never left it and will never leave it. St. Thomas says that the faith of the church is always "formed" by charity.[91] Some people in the church sin in all kinds of ways, and individually taken, all the members are fallible. They are all, with the exception of the holy Virgin, effectively sinners. The Virgin Mary is an exceptional member of the church (and also an image of the whole church). But the community itself is holy, and it cannot separate or turn itself away from God (not only with respect to its constitutive principles but also with respect to at least some part of its members at any given moment).

On the one hand, there is an election that affects the people as a whole and that cannot defect at the group level, even despite failures of one or another member.[92] On the other hand, there are God's formal promises concerning the fidelity and indefectibility of his church (cf. Luke 22:31-32; Matt 16:18, 28:20, etc.). That is why the more we are inserted in the communion of the church, the more deeply we are established in holiness and truth.

While the community as such is always united to the Holy Spirit, and therefore always holy, always spouse, individual souls may or may not be united to God. The gifts by which the Lord constitutes his church are twofold. There are gifts of service—gifts of ministry—and we can use them well or poorly, exercise them well or badly. And there is the gift of life itself—life in Christ—interior justification and the fruits of the Holy Spirit within us; and we can receive or refuse them, honor or betray them. This question of the use of the gifts of ministry and of fidelity to the gifts of life is one where human liberty plays its role. This is where by human fallibility we can thwart God's gifts. We are able to walk according to the Spirit or according to the flesh (Gal 5:24-25).

---

[91] *In Sent.,* III, dist. 25, q. 1, art. 2, ad 4; IV, dist. 6, q. 1, art. 3, q. 2, ad 3; *Summa Theol.* IIaIIae, q. 1, art. 9, sed c. and ad 3; q. 2, art. 6, ad 3.

[92] This is true not only for Israel in the Old Testament but also for the Israel of the New Testament: cf. Eph 1:4 (as to the "us" in the text, see the commentary of Armitage Robinson on v. 4; cf. Col 1:12-14). For the "Twelve," see John 6:70 and its use of the word "Twelve."

The expression of St. Paul, the "body of sin" (Rom 6:6), has sometimes been applied to the church—an expression equivalent to "the body of the flesh" (Col 2:11). It is not that bodiliness as such is evil, either for the faithful for whom the body can be an instrument of justice (Rom 6:12-13; 12:1, etc.) or for the church for whom bodiliness is the church's exterior form and a sensory element necessary and good in itself.[93] It is not the church, then, even as community, that sins; it is individual human beings who are tempted and who sin. Through them and in them (who belong to the church), the church knows temptation and sin; through them and in them, the church is spotted by diverse stains.

Every evening at Compline (in the Latin Rite), the church has us read St. Peter's warning: "Keep alert: Like a roaring lion, your adversary the devil prowls around, looking for someone to devour. Resist him, steadfast in your faith . . .," and the text goes on to say, "For you know that your brothers and sisters in the entire world are undergoing the same kinds of suffering" (1 Pet 5:8-10). The people of God are a people tempted, and the years that Israel lived in the desert between Egypt and the Promised Land we are now reliving in the present time, between this earthly world and the kingdom. These are essentially years of temptation. Thus there is often sin, and then penitence.

The church in the collectivity of human beings which compose it, both individuals and hierarchical persons, is subject to temptation, to sin, and to the call to repentance. This is why St. Ambrose, whose views we have already examined, says that the church sheds tears of penitence, but it never ceases to beg God to heal its wounds, and it approaches Christ with the sentiments of the woman who said, "If only I can touch his garment, I will be healed . . ." This is why St. Augustine, returning to what he had written, says, "Wherever in my books I spoke of the church having neither spot nor wrinkle (Eph 5:27), it is necessary to understand this not as if the church were already like this, but in the sense that she is preparing herself to be, on the day when she will appear in her glory. At present, by reason of the ignorance and infirmity of her members, she has reason to say every day, 'Forgive us our debts.' " It is also in this sense that a dignitary of the Roman Church remarked, "The Church recites the *Confiteor* . . .," and the encyclical *Mystici Corporis*

---

[93] This is clear in the vocabulary of the New Testament, which makes a distinction between σάρχινος (*carneus*, meaning fleshly) and σαρχιχός (*carnalis*, meaning carnal); cf. Westcott, *Epistle to the Hebrews*, pp. 186–187 (with respect to Heb 7:16). Of course the body of the church can become "carnal" here or there.

applies to the church the petition of the Our Father, "Forgive us our trespasses . . ."[94]

We are not dealing here with a temporary situation or with a period of decadence. Others have quite correctly pointed out the imaginary quality of an image of the primitive church—even of the apostolic church—that is too beautiful.[95] That church also had its flaws, as the New Testament gives us enough evidence to see. The heroic church, the church of the martyrs, was itself sometimes also a weak church, rich in sinners and renegades. The persecutions of Decian and Domitian tragically brought the church to understand this and forced it to think theologically about the fact of the failure of the members of the body of Christ.[96]

However, the error that holds that the church could only be composed of the just and the predestined periodically reappeared in Montanism, the Schism of Novatian, Donatism, and later the Cathars, Wyclif, John Hus, and the Anabaptists (this last group vigorously refuted by Calvin himself).[97] In their different ways, each of these groups deviated from the Catholic tradition in misunderstanding an essential trait of the mystery of the church.[98] For the presence of sinners in the church is not something accidental, a peripheral phenomenon; it represents something structural. The whole idea of the church is involved here.

If the church is only a completely spiritual communion with God, then one has to leave the church because of sin (even interior sin) to the degree that one commits it. Sinning, in effect, would destroy communion with God in Christ. But the church, at the same time that it is communion with Christ, is also the means of this communion—the means of procuring it through the proclamation of the faith and baptism, the means of nourishing and bringing it to perfection through everything which en-

---

[94] AAS, 1943, p. 225. For St. Augustine on this point, cf. *supra*, n. 43.

[95] D. Franses, *Radicalisme in de eerste eeuwen der Kerk* (Bois-le-Duc, 1936); H. Pinard de la Boullaye, *Carême de 1937*, 6th conference (pp. 248f.), cites 1 Cor 3:3; 5:1-6; 1 Tim 1:18-20; Jude 4; Rev 3:15-17, etc.; P. Simon, *Das Menschliche in der Kirche Christi* (Freiburg-im-Breisgau, 1936), ch. 3 on the "human" in the apostolic church.

[96] Cf. G. Bardy, *La théologie de l'Eglise de saint Irénée au Concile de Nicée, Unam Sanctam* 14 (Paris, 1947), pp. 167–191.

[97] *Institutes*, vol. 2, pp. 148f. Rather than undertake a discussion of principles, Calvin looked in the OT and NT for examples of sinners who still belonged to the people of God.

[98] Cf. Franses, op. cit.; K. Rahner, "Kirche der Sünder," *Stimmen der Zeit* (June 1947), pp. 163–177 (and as a booklet from Herder, Vienna). Rahner clearly shows how the church is a church of sinners. Cf. n. 39 above, on the *De Poenitentia* of St. Ambrose.

lightens the faithful—the means of pastoral help and of grace, the means of repairing the Christian life through the exercise of the power of the keys . . . Sinners belong to this church that is their means of grace as long as their sin does not bear expressly upon this ecclesial affiliation (heresy, schism, apostasy) or does not lead to excommunication. While the impure and sinners have no part with Christ, the church here below is like a net full of fish of all sorts, good and bad, like a field where weeds are mixed with wheat; both Cain and Abel can belong to it.

The church's proper work is precisely to ceaselessly purify sinners from their sin. The church is itself the place and the instrument for the application of Christ's redemption. This redemption is accomplished as far as Christ is concerned, but it is brought about in us only through an implementation repeatedly pursued again and again—"*Opus redemptionis exercetur*" (the work of redemption will be carried out), as the liturgy says. "The mystical body, the holy mystical body, is a body where redemption is both accomplished and not accomplished; where then sin is always present and active. Each generation which arises gives new expression to sin in some way, thus giving sin new life. The mystical body is the place where sins must be cast out, the place where trials arise—the place where redemption is at work . . ."[99]

The liturgy, which is so revealing to those who pay attention to its profound meaning, helps us to understand the nature of the church's mission when it assigns the pericope about Zacchaeus (Luke 19:1-10) as the Gospel for the Mass of the Dedication of a Church. Zacchaeus is a sinner (or has that reputation). But when Jesus comes under his roof, he acknowledges that he is a sinner, and he rectifies the injustices that he has committed. With Jesus, salvation entered his house; the publican, excluded from the people of God, has become a son of Abraham as well: "For the Son of Man has come to seek and save what was lost." This sheds great light on the work of the church: to help humanity to pass from the "world" into the people of God (making Jesus present and active) and to pass from sin to justice, from perdition to salvation. The church according to its first meaning (as institution of salvation) incessantly brings holiness into the church in the second sense of the word (as the community of the faithful and the people of God).

So we see where sin is situated in the church. The church is neither the principle nor the subject of sin—it is rather the members who are the

---

[99] Emile Mersch, *La théologie du Corps mystique*, vol. 1 (Paris-Brussels, 1944), p. 366.

principle of sin, the human beings who make up the church. From this point of view, the traditional response to the problem of evil in the church appears correct and satisfying: the weaknesses are not the action of the church itself but of its members. We can see why Dom Vonier preferred to speak of the faults of the "people of God," not of the church.[100]

In *L'Esprit et l'Epouse* he had considered the church as the spouse of God, that is, as completely holy—whether seeing it in its powers and its sacramental and liturgical activity or whether according to its value as a quasi-personalized community. In *Le Peuple de Dieu* he looked at the church according to the second sense that we have distinguished here, that is, in its concrete historical life, at once personal (in individuals) and social. Dom Vonier succeeded better in speaking of the Church-Spouse than in speaking of the people of God. But his distinction accords with mine, and he contributes a poetic feeling that the ideas of *formal cause* and *material cause* don't convey to the same degree.

b) *The area of social-historical mistakes.* These are the mistakes that particularly bother our contemporaries. Even though this is a decisive question, I can only give a rapid overview here. Since this topic relates to the chief concern of reform, I will study it closely in the following chapter.

In any given society people share a whole world of received ideas and attitudes pertaining to their social grouping. These are things that have explanations and sometimes historical justification. But people scarcely ever call them into question because they make up the very milieu they are immersed in and live in. They do not represent the church as such, but rather the forms of Christian thought and existence; however, they are inherited from concrete historical situations and become fixed into received ideas and habits.

Sociological reality that is religious at its root and human in its manifestations is inevitably shaped by human beings when they become the people of God in history. We see this above all when we realize that the habits, the attitudes, and the "mentality" of this people are shaped less by the deep structures of the church than by concrete sociological structures. In brief, people are shaped by a "Christian world" that has its good sides, certainly, but also its limitations, its stolid resistance to cultural innovations, and its rigidity and narrow attitudes.

We should note, by contrast to what happens with sins properly so called, that here the more one moves toward the collective, the greater

---

[100] See especially *Le peuple de Dieu* (Lyon, 1943), pp. 122–123.

is the danger of corruption. Although the church constructs itself most fully through a spiritual communion in faith and the sacraments of the faith, it more or less betrays itself and hides its genuine features beneath the forms of the "Christian world" elaborated throughout history.

In our time, in a country like ours, the corruption of the Christian world does not so much compromise the church as hide it. The proof is that in countless cases, the rediscovery of the true mystery of the church comes not from official organisms of the Catholic milieu but from little groups that return to the Tradition by rediscovering the liturgy and theology through their own practice (see above, intro., pp. 45f.). It would not be hard to show how throughout history, but especially in our time, the church reappears and shines forth more clearly when the conventional (but inauthentic) facades of the Christian world fall apart. I can even say that the church only begins to be purely and fully itself when it is pushed out of certain positions that it held within a "Christian world" (which is sometimes almost the same thing as the "world" as such).

I know that some people, especially Protestants, consider this distinction between church and Christian world to be gratuitous and mere wordplay. That follows from the tendency of Protestant thought that misunderstands the distinction between the church as institution and as mystery so as to see in the church only the congregation or the people made up by the faithful. I examine the texts and the outcomes of this position in the third part [omitted in this translation]. However, at the point that Protestants rediscover this aspect (as is happening at this time), they return to positions rather similar to ours.

The Church as the Ensemble of Churchmen or Hierarchical Persons

In this third meaning of church, the church means hierarchical figures. It is easy enough to admit that there are members of the church who sin and who fail. But there are also faults and defects of hierarchical figures —churchmen—who not as individuals but precisely as hierarchical personages are at fault in the very exercise of their ecclesiastical functions. Are not such faults and defects, then, the faults and defects of the church?

Yes, in the third sense of the word "church," we should say so. We have to stop and recognize that many faults that give scandal and give the impression of being failures of the church itself are fundamentally situated in this area.

A preliminary answer comes to us from dogma and theology on the level of principles and of what *can* be a priori. There is a domain of action where the hierarchy (that ensemble of men who have received the ministries derived from Christ and the apostles) is sinful and fallible. When it is a question of acts of the *priesthood*, it is a matter for the most part of sacramental actions that pertain to that objective order of holiness, independent of human persons, that we have already discussed.

But the celebration of the sacraments is also (and first of all) a prayer, a ceremony that bears witness to faith and invites us to pray. In this respect, the personal holiness and unworthiness of the minister are dispositions of capital importance. Pastorally they either nourish or destroy Christendom.[101] The sacraments in themselves, the Eucharist in itself, insofar as they come from Christ, are completely holy, pure, and perfect. But, with respect to their celebration by priests, they become the worship of a particular community . . . We well know how miserable their celebration can sometimes be. It is also clear that the liturgical or ritual forms, instituted at a given moment and in a given cultural context, can present limitations and more or less serious handicaps.

It is enough to think of the inevitable problem of Latin, of the failure to adapt our liturgy for the good of mission lands, of the demands made by the present liturgical movement, for example, in order to see that the existing priestly ministry of the church is imperfect. Further, isn't this just what the encyclical *Mediator Dei* (November 20, 1947) recognized? This great text clearly distinguishes between the divine and the human elements of the liturgy, and it recognizes, on the human side, possibilities for development as well as for abuses. This lays the groundwork precisely for the exercise of an activity of reform (cf. *Mediator Dei* 50).

From the point of view of the magisterium, there is a guarantee of infallibility under certain precise conditions, whether for the whole church in its unanimity with respect to what it professes to believe, or for the episcopacy dispersed throughout the world but teaching as doctors of the faith in a unanimous way, or for the episcopacy legitimately assembled in council and defining the faith, or finally for the pope "when he speaks *ex cathedra*, that is, acting as the universal pastor and teacher and drawing upon his supreme apostolic authority when he defines what must be held by the whole Church as a doctrine concerning faith or morals."[102] This infallibility is not the fruit of an *inspiration* but simply

---

[101] Blanc de Saint-Bonnet wrote: "A holy clergy make for virtuous people, a virtuous clergy make the people honest, a bad clergy make the people ungodly" (cited by Leon Bloy in *Celle qui pleure*, p. 91). The same idea is expressed in a less literary way in St. Gregory and throughout the Middle Ages.

[102] First Vatican Council, Denzinger, no. 1839.

of an *assistance*—a guarantee bearing upon the final expression of the work. But this work itself, as it unfolds, follows normal human pathways, again with God's help. The history of conciliar definitions is often a very human history. The work of the persons involved remains influenced by their own limitations, even in the final product, the definition of dogma. God's guarantee to spare the church of error is nonetheless marked by circumstances, and the resulting human statement is not beyond improvement.

Besides the question of infallibility, a charism that is needed in order to assure the first of the formal principles of the church, there is the habitual governance of the Holy Spirit over the church. But this governance does not rule out particular failings, nor does it always supply for the limitations or the ignorance of churchmen, even those placed in the highest roles. Even if it is certain that the church as such will never teach error, nonetheless the part left in the church to the activity of human beings means that the church will not necessarily always, at each moment and in each circumstance, enjoy the best manner of teaching or the greatest plenitude of teaching.

In a way that was unanimous and formal, the Middle Ages admitted the possibility of a heretical pope with respect to his private person. The treatises on theological criteriology (*De locis*, etc.) are likewise unanimous in admitting that isolated bishops, the Fathers of the Church, and theologians, not only as isolated persons but in groups (theological schools), at certain times can be mistaken in their teaching. Examples of each one of these cases would be easy enough to cite. There would be examples as well of the slowness to respond or of the accidents that can be found in the development of doctrines. There are in the history of Christian doctrines examples of obscurantism; there are cases of slowness of response, even detours in the development of ideas. On several points (for example, in the area of social doctrine), the development of theological truth is conditioned by the state of the world. In summary, the cooperation of human beings plays its role in many ways, bringing with it, outside of those determined cases where it benefits from a formal guarantee from God, possibilities of bad results and failure.

If we consider that the magisterium includes the whole area of pastoral preaching, we suspect that churchmen may be judged lacking in the exercise of one of the hierarchical acts that is most essential. Think about the failure of preaching in the past, sometimes even in the present; think about how the altogether analytical and scholastic approach of modern catechisms represents a narrowing and mediocrity of adaptation . . . If preaching and catechesis are precisely the object of the major concerns for reform at present, it is because they have been shaped by ideas received from the past and are not what they ought to be for the present.

In essence this is a question of the function of the ruling power of the church. This too is the object of a general assistance of the Holy Spirit (who governs the church). I can even admit (with the Swiss theologian Charles Journet) the idea of a practical infallibility of the church in the order of prudence, analogous to its dogmatic infallibility, but also *limited* (as that is, of course). That does not prevent, however, that in this area certain hazards are at play with respect to human cooperation with the work of God. There are hazards above all in this area, I would say, since it is even further away from the formal magisterium and from the sacramental order where human instrumental causality is in interplay with divine assurance and infallibility. Government in the church is a power received from God but, operating by juridical practice such that the church fully exercises it through itself and *positis ponendis* (taking all necessary distinctions into account), exercises it as a political authority would exercise its own power of government.[103]

Père Emile Mersch writes the following:

> Wherever humans act as humans, in everything that Christians do—even the best, in all that ecclesiastical leaders do, even the most dignified, human weakness and human malice and the trace of human sins inevitably betrays itself—and does so often. The saints themselves do not totally escape from these bad moments except at the moment of their full spiritual maturity when they're dying. Grace, as we ought to believe, should preserve the pastors of the church and even more their most important actions, but it does not suppress their failures—that would be to suppress their humanity. There is then, even there, beyond authentic faults, the interference of selfish viewpoints and worldly calculation even in the perspective of the most apostolic persons; there are prejudices and unconscious ignorance, vanity that renders people inattentive, touchiness that nourishes unacknowledged grudges, prideful stubbornness which insists upon respect for the role they play, impotence to have and to keep a genuinely right intention in the spirit of true humble abnegation, etc. . . .[104]

---

[103] See my "Ordre et Juridiction dans l'Eglise," in *Irénikon* (1933), pp. 22–31, 97–110, 243–252, 401–408 (reprinted in *Sainte Eglise*, Paris, 1963).

[104] *La théologie du Corps mystique*, vol. 1, p. 368.

This last idea of Père Mersch ought to receive our attention. One of the temptations of churchmen is certainly to identify in their own minds what they do concretely with the sacred function in itself. Yet these men who exercise the most sacred authority can be lacking in information or intelligence.[105] They can spoil occasions, alienate people, provoke irreparable damage by their narrowness or their lack of understanding. People agree in thinking that Cardinal Humbert acted brutally in the matter of the Patriarch Michael Cerularius, who himself bears terrible responsibility. St. Clement-Marie Hofbauer said that he had tried in vain to make the Curia understand the true cause of the Reformation, and he considered Rome responsible for the state of affairs in Germany and in Austria.[106] What might we say of the religious history of Bohemia in the fifteenth century?

Churchmen can also lack character. St. Peter agreed dogmatically with St. Paul about the question of Christians coming from paganism (Gal 2:11f.), but he took an equivocal attitude (and it is not impossible that he lacked character). Such is the case, later on, of Pope Liberius signing the formula of Sirmium and of Pope Honorius misunderstanding what Monothelitism meant and consequently showing himself indulgent toward it, the case of Pope Paschal II when the emperor Henry V extorted from him a renunciation of his rights of investiture, and of Pope Pius VII signing the Concordat of Fontainebleau . . .[107]

If after examining dogma and theology, we now look at history, we discover an unequivocal answer. Churchmen, charged with hierarchical powers and responsibilities, failed over and over not only in their personal lives, but also in the exercise of their administration. They failed to the degree that they were not pure instruments of the action of God (as

---

[105] At various moments in history, we meet up with a veritable hatred for priests, going so far as to inspire their murder. I have collected several examples of this, both between 1500–1530 and between 1820–1850.

[106] Cf. J. Hofer, *Der hl. Klemens Maria Hofbauer: Ein Lebensbild* (Freiburg im Breisgau, 1921), pp. 276 and 383–384. After quoting the famous letter in which Perthes describes his interview with the saint on the religious meaning of the Reformation, Hofer cites the following letter of E. Veith from Apr. 21, 1863: "*Nicht ohne Grund hat Hofbauer, der ein wirklicher Heiliger war, fast täglich wiederholt, Rom sei an allen Uebel schuld*—Not without reason did Hofbauer, a genuine saint, repeat almost daily, Rome is guilty for all these evils . . ." (ibid., p. 384, note).

[107] I borrow these four examples from F. Mourret, *Le Concile du Vatican d'après des documents inédits* (Paris, 1919), pp. 314–315.

in the celebration of the sacraments or the charism of infallibility linked to their function), that is, to the degree that they expressed themselves.

The church itself, through the voice of its most important pastors, has several times admitted this. I cited above some texts from the period of the Reformation which are clear in this respect. "All this evil has come from us," said Hadrian VI; likewise Contarini, Carafa, Pole, and Sadolet, addressing Paul III, the legates opening the Council of Trent, and Cardinal de Lorraine at the end of his life's work. To that we could add other texts of Sadolet, statements of Pope Pius V, St. Vincent De Paul,[108] Bossuet, and lots of others. There is no point in going into detail about the faults of so many popes, bishops, priests, and religious. This history is rather well known and the church has suffered abuse because of it. Rather, let's see if we can understand a bit the meaning of all these facts.

In the preface which he wrote for the 1877 third edition of his *Via Media*,[109] Newman, wanting to address the criticisms that he had formulated against Catholicism as an Anglican, took up this problem. He showed how from the moment that the principles of the church in its three prerogatives of power (priesthood, magisterium, and government) are concretely exercised in history, they are necessarily mixed up with circumstances and cease being concretely or historically pure. They interfere and react one with another and end up limiting themselves. An *idea* is able to be pure, but *life* takes place in the world where one cannot escape being mixed up in some kind of compromise or blemish.[110]

In this perspective sketched out by Newman, I discovered some light on the subject in his idea of historical conditioning. From the moment that the priesthood, the magisterium itself, but above all the power of government are concretely exercised in history, they are touched by the conditioning of historical situations. They take concrete forms which are limited, and in part determined, by the conditioning that the state of ideas and morals, politics, and even economics imposes. They take on modalities which do not pertain to them essentially, but which phenom-

---

[108] "The church has no worse enemies than its priests"; "It's because of priests that heretics have prevailed and that vice has overcome and ignorance pitched its throne among the poor . . ." (St. Vincent de Paul, quoted by J. Delarue, *L'Idéal missionnaire du prêtre d'après saint Vincent de Paul* [Paris, 1947], p. 283).

[109] Pp. 36–94. There is a French translation of these pages in J. H. Cardinal Newman, *Pensées sur l'Eglise* (*Unam Sanctam* 30 [Paris, 1956]), pp. 306–343.

[110] Cf. H. Pinard de la Boullaye, *Carême 1937*, p. 269. This idea makes me think of the Legend of St. Nicholas and of Cassian that Soloviev tells at the beginning of his *La Russie et l'Eglise universelle.*

enologically or historically enter into their concrete exercise. The priest-hood becomes linked to all sorts of cultural forms, to devotions where human piety enters strongly in; the magisterium, at least in its minor expressions, is linked to a specific level of information[111] and means of expression. As to governance, it is much more associated historically with particular forms of authority, and it includes, even in an area as holy and pure as that of the missions, for example, delays, limitations, and narrowness . . .

Within extremely complex circumstances, drawing from a large his-torical canvas, the bishops and above all the popes took on secular titles in the context of feudalism after Constantine, the fall of the Roman Em-pire, and the Carolingian Empire. The structure of Christendom has made of the church and of the secular city one single society, the "Chris-tian Republic," in which prelates and popes have exercised powers de-riving from another competence than that of their strictly spiritual jurisdiction: rights of overlords, arbiters, moderators of Christendom, judges of the Christian princes, etc. Pius IX expressed this clearly when speaking of the deposition of kings: "This right has been exercised by the popes in extreme circumstances, but it has nothing to do with pon-tifical infallibility. Its source was not infallibility but pontifical authority. That authority, according to the public law then in force and with the consent of the Christian nations, recognized that the pope was the supreme judge of Christendom, and his authority extended to the right to judge, even in temporal matters, the princes and the states. Of course the present situation is completely different."[112]

Pius XII made a similar application of the distinction between the pure substance of papal power and its historical application, where all sorts of elements become involved. In question was the organism in the church that defends the body against heresy and which has taken, at certain times, the form of the Inquisition. "Without doubt," said Pius XII, "through the centuries the tribunal charged with the defense of the faith took on forms and undertook methods not demanded by the nature

---

[111] This explains some cases (rare, indeed) like that of Pope Honorius approving Monothelitism. In the case of the condemnation of Galileo, a lack of knowledge was joined to an excessive claim of authority with respect to an area where the church has no competence.

[112] Speech of July 20, 1871, to a delegation of the *Accademia di Religione cattolica* (cf. *La Civiltà Cathol.*, series 8, vol. 3, 1871, p. 485), quoted by J. Lecler, in *L'Eglise et la souveraineté de l'Etat* (Paris, 1946), p. 87.

of things, but which can only be explained in the light of the historical circumstances of the time. It would be false however to try to create an argument against the legitimacy of the tribunal itself."[113] So one of the things which nourishes the bulk of complaints and accusations against the church, according to historical analysis, is the way it carried out its mission.

During the centuries in which the West was developing, the popes and many prelates added the exercise of essentially secular powers to their sacred functions. More than once, they used their secular power for the benefit of the church, whether in favor of their spiritual jurisdiction (above all) or for temporal interests. Inevitably, it happened that they abused their power, treated secular questions with methods drawn from another order—methods of authority and tradition that work in theology but do not belong in the realms of science or politics. Or, on the contrary, it happened that they sometimes treated spiritual questions with methods borrowed from the temporal order, using physical compulsion, for example. Inevitably, again, they sometimes succumbed to the temptation of power, and the "secular lord" in them sometimes overshadowed their responsibility as pastors of souls. Again, when the profane world became secularized, it violently rejected the guidance of churchmen and nurtured a kind of resentment against them which often turned into revolt.

Reflecting on this, we perceive that a good part of the failures that people blame on the church fall under the perspective of what we noted quickly above: acts of simony, nepotism, abuse of power, violent constraint, use of spiritual arms for temporal ends—the Galileo affair, etc. . . . These are essentially consequences of the fact that the spiritual power linked itself to secular practices and, even more deeply, the fact that in a world subjected to the church, the spiritual power naturally took on a spirit of jurisdiction. But these are practices whose explanation needs to be researched and at least contextualized by history. We're talking about facts that have to be seen historically, that have a date in time; and it would be not only unjust but stupid to judge them according to our ideas in the present. History is the great mistress of justice and truth. She permits us to distinguish things and to give them a concrete context. History provides us with criteria according to which we can judge with justice and objectivity the human role in the exercise of the powers of the church.

---

[113] Speech of Oct. 6, 1946, to the members of the Tribunal of the Rota (*Doc. Cath.,* Oct. 27, 1946, col. 1187).

Churchmen, yes—but laity too. To the degree that they have had an influence, shaped the opinions of Catholics, or exercised leadership, what we said about bishops and their government applies to laity also. In their own way, they have affected the collective behavior of Catholics and so, amazingly, they have shaped the attitudes of the church as a concrete reality and as a historical phenomenon. Think of Montalembert or Veuillot, of the Catholics of the Second Republic or of the Second Empire, against whom H. Guillemin has made a pitiless indictment.[114] Think of what Pius XI says, in *Quadragesimo Anno*, about Catholic employers who are unresponsive to papal directives: "These people are the reason why the church, without in any way meriting it, can seem to be, and can be accused of, taking sides with the wealthy and to lack sympathy for the needs and the suffering of those who are deprived of their share of well-being in this life . . ."

From a historian's perspective, the concrete means chosen by spiritual authorities make an impression. The behaviors of the Catholic population are given voice by their leaders. Historians don't look at the church in the first sense given above, the one that derives its meaning from the faith. Rather, they look at the church in terms of the concrete shape of the "Christian world," since they can only grasp it as a concrete sociological grouping, directed by a hierarchy operating under specific circumstances in which contingent means become fused with their structural power.

Further, the church, seen in its human incarnations, may appear to be an impressive reality but not too much different from others. The scandal comes precisely from the contrast between these concrete experiences of the church, on the one hand, and the church's claims to a supernatural sanctity, on the other, without distinguishing between the two contexts so as to see the facts about its holiness and its failures.

Often scandal also comes from the fact that, despite all these imperfections in the church's history, we find in the church a sort of intransigence bordering on pride. But in the light of what we have seen, the church's intransigence can be understood, as well as its failings. Even though, when it is a question of human beings, any kind of failure is possible, still the church needs to safeguard the purity of whatever is even remotely linked to the formal principles of the church (first sense).

Once again, Newman can really help us here. We saw how he explained that the church, in carrying out its sacred ministries in the framework

---

[114] "Les catholiques français et la IIe République," *Esprit* (Dec. 1945), pp. 875–898; *Histoire des catholiques français au XIXe siècle—1815–1905* (Geneva-Paris-Montreal, 1947)—a "history" that is both fragmentary and biased.

of human history, was led to allow itself to adopt concrete expressions that were somehow unworthy. In this same perspective, he came to distinguish between two conditions of Catholicism (or of Anglicanism).[115] First there was the level of principles, for example, the formal dogmas of the church, and then there was the level of religion lived spontaneously and concretized in the passage of human history—namely, the common doctrine expressed in popular beliefs and practices, deriving from controversies and historical circumstances. In sum, this is the difference between Catholicism (or Anglicanism) *at rest*, and Catholicism *in action*.

In changing the frame of reference a bit, we might call this today the difference between "Christianity" and the "Christian world." Newman went on to add that the objections and the oppositions of Anglicans and Protestants to Catholicism were in general due more to Catholicism "in action" than to Catholicism and its principles "at rest." Newman thought that Anglican opposition to Catholicism was situated less at the level of principles than at the level of concrete historical and popular religious expression. Their opposition didn't concern Catholicism in itself, but rather what Newman called, along with his colleagues, "Romanism." Anglicans' opposition arose less from authentic Anglicanism than from their tendency to fall into Protestantism (using the Anglican vocabulary here). Their opposition focused more on a *mentality* than on doctrine. Further, according to Newman, they often erred in attacking a political or popular expression in the name of pure principles, attacking "Romanism" in the name of Anglicanism—simply put, attacking exaggerations or deformities in the name of pure theoretical principles.

Later on we will see that Soloviev blamed Khomiakov for making a comparison between a concrete Catholicism and an ideal, abstract, and unreal Orthodoxy.[116] Alas, this is the constant tendency of any polemic; and isn't there a certain element of polemics in any apologetics? Even further on, Péguy, after making his famous distinction between the *mystical* and the *political* (which resembles Newman's opposition just noted), remarks that often authors are unjust in comparing not mystical doctrines among themselves or political doctrines among themselves, but rather comparing a mystical doctrine with a political doctrine or a political

---

[115] Cf. the introduction to his *Via Media* (n. 109 above) and the first volume of this work, reproducing *The Prophetical Office of the Church* (from 1837); also his *Apologia* (French trans. by Michelin-Delimoges: Paris, 1939), pp. 112f., 141, and 232f.

[116] Cf. D. Stremooukhoff, *Vladimir Soloviev et son oeuvre messianique* (Paris, 1935), p. 203.

doctrine with a mystical doctrine.[117] Still, staying close to Newman's meaning, Péguy adds that the "mystical doctrines are less opposed to one another than political doctrines among themselves—and in a different way. You don't have to attribute to mysticisms the evil of dissensions, wars, or political bad feeling. Nor is there among them the restless resentment of the political order" (p. 82).

It is easy to see how such ideas contribute to clarify both our problem here as well as any ecumenical program. From the point of view of an irenic effort to create mutual understanding, we can see the big part that false contradictions arising from prejudice, the clash of different mentalities, and a historical legacy of quarrels and resentments play in the divisions among Christians. From the point of view of our problem [concerning evil in the church], we can see an application and confirmation of the basic distinction between the weakness of churchmen and the purity of the church in itself, that is, between the kind of discredit that ecclesial realities undergo when they are employed by human agents and the same activities viewed according to their essence and their principles.

The Concrete Church, Synthesizing the Preceding Elements

Finally, we need to reunite the elements that we have distinguished during this analysis. If a purely profane history sees the church as a sociological reality composed of men and women linked to concrete means of expression and committed to conditioned circumstances of time and place, the faithful cannot be satisfied to simply juxtapose with this completely exterior perspective an affirmation of transcendence. Let me say it again: I have only distinguished the different aspects of one, single church that are reunited in the church's concrete reality. Yes, there is only *one* church.

The very church that a strict historian sees as a human society (second and third senses) possesses, as the faithful know, truly divine internal principles (first sense). They know it is the very church whose mystery consists precisely in this fusion of the divine and human that is so difficult for us to perceive. As the encyclical *Mystici Corporis* (June 29, 1943) solemnly recalled, there is only one church and thus only one adequate meaning of the word—the one that reunites the three aspects we have just distinguished.

---

[117] *Notre Jeunesse (Oeuvres compl.*, ed. NRF), p. 62.

The church is the human community to which the divine energies communicated by Jesus Christ, the Incarnate Son, are entrusted, and in which they become active so as to bring human beings together in communion with the life of the Father. Or in other words: the church is human beings gathered up into the bosom of the Father by the action within them of the energies of Jesus Christ made present in their midst through his Spirit, his sacraments, and his Word, whose ministry has been confided to the corps of the apostles. Or finally: the church is the communion of men and women in whom the Spirit and the energies of Jesus Christ are active and at work. The corps of the apostles has received the ministry of this spiritual work and thus they have within them the animating power of Jesus Christ, the second Adam.

We can see how, if we take the church in its *concrete but adequate* sense, this church is both holy and full of sinfulness, both indefectible and fallible, both perfect and still subject to many historical imperfections. In the church, what comes from Christ is holy and without defect, but what comes from the exercise of human freedom is subject to mistakes. However, both the one and the other truly pertain to this concrete body which, if we take it for what it really is, is the church.

In this concrete body there is a divine part and a human part. The divine part is truly interior to the church and constitutes the array of its formal principles. But the human part, with its inherent weakness, is also a reality inside the church. So the church in its internal principles is without either weakness or sin, but the human matter that enters into its concrete structure is fallible, and that brings sin into the church—without, however, dishonoring the church itself. St. Ambrose spoke this way: "*Immaculata ex maculatis*—the Immaculate is made up of the sinful." For the sins and limitations of persons who are in the church remain the sins and limitations of these individuals, even if they exercise hierarchical functions and if they sin even as they exercise these functions.

All the same, there is a sense in which these faults are the faults of everyone, and so they are the faults of the body, since "we are all members of one another." Deeper than the solidarity of example and of social practice, there is an organic solidarity in virtue of which every sin sullies the whole church because it sullies the body.[118] On the other hand, every expression of goodness also affects the whole body as well. Evil and especially good coexist so closely in the church at this point that the one

---

[118] See the texts of Augustine, Tertullian, Origen (*In Jesu Nave*, hom. 5, n. 6), etc.; in H. de Lubac, *Catholicisme* (1st ed.), p. 45, n. 3; (4th ed.), p. 51, n. 1.

always compensates for the other to some degree. There is a social or, more exactly, an ecclesial aspect of penance, which formerly was clearly expressed in public penance; this is still a reality and it is observed in the text of the *Confiteor* and its recitation at the start of the celebration of the Eucharist. As St. Ephrem said, "The whole church is the church of penitents and the whole church is the church of those who were perishing."[119]

Solidarity plays out in a way that is both truly collective but also truly personal in this area of historical faults and group behavior. Each person affects all the others to some degree and contributes in constituting, maintaining, or transforming a situation where human weaknesses affect all the members of the group. It was inevitable that along with the awareness of an order of historical or social failures, the question of collective responsibility would be raised. This question can also be addressed to the people of God (something that I will look at further in an appendix).

It was understandable to have recourse to the idea of the body and to the notion of the incarnation in order to think through this union of the divine and the human. I myself said that the *Ecclesia de Trinitate*, pure and simple, and the *Ecclesia ex hominibus*, fallible as it is, meet *in Christo*. From that fact we justify the presence in the church of an element of light and an element of weakness. This is a bit like what is the case in Christ: there was weakness in him but it stopped at the threshold of sin. Without going so far as to develop a notion of *kenosis* so dear to some Protestant theologies,[120] theologians have often applied to the church the idea that it replicates the conditions of Christ's life,[121] but in the church as in Christ the divine is present as incarnated, in the condition of humility, in the

---

[119] Cited by V. Lossky, *Essai sur la théologie mystique de l'Eglise d'Orient*, p. 177.

[120] A christological theory arose out of Lutheran dogmatic theology that, drawing from Phil 2:7, claimed that Christ was stripped of his divine attributes. To see this applied to the church, see W. R. Carson, "The Kenosis of the Church," in *Reunion Essays* (London, 1903), pp. 157–172. The whole tone here is both bold and timid, childish and ill at ease, like the atmosphere of the Modernist period.

[121] For example, Msgr. Benson, *Le Christ dans l'Eglise* (Paris, 1920); Mersch, *Théologie du Corps mystique*. Elsewhere I will point out the criticisms to be made of too organic and biological an interpretation of the analogy of the body. In some treatments the activities of the church-as-body of Christ are presented too much as being the activities of Christ himself. See my contribution to vol. 3 of *Chalkedon: Geschichte und Gegenwart* (451/1951), published by the theological faculty of St. George in Frankfurt and reprinted in *Sainte Eglise* (Paris, 1963), pp. 70–104.

form of a slave.[122] In this perspective we are brought to recognize a kind of essential and general weakness of the church and to situate this weakness in the earthly and created element as such, in the visible forms in which the divine principle is realized and becomes manifest.[123]

This point of view is altogether correct. It easily opens out upon an eschatological perspective (explicitly so in Karl Adam); that is, it leads to a perspective closely related to the final and glorious accomplishment of God's work. This is somewhat similar to some Protestant viewpoints and thus risks being attracted to the separation in that Protestant perspective between the divine and the created, the spiritual and the sensible . . . and thus risks also to identify the *body* with the *flesh* and to confuse what St. Paul called "the body of sin" with bodiliness as such. That evidently would be an error and would make it very difficult to think correctly about ecclesial reality.

Excursus: Evil in the Church in the View of Several Contemporary Theologians

It will be interesting here to see the way in which some theologians who have studied the problem raised in this chapter have proposed to resolve it. This is a way for me to confirm or complete my own approach. First, the study done by M. Villain and J. de Bacchiochi (*La vocation de l'Eglise*, Paris, 1953) and H. de Lubac (*Méditation sur l'Eglise*, Paris, 1953, pp. 78f.) are similar in their views to mine.

Père Pinard de la Boullaye twice touched on this question in his conferences at Notre Dame. He first of all took up the argument, still useful, of the Catholic apologetic about the weaknesses of the popes: these weaknesses are personal, so that the properly hierarchical or dogmatic action of these popes is beyond reproach.[124] Next he showed that the church is made up of humans who are subject to human weakness, and

---

[122] P. Simon, *Das Menschliche in der Kirche Christi*; K. Adam, "Le mystère de l'Eglise: du scandale à la foi triomphante," in *L'Eglise est une: Hommage à Moehler* (Paris, 1939), pp. 33–52; Fr. P. Sladek, "Göttliches und Menschliches in der Kirche: Ein Beitrag zur Frage aus der Sicht des Grenzlandes," in *Theolog. Quartalschrift* (1941), pp. 175-190 (*kenosis* is mentioned on p. 183). I only became aware before the 2nd ed. of the recent article by Karl Adam, "Das Problem des Geschichtlichen in Leben der Kirche," in *Theolog. Quartalschrift* (1948), pp. 275–300, pages that show the presence in the life of the church of both a human, historical principle and of a transcendent principle, drawing from well-chosen historical examples.

[123] You can find this idea in Adam and Simon (op. cit., pp. 48f.).

[124] *Conférences de Notre-Dame*, 1931, 5th conference, p. 216.

that it has always been such. The church can't live on earth without soiling the hem of its vestments a bit. Nonetheless the church has enduring promises to convey so that, instead of doubting the church, we should rather humbly mistrust ourselves.[125] There is nothing here that doesn't accord with my own exposé.

At the time of violent Nazi attacks against the church, J. Bernhart made a distinction between the divine and the human in the church by distinguishing between *Wesen* and *Geschischte*[126]—an approach that resembles a lot my distinction between *structure* and *life*.

We have already seen how Dom Vonier, in distinguishing between the church itself (that is, its principles received from God) and the people of God, practically expresses what is essential in my distinctions. Cardinal Journet formulates these in precise concepts: the church does not lack sinners, but it is itself without sin. We are pure in everything that links us in reality to the church. The degree of evil that we shelter measures the degree of disfigurement that we introduce by our participation in the church.[127]

I came close to saying this myself in returning to the question in 1961.[127a] However, I introduced a third term between the "sinless" church as such and our sins, namely, the pitiful things, the more or less seriously harmful things, that happen to the church itself and to the exercise of its ministry. There are "pitiful things," things that need to be corrected, that are clearly linked to the actual sins of members of the church.

Karl Rahner took up this question with characteristic energy and frankness.[127b] We can't just talk about a kind of completely ideal Platonic church untouched by the actions of its members. If its members are sinners, then we need to speak of the church of sinners. However, this does not injure the church's holiness, for the church has the power within itself to purify its members from their sins and to sanctify them. The church ceaselessly goes about doing just that. It is the "holy church of sinners."

[125] Conferences for 1937 (*Jésus vivant dans l'Eglise*), 6th conference: "L'Eglise idéale et l'Eglise réelle," pp. 247f.

[126] "Göttliches et Menchliches in der Kirche," in *Die Kirche in der Zeitwende*, ed. E. Kleineidam and O. Kuss (Paderborn, 1935), pp. 238–268.

[127] Journet, *L'Eglise du Verbe incarné*, vol. I: *La hiérarchie apostolique* (Paris, 1941), pp. xiii–xiv, 124f., 314, etc.; vol. II: *Sa structure interne et son unité catholique* (Paris, 1952), pp. 489, 904; *Théologie de l'Eglise* (1958), pp. 236, 244.

[127a] "Comment l'Eglise sainte doit se renouveler sans cesse," *Irénikon* 34 (1961), pp. 322–345, reprinted in *Sainte Eglise* (*Unam Sanctam* 41 [Paris, 1963]), pp. 131–154.

[127b] "Die Kirche der Sünder," *Stimmen der Zeit* 140 (1947), pp. 163–177.

In a brief article Abbé Couturier proposes three levels that he calls the sacral, the ecclesial, and the ecclesiastical.[128] The sacral corresponds exactly to my first sense of the word "church." The ecclesiastical belongs to the human context that I have analyzed under the second and third senses. Between the two, Couturier posits an *ecclesial* level that represents, if I understand him, the bodiliness of the sacral, "the human container, which is thus perfectible, but guided by the Spirit." For example, "the scriptural texts which could have been different and whose interpretation is constantly in progress, the texts of the rites and of the Missal, whose adaptation ought to be modeled on the psychological structure of human persons that is itself variable in time and space, dogmatic texts that are indefinitely perfectible, and the secondary social structure of the church—a structure expressive of the church's immutable sacred architecture" (p. 65). In summary, it is a question of the sensible forms assumed by the divine principles of the church. These are institutions with a human form that derives sometimes from God, sometimes from the church guided by the Holy Spirit.

The *ecclesiastical* is a concrete implementation by the members of the church, both hierarchy and faithful. Summing up, Couturier writes: "The church is infinitely holy and unchangeable because it is *sacral*; it is holy and perfectible because it is *ecclesial*; and it is terribly sinful and in need of sanctification because it is *ecclesiastical*. In speaking of the church as such, then, we can say—we ought to say—that it is holy, changeable, and sinful" (p. 67).

Couturier's categories are interesting. They grasp well the bodiliness of the church itself: the earthly form of the church, on the one hand, and the area of sin, on the other hand. In my categories, however, these things are found between the first and the third meaning of the church. Scripture belongs to the first sense; the "secondary social structure of the church" belongs to the third. That third sense is the area where failure can exist, but where the Holy Spirit is ceaselessly at work and in a way that is increasingly powerful and effective to the degree that we draw closer to the constitutive principles of the church as the instrument of our salvation.

---

[128] "Chaque chrétien est responsable de l'Eglise," *L'Amitié* (Jan., 1947), pp. 57–69. These distinctions are taken from Damasus Winzen, "L'Eglise mystère," *Oecumenica* (1934).

Chapter 2

Why and in What Way Do the People of God Need To Be Reformed?

I. God's Plan and How God's People Should Respond to It: Situating the Problem of Reform

1. It takes work, but eventually we can see and be excited to understand that the whole Bible shows us how all God's activity is both a history and a development. This holds true not only for God's work of creation, where it is so obvious, but also for the work of grace and salvation. God did not do all this in a timeless heaven of ideas, but rather within our history and our time, thus giving meaning and value to time itself. Everything in God's plan begins from a seed and develops through stages, moving toward fulfillment. This continually happens in nature, where everything begins with a seed, then grows, matures, and bears fruit. This happens in human history as well,[1] where life, as it matures and brings forth new ideas, poses new problems as well. By confronting these problems with the resources of a given period of time, humanity is led to push beyond its available resources and to discover new values and new forms. This is what emerges in God's work, as we see in the work of the Revealer and Redeemer to whom the Bible bears witness.

---

[1] However, human history does not grow in the manner of a biological or "natural" type; human history is the area of human creative freedom, and what develops there by way of innovative "seeds" is not strictly contained in the potency of what went before.

Here everything is based on God's initiatives, and that explains why development does not mean a sort of automatic continuity but rather is governed by the distinct "vocations" that God offers to human beings who are, in the most special way, "those who belong to God" or, as we will see, the prophets.

From one end of the Bible to the other, the gifts of God are first given to one person or to a small group, but with the idea of a gradual offering of the gift to everyone. Adam is given breath "in the image of God" but in order "to grow," to multiply and fill the earth. Abraham is chosen and called but in order that in him "all the nations of the earth shall be blessed." All further development takes its point of departure there. Earthly humanity is only the development of Adam, while religious and redeemed humanity is only the development of Abraham.[2] We are talking about the people of God coming forth from the promises addressed to Abraham—realized first of all in Israel, then beyond Israel, in the church. The final reality is only the development of what had been given and foreseen from the beginning. It was given in the form of a seed with the prospect of its complete realization; the final reality was contained in the beginning, but it was *called* to develop even to the fulfillment where this beginning will finally reveal what it had contained and the reason why it had been given.

Israel, the people of God, is already there in the patriarchs. What the patriarchs lived prefigures and engages the whole destiny of the people who will come forth from them. The twelve tribes come from the twelve sons of Jacob-Israel. The tribes are really only the extension and the realization of the children of Jacob. The church will come forth from the twelve apostles and will only be the developed reality of their experience (cf. Jas 1:1)—one of the reasons, not the least important, why the church is called "apostolic."

We could reread the entire Bible from this point of view.[3] But that exceeds the possibilities of this present study. Let me simply summarize the conclusions that would come from that kind of analysis. Everywhere we look, God's gifts are given first in the form of a seed. This seed, even

---

[2] This is something that the liturgy maintains with a luminous awareness. Cf., among others, the prayers following the third and fourth prophecies in the office of Holy Saturday in the ancient Vigil of the Roman rite.

[3] I have gotten much personal profit from reading W. Vischer, *Das Christuszeugnis des Alten Testaments*, vol. I (Zollicon-Zurich: French trans., *La loi ou les cinq livres de Moïse*—Neuchâtel and Paris, 1949).

at the beginning, contains in a hidden and veiled way the fullness toward which it is directed. But it only develops this content progressively through stages. It is destined to result in the full manifestation of what it possessed from the beginning, but this only happens progressively and always imperfectly.

It is not only the Bible that begins with a Genesis and ends with an Apocalypse—that is, a revelation. Everything is a gift; everything is God's own work. Everywhere, there is first promise, then realization of the promise, but only a partial one still calling for a final fulfillment. Everywhere, the meaning is discovered in the final fullness. The Old Testament moves toward the New, where its promises and expectations are fulfilled. The Gospel itself, a reality with respect to the promise of the law, is still a seed of promise with respect to the church, toward which it moves and in which it fulfills itself. And the church, the reality of the promises that became fulfilled in Jesus Christ, is still awaiting its last and definitive fulfillment.

Even though the seed is oriented from the very beginning toward the fullness and perfection that will only be revealed at the end,[4] it nonetheless only develops the potential it holds within itself progressively and by stages. It works within time, drawing upon the resources of time. If God were the only one to do everything, if everything were pure gift, if truth and salvation, while being given by God, did not become realized also through our agency as well, then there would be no need for a progressive development, or for delays and stages of emergence. If, however, the gifts of God require our response, if they represent a divine condescension that requires and calls for us to rise up, if they leave to the one who receives them a piece of the action, an element of cooperation and of preparation, if God, finally, is not only the one from whom everything proceeds by pure grace but also the one to whom everything is destined to arise and return through an effort that God makes it possible for us to do but which we nonetheless do—then, of course, we can understand why there needs to be development, movement from promise to reality, the unveiling or the unfolding of what was already contained in the seed. In that case we can see why God's action must be progressive and carried out in stages. This is indeed how God's work happens, as it is portrayed by the Scriptures.

---

[4] In this context the end means not only the *conclusion* but also the *goal*. Here, *end* means both of these things.

2. We can describe God's plan revealed in the Bible as a process of going from the outside to the inside, from figures and symbols to a reality within human persons themselves. We know the classic structure, devised by the Fathers and used by iconography and Christian liturgy as well (and even before them in the interpretation of the New Testament). The meaning of things in the Old Testament was as a prefiguring, a prediction, a promise, or a stage of development. Their true meaning is found beyond themselves. The Fathers called them *Sacramenta Veteris Testamenti*—sacraments of the Old Testament.[5] More precisely, we can say that things in the Old Testament that had the character of a prediction or a preparation remained somewhat exterior. Once within the new covenant, however, they have to become internalized within human beings themselves—become spiritual and interior. It's easy to show this by referring to the ideas of the Epistle to the Hebrews that make the contrast between the situation of the old covenant and that of the new. The elements of comparison are the law, priesthood, sacrifice, temple, or presence of God. For the present, let us examine the question of sacrifice, which requires a priesthood, since the act of sacrifice structures priestly functions, and finally the question of the temple.[6]

Throughout the Bible, God requires worship and sacrifice. In the old dispensation worship and sacrifice are governed by regulations and carried out in a certain number of prescribed external actions. In particular, the Old Testament prescribed sacrifices of animals and the offering of first fruits. However, we see the prophets criticize sacrifices and even claim that God holds them in disdain.[7] Some historians have been so carried away by this that they came to think that this meant a condemnation of worship as such.[8] But the same prophets who repudiated sacrifices in this way go on to call people to make a perfect sacrifice[9] that the old law was powerless to produce. The old law was unable to bring anything to its perfection (Heb 7:19).

---

[5] To understand this patristic idea of sacrament in the wide sense, nothing is more helpful than H. de Lubac's *Corpus mysticum* (Paris, 1944). English translation: *Corpus Mysticum: The Eucharist and the Church in the Middle Ages—An Historical Survey*, trans. Gemma Simonds et al. (Notre Dame, IN: University of Notre Dame Press, 2007).

[6] For the idea of the law, see Augustine's *De spiritu et littera*; the principal ideas of this work are used by St. Thomas in his treatise on the "new law."

[7] Cf. Hos 6:6; Amos 5:25-27; Isa 1:11; Jer 7:21-23; Mic 6:6f.; etc.

[8] E.g., A. Lods, *Les prophètes d'Israël et les débuts du judaïsme* (Paris, 1935), pp. 74f. (for Amos, p. 95; for Hosea, p. 106; etc.).

[9] Malachi 1:6-14 (v. 11), and see Hebert, [*note 10, below*], pp. 117–118.

There are passages in St. Augustine, in Pascal, in L. Bouyer's *Mystère pascal*, and in the writings of the Anglican theologian Gabriel Hebert[10] that show how God, under the old covenant, asked for sacrifices and at the same time announced that he did not want them. The prophets were commissioned to establish and to oversee the development of religious institutions and the fulfillment of God's plan. They said at one and the same time: yes, this is what God wants; and no, this is not it. God wants it, and he doesn't want it. He wants it, but not in the way that you imagine and that you practice it. He wants it, but in another form, done in another way, going beyond what you are presently doing . . . So God wanted a sacrifice, but not what the old law, with its imperfections, prescribed to be offered to him, namely, the blood of bulls and goats. He wanted a sacrifice, but only that of the human person himself: openness, conversion, and the gift of one's heart.

Here as elsewhere "fulfillment" of the law by Jesus will consist not in adding to the prescriptions set down by Moses some supplementary and more perfect norm, not a new obligation, either more rigorous or more general. What God sought was to isolate and reaffirm, within the law, the fullness and the purity of meaning that pertain to the intention that God had from the beginning, which was none other than the perfection of love. God wanted to deploy a fullness which had been tied to historical conditions within which, in each one of its stages, the people of God realizes the plan given to them to fulfill.[11] From the point of view of sacrifice, this fulfillment seeks a sacrifice that cannot be anything exterior, but only the person himself. Jesus Christ achieves this new interior sacrifice and then, after him and thanks to him, we join ourselves to him, even to the point of forming with him only one single body.

We need to read the admirable texts of St. Augustine, written at a peak of theological contemplation, where this doctor of the church shows how the true sacrifice of the Christian, with respect to which the other sacrifices are merely "sacraments" (that is, means of achievement meant to

---

[10] Augustine, *City of God*, bk. X, chs. 5 and 6; Pascal, fr. 659f.; L. Bouyer, *Le mystère pascal* (Paris, 1945), pp. 273f., 456f. (See his translation of this great text of Augustine); G. Hebert, *The Throne of David* (London, 1941), pp. 111–222. For this example of sacrifice, as for the questions of purity, marriage, and universalism, I have found a remarkably good analysis in chapters 4 and 9 of this work of the Anglican theologian; I have myself used this work in a course on the Bible. After I wrote these pages, *Le Trône de David* has appeared in French translation (Paris, Aubier).

[11] On the meaning of this fulfillment of the law, see W. Vischer, op. cit., 6th ed., pp. 309f.

be surpassed)—the true sacrifice is nothing other than the body of the whole Christ, the *tota redempta Civitas*—the whole redeemed city, that is to say, ourselves who have become, even though we are many, a single body in Christ.[12] St. Augustine explains the "truth" of the priesthood in a way that corresponds exactly to these ideas. But that would take us too far afield. Consider instead a parallel idea, namely, the great reality of the indwelling of God and the existence of something which might be called God's temple.

Ever since Moses, God had promised to dwell in the midst of his people. During the Exodus, he had manifested his presence in an extraordinary way through the ark of the covenant. When David, who had made his capital in Jerusalem, wanted to build a temple to shelter the divine Presence, God told him through the prophet Nathan what he really wanted in this respect, and that became a promise of decisive importance (cf. 2 Sam 7). David would not build a house for the Lord, but his son would. And God announced that from this son, his posterity, he would make for David a lasting house. God solemnly promised that this would be an unending bloodline, and God's grace would remain with it forever.

When Solomon had constructed a glorious temple, he thought that he had really fulfilled what Nathan had predicted to his father. He believed that the program of the temple and the indwelling of God among his people had been achieved for good.[13] However, in coming years, the prophets announced that God was going to leave this dwelling place and that the temple would be destroyed.[14] And indeed it was. The ark was lost, and the flower of the chosen people was taken into captivity.

It was then that the voice of the prophets was raised anew. There is no longer a temple, they said. However, the promise that God made to dwell in the middle of his people is more valid than ever.[15] God remains and will remain in the midst of his own.[16] As Isaiah said, God dwells in the hearts of the contrite.[17] In short, we rediscover here the dialectical

---

[12] Cf. *City of God*, bk. X, chs. 5 and 6 (PL 41:281–284); cf. *Tract. XXVI in Joan.*, ch. 6, nn. 15 and 17 (35:1614).

[13] 1 Kgs 2:24, 33b.

[14] Mic 1:2-7; Ezek 9:3; 10:18f.

[15] Zech 6:12-15.

[16] Hag 2:3-9; Jer 3:16-17.

[17] Isa 66:1-2.

affirmation so characteristic of the prophets that we have already seen with respect to sacrifice. It is like this, but no it's not; it is true, but not as you imagine, not as you believe it to be and have experienced it . . . So the prophets affirmed at one and the same time the imperishable validity of the promise but also that it would be necessary to look for its fulfillment beyond the outcome of what had already happened.

In fact, Jesus teaches us that it is neither in Jerusalem nor on Mount Garizim, nor in any other particular place, that we should worship the Father. Rather, we should worship in spirit and in truth (John 4:21-24); or better, Jesus tells us what really is the temple of God, the place of his presence and so the place for true adoration. This is the temple of his body.[18] Then we can understand what was the object of God's promise from the beginning to dwell among his people and what was the meaning of Nathan's prophecy. God was not going to dwell in a house made of stone or in anything made by human hands.[19] We then understand these apostolic claims: we are the true temple of God; we are members of Christ and collectively form one body with him.[20] The one true temple of God is the son of David and it is also, just as truly, his people, the fraternal community of the faithful who are the members of Christ. In short, the true temple is nothing other than humanity itself, when it is renewed through Jesus Christ and reunited in him. Humanity here is in truth made to the image of God. There is no other true sacrifice, no other genuine altar, no other true temple than humanity reaching its fulfillment in the body of Christ.

Look again at the splendid text of the *City of God* that we mentioned above. St. Augustine saw the whole economy of salvation not only in the lives of individuals but in the great collective movement that starts with Abraham (even with Adam) and moves to the heavenly city, rising by stages to the point where everything is fulfilled. That fulfillment is the perfect interiority of human beings one with another through the unity of *all* in *one*, and the unity of God becoming truly "all in all." This is the endpoint of the huge trajectory of God's purpose, or of the work of God, which is brought to completion in his people and to which the Scriptures bear witness.

---

[18] Mark 14:58; 15:29; John 2:19-21.

[19] Cf. Isa 66:1f.; see also St. Stephen's remarkable discourse in Acts 7:44-50. It was for *this* that Jesus and later his disciple, the first "martyr," died.

[20] Eph 2:19-22; 1 Cor 3:16-17; 6:19; 1 Pet 2:2-10; Letter of Barnabas 4:2; 16.

3. However, this trajectory is achieved in stages, through a development made up of successive and gradual outcomes. This forward movement will succeed and reach its goal, intended from the start, only if it does not stop at one of the intermediate stages. There is always the danger that some stage already achieved will refuse to yield to further development, that the group or the individuals who carry out the promise, who are the stewards of the seed and of its future, become stuck. There is the danger that they may imagine their present experience to be unchangeable and definitive in terms of the forms in which the living idea finds itself already realized. Yet the dynamic power of the seed or of the promise eventually has to surpass all the intermediate stages. This is exactly the temptation of the synagogue. I will explain this more clearly in borrowing examples from salvation history.

In the Old Testament we find an insistence upon purity that would only be fulfilled in an interior and spiritual holiness surpassing all external and legal purity. In many texts a moral and interior meaning already had been given to legal purity, and the essential role of gratuitous divine mercy in the justice of the law had been affirmed. The development of the Old Testament itself, through the writings of the prophets, reached out toward what would be the message of the Gospel. But the Jews, clinging to the given historical form of the divine requirements for purity, although in its preliminary stages, remained caught up in observances of the law and refused to recognize the fulfillment of this demand in the Gospel. In a way, they refused the Gospel by being faithful to the gift and the commandment of God; and so there is something tragic and poignant in seeing them turn away from the fulfillment of the gift out of fidelity to the gift such as they understood it. We will find comparable situations in the church.

Marriage had been given from the beginning with an eye to its perfection. It had been willed and instituted as monogamous. Even in Israel, despite God's condescension to allow polygamy and divorce sanctioned by the Mosaic Law, the purity of conjugal union was maintained. The idea of a spousal union between God and his people, powerfully presented by the prophet Hosea, is exclusive and definitive. When our Lord, who came not to abolish but to complete the law, affirms the obligation of a monogamous and perpetual union between couples, he presents this reform as the reiteration and completion of what had already been instituted from the beginning. Transcending the valid form given in a certain stage of life of the people, the Lord gave meaning and development to the seed that had been planted from the beginning with an eye to its fulfillment.

All the "fulfillment" of the law declared solemnly in the Sermon on the Mount corresponds to this same intention.[21] Throughout all statements of the type, "You have heard that it was said to those of ancient times . . . but I say to you," this "fulfillment" consists not in Jesus adding to the prescriptions of the Mosaic Law some further precision, some new obligation that is more rigorous or universal, but rather in reaffirming the law in its fullness and its purity, such as was intended and implicit from the beginning. However, the law was given historically, at a certain time, and it carried within its expression limitations that its "fulfillment" had to surpass. Not an iota of the law will be removed until it is entirely "fulfilled." But this fulfillment is only possible if the limitations of certain historical forms corresponding to the stages of development have been surpassed. This is the kind of dialectic, essential to any development, in which the already acquired reality is at once both denied and affirmed, both surpassed and fulfilled, and which rests, *positis ponendis* (particular details attended to), a rule for the church itself.

My last example here is that of the universality of God's plan, tied to God's dwelling among his people. An appeal to the universality of the true religion is often found in the prophets of Israel. For them, Yahweh was the God of all human beings and of all peoples. But Yahweh dwelt in Israel, in the temple of holy Zion, and the conversion of the nations to the worship of God was described as a conversion to Judaism, coming to Zion. It becomes the gathering place for all the nations (cf. Isa 3:2; Ps 49:1-3). The nations must come to the temple, from which will flow the water of the new paradise garden (Zech 14:8f.).

Already, even before the destruction of the first temple, Jeremiah had claimed that religion consisted in interior, personal prayer. In Jerusalem the saving actions of the Messiah unfold; there Christ dies and rises again. By his death and resurrection Jesus achieves what he had proclaimed: "Destroy this temple [made by human hands], and in three days I will raise it up." But he said this, explains St. John (2:21), about the temple of his body. In the body of the risen Christ, the new temple is the church—the New Jerusalem; the church, the body of Christ born in Jerusalem from the passion and the resurrection through the gift of the Holy Spirit; the church, the spouse of the Lamb. From now on, the hour has come that Jesus had proclaimed to be near (John 4), when the Father will raise up true adorers. This true adoration is focused neither in Jerusalem nor on Mount Garizim, but rather focused upon this body of Christ in spirit and in truth. The body of Christ is the spiritual temple

---

[21] Cf. W. Vischer, op. cit., pp. 109f.

of God, constructed of living stones through our faith and our love. There is no longer a local temple. The city of redeemed souls is itself the temple of God (cf. Rev 21:22). Every soul who responds with a personal act of faith to the preaching of the apostles, sent out and dispersed from Jerusalem by the Spirit's breath at Pentecost, has become Jerusalem, the temple of God, a living stone of the body of Christ, a new and definitive tabernacle of God.

Here again, the living seed of the Old Testament, anticipating its fulfillment from the beginning, achieves its fullness and reveals its meaning only through the negation and the rejection of the limited forms in which it had been carried and realized through the preliminary stages of its development. Jesus came precisely to bring about this fulfillment (John 11:52); it is Christ that the Old Testament proclaims. It is for the fulfillment of the promise that he is condemned (Matt 26:61); it is for that same fulfillment that he is crucified. For this same reason Stephen will be stoned after having uttered his sublime testimony (Acts 6:11, 13-14; 7:48-50), and Paul will be seized by the Jews and imprisoned (Acts 21:28; 24:6). In sum, it is precisely this fulfillment that the synagogue rejected, and this is the meaning of what I mean here by *"Synagogue"*—the rejection of the fulfillment of the promise when confronted with the church that was born on the cross and at Pentecost. It is not so much that the synagogue denies a certain universality implicit in its profession of God's oneness; but it insists on maintaining it in forms linked to the past, tied up with the Mosaic Law, with the temple, and with the city of Jerusalem.

The "synagogue" acted out of fidelity to its tradition. But this *fidelity* to a cultural form became an *infidelity* with respect to the principle (the origin) of which the cultural form was merely an imperfect and historical realization. The principle is what gives meaning to its historical expressions, and here it needed to surpass what had existed in order to achieve and reveal its authentic fullness. There are cases where fidelity to the principle can only be achieved by a kind of infidelity to the transitional form in which it is expressed.[22] Perhaps we shouldn't really call it "infidelity," since it is only imperfect in the perspective of its genuine fulfillment. Israel lost their character as the true people of God not because

---

[22] Cf. the remark of M.-J. Nicolas with respect to the meaning of the end of marriage in the theology of St. Thomas: "On this point of theology as in several others, faithfulness to the thought of St. Thomas allows us to go beyond his formulas almost to the point of seeming to change them" (*Révue Thomiste* [Dec. 1939], p. 793). See what I have to say below on the question of two kinds of *fidelity*.

the promise of God and the proposition of God's grace were nullified but because Israel refused the new disposition, the new forms, in which Jesus fulfilled the promise and the proposition of grace. By false fidelity to the letter, Israel lost its true fidelity to the spirit. It misunderstood that the trajectory of God's plan had to reach out to its fulfillment, the goal that we have called here the *interiority* of the religious relation within the very heart of every person.

The case of Israel, important as it is, is an example of every reality meant to develop. Every historical form is tempted to stop developing, to refuse its further evolution—and this is what I mean when I use the expression here of the "synagogue."

4. Is it possible to apply these ideas, transposing them from the situation of the Old Testament, to the church, with respect to the fulfillment of God's promises and gifts? If the period of the law represents a *prefiguring* with respect to the Gospel, a preparation and a promise, then the church is *already* the reality of the new and definitive covenant. The church is the people of God no longer waiting for their salvation but living in messianic times, drawing from the abundance of the gift of new life. However long the wait will be between Pentecost and the glorious return of Christ, that is where we find ourselves. This is the time of the church. We are, even in the present, living in the last times, in that order of things beyond which there is no further dispensation to look for or to wait for.

In the preceding paragraph, we said that the realization of God's purpose includes various steps, but after the coming of Christ there is only one—or rather we are *in* that last stage—whatever the chronological duration of this "time of the church" may turn out to be. One of the errors of the movement of Joachim of Flora was to imagine and to proclaim the coming of the Church of the Holy Spirit that would follow that of the Church of the Son, which had been inaugurated by the incarnation, just as the Church of the Son had followed the Church of the Father, represented by the Old Testament.

This idea failed to understand that with the coming of the Son and the sending of the Spirit, we have already entered the last times, as the Letter to the Hebrews (1:2) explains. We are under the conditions of the new and definitive covenant. This means that essentially there will be no further culmination. The deposit of apostolic faith, of the sacraments, of the apostolic powers (priesthood, magisterium, and governance), in brief, everything that structures the church, has been given to us. This is definitive; it is unchangeable. I pointed this out already in the last chapter.

However, if the church can no longer yield to another and greater "fulfillment" of the kind that the Old Testament knew, who would deny that there is still further development to be accomplished? I will examine this development under two headings.

a) Even if we are now in the period of the last things, we do not yet enjoy their full expression. Although in fact we have entered the "new and eternal covenant" that we celebrate each day in the Eucharist, we still only possess it in an incipient way, partially, as though veiled, in an imperfect and unstable manner. The full realization of our redemption and of the new alliance belongs directly to God as well as the elimination of everything that goes by the name of evil or death: ignorance, suffering, injustice, sin, error, and corruption. We now possess the fullness of this new covenant only by way of promise, as a seed. As promise, this is already something great, but it is also the seed and the beginning of the reality, its first fruits. This is what St. Paul called the "first installment" of our inheritance. The New Testament reveals, explains, and brings about what was promised in the Old; just as the church reveals, explains and brings about the New Testament; and finally the heavenly Jerusalem will explain, reveal, and fulfill the meaning of the church. It will be the reality, the full and true reality of our sacraments, prefigurings, and concepts.

All these things, mirrored in all the activities of the church on earth, are meant to pass over finally into the reality for which they are the preparation. The earthly church is a means toward that definitive reality which will consist not in anything exterior to God and humanity but in a perfect presence and perfect interiority of one to the other. In its external activities the earthly church is like a sacrament that is meant to provide grace, but that in itself is only a sign, a means (St. Thomas said "*inductivum ad gratiam*—leading us to grace"[23]). The church belongs to the order of means that will have to pass away, just as we gather up straw into sheaves and throw them on the fire once their stems have matured into grain and the harvest is complete.

Beneath the external signs, the rites, and the words spoken, the sacrament has the power to achieve an interior change. This is the whole point of the sacraments. Everything that we said about the trajectory of God's gifts in the Old Testament applies here. God's goal was not to produce signs, but rather to bring about the interior and spiritual reality that the

---

[23] *Summa Theol.*, IaIIae, q. 106, art. 1.

signs lead to. The point is not the water, the oil, the bread, and the wine, not the ceremonies of baptism and Eucharist. All these things are for the sake of the interior grace, the awakening of faith and love. Because we have not yet arrived at the completely spiritual and free condition of the heavenly Jerusalem, we need these signs, ceremonies, words, and all the apparatus of the church, with its sacraments, dogmas, and government. But again, all these things are only means, and what God wants to achieve with them is that human beings themselves become united to God in mind and heart.

Further, the sense of the church as it continues to celebrate the sacraments with vigor and fidelity, to preach holy doctrine, and to govern spiritually (the three great acts of the apostolic mission—itself evolving from the Twelve and from Pentecost) is to recognize that none of that is an end in itself. Everything it does as church it does as *means*. The church has not achieved what it was created to do until, at a level deeper than its conduct, its catechesis, and its institutions, it has actually led souls to a personal interior contact with God. When its sacramentality, its rites, and its symbols become themselves the content of what is sought and celebrated, then the church becomes an *obstacle* instead of a *means* to life with God.

b) Christianity comes from above. By the ministry of the faith and the sacraments of the faith, the church's task is to communicate to people the divine good that is the grace and truth offered us in Jesus Christ. So Christianity and the church transcend time, and we are right to say that they do not share in time's contingency. Nonetheless, the work of transcendence that belongs to the church by its very nature has to be carried out within the flow of time. The church's job is to bring to the whole of humanity (the Gospels say "to every creature") grace and truth. Further, since all salvation comes from this one Savior, since only one will go up to heaven, the Son of Man who came down from heaven, what must be done is to incorporate into Christ everything that he came to save, namely, all human beings, made from the beginning in the image of God.

Elsewhere I have explained the essentials of such a program.[24] Basically it is a matter of the encounter *in Christo*—in Christ—of what proceeds *de Trinitate* (from the Trinity) and what is *ex hominibis* (from human

---

[24] *Chrétiens désunis* (Paris, 1937), ch. 3: "La catholicité et l'Eglise une"; and my article "Catholicité," in the encycl. *Catholicisme* (Paris: Letouzey), reprinted in *Sainte Eglise* (Paris, 1962), pp. 155–161.

beings), that is, the encounter of a source from on high and a source from below. In Jesus Christ, God gives us his life, making Christ the second Adam, the new principle of life for all those who descend from the first Adam by physical birth. All those who are descended from the first Adam and who symbolize a part of his living substance must receive a new kind of life, a life of which Jesus Christ is the principle and source. In this way they must all form the body of Christ, the body of the *redempta Civitas*—the redeemed city about which St. Augustine speaks.

Now this humanity that descended from Adam does not exist as a kind of timeless and changeless entity, like an inert stone. It lives and grows in conformity with the blessing which was given to it at the beginning: grow, multiply, and fill the earth. It does fill the earth, becoming diversified through a multiplicity of races, languages, cultures, situations, conditions, and involvements. Humanity lives, grows, and becomes diverse, evolving even across time, filling up the changes of time as it fills the space of its progressive developments. The seed of Adam evolves and develops, expands and becomes fruitful by pouring out its potential into space and time.

The church's program is to convey Christ's truth and grace to every human being and so to lead all of Adam's progeny (and the whole world) back to God in Christ. Therefore the church (even though it is changeless with respect to what it receives from on high) has to follow humanity in expanding and evolving and thus experience a parallel development within itself. If the church failed to do this, it would leave between itself and part of humanity a distance or hiatus, and in this way would fail to carry out God's plan. From this it becomes evident why the church needs to pass through stages of development in order to realize God's plan.

In the old covenant, the stages of development had to do with *bringing forth* the principle of salvation itself, that is, the very structure of the church. Now, however, the stages that challenge us have to do with *applying* the principle of salvation in the present. This has to do with the life of the church. These stages of development have no less importance, and we should be conscious of that.

What is at issue is the church's relation to the world. Clearly the church cannot avoid it. In order to bring to a changing, developing world the eternal treasure of which it is the steward, the church has to mirror the world's development with respect to what is adaptable and changeable within it. This is how problems of growth, adaptation, and renewal are posed for the church—problems that we have already encountered, and problems that we will soon take up again. Although in its essential structure the church is eternal, in its visible structures it must remain in contact with the world.

This necessitates conversation and dialogue with the world. The church will have something to give and *it will have something to receive.*[24a] We understand what it has to give, but what might it receive? First of all, it receives the context of its life as well as some understanding about the conditions in which it lives. The church does not belong to the world, but it lives in the world and, in a way, the world "provides its bed"—a "bed" that is inflexible, because it is the bed of history. For the people of God historical developments have often prepared the contexts and the forms of life that they have received and adapted. The activity of Israel's great prophets and their universalizing message took place in a world that had entered into a context of *Weltgeschichte* (world history), to use the categories of the German historians. Later, the church would see an analogous development.

The idea that Greece and Rome had prepared the way for Christ is banal and perhaps too vague for my argument here. Nonetheless, it was understood that the administrative structures of the church should take over the riches of the world (temporal and perishable) that God certainly didn't need. But those historical conditions made it possible for them to be offered to God in Christ. The people of God grow in number in Egypt, and they do not leave their land of slavery without bringing Egypt's treasures along with them; idolaters help build the temple (1 Kgs 5:15f.), and the nations are invited to contribute their riches (Hag 2:7, etc.). Literally, the body of Christ needs to be made from the physical matter of the body of Adam, from living persons throbbing with life.

The church also receives questions from the world. The temporal order questions the eternal, seeking a word to illuminate its problems and its path. The church has to understand these questions and respond to them, and, for that to happen, the church is compelled to clarify things that it has held in its treasury, long obscured or even buried perhaps.[25]

[24a] See on this point *Gaudium et Spes* of Vatican II, no. 44.

[25] Consider this text of Paul Claudel: "The complicated Dreyfus affair and the protests that it stirred up along with their reverberations had a twofold character in common: they were spontaneous, and they happened outside the church—even though they may have been in contradiction or even in opposition to the church. But as St. Paul poses the question to our Mother [the church]: '*Who asks a question without questioning me?*' The church speaks not only to her [unaware] new friends from all points of the horizon, but also to her enemies when she cries out: 'I was waiting for you. Here I am: and all I can tell you is this—Blessed are they who come to me in the

Sometimes the world brings to the church not only questions but also partial answers, positive values that are still rather rough or unworthy. Such things evolve in the world of ideas and lead to new perspectives from which the people of God can profit. Further, the world often ends up giving back to Christianity in this way something it had already received from it in germ. In any case, one part of Christian progress is made up from elements coming from non-Christians. Currents of thought that Christians have sometime neglected are revived by passing through the hands of those more industrious than themselves, perhaps we could say after passing through a sort of "season in hell."

Sometimes the kingdom is given over to those who make it fruitful, and the vineyard is rented out to those who can be more useful . . . It can even be the case that, in expressing criticisms and even very severe judgments about the life of the church, in seriously calling into question certain attitudes among Christians, the world, without realizing it, pronounces God's own judgment. Many revolts against the church are linked to the church's disobedience to God. What Yahweh said to Samuel with respect to Israel's insubordination could often enough be repeated with respect to the church: "They have not rejected you, but they have rejected me from being king over them" (1 Sam 8:7). It also happens that under the form of questions that the world poses to the church, God interrogates his people, standing at the door and knocking with raps made up of facts and events, these "instructors" that God sometimes gives us himself . . . The church has to listen to such things and to allow itself to be called into question, reserving judgment, of course, about the importance of such events. There is a movement in history that the church can't refuse without failing in its duty to the world or, if you prefer, failing in its duty to God with respect to the world.

Although almost normal, it is nonetheless fatal that the church is so slow to welcome the questions and the contributions of the world. The church belongs to the eternal; the church is tradition. It sometimes agrees to add things, but it doesn't like to face up to what is useless, to suppress

---

name of the Lord! If you knock me down, it is because you need me. Knock and the door will be opened! Knock, and you will not be disappointed! Your many questions, however brutal and insidious, are not too much for me. They draw out of me what is mine and belongs to you, that part of the Word of God hidden away but intended for you—the Word within me that corresponds to your needs and is indispensable for you'" (address on his reception at the Académie française [*Doc. Cathol.*, Mar. 30, 1947, col. 441]). Cf. Origen, *In Matth. Com.*, ser. 27 (GCS VIII, p. 175; cf. H. Urs von Balthasar, *Parole et mystère chez Origène* (Paris, 1957), p. 130, n. 25.

it, or to replace it with something else. This is evident in the church's liturgy. The church has added a great deal there, but it dislikes taking anything out. Rather, it lets the new enter and combine with the old, even at the risk of weighing down the liturgy. The church likes to hold onto old habits that it has received from a past. That, for her, has the value of tradition. On the other hand, when something new arises, the church was there first—and the church feels immediately the contradiction of something presented as new and looking for acceptance. Yet when the new element has been accepted, it is no longer experienced as a negation but as a reality, and the church opens itself to it. People judge this to be a belated and self-serving response, and sometimes that's exactly what it looks like. However, the issue is much more serious. The church ought to express within the world an energy linked to the energy of the world, but it shouldn't follow or accept just anything, or just give the appearance of being in sympathy.

5. These discussions—(§ 1) of the development inherent in God's initiatives among his people, (§ 2) of the endpoint of this development which is the interior possession by the human heart of the spiritual reality, (§ 3) of the obligation that this vision entails not to refuse to move forward through stages of development, and finally (§ 4) of the conditions in which the church lives out these dynamics—may seem to the reader far from the problem at hand, namely, the question of reforms in the church. However, all of that was necessary to allow us to situate precisely where reforms fit in and to understand theologically what makes them necessary.

Seeing the church in this light, there is a twofold danger or temptation. On the one hand, there is the temptation to forget that religion is only true in human experience and to become completely preoccupied with "things." This is the temptation to allow observances or means to become ends—here I'm going to call this the temptation to *Pharisaism*. On the other hand, there is the temptation to refuse to accept any progress in the development of the forms by which we celebrate God's work, forms situated and fixed in a given moment in time. When these forms are absolutized, they slow down or stop development and impede the source or the seed from bearing its proper fruit. This is the temptation of the *Synagogue*. We can see from these names that these two temptations existed already in Israel.

I have shown how these questions have arisen in a completely different way within the church but also how they continue to arise. Since the church still possesses a whole structure of means ordered to an end not yet achieved, the temptation of Pharisaism still exists. On the other hand, for the church as a dynamic entity still in evolution, the temptation to refuse to develop or to adapt her forms to new realities is also still a challenge for her.

There is a truly impressive parallel between these two temptations and the motivations for reform that we noted earlier. We discussed first the desire to give truly spiritual meaning to acts that have become routine, and second the desire to better adapt some of the forms of ecclesial life to the needs of new circumstances. In reality, these two points about which the modern world is so sensitive are the two points which the Old Testament prophets and religious reformers of all times also addressed. Just a bit of attention to history persuades us of this, and the rest of this chapter will demonstrate it.

So then, we see two great titles that remind the people of God to be attentive to reforming themselves. This is not a question of reform in the church's essential structure, but rather in its life. These two themes are Pharisaism and the danger of acting like a Synagogue.

In truth, by interpreting the two great themes of reform in this way, we discover something of a plan for addressing the general dynamics of ecclesial life. This raises the immense problem of the church's complicated historical growth. While expansion is made necessary by the external context, it is guided by an interior law of development and by a transcendent impulse of the Holy Spirit. With respect to such a complex problem, "reform" is only one act, one particular moment. It would be wrong to suggest that "reform" is coextensive with the whole process of the gradual self-realization of the church's life. I have no intention of doing that. The fact of adaptation, before ever being considered as a possible motive for reform, is a positive fact about the life of the church. The church usually lives peacefully through its periods of adaptation.

All this is unquestionable. I have no intention of reducing the whole vast life of the church to the special problem of the instinct for reform. Still, this problem seems to be located and to find its explanation in the context of the process of development, and even more especially in the context of those two hazards that come up in the course of the church's life and that we are about to study more carefully. As one part or as an occasional event in the life of the church, "reform" as a fact can only be studied properly in the context of the whole. How could we examine one aspect of a vital process without at least evoking the complex reality of the whole? Furthermore, this present work is only one part of a group of studies in which other aspects of the Catholic communion (of the life of the church) will be examined theologically.

II. The Need for Reform in Light of the Temptation to "Pharisaism"

The first danger is the risk, faced by every institution, of turning *means* into *ends*. In the case of the church, there is the risk that the ecclesiastical apparatus might overshadow the Spirit and the grace of God in people's attention.

In fact, this is a general problem concerning *spirit* and *life* and the *forms* in which spirit and life are embodied. Sometimes this problem has been raised in terms of a tension between *life* and *form*.[26] This tension is a question of the relationship at once of opposition between the two poles of reference, and of the necessary mutuality of the two poles with one another. These are interesting categories, but they are too static, perhaps, because they don't take enough account of the influence of time.

Bergson's categories might fit my analysis better—*élan vital* versus a spirit that has fallen or cooled off; a process of *becoming* versus a state of being *all finished*; *closed* versus *open*—especially if we take these ideas according to Péguy's understanding.[27] Péguy gave us a sort of phenomenology of emerging life: the freshness and youthfulness of life become transformed into hardened routines, petrified memories . . . and then aging. He spoke of mysticism transformed into politics. His analyses are important and true. You can't just dismiss them as imaginative descriptions or poetic fantasy. A great deal of the Book of Revelation falls under the same literary genre. In reality, using simple and beautiful images, Péguy managed to portray our common experience: verve and spirit are replaced with structures, that is, with solid external forms—forms that human verve and spirit need to enliven or to borrow if they are to continue to exist.

If human history teaches us anything, it teaches us that it is impossible for a spiritual impulse to survive in our world without somehow confronting the devouring logic and the sheer necessity of taking on a fixed expression, becoming locked into habits, memories, and institutions. This means the risk of growing old. The story of St. Francis—not the saint personally, but his achievement—is a striking illustration of this point. There is something deadly here that we have to understand and

---

[26] A. Rademacher, *Religion und Leben* (Freiburg im Breisgau; French trans.: Brussels, 1934); J. Hessen, *Luther in katholischer Sicht* (Bonn, 1946), pp. 16f., and *Religionsphilosophie*.

[27] Cf. especially his *Mystère des saints Innocents*; *Note sur M. Bergson*; *Note conjointe sur M. Descartes*; and also A. Rousseaux, *Le prophète Péguy*, vol. I, pp. 111 and 256f.; P. Duployé, *La religion de Péguy* (Paris, 1965).

accept, all the while doing everything possible to avoid letting the spirit sink, decompose, and turn entirely merely into its body and its shell.

Péguy writes: "Everything begins in the mystical—a given mystical experience—in one's own mystical experience, and everything ends up in the political . . . What is interesting, the real question, the essential here, is that in every order, in every system, the mystical should not be swallowed up by the political to which it gave birth."[28] The danger here is that the principle or end might become overshadowed, blocked out, and finally replaced by what should remain merely a means. Writing about socialism, Henri De Man[29] analyzed the process through which every social movement risks finding its ends masked over or even replaced by means. The organization and the means can become the chief obstacle to the realization of the authentic end. This is why, as De Man says, it is desirable to maintain the same psychological flexibility in the application of the means as in the pursuit of the end.

History and daily life show us many examples of this substitution of means for ends. Let me give some examples.

The Fourth Crusade, launched for the conquest of Jerusalem, turned into the siege and conquest of Constantinople (a complex drama in history). For more than one crusader, the other Crusades became an opportunity to seize a fiefdom or principality. (This is why you can't tell their story—not even that of the First Crusade—using only texts about the ideas that explain their hopes and objectives, as M. Paul Rousset largely seems to have done.) The Spanish or Portuguese conquests of the fifteenth and sixteenth centuries, undertaken principally to propagate the Gospel, quickly became the conquerors' quest for profit. The goods and privileges of the nobility, which previously had been the counterpart of an important role in serving the community, ended up becoming things sought for and clung to for themselves. Something similar happened, to a lesser degree, among the bourgeoisie.

In an inverse manner, the idea of equality of opportunity and rights as a factor in social life frequently turned into a fanatical egalitarianism (and rather quickly at that). So conceived, that means that another person ought never to have more than one has oneself.

Any social movement, group, or party that starts out with the ideal of pure justice and brotherhood will always risk being derailed by democratic competition, lies, blackmail, or simply by the growth of its own

---

[28] *Notre jeunesse*, in *Oeuvres complètes* (Paris, N.R.F.), pp. 59–60.
[29] *Au-delà du marxisme*, ch. 9.

organizational structures. You can see some of that in the history of the Congregation under the Restoration.

All these examples bring personal interest into play. It would be easy to find other examples of the same danger in other areas of life . . . We say that anyone who wants peace should be prepared for war. But when we build up a stockpile of arms, we create a mentality that, at a certain point, finds it logical to use the weapons. We take the necessary measures against another possible German invasion, but what was supposed to be a means turns into an end, and then wiping out Germany looks like an objective.

Looking closely at what Père Clérissac aptly called "scholasticism gone to seed," it is clear that here too there has been a similar substitution of means for ends. Of course, theology had, and always has, as one of its tasks the responsibility to save and to transmit the enduring articulation of sacred truths to new generations. It has done that, and my criticism is not about that, but rather about the excessive and stifling place given to its scholastic formulas, ritualistic exercises, and defensiveness about articulated positions. Although in reality only means, such things have for all practical purposes been made into ends—as Papini blames the monks for doing even today.

The [medieval] schools were created less to prepare ecclesial servants for the people of God or creative thinkers than to produce "doctors" capable of brilliantly arguing in scholastic disputations with a view to augmenting their number and prestige and perpetuating the scholastic system itself. "Scholasticism gone to seed" did nothing more than reproduce itself. It is easy to illustrate what I mean by looking at the scholasticism of the sixteenth, seventeenth, and eighteenth centuries and what it produced, for example, in my area of apologetics and ecclesiology. The results are similar to the source and the method that produced them. I find a parallel here between this "scholasticism gone to seed" and the phenomenon of academicism in the arts, so well analyzed by Père Régamey.[30] In both cases, the output is fixed and constricted. Instead of valuing creativity in the principled use of a living tradition and looking at the problems and the data of their own time, rather they imagined an unchanging perfection and tried to set about reproducing it.[31]

---

[30] Cahiers de *L'Art sacré*, 10 (Oct., 1947).

[31] Since life is logical, this parallel could be pushed further into other domains to find analogous examples. Here and there we find differences between *schools* and *living experience*—here, between art schools and professional workshops; there, between

For the moment these examples will suffice. They help to support my suspicion that there is a pattern in these matters. We have to turn now to the life of religion and the church. Here, the typical example of this process of deterioration is the case of Pharisaism. In the beginning, the pharisaical movement had been both sincere and worthy. One hundred sixty-five years before Jesus Christ it had been essentially a movement of spiritual resistance, a concentration in Judaism upon the purest meaning of its origins, a reaction against the danger of Hellenization and of allowing oneself to be led astray by foreign and idolatrous influences. The movement had its martyrs. But as Canon Guignebert has written, the movement had survived "for a long time after its reason for being had passed away."[32] The movement had turned into a system and had become a kind of end in itself.

Inside the system of the Pharisees there was a quest for legal purity, going from one subtlety to another and ending in the narrow and inhuman legalism that our Lord fought against and that we know about through the Gospels. The very *idea* of the Messiah and his kingdom had been "politicized." Although Jesus is, of course, much more than a reformer, he is nonetheless a reformer in the larger sense that this study accords to the word. Jesus opposed this obscuring of God's plan, this replacement of the end with the means. His reaction to a religion that had deteriorated into Pharisaism can be summed up in this question that we can never consider too often: "Was the Sabbath made for humankind, or humankind for the Sabbath?" (cf. Mark 2:27).

There have been periods in the life of the church when excessive external practices have obscured the spirit of the Gospel which, however, remained still alive. That was doubtlessly the case with the period preceding the Protestant revolt. A number of contemporary texts tell us to what degree almost everywhere there was a desire for religion that would be something other than "practices" (pilgrimages, the veneration of the relics of the saints, indulgences, confraternities of one kind or another, diverse ways of being attached to a religious order, questions of fasting,

---

religious schools and the pastoral life of the church—as well as between schools and the "public," between schools and the laity. It has even happened that pontiffs, holding the key of knowledge, prevent others from entering into understanding: we have seen sometimes the most creative people removed from office or kept on a leash. In every generation, they were first treated like revolutionaries and then, fifty years later, almost everything vital has become nourished by their work.

[32] *Jésus*, p. 493.

abstinence, holidays, etc.)—a desire for religion that would constitute a personal relationship of the soul with God.[33] Luther's preaching was a thunderous success first of all because at last people heard in it words like Gospel, grace, Christian freedom—indeed, Jesus Christ.[34] A member of the bourgeoisie from Lorraine who went over to the Reformation with his whole entourage said that he was passing over "into the kingdom of Jesus Christ."[35] This is only one example among thousands. This is what justification by faith (alone) meant at the beginning for a vast number of people. . . . In place of a political church, of a huge juridical organization, they finally found communities where they could hear the word of God and sing his praises with simplicity. At least that was the ideal.

The reform spirit of Erasmus expressed itself essentially by denouncing in the church of his time a "Judaism"—that is, an invasion of all sorts of heavy obligations, worse than those of the Jews, or of external practices like those carefully undertaken and transmitted by the monks[36] or even by the leaders of the Roman Curia (whom he called the Pharisees).[37] For Erasmus, that "Judaism" had replaced the simple spiritual meaning of the Gospel. Erasmus may not be a perfect model for understanding Christianity and the church, but he had a real sense of them both (see below, "Conclusion," pp. 327f.). He was not radical and unilateral the way Luther was. He was willing to hold onto the status quo as long as it underwent purification and was accepted in moderation. Finally, he put his finger on the real problem of Catholicism in his time almost everywhere: the *pastoral* had been overshadowed or effaced by the *feudal*, the Gospel spirit by the excrescences of flamboyant piety, *faith* by *religion*, and religion by practices . . . You can understand how, faced with people

---

[33] For example, see A. Renaudet, *Etudes érasmiennes (1521–1529)* (Paris, 1939) passim and, e.g., pp. 238, 300; also *Augsburg Confession*, art. 20.

[34] P. Imbart de la Tour, *Origines de la Réforme*, vol. IV, pp. 240f.; L. Febvre, "Une question mal posée: les origines de la Réforme française et le problème général des causes de la Réforme," *Revue historique* 161 (May–June 1929), pp. 1–73; H. Dannenbauer, *Luther als religiöser Volkschriftsteller* (Tubingen, 1930). See the characteristic reaction of Albrecht Dürer upon hearing of Luther's death on the way home from Worms in 1521: *Dürers schriftlicher Nachlass auf Grund der Originalhandschriften*, eds. K. Lange and F. Fuhse (Halle, 1893), pp. 161f.

[35] Cited in J. Aynard, *La bourgeoisie française*, 2nd ed. (Paris, 1934), p. 227.

[36] Cf. A. Renaudet, op.cit., passim; esp. pp. 41, 148–150, 163–164, 166–168, 172, 176–184, 215–216, 300. Cf. Renaudet, *Préréforme et Humanisme* (Paris, 1916), pp. 431f.

[37] Op. cit., pp. 215–216.

that had fallen into the Judaizing attitude of the Galatians, Luther had articulated his protest drawing upon the themes of the letter of Paul and exaggerated them in a dangerously unilateral way.

Canon J. Leclercq recently called attention to this danger of replacing the end with the means.[38] He did so with all the serenity and finesse of his intellectual and apostolic experience. First, he shows how in a religion composed not only of saints and heroes, routine becomes a real danger. It calls for doing certain actions without insisting on the spirit that gives meaning to their observance. Carrying out the function, executing the rite, or performing the obligation becomes the objective and the content of the action. This leads to religious formalism, similar to that of the Pharisees, with perhaps less rigor than they might have had.

From my point of view, the danger is graver when it is a question not of personal conviction and initiative, but rather of Christianity as a religion of the masses into which one is inserted by birth, education, and social conformity.[38a] Tertullian proudly said that people are not born Christian, but they *make themselves* Christians. However, from the day that people *were* born Christian, or from the day that the faithful formed a numerous group of people for whom there was no longer any question of conversion or choice, the risk arose that the real content of Christianity would be less its spiritual meaning than its habits, its external obligations, its rites, and its visible social reality.

We should note that carrying out the means can be absorbing, interesting, and engaging. In a sense, practically speaking, this is what fills up our life. We become involved in the proper execution of liturgical ceremonies *in order to* praise God, we study and write *in order to* spread the kingdom of God, *in order to* love and to help others love God more deeply; we take our rest "so as to serve God better." Our study or rest or work in the kitchen—our life—is filled up, at least concretely, not with acts of love of God but with singing, studying, or some other demanding activity. The risk is that the real end that we pursue might not be God's service or love, but rather these occupations that fill up our days and give shape to our life. The risk is that the genuine end of our activities might become not the reign of God and the service of others but the smooth functioning and the success of our work—the things we do in

---

[38] *La vie du Christ dans son Eglise—Unam Sanctam* 12 (Paris, 1945), esp. part 1, ch. 7, "La lutte pour l'esprit du Christ dans l'Eglise"; and part 2, ch. 1, "L'Eglise militante."

[38a] Profitable here is Pascal, *Comparaison des chrétiens des premiers temps avec ceux d'aujourd'hui* (Petite édition, Brunschvicg), pp. 201f.

themselves. The risk is that all these noble activities, theoretically filled with the spiritual meaning that Catholicism imposes upon us and makes us do, might become mere actions, rituals cut off from their frame of reference in divine life.

Even more serious, we live in a world infatuated with sincerity in which there is a pitiless critique of everything that seems to claim to give sublime, religious, spiritual, or disinterested motivation to our actions. We live in a world where, faced with brutal opposition and with mysticisms that demand absolute devotion, Christianity is expected to be absolutely sincere and can be professed only on the condition of representing what is genuinely true, what one really believes, and what one is willing to invest in.

The spiritual deterioration I am warning about is even more dangerous if Christianity has "succeeded" in winning the favor of those in power or of society as a whole. Success is a terrible temptation for any social movement bearing witness to an idea. The end of the church is spiritual, apostolic, and supernatural—to bring souls together through faith and love in Jesus Christ and to promote in this way the kingdom of God. We can't confuse this spiritual end with either external success or the flourishing condition of an ecclesiastical organization. The danger in this case is to believe that we have fostered the kingdom of God to the exact degree that we have succeeded at the level of means—for example, because we have filled the church thanks to an extraordinary musical performance.

In one sense, the very will to succeed presents temptations. It is always looking for the satisfaction of being able to judge that it has succeeded. By that very fact its mentality is focused on identifying the "success" of God's work (which is what we are after) with the success of the means at hand. Or to be even more subtle, the danger is no less real of confounding zeal for the Gospel with a certain mentality of triumphalism. This is a delicate question. We always want to succeed: the saints always looked for maximum efficacy in what they did. But we can never let go of the margin of mystery that stands between the recognition of success in the implementation of our means and the feeling of success for *God's* work— a mystery that needs to be respected without trying to clarify everything. We don't really know, and we shouldn't try to know, the results of our work for the kingdom of God. For us it is time to sow, not to harvest—not a time for calculating results. We have to do our very best using the tools of the Spirit, but we also have to know that when we have done everything we need to do, we remain useless servants and let the Master judge the results.

Some time ago I published a study on proselytism and evangelization in which I made a contrast between two attitudes that we can adopt.[39] Using these two terms, we can see how we pursue the success of the institution of which we are ministers (proselytism) rather than seeking the spiritual good of others and their grounding and progress in Christ (evangelization). Looking at our real motives and the spirit of our actions, we perceive sometimes that we have allowed ourselves to be overtaken by enthusiasm and by a preoccupation with what is easy and immediate. So ultimately what we're looking for, it seems, is converts to our group, numbers in our organizations, growing influence, and the support of influential people. In this way the church's organizations, its influence, its youth groups, the participants in its movements, the statistics, the number of Easter communions, the visible effect (for a good cause, naturally) have become the real motivation for our actions. The *means* has become the *end*—even though maximizing the means requires personal detachment and often a lot of zeal. However, this zeal is poisoned by clericalism: no longer a political, but a moral and psychological clericalism which, while unconscious, is strongly resented by those who observe it. They are able to perceive this fixation on means and they are afraid of getting caught up in the system and of being manipulated.

Unaware of the way others see us, we are sometimes surprised and pained to discover that others don't trust us. Recognizing this can lead us to reflect and to question ourselves, wondering if we don't look more like servants of the clerical apparatus than servants of God and of humanity. In truth, have we really been working for the success of the ecclesiastical system? Haven't we often confused the spiritual with the ecclesiastical, and the essential relation to God with the mere observance of means and external forms?

This danger becomes still more acute when the church, established as a sacred institution in society, enjoys honors, riches, material advantages, and easy influence. Then someone might become attached to the church not in order to find Christ but to find success—personal success or success for their group. This danger is even greater when, not only enjoying the advantages of power, the church itself holds and exercises power, as was the case in the Middle Ages under the bureaucratic-hierarchical structures of Christendom.

The great danger in this kind of symbiosis between the church and society is that the church might take on externally and sociologically the

---

[39] See my "Prosélytisme et évangélisation," *Rythmes du Monde* 2 (1946), pp. 58–68; reprinted in *Sacerdoce et Laïcat* (Paris, 1962), pp. 51–64.

aspect of a "Christian world." The fear is that under these conditions the lives of a great number of the faithful and the pastoral activity of priests may become guided by the ideas and behaviors of the group, of the "Christian world," following the ideas of the "already finished," of "closed or sociological religion" in Bergson's sense, of the "political" in the sense of Péguy, of the "mentality" as contrasted with the "spirit" in the sense of Jean Guitton, of "conformity" more than "orthodoxy" in the sense of Gabriel Marcel.[40] I could cite still other authors and different categories, but it is fundamentally always the same problem. The actions of Christians should be true and should arise from a spiritual source; the forms of religious expression should manifest the spirit and not replace it; religion should truly have its authentication in the heart of human beings, and not only in their rituals of thought and action as well as their worship.

The prophets took a stand against any spiritual deterioration of this kind. The reformers rose up against such things in the church. Both prophets and reformers have repeatedly brought external actions back to their deepest meaning, from the letter to the spirit, from the means to the end.

Nonetheless, they did not fail to recognize the role that form plays, nor did they deny that forms remain an essential means, even as they insisted upon avoiding that the liturgical or hierarchical apparatus might become an end. Between these two positions the whole fate of true or false reform is at play. It was a tragic excess on Luther's part, from which Protestantism has never totally escaped, to consider every "form" as an expression of a "letter" that inevitably betrays the spirit. By criticizing the church, which was weighed down with bureaucratic excrescences and in which too many secondary forms threatened to obscure what was essential, Luther sought to be the prophet of a return to pure Gospel. But he was too impassioned and incapable of submitting to any external regulation of his personal experience. He thought in too concrete a way, and he presented only the choice between the pure Gospel or the work of Satan.

Luther did not sufficiently avoid identifying Christianity with the interior man and with the purely spiritual, thus relegating every external reality to the worldly and the carnal.[41] But in fact he rather quickly discovered the impossibility of conceiving the church in these categories,

---

[40] *Du refus à l'invocation* (Paris, 1940), pp. 237f.

[41] This is so especially in "The Freedom of the Christian" (see my *Chrétiens désunis*, pp. 157–158; also see part 3 of this study [not included in this translation]).

and to a certain degree he sought to re-empower the ideas of "ministry" and of "function," the objective character of *word* and *sacrament*—both external realities needed for church unity.[42] Unfortunately, he infected Protestantism with a fatal tendency to oppose form and spirit, "this Protestant mistake that claims to identify inspiration with the absence of a method or a plan."[43]

I cannot treat the serious problem of form and spirit here. However, with respect to what has been said already, let me remark that the necessity of external forms is linked precisely to the present condition of the people of God, which is that of "being at home in the body [and] away from the Lord" (2 Cor 5:6); of not yet being in the state of the heavenly Jerusalem—a state of freedom; of being still under a law, even though we are already in the economy of grace. The Antichrist is "the lawless one," *anomos* (2 Thess 2:8; Acts 2:23). As a result, by way of a curious

---

[42] On this topic, see O. Piper, "Vom kirchlichen Wollen der deutschen Reformation," in the collection *Luther in ökumenischer Sicht* (Stuttgart, 1929), pp. 93–110; cf. remarks of H. Preuss, *Martin Luther: der Prophet*, pp. 192f., where we also see that the teaching of a "prophet," as soon as it is transmitted, is institutionalized and becomes a *tradition*, or school of thought. Lutheranism, like Calvinism (even more so), developed from the middle of the 16th century into a scholasticism that was not much better than medieval scholasticism. This is remarkable and also generally the case: most reformers who first cried out against outward forms, ended up restoring much of the structure and organization of the church. This is so with Calvin, who never shared in the anti-juridical concerns of Luther and whose evolution in this regard can be tracked in the successive editions of *The Institutes of the Christian Religion*. There is a similar development in Schleiermacher. H. P. Douglass (*Church Unity Movements in the United States*, p. 152) has observed a rapid evolution toward institutionalization and tradition among American sects. Many (even churchmen) who once had an open mind took on the positions of those in authority and of the tradition once they found themselves in positions of power. This was the case with Gerbert, who became Pope Sylvester II; Aeneas Sylvio Piccolomini, who became Pope Pius II; Carafa, who became Pope Paul IV; and even Nicholas of Cusa, etc.

[43] W. Monod in *Le Christianisme social* (July 1933), p. 15. This partisan inclination to build upon an opposition of form and spirit has filtered into German Catholic writings concerned with reform. For example, in the article of "a Roman Catholic priest," "Gedanken zur Eneuerung der Römischkatholischen Kirche," *Eine Heilige Kirche* (Jan. 1934), pp. 50–57, the author calls for "more Christ and less church," "more gospel and less church," "more love and less church," as if all these things were opposites. The same kind of false claim can be found earlier in A. Pichler, *Die wahren Hindernisse und die Grundbedingungen einer durchgreifenden Reform der katholischen Kirche, zunächst in Deutschland*, 1870. The article of Ida Görres cited above (1950 intro., n. 19) contains a good critique of this misleading assumption. Perhaps this is a sign that the tendency is emerging again; at least, it is a sign that my idea of reform is not like that of the leaders of the "Reformkatholizismus."

paradox, Luther's protests in favor of a pure spirit must be placed within the logic of the heavenly Jerusalem, and we then see how they misconstrue the real condition of the pilgrim church. In this way he represents a kind of *theologia gloriae* (theology of glory) rather than a *theologia crucis* (theology of the cross), to use the very expressions (beautiful ones!) so dear to Luther and to Protestant theologians.

Conscious of these dangers and moved by the needs of a "spiritual apostolate" (the formula of Père de Montcheuil), Canon Leclercq concluded that the church is in a better situation when it has to face up to some kind of opposition. Then it purifies itself and reawakens to the demands of its ethical principles. A church grown fat and fixated on its works, its successes, and its securities risks becoming more worldly and forgetting its true purpose: through whom and for whom it exists. On the frontier of the "land that flows with milk and honey" to which he guided Israel, Moses foresaw the weakening of the spirit in Israel when they became settled in a rich and cultivated environment:

> Jacob ate his fill; Jeshurun grew fat, and kicked.
> You grew fat, bloated and gorged!
> He abandoned God who made him,
> and scoffed at the Rock of his salvation . . .[44]

In later times the prophets would refer to the time that Israel passed in the desert in poverty as a time of freshness and fidelity to God.[45] Periods of easy and sumptuous life are not the best for the church, nor for Israel, nor for any people or individual. Speaking of the years of favor and prosperity before Diocletian's persecution, Eusebius noted how this kind of euphoria had ended by creating a softness and laxity that fostered divisions.[46] After the peace of Constantine that allowed the felicitous

---

[44] Deut 32:15; cf. ch. 8. Cf. Ronsard, *Elégie à Guillaume des Autels*:

Que dirait-il de voir l'Eglise à Jésus-Christ	What might he say in seeing the church
Qui fut jadis fondée en humblesse d'esprit.	That once was humbly founded
. . . .	. . . .
Et la voir aujourd'hui riche, grasse et hautaine . . .	To be now rich and fat and haughty . . .

[45] Cf. Hos 2:16-17; 11:1, etc.; Jer 2:1-3.

[46] *Hist. Eccles.*, bk. VIII, ch. 1, no. 7. Cf. Bardy, *La théologie de l'Eglise de saint Irénée au Concile de Nicée—Unam Sanctum* 14 (Paris, 1947), pp. 255f. On the other hand, Origen, who lived through the persecutions, said that one is not truly Christian *unless it is difficult and dangerous to be so* (*In Jerem.*, hom. 4, 3, cited by J. Lebreton, in *L'Histoire*

unfolding of the church's life, the Fathers of the fourth and the beginning of the fifth century made note of the dangers of success and of official privileges. St. Gregory Nazianzen,[46a] St. Jerome,[46b] St. Ambrose,[46c] and St. Augustine rejoiced at the church's victory and its glory but also noted the dangers it faced—at the very moment when it had to respond to the Donatists who were the very incarnation of a refusal to accommodate to power and to the world.[46d]

Analogous situations produced similar effects at many moments in history.[46e] Augustine formulated a general warning about which we can always reflect with profit: "We shouldn't say that the Church is glorious because the earth's rulers serve her; this precisely is her greatest temptation."[47] St. Augustine is not alone. Before Pascal wrote with some bitterness that "the church is in a good state when it is supported by nothing but God,"[48] the church heard more than one message (not only written, but lived) of this profound conviction that, despite appearances, applies to her. St. Ambrose, whose independence as a bishop is well known, said that it would be better for the bishops to be persecuted by rulers than to be their friends.[49] Pope Hormisdas wrote at the beginning of the sixth

---

de l'Eglise of Fliche and Martin, vol. II, p. 252). Given his fervor, he thought that baptized Christians of his time were no longer like the converts of the apostolic age and that they were too much influenced by the spirit of the world. See *Com. in Rom.*, V, 8 (PG 14:1040b); *Com. in Mat.*, XVII, 14 (GCS Orig. X, 652).

[46a] *Carm.* II,11; *De seipso*, XI; *De vita sua*, 20f. (PG 37:1031).

[46b] *Vita Malchi* (PL 23:55): "Christi ecclesia . . . postquam ad christianos principes venerit, potentia quidem et divitiis maior, sed virtutibus minor facta sit—the church of Christ, after showing favor to the Christian princes, was made stronger in power and riches, but weaker in virtue"; cited by G. B. Ladner, *The Idea of Reform* (Cambridge, MA, 1959), p. 252, n. 57.

[46c] *Ennar. in Ps. 118*, XI, 21 and 22 (PL 15:1428–1429).

[46d] Cf. *Ennar. in Ps. 7*, 9 (PL 36:103): "*Nunc postquam in tanto culmine nomen coepit esse christianum, crevit hypocrisis*—Now after the name of Christian begins to be used everywhere, hypocrisy is growing." Cf. *In Ioan. Evang.*, tr. XXV, 10 (PL 35:1600); A. Vecchi, *Intoduzione al "De Civitate Dei"* (Modena, 1957).

[46e] See, e.g., the testimony of the Bishop of Castres in 1708 on the decline of Catholicism because of conversions without conviction following the revocation of the Edict of Nantes; cited in *Annales* 10 (1955), p. 256.

[47] *De perfectione justitiae*, n. 35 (PL 44:310). Cf. St. Hilary, *Contra Constantium imper.*, 5 (PL 10:581–582).

[48] Pascal, frag., 861.

[49] *De obitu Valentiniani*, n. 39 (PL 16:1371c). Cf. H. Rahner, *Abendländische Kirchenfreiheit: Dokumente über Kirche und Staat im frühen Christentum* (Einsiedeln, 1943), p. 377.

century: "My brothers, trials are not new for the church; for the church, moments of humiliation or loss that seem an affliction, are in fact her enrichment."[50]

We will discover a similar idea with respect to the second temptation. We will see that it is sometimes good for the church to be led by poverty to rediscover the truth of its mission and the full freedom of her apostolic action. In a way, it is good to be pushed back by the resistance of the world in order to reclaim the church's evangelizing spirit. Isn't this a frequent theme of the apostolic writings? Persecutions, temptations, even heresies are needed so as to test the faithful and to purify the people of God.

III. The Need for Reform in Light of the Temptation To Become a "Synagogue"

In this between-times, which both separates and links the first and second comings of Christ, this time of Pentecost (as both beginning and fulfillment), everything is in a state of development. On the one hand, there is the perfect kingdom that Christ's return will establish, but, on the other, there is also the kingdom germinating and growing in our midst—in us and through us. This latter is the kingdom that is revealed to us under the images of a seed, a grain of mustard, the yeast in the dough, and which acts upon the dough *donec fermentatum est totum* (until all of it is leavened, Matt 13:33), *donec omnia fiant* (until all is accomplished, Matt 5:18). This is the seed of the word of God, the grain of mustard of the faith, the leaven of the Holy Spirit . . .

This is the way the church, in which and through which the kingdom grows, has to develop in the *field* or in the *dough* of the world. In this sense the church is also essentially apostolic or missionary. Utilizing the two great functions of its ministry, preaching the faith and celebrating the sacraments of the faith, the church's pattern is progressively to help the kingdom of God to come into a humanity which has (for its part) received the mandate to "grow, multiply, and fill the earth." The church's mandate is to bring about the transition, bit by bit, of the passage of the whole substance of the first Adam into that of the second—to progressively recapitulate the whole of humanity in Christ.

---

[50] *Coll. Avellana*, 140; *Corpus Script. Eccles. Latin.* 35, 2, p. 572, l. 18–19. (Cf. H. Rahner, op. cit., p. 252). Cf. St. Hilary, *De Trin.*, VII, 4 (PL 10:202a).

The church has to develop, then, and to make progress in the world along with the world. This is the case not just for the group of apostles (its primitive cell) nor just a matter of making contact with an unchanging world. The church is obliged to follow the ceaseless development and variety of the ever-growing innovation and new situations of humanity. The church has to move forward on the human journey. R. Dumaine summed up a study day consecrated to the future of the church in the November 1963 *Semaine des intellectuelles catholiques français* with the phrase, "the future of the church means to be present to the future of the world."

With respect to this obligation, the church finds itself confronted with temptations similar to those to which Judaism gave in. Here it is not a question of fulfilling the law with the Gospel or fulfilling figures with reality. Rather, the church runs the risk of becoming attached, with respect to its own proper development, to familiar and established forms and then of failing to hear the call for new needs and for new growth requiring new forms. Throughout the world humanity has a longing for new solutions—for fresh adaptations, ideas and ways of seeing things. Everywhere, continuously, these new forces are looking for new values. The variety of these innovations across time exceeds the variety of types and experiences expressed in different places. The catholicity of the church ought to be able to integrate these innovations. A keen awareness of this problem becomes upsetting for many, however, and leads to the kind of discomfort that led a priest (in 1946) to propose the following description: "The church's body has grown, but not its skin. So it is in danger of splitting open . . ."

Great transformations come about in phases; great developments come in stages. Using spatial images, we see large, extended uniform areas, and then a change of climate or of ethnic perspective or of culture. As to time, there are periods of tranquility and then, sometimes after long preparation, moments of profound renewal, crises of transformation, moments where opportunities for the future come together. This is what Péguy has called the "epochs."[51]

There is little doubt that, from the point of view of human affairs, we are living in one of these epochs. Forces whose meanings have yet to be recognized are struggling to be expressed. Naturally these forces are linked to the most active social elements, called the rising class, without

---

[51] *Notre Jeunesse* in *Oeuvres complètes* (N.R.F.), pp. 53, 102; and cf. A. Rousseaux, *Le prophète Péguy*, vol. I, p. 187; vol. 2, pp. 273f.

necessarily appealing to Marxist theory.[52] These new forces confront the forces representing established, already acquired and entrenched social realities. These latter have the tendency to remain in possession of social authority and to perpetuate the structures in which they are expressed. There is a great risk that the old forces will slow down social development and that they will impede the forces of openness, innovation, and integration from making their impact upon history.

Feudalism sought to obstruct the Commune movement, the bourgeoisie sought to forestall the coming of a true economic and social democracy in 1848, etc. There is a whole order of people in place who feel and believe themselves linked to these social or cultural forms that are being called into question by the movement of history. Most theologians, especially those from religious orders, reacted in this way when faced with the cultural and theological innovation of modern humanism.[53] When the present becomes frozen in the past, it blocks the flow of life. There is never a shortage of motivations, either *really* or *apparently* noble and urgent, for refusing to run risks, and above all to run the risk of modifying our articulation of the deposit of faith. As for the Synagogue of old, *fidelity* is often the reason given for turning away from change. But just as with the Synagogue, an excessive attachment to the historical forms that give the church its cultural expression, and are by that very fact dated and partial, can lead to an inappropriate blocking of the church's fidelity to its living principle.

In every generation those who have accomplished something (for which they deserve great respect), and who are thus "in charge," tend to try to impose their view of things on those who have only fresh energies and ideas to contribute. What parent has not known the temptation to impose the same rules on their children that they themselves had to follow—times for returning home, things to read, types of entertainment, and how to feel or how to express themselves? These are all the things that a new generation wants to do for itself, with its own ideas, experience,

---

[52] In the 12th century the "apostolic" movements and sects were recruited from among the weavers and the rising bourgeoisie. (I take this from L. Spätling, *De Apostolicis Pseudoapostolis, Apostolinis* [Munich, 1947], pp. 94f.). It was the middle class that favored and followed Wyclif (A. Humbert, *Les origines de la théologie moderne* [Paris, 1911], p. 73), and it was the bourgeoisie that most easily embraced the Reformation (cf., among others, the studies of A. Schultze on the urban communities at the time of the Reformation).

[53] Erasmus's diagnosis here is precise and accurate: Cf. Renaudet, *Etudes érasmiennes*, pp. 46–48, 49–52, 175, 190, 270f.

and creativity. The reaction of children against their parents is a major theme in life, before becoming one in literature or in theater.[54]

Having geriatric leaders can only make this difficulty worse. After a certain age, it is very rare that someone can really think through problems in a new situation, even if they want to. We saw this in 1940 . . . It was said (a bit unjustly and with some levity) that the General Staff are always behind in waging combat, and the church is always late in recognizing a revolution.[55] There is a lot more to say about this, and perhaps that is the way it should be.

Genuine success can be the source of significant temptation. The historical periods and the structures that have succeeded too well have attempted to exercise a sort of perpetual hegemony over later generations by reason of their classical status and their success. Such is the case with medieval Christendom, with scholasticism, with the Grand Epoch in France. In a way, the revolt of the modern world against the church is precisely a revolt against too great a success in its administrative supervision—a guardianship opportune for its proper time but held onto long after it was no longer appropriate.

Even aside from their character as the "personnel in charge" (and for deeper reasons as well), it is understandable that the church hierarchy, who are responsible for guarding the "deposit of faith" by which the church maintains its deepest structure, would have a conservative spirit and be mistrustful of innovation. They have serious reasons for exercising pastoral prudence[56] that may block demands for renewal, at least at first, even if these demands are perfectly legitimate.

Some things in the church are unchangeable because they are of divine institution and they represent the very foundations upon which the church is built. Among these, for example, are dogma, the sacraments, and the essential structure of the church. Other realities, without being

---

[54] Marcus Aurelius placed strict limits on the gladiators' combats; his son Commodus dreamt of becoming one. Hitler, the son of a minor bureaucrat in the customs office, fashioned himself in reaction to the model of the lower-middle-class bureaucrat that his father represented.

[55] G. Mounin in *Esprit* (Aug.–Sept. 1946), p. 216; cf. a younger and lighter account by M. Dupouey in *Esprit* (May 1946), pp. 710–717.

[56] I am struck by the fact that for almost any question, out of concern for pastoral "prudence," the doctrinal arguments that support the hierarchy's attitude are multiplied. I pointed this out, for example, with respect to ecumenical meetings (*Chrétiens désunis*, 1937, pp. 179f.) and with respect to [magisterial] teaching (*Esprit*, Mar.–Apr., 1949, pp. 419–421).

as essential as that, are so deeply linked to the essence of the church that they cannot be fundamentally changed; they demand our docility and our respect. (Here, for example, are found formulas of doctrine, even those that are not dogmatic formulas properly so called.) We should not rush to judge or change things that are linked to centuries of discernment, to a "Catholic" sensibility, like the customs of the church.

Ecclesial institutions, even those that are not strictly of "divine right," represent a treasury of truth, wisdom, and practices that come from God. We would have to reflect long and hard, with great docility to the church's tradition, before condemning some form of ecclesial life in the name of development. Judgments made too quickly are prone to errors that a more careful consideration of the matter would show to be super-ficial. History shows that it is wise and indeed more true if we do not let ourselves too quickly give credit to a judgment that ecclesial institu-tions may be out-of-date or obsolete. Often we are happy, finally, that the church hung onto what once appeared as anachronisms, that it knew how to appreciate such things in the light of its long experience.[57]

The church's experience, shaping its consciousness and guiding its discernment, also teaches us that it would be dangerous always to call into question just anything, even things that are in themselves debatable. St. Thomas, following Aristotle here, says that since laws take a lot of their force from habit, they shouldn't be changed easily.[58] Contemporary psychologists support this conclusion from the point of view of the individual, when they observe that people become nervous or exhausted when faced with too many questions and too many options. The literary forms of scholasticism, as those of the theater in the classical period, may have been excessively rigid; but history shows us how this "rigor" worked in favor of creativity for the best minds, who thereby were not forced to exhaust themselves by inventing new structures to use.

---

[57] Thus Möhler was mistaken when he believed that religious orders were finished as well as when he rejoiced that the French Revolution had succeeded in liberating the church from this dead weight: cf. E. Vermeil, *Jean-Adam Möhler et l'école catholique de Tubingue* 1815–1840 (Paris, 1913), pp. 381f. Möhler failed to distinguish sufficiently between that part of the life of religious orders that died in the 18th century and that part of their lives that would be revived in a magnificent, purer way in the 19th century. Nonetheless, as a historian of the church, he still did justice to the religious orders, and he grasped the deep influence of monasticism on the life of the church. Cf. A. Gunthör, "Johann-Adam Möhler und das Mönchtum," *Theol. Quartalsch.* (1940), pp. 168–183. For other examples, cf. pp. 309f.

[58] *Summa Theol.* IaIIae, q. 97, art. 2, ad 1; Aristotle, *Politics* V, 14 (1269a 20).

History also shows that an attitude of permanent dissatisfaction or perpetual questioning undermines the spirit of the people. That is what happened in the fifteenth century in the face of the critique of the church: Catholic consciousness rather easily collapsed after the shockwaves of the Reformation. Monasteries, more detached from the events of the day, resisted the best. Péguy's distinction between epochs and periods of history might be applied here in a way he did not foresee. Not everything should be considered a crisis or a question. There are periods of development as well as periods of tranquility. And careful attention should always be given not to weaken anything that pertains to the very substance of the Tradition.

Above all, we should not imagine that the ancient forms of the church are out-of-date simply because they come from the past. There is a continuity in Christian development which resists automatic or mechanical substitutions or replacements for ecclesiastical forms. Newman, at the beginning of his "Essay on St. Benedict's Mission,"[59] shows that Christian teaching passed through three periods: antiquity, the Middle Ages, and modern times. In each of these, Newman said, we find a great religious order and the personality of the founder that characterizes the times. St. Benedict was gifted especially with a poetic character. St. Dominic possessed a scientific character. St. Ignatius had a practical character. These three orders somehow reproduced in themselves the successive stages that a human being goes through in human development: childhood (living by imagination, with poetic feeling), adulthood (given to logic and reasoning), and finally, with age, experience . . . We shouldn't forget, however, what Newman adds to this:

> The Catholic Church never loses what she once possessed . . . instead of passing from one phase of life to another, she carries her youth and immaturity into old age. She does not leave behind what she once possessed, but accumulates experiences and, according to the Gospel expression, she draws treasure from both the new and the old. Dominic did not make her lose Benedict; and she still possessed both of them as she became the mother of Ignatius.

It would be a great mistake to interpret my goal here as a call for change for the sake of change, and as the relativization of the church's

---

[59] Article in the *Atlantis* (Jan. 1858), French trans. in *Saints d'autrefois* (Paris, 1908); cf. pp. 223f. The text cited here is on p. 227.

life into just a series of transitory historical expressions. Development, which is a law of life, requires respect for institutional structures and for the past, for fidelity, and for rootedness and continuity. But development also respects mobility, growth, and adaptation, and this is the point of view that my theme presses us to examine most particularly.

Refusing anything new in principle is no more likely to lead to the truth than always insisting on innovation. Yet this is a natural reaction, which seems even more justified in the area of religion, where tradition has a status that can make "novelty" seem synonymous with error. What matters is to know if tradition represents only intransigence, or if it also accepts development. . . .[59bis] It would be unjust to the full meaning of tradition to see it exclusively as representing immobility and inertia. When St. Jerome made a new translation of the Bible, he was accused of disturbing the peace of the church and of weakening the foundations of the faith . . . This was to confuse the absolute and relative. The church has many human institutions. Even its core elements, which are essentially untouchable, have taken on in the course of history modes or forms of expression which are themselves contingent, historical, and subject to change. Christianity is eternal, but the forms in which it is expressed and currently embodied in Christian civilization, the actual organization of its apostolic life, the universal and local administrative structure of the church, even the celebration of worship and certain elements of the Christian philosophy of man and of society—all these in great part are linked to history and conditioned by a given stage of development.

To desire to ascribe the value and the permanence of all these things to Christianity itself would mean absolutizing what is actually relative. This is a kind of idolatry related to the mistake of relativizing what is absolute. Furthermore, this represents a serious failure in intellectual judgment and perhaps a sign of narrowness and lack of culture. At the risk of repeating myself a bit, I want to clarify the distinction and the

---

[59bis] See my *La Tradition et les traditions*, 2. Vols. (Paris, 1960 and 1963); *La Tradition et la vie de l'Eglise— Je sais, je crois* (Paris, 1963). Erasmus said that to identify novelty with heresy was the same as identifying orthodoxy with ignorance. Pius XII, in his "Discourse to the Roman Nobility" (Jan. 19, 1944), said: "Tradition is something very different from a simple attachment to a distant past. It is the complete opposite of a reaction that mistrusts healthy progress. . . . Tradition means going forward, a continuous advance that takes place with calm and vigor, following the dynamics of life" (*Relations humaines et société contemporaine*, texts collected by A. F. Utz and J.-F. Groner (Fribourg, 1956), no. 1309).

connection between what is permanently valuable and what by its nature can become obsolete.

Most people don't live Christianity at the level of principles but at the level of habits. Such habits are less personal choices than the custom of a sociological group, behaviors belonging to a cultural milieu. Practically speaking, they confuse received ideas with tradition. Imagining that they are maintaining fidelity to principle, in fact people cling to a simple translation of said principle into the language of a cultural period.

There's no better example of this than the condemnation of Galileo, where the *libellus* [statement] of condemnation is so revealing:[60] The ecclesiastical judges refused to budge concerning two or more conceptual links that the progress of science was just then in the process of opening up. A century earlier, when Erasmus had published his Greek New Testament, he was accused (among other things) of denying the resurrection because he had reestablished the exact text of 1 Cor 15:51[61] (the Reuchlin affair had just barely terminated [1520]). In all these matters church leaders thought they were defending the Tradition, and I don't want to say that there was nothing of that in these cases; but above all they were defending received ideas, habits, and expressions that were, in themselves, contingent but which they treated as if they were essential to expressing the truth. At the same time, the treatise of Lefèvre d'Etaples on the three Marys caused such a storm that the author was obliged to leave Paris, with the result that his translation of St. Paul, itself important, failed to gain the attention it deserved. How true it is that our routine understandings are more devoutly cherished than what is essential.

These examples from the distant past, about which no one would argue, suffice. Every period can provide us similar examples, and on occasion I will refer to some others. Clearly, we have often failed to distinguish between spirit and mentality, orthodoxy and conformity, tradition and received ideas. Often we have taken "the survival of the past for the permanence of the eternal. This mistakes the unchanging for the immutable."[62] To hold on to something of permanent value expressed in the forms of an outdated world is an anachronism. They say that the Sisters of the Visitation still keep their accounts in *aunes* and

[60] The original is in Italian. The text is in Latin in Mirbt, *Quellen zur Geschichte des Papsttums*, n. 515 (for references for other works). For excerpts in French, see Vacandard, *Etudes de critique et d'histoire*, 1st series (Ital. text in the appendix).

[61] Cf. A. Renaudet, *Etudes érasmiennes*, p. 46.

[62] R. Remond, in *La Vie Intellectuelle* (Feb. 1948), p. 15.

denariuses because that's how it was done at the time of their foundation (but that has to be a calumny) . . .

Here is an example from world history. Soloviev comments that Spain in the Middle Ages fulfilled its mission of providing security for Christianity by fighting the Moors. However, he remarks, instead of adapting this responsibility to new historical conditions, Spain remained fixed in its old ways, particularly by continuing to use force and constraint, and in this way it lost its ability to respond to the reality of history. The author from whom I borrow these remarks concludes for his part: "Through formal fidelity to its earlier calling, Spain became unfaithful to its deepest vocation."[63]

We have to be faithful to the deepest meaning of the principle, even if that requires letting go of the forms that it has taken at times. This allows the living principle of tradition to develop new forms of application or expression in a style that is most meaningful and effective for its own period of time. In doing this, we need to be sure that, while recognizing the evolution of structures, we always honor the principle that was previously applied in a different way. For example, I think that certain criticisms of the present form of Christian teaching forget the basic principle that has to be honored under any circumstance, namely, the church's responsibility to provide Christian education.

On the other hand, when we try to reinvigorate and adapt forms in a spirit of fidelity to principle, it often happens that by going beyond or setting aside forms that have deteriorated into mere routine, we rediscover the original actions—even materially. This is what we find in a number of actual pastoral practices and liturgical and community usages that draw from a living logic and intuition deeper than mere reaction to outdated forms.

This example is very concrete and quite harmless: in hopes of restoring to religious life practices that are adapted and truer for the present time, in some places the "spiritual conference" is given in a dialogue form, as a kind of study circle or group discussion.[64] Those who knew

---

[63] J. Gauvain, "Vladimir Soloviev et le problème russe," *Nova et Vetera* (July 1945), pp. 240–258; cf. pp. 249–250. Cf. the remark of Père de Montcheuil that has often been cited in recent years: "Those who carry on the tradition are not those obsessed with the past, but those who have deep insight" ("Vie chrétienne et action temporelle," in *Construire*, Cahier 12 [Notre Tradition Catholique, 1943], p. 109).

[64] This actual example is given by Père Victor de la Vierge, novice master for the Carmelites, in *Le Supplément de la Vie Spirituelle* (May 1948), p. 40.

the "classical" spiritual conferences based on the Sulpician tradition may find the new style somewhat surprising. But, in fact, this innovation corresponds exactly to what St. Francis de Sales did at the convent of the Visitation and what St. Vincent de Paul did with candidates for holy orders . . .[65] The idea of the seminary conceived by the Mission de France might appear new or even rash, but it has hardly done much more than apply rather literally the priestly formation program of M. Bourdoise and St. Vincent De Paul, or indeed St. John Eudes and M. Olier . . .[66]

This leads us to distinguish between two planes or levels of fidelity. This observation is of key importance for the present subject as well as for some others—in particular, for ecumenism, which will rise or fall with this distinction. Our fidelity can be identified with two aspects or conceptions because truth entails two levels, and, even more, reality does as well. Fidelity exists fundamentally in its principle, which gives it its deepest truth, and it exists also in a certain state or form or formula that it takes on historically. The two aspects are of course meant to coincide, but they only coincide ultimately, when the realization of the principle arrives at its absolute perfection. To the degree that we are not there yet, what we perceive is a truth still searching for its expression, to use the phrase of St. Isidore that St. Thomas applies to dogmatic expressions.[67] Everything in the church is "militant," on the way toward its realization of a principle that was established by God.

Apply this to the question of fidelity. One kind of fidelity exists only at the level of articulated forms and formulas. But there is also a fidelity that includes the possibility of surpassing these forms (without mistaking one for the other), through a deeper penetration into the principle or through a more intense movement toward fulfillment. The choice: fidelity to the letter or fidelity which includes development. (See appendix 2 about these two levels of fidelity.)

It is even possible to oppose legitimate development for the sake of "fidelity." We have just seen some examples. Père Régamey[68] quotes the

---

[65] Cf. J. Calvet, *La littérature religieuse de saint François de Sales à Fénelon*, p. 33.

[66] Cf. J. Delarue, *L'idéal missionnaire du prêtre d'après saint Vincent de Paul* (Paris, 1947), pp. 302–308. The author makes this connection deliberately on p. 307, note.

[67] "*Perceptio divinae veritatis tendens in ipsam*—a glimpse of divine truth moving us toward that Truth" (*Summa Theol.* IIaIIae, q. 1, art. 6, sed contra). St. Albert and St. Bonaventure also invoke Isidore, but this text has not been found in his works. Cf. J.-M. Parent, "La notion de dogme au XIIIe siècle," in *Etudes d'Histoire littéraire et doctrinal du XIIIe siècle*, vol. I (Paris and Ottawa, 1932), p. 149.

[68] *L'Art sacré*, 10 (1947), p. 262.

resolute opposition of Ingres: "We have to resist the barbarians," by which he meant Géricault and Delacroix—painters who were knocking on the door of the future. I wonder if sometimes in the history of the church people who believed they were defending tradition, but who were in fact defending custom, didn't take advantage of the prestige and power they had to create roadblocks for authentic appeals for renewal. In the Constitution *Sollicita ac Provida* about the Index, Pope Benedict XIV makes his own the warning of the *Opus imperfectum in Matthaeum*, addressed to those who want to hold on to what was previously said and oppose anything new: their attitude leads us to think they would have responded the same way to the ancient authors, whom they profess to venerate, as they respond to their contemporaries.[69] Why are genuinely good Catholics so often accused of "novelty" and forced to wait for justice from the Father who sees in secret or from the passage of time to finally prove them right?[70] Why have so many people been accused who were correct, but who upset received ideas; why have they not been recognized before their deaths, if not for their heartfelt loyalty, at least for the rectitude of their judgment?[71]

---

[69] *Constitutio "Sollicita ac Provida"* (July 1753), n. 28, in *Bullarium Benedicti XIV*, vol. IV (Venice, 1778), p. 53. The text is taken from the *Opus imperfectum in Matthaeum*—not from hom. 42, as it says, but rather from hom. 45 (PG 56:887).

[70] Cf. St. Augustine, *De vera religione*, ch. 6, n. 11 (PL 34:128): "Often . . . divine providence permits even good men to be driven from the Christian congregation by the turbulent seditions of carnal men. When for the sake of the peace of the church they patiently endure that insult or injury, and attempt no novelties in the way of heresy or schism, they will teach men how God is to be served with a true disposition and with great and sincere charity. The intention of such men is to return when the tumult has subsided. But if that is not permitted because the storm continues or because a fiercer one might be stirred up by their return, they hold fast to their purpose to look to the good even of those responsible for the tumults and commotions that drove them out. They form no separate conventicles of their own, but defend to the death and assist by their testimony the faith which they know is preached in the Catholic Church. These the Father who sees in secret crowns secretly. It appears that this is a rare kind of Christian, but examples are not lacking. Indeed there are more than can be believed" (Eng. tr., *St. Augustine: Of True Religion*, trans. by J. H. S. Burleigh [Chicago: Regnery, 1959], pp. 12–13).

[71] Sometimes this recognition is notable even during the life of those who have known suspicion: such was the case of Cardinal Dechamps, whose ideas had first been taken badly (Mourret, *Concile du Vatican*, pp. 97–98), or the case of Cardinal Mercier, who underwent a veritable disgrace at Louvain (cf. A. Vermeersch, "A la pieuse mémoire du cardinal Mercier: Notes et souvenirs," *Nouvelle Revue Théologique*

But truth always comes into the open in the end; the sap makes the bark expand—there are breakthroughs. There comes a time when "received ideas" can no longer block new ideas because they are no longer "received." In 1660, a certain Père Fabri could still claim in the name of the condemnation of Galileo that to be Catholic, one had to be anti-Copernican. However, many ecclesiastics upheld the system of Copernicus,[72] and finally Galileo's condemnation was revoked . . .

I said above that the church cannot admit a situation of being called into question all the time. But at least, at certain epochal moments of great transition, the church ought to be able to accept in some way a kind of revision of its "received ideas," a critique of the previous period and, at least, of certain historical forms derived from it. For with respect to development—with respect to that which doesn't yet exist but aspires to become real—these established forms can act as a brake or a bottleneck for the needs of a new (sometimes tragic) apostolic situation. You can't put new wine into old wineskins; let the dead bury the dead.

This is the real significance of the church's present crisis as well as of the self-criticism that it experienced between 1945 and 1950. We have already seen that this crisis and this self-criticism have nothing to do with the Modernism of the early twentieth century. They arise not out of ideas about the dogmatic, sacramental, and hierarchical structure of the church but out of a consideration of facts concerning the apostolate. They began, as I showed, in the awakening of apostolic concern prompted by the method of inquiry [observe, judge, and act]—so much so that probably people's attitudes could be classified according to one or other type of *fidelity* just examined and linked at first glance to whether they have really analyzed the present circumstances or not. The *former* have critiqued some of the forms or structures that present-day Christianity has received from history; the *latter* have not. This is what is at issue.

It's not about dogma. At least, church dogma was not called into question by the reform spirit before Vatican II. If dogma is in question

---

[Apr. 1926], p. 244; Msgr. Laveille, *Le cardinal Mercier* [Paris, 1926], p. 85). Sometimes death puts an end to unmerited suspicion. Sometimes there is a partial justice done: this is the case of Cardinal Newman, to whom the Roman purple gave a striking justification for accusations that had really handicapped him; yet, on a point as important as Catholics going to the great universities, people only rallied to his position long after his death . . . Cf. A. Adam, *Spannungen und Harmonie* (1940), 2nd ed., p. 64, from which I took the text of St. Augustine cited just above.

[72] For this significant episode, cf. H. Busson, *La religion des classiques* (Paris, 1948), pp. 102f.

today in some writing or another (or if people think that it is), that is because things have changed. However, this book was written between 1946 and 1950 in a situation in which dogmatic issues were not being called into question any more than in any other of the great moments of the church. The real objective, rather, has been to grasp church dogmas according to the deepest meaning of the tradition.

What really mattered was how to do catechesis, how to preach. The question was whether in some areas there is not some way (some obligation) to go beyond the way we habitually presented Catholicism, but that did not do justice to the fullness of its doctrinal traditions.

For instance, in the light of a renewed understanding of the divine "economy" and of eschatology, can't we say more concerning the "last things" than what we find in most familiar treatments? If so, then naturally some improvements appear desirable in clergy education and in seminary book lists. We can find no example of an ecclesial reform that was serious that did not require a new perspective, a renewed impulse, and a return to the deepest wells of tradition—as well as a revision of clergy education.[73]

The sacraments are not being called into question. Doubtless, the liturgical movement, which had Dom Guéranger as one of the founders and St. Pius X as one of its most important figures, has played a key role in the present wave of reform. The challenge is to bring the baptized neo-pagans of our world into the living reality of liturgical prayer, and perhaps also to rediscover more accessible forms of worship in and through the tradition. (I am convinced of this.) In any case, the goal of the reform is to produce something that is less like formalism, less

---

[73] Some examples: the Carolingian reform (cf. F. L. Ganshof, "La revision de la Bible par Alcuin," in *Bibliothèque d'Humanisme et Renaissance: Travaux et Doc.*, IX [1947], pp. 7–20); Innocent III, the Lateran Council and the Dominican project (cf. A. Luchaire, *Innocent III, le Concile de Latran et la réforme de l'Eglise*, p. 20; P. Mandonnet, *Saint Dominique*); the humanist reform movements (A. Renaudet, *Préréforme et Humanisme*, p. 342 [Standonck]), (Lefèvre d'Etaples, pp. 505, 514), (Erasmus pp. 431f.), etc.; the Spanish Catholic reformers of the 16th century who are so interesting (John of Avila: cf. the article of A. Duval in *La Vie Spirituelle: Supplément*, Aug. 1948; Luis de Leon: cf. A. Guy, *La pensée de Louis de Léon: Contribution à l'étude de la Philosophie espagnole au XIVe siècle* [Paris, 1943]); the Council of Trent and the French renewal of the 16th and 17th centuries; the projects and proposals of Drey, Hirscher, Möhler in the 19th century (cf. Ed. Vermeil, op. cit.) or even of Lamennais (cf. P. Broutin, "Un aspect de l'oeuvre menaisienne," *Nouv. Rev. théol.* 64 [1937], pp. 969–985, 1091–1102, etc.); cf. below, n. 79, and pp. 243f.

esoteric, less done for show and something more *done for* and *done with* us—something that is genuine community prayer.

In the reform spirit of 1945–1950 hierarchical authority was not being questioned. People recognized that *everything* falls under its competence. But they were looking (and are still looking) for pastoral structures that respond better to a condition that is no longer that of Christendom (in France at least). Our world is no longer a world accustomed to respecting the church, but rather a world that is largely pagan, selfish, and fundamentally secular.

People are looking for more communitarian and mission-oriented forms of church, for a better adaptation of our parishes, schools, and Christian works, and eventually for a better organization of ministry. In addition, they want to introduce more genuine rapport between the grassroots and the leadership, along with a clearer understanding of the role of the laity in the ecclesial system.

Finally, Christianity is not being called into question. In a sense, the whole point of the reform effort is to focus upon Christianity. What is being questioned are certain features of the historical profile that the church received from another world, different from the one we live in. Possibly many of our contemporaries reject Christianity itself, that is, God and Jesus Christ. But surely what they reject has often appeared to them to be wrapped up in sociological forms they find unacceptable. Precisely because people do believe in Christianity and are not calling it into question, this makes me wonder whether the crisis is not really that of a particular "Christian civilization,"[74] a certain "Christian world," a certain Christian "mentality"—ultimately a crisis of sociological structures that represent, not Christian reality, but rather a certain *concrete expression of the way things are done.*

We are thus positioned better to define the scope of potential reform in the church, the precise nature of which has not always been well understood. We habitually think of two distinct types of reform for which there are many examples in history: a simple reform of abuses, on the one hand, and a doctrinal revolution in the style of Protestantism, on the other hand.

[74] Cahier 5 of *Jeunesse de l'Eglise*, which was much discussed at its publication, was entitled "La crise de la civilization chrétienne."

However, there is another platform on which reform can take place, and the preceding pages allow us to imagine what it is. It is deeper than questions about abuses but does not involve criticizing the dogmatic, sacramental, and hierarchical structures of the church. This is the platform of the *state of affairs*, the historical form that the church as a community of the faithful expresses in its inherited practices. I'm speaking about *ecclesial structures*—a word that may be debatable but which is understood (cf. introduction, n. 50).

Take the historical example of what happened in the sixteenth century. Luther's critique turned into an attack on the essential structure of the church. That is something that can be explained by history. In ecclesiology and theology, however, it can only be condemned. However, the most recent Catholic historian of the Lutheran Reformation, Prof. J. Lortz, looked at the condition of the church at the beginning of the sixteenth century, and after having analyzed and given examples of different types of abuse universally acknowledged, and then having shown how (despite everything) faith and religious practice remained vigorous, he suggested the following clarification.[75]

You can point to many abuses, but with equal veracity you can point to the prosperity, indeed, the vitality of Catholicism around the year 1500. What was wrong was a *state of affairs*: not the life of religion in itself but the idea that many people had of it as well as dubious behaviors that were tolerated rather habitually. The problem was not hierarchical power as such but the sense of pastoral deficiencies that were due to widespread practices, ingrained without being disavowed, right up to the highest levels of the hierarchy. The problem was not the sacraments or the doctrine of grace as found in theological writings and the liturgy but instead a generalized state of *practices*, coupled with a theology of grace that arose from Nominalism and a widespread preaching of dubious practices [e.g., indulgences]. In a sense, this was more than a question of abuses; it was a *state of affairs*, a repertory of received ideas that called for an overall reform of considerable depth in the name of a return to the sources of Catholic doctrine.

This distinction between "abuses" and a "state of affairs" is plain enough, in the light of the *means* of reform that correspond to each one. To reform abuses, it is sufficient to recall and apply the rules, that is, in

---

[75] *Die Reformation in Deutschland*, vol. 2 (Freiburg im Breisgau, 1940); *Die Reformation: Thesen als Handreichung bei ökumenischen Gesprächen* (Meitingen, 1940); *Die Reformation als religiöses Anleigen heute* (Trier, 1948), pp. 96–99.

ecclesiastical language, the canons with their prescriptions and sanctions. At most, it may be necessary to formulate new canons, but of the same kind. In fact, this is what happened (often) in the course of the fourteenth and fifteenth centuries; in the first years of the sixteenth century this same approach was taken by zealous reformers of abuses (a history that has been sketched by A. Renaudet).[76] In fact, several of these reformers were led to new ideas—not about doctrine but about pastoral practice. There should have existed already a noteworthy foundation for useful pastoral thinking, if only church leadership had seized the opportunities for reform. On the whole, however, what happened was a reform of observance, a return to the strict practice of sacred laws. So there was a reaffirmation of the disciplinary system without, however, a real return to sources.

In truth, the need for reform required more than that. There was a need to deal with widely accepted theological doctrines tainted with Nominalism, dubious devotional practices, the role of the mendicant orders in the church, the exercise of papal power, the system of government practiced by the Roman Curia,[77] and the way a great number of bishops conceived of and lived out their episcopal role . . . In summary, the problem was not a matter of particular abuses but rather of a taken-for-granted and entrenched *state of affairs*. What was needed was not simply to reestablish good order or to reconstruct a happy past but to look deeply into the sources of the church for the truth of things and to renew the church's spirit at its roots.

In this respect Erasmus was right. He said (Luther said the same thing, but he would draw completely different conclusions) that reforms in the monasteries will not do anything as long as they deal merely with questions such as the religious habit or ceremonies. What was needed was to renew the very idea of the Christian life,[78] a reform of the way we think and conceptualize—reform that Erasmus argued, quite correctly, had to begin with teaching.[79] Basically, he recommended an "evangelical" reform, that is, something other than a mere restoration and return to canonical prescriptions. This requires, as Jesus himself had done, a return to the genuine meaning of what we consider our *origin* and our *end*.

---

[76] Cf., for example, *Préréforme et Humanisme à Paris* (Paris, 1916), pp. 160f.

[77] These two last points had been analyzed with great precision in the memorandum addressed to Paul III by the Commission of Cardinals and Bishops in 1537.

[78] Renaudet, op. cit., pp. 608–609.

[79] Ibid., pp. 431f.; above all, p. 435. Cf. n. 73 above.

This type of reform requires not only recourse to stricter rules than those needed to correct abuses but also the discovery of fresh energies. It is not easy to breathe a new spirit into old institutions. The weight of old habits is too heavy. In the fifteenth century religious reform came off better in the new orders than in the old ones, for example, in the Brothers of the Common Life or the Canons of Windesheim or the Minims of St. Francis of Paola. When what is needed is a new spirit, the renewal of a whole system, and not just the correction of abuses, it is often necessary to call upon new leaders. Those who have grown up inside a system are often prisoners of the system. They have neither the desire nor the ideas required to call the status quo into question. I will come back to this idea in the second part of the book. Further, we will see how such reforms require different types of "prophets" . . .

Let me terminate this section (as I did the preceding) by noting that when prophets are lacking or are not listened to, God sometimes sends us events to reshape our understanding. Such events are sometimes harsh teachers.

Sometimes a church that is too entrenched in its "received ideas," in its "Christian world," has to be led back to its principle—the one thing necessary, a return to its beginnings—by the hardship of poverty. Recently in France, a lot of people have read Graham Greene's *The Power and the Glory*. Here is a novel which ends up showing us an apostolic *ressourcement* in the stripping away of the protagonist's dignity. We get a glimpse of what an established church can become: full of authority and self-assurance, rich for that very reason, but scarcely apostolic and mediocre in evangelization. In the novel, a priest coming from that "Christian world" that was stripped away by the Mexican Revolution, who was pursued by the police, who lost everything including his reputation (even in his own eyes), rediscovers his ministry in poverty in the name of the Lord in all simplicity.

This is not only a novel; it is truth as only great poetry can tell it. Its lesson is important not only on the level of the spiritual life but on the level of religious sociology as well. It suggests that there is a deep relation between evangelical thinking and behavior, on the one hand, and evangelism in structures and conditions and style of life, on the other. There are "things that we will only understand when we have been completely crushed"[80] not only in our moral life, or in our spiritual relations

---

[80] Père Couturier reports this profound remark of a Spanish woman in *L'Art Sacré* (Jan.–Feb. 1950), p. 29.

with God and with our neighbor, but also in our apostolic work and in relation to society and history. We cannot be completely evangelical in our thinking if we are not living in conditions or in a lifestyle that is evangelical. But there still can be an exceptional success on the part of an individual who is not characteristic of the social group. The most sincere and generous desire to imitate the "primitive church" will end up frustrated as long as we continue to live in the structures and patterns of the Constantinian church. Only from the perspective of religious poverty, as I have shown, is it possible to understand Christ's spiritual kingship revealed to the church and how it implies no temporal domination.[80a] This problem of sociological structures for ecclesial life is really a very deep problem, and the problem of reform corresponds to it exactly, because it is linked to the demands of the Gospel itself.

The question of sociological structures is also formally and deeply linked to the general perspective that I have considered necessary for situating the whole question of "reforms" in the church. History shows us that the church has only been able to develop in all the necessary ways when certain structures have been left behind. Take, for example, the Gospel's ideal of justice and fraternity.

Should we not be scandalized that it took long centuries to eliminate slavery, and then serfdom, and that the church has not yet succeeded after two thousand years to eliminate the proletariat and war? Or might we say that the principle of justice and fraternity, found at the heart of Christianity, could be understood only when structures of slavery and serfdom had been abolished? The principle of justice and fraternity will not be fully understood until the social structures that make the condition of the proletariat and conditions for war seem inevitable have disappeared. Basically, in all these cases (and others) there is a principle that is sometimes actualized in ecclesial structures and sometimes constricted or bound up (like Lazarus in the tomb).

We have to leave behind the false idea of some kind of "pure" spiritual life that *realizes itself* independently of all concrete influences. Concrete influences have a role to play not only in the implementation of the idea but also in our understanding of its implications. The Gospel's teaching about God as the Father of all humanity (and the implication of the fraternity of all persons) was the reason for overthrowing slavery; and it will be that teaching which one day will abolish the proletariat and war. Nonetheless, to understand the full meaning of the Gospel and

---

[80a] See J. Leclercq, *Jean de Paris et l'ecclésiologie du XIIIe siècle* (Paris, 1943), pp. 98f.

how to bring it to life, certain structures have to pass away so that the fundamental principle can be realized in experience.

These remarks lead us to an important clarification. Several Catholic authors at the time of Modernism or of the protests that prepared for it undertook to defend the church's tradition by insisting particularly on the moral, interior, and personal aspects of the spirit of reform.[81] Faced with an impulse that wanted to change Catholicism from the outside and which also called the actual structure of the church into question, it was normal to react. Faced with a type of reform that was revolutionary, beginning from outside in order to substitute new doctrines, it was understandable that the primacy of reform from within, calling nothing within Catholicism itself into question, should be affirmed. In place of a "commissioner," they proposed a *yogi.*

Perhaps this represents something of that spirit, widely found among Catholics, that sees almost nothing but the moral aspect of problems and believes that everything will be okay if our intentions are right and pure. However, I see more and more clearly that the *yogi* is not the answer to the Christian reform movement. Intentions matter, but so does effectiveness. There is history, but there are also the ways that history comes into being . . .

Père Chenu, by looking at some of the great reform movements (in a study already referred to in the introduction, n. 45), shows how the full expression of an evangelical reform only succeeds by basically calling into question certain social structures, or the way the church is involved in the structures of society. By putting forward the reform movement of

---

[81] Cf., for example, A. M. Weiss, O.P., *Reformbestrebungen* (a text from 1905 that became ch. 6 of *Lebens-und Gewissensfragen der Gegenwart*, vol. 2 [Freiburg im Breisgau, 1911], p. 1–145), especially pp. 57–64, 65f., 85–100, 118f., 134–145. Cf. *Vraie et fausse réforme: Discours de Msgr. Keppler . . . 1er décembre 1902*, a text taken from the third edition by Abbé Bègue (Fribourg en Suisse, 1903): Msgr. K. shows that true reform in the church is not a reform of doctrines but of the human side of the church, of Catholic life, of the formation of the character of Catholics. True reform is interior and spiritual, and it goes from the interior to the exterior: it touches people intimately so as to perfect them. In this sense the church will always need to be reformed. Msgr. K. makes note of and critiques the cerebral and intellectual character of the modern reform spirit which became the early warning sign of Modernism. However, he admits that "doubtless there are many questions concerning details of ecclesiastical discipline and Catholic life—secondary points—where there is room for reform, where it is even necessary—for example in the areas of science, education, ecclesiastical administration, lay movements, the press, etc." (p. 31). Cf. below, part 2, nn. 35 and 42.

the mendicants at the beginning of the thirteenth century as the example of his own thesis (if that movement really does represent an exceptional harmony of a spiritual movement with the emerging human cultural and social dimensions of the world), Chenu explains the full meaning of the Gregorian Reform. In the first volume of his *Réforme grégorienne*[82] Fliche has clearly shown how two platforms of reform were involved: what he calls the "Italian" plan (Atto of Vercelli, Peter Damian) that sponsored a purely moral reform of preaching and good example, and what he calls the "Lorraine" plan (Wason of Liège, Rather of Verona, Cardinal Humbert)—who, in addition to moral change, recommended action with respect to institutions and structures, hoping to destroy simony and Nicolaism by attacking them at their roots in lay investiture. St. Leo IX, someone from Lorraine in fact, did not follow these recommendations. And in his second volume Fliche shows how Hildebrand first preferred the "Italian" program and then went over to the "Lorraine" program, which he supported through a theological program of papal prerogatives, the *Dictatus papae*.

Something similar had already been done in an earlier reform that was originally purely monastic but radical in spirit. It had an almost universal influence because of its effectiveness. This was St. Benedict of Aniane's reform at the time of Charlemagne and Louis the Pious. A recent historian of the saint and his work[83] has shown how Benedict must have

---

[82] A. Fliche, *La Réforme grégorienne*, vol. 1: *La formation des idées grégoriennes*, vol. 2: *Gregoire VII* (Louvain, 1924 and 1925); see also D. B. Zema, "Reform Legislation in the 11th Century and Its Economic Impact," *Catholic Historical Review* 27 (1941), pp. 1f.; and Zema, "Economic Reorganization of the Holy See During the Gregorian Reform," *Studi Gregoriani* (Rome, 1947), vol. 1, pp. 137–168 (showing how the misfortunes of the church were related to the economic state of affairs, the system of ecclesiastical properties, and how Gregory VII addressed the causes of the problem). See also G. Schreiber, *Gemienschaften des Mittelalters* (Munster, 1948), pp. 306, 370–372. Schreiber explains how the canon "*ut omnis christianus procuret ad missarum solemnia aliquid Deo offerre*" is linked to Gregory's action in favor of the independence of the churches from the system of *Eigenkirchen*: the priest would live from the gifts offered by the faithful. There is here an element of returning to earlier Christian practices (pp. 309, 318); and an aspect of a liturgical reform spirit (pp. 318, 321, 331, 333, 336, 368). A comprehensive study is needed of the idea of returning to the ideals of the early church in the Gregorian Reform and in the canonical reforms that follow. See, e.g., Ch. Dereine, "Vie commune: Règle de saint Augustin et chanoines réguliers du XIe siècle," *Rev. Hist. eccles.* 41 (1946), pp. 365–406, e.g., p. 389, St. Peter Damian; cf. his *Epist. I*, 1 from the year 1045 (PL 144:205c); and in the 12th century, Gerhoh de Reichersberg, *De Aedificio Dei*, ch. 30 (PL 194:1271f.).

[83] J. Naberhaus, *Benedikt von Aniane: Werk und Persönlichkeit* (Munster, 1930).

been led logically to attack the Germanic institution of private churches (*Eigenkirchen*) that were the source of so much abuse. Like Gregory VII, he was also attacking the political and economic implications [of lay investiture], symptoms of a *state of affairs* that was causing serious harm to the church. Let us hold onto these three conclusions, which can serve as a hermeneutical norm:

1. A purely moral reform is insufficient because it does not affect the structural causes that underlie the problem and so fails to put into effect dynamic means that will change history (Gregory VII).

2. There can be no realization of an evangelical spirit in the religious context without an evangelical spirit that also affects the conditions (even external and economic) of the way people live.[84]

3. There will be no full adaptation or renewal unless the church, sustained by the impulse of the Gospel as its source, generously agrees to attune itself to the structures of the emerging world and of a renewed society—which it also needs to baptize . . . (cf. Chenu on the example of the mendicants).[85]

[84] It is noteworthy that the "Lorraine" reform impulse, which Gregory VII took up and extended, is linked to the first expression of the idea of the *vita apostolica*, an idea which will spread very widely and sometimes in a disordered fashion after the Gregorian Reform, and which will culminate in the mendicant movement at the beginning of the 13th century. For this connection, see Spätling, *De Apostolicis*, p. 43.

[85] Facing a situation which still causes us great concern, Péguy contributed this prophetic perspective: "The church will not reopen its workshop, and it will not reopen to the people, unless like everyone else it pays a lot to bring about a revolution in the economy, a social revolution, an industrial revolution—in other words, a temporal revolution for the sake of eternal salvation. Such is eternally and temporally the mysterious subjection of the eternal to the temporal. You have to pay the economic, the social and the industrial, that is, the temporal dues. Nobody or nothing is exempted, not even the eternal, not even the spiritual, not even the interior life" (*Notre Jeunesse* [*Oeuvres compl.*, vol. 4, ed. N.R.F.], pp. 171–172).

Chapter 3

Prophets and Reformers

So that the sap of Christianity can still thrust its shoots through the crust of history, the Holy Spirit, watching over the church, raises up servants whose fidelity goes beyond conformity to the status quo. "Twice-born" persons are needed for this.

Of course, all members of the church have been born "of water and the Spirit" in Jesus Christ. Their whole life in the church is a sort of ratification and exercise of the baptism through which they were inserted among the people of God. From the point of view of their personal salvation, they find themselves in the Ark of Grace—and that is enough. They can be sanctified; they can love and serve God and their fellow human beings without ever questioning the "state of affairs" in the church. Further, we might say that if they are genuinely religious and personally united with God, then they resolve the issue of formalism or Pharisaism by the way they live.

However, this sort of deep personal investment can still exist in the midst of a "state of affairs" in which formalism plays a big role and in which ecclesial structures are poorly adapted to the needs of the world, to their effectiveness, and to the impulses of the Holy Spirit. Naturally, reforms would best be carried out by persons chosen by Providence who are also saints. But history shows that being a saint isn't enough to change the "state of affairs" and that sanctity has sometimes flourished in an environment or a collective state of affairs in need of reform. The ecclesial institution itself is holy and penetrated by the means of sanctification, so much so that whenever people submit to the church, the church produces in them abundant fruits of the Spirit. That can be seen in the countries and the epochs of Christendom. But there are still other situations in the church, other needs—those which this chapter is going to explore. In addition to the new birth of baptism that opens the door to salvation, people need another "second birth."

This expression is not understood here in the dogmatic sense of Jesus in his meeting with Nicodemus but more in a psychological or moral sense. Here it refers to the idea of the distinction between two types of persons, the *once-born* and the *twice-born*.[1] Some people have experienced a kind of revelation, a new birth; they have discovered a new personal set of values and a kind of change has come over their lives. They live their lives no longer in conformity to the received ideas of their social milieu but according to their own personal convictions. This is something like what Kierkegaard called *hin Enkelte*, meaning the "individual" or the "person," by contrast with the "general group of people."

There are, of course, those who simply live according to the expectations and habits of their social group. They maintain the established ways of their milieu. They exist less in themselves than in a tradition. Their number makes up a great crowd of nice people. However, ultimately, by way of a certain negative transformation of faith into custom, there are (if I may use the expression of a nonbeliever) "all the lazy believers in the churches—clerics and laity alike—who don't believe anything by themselves, but remain sprawled out in the barn where they have been cooped up in front of a manger full of convenient beliefs that they only have to take and chew on" (Romain Rolland).

Clearly, if beyond personally using the means of grace in a saintly way, people are to do something about the "state of affairs," they need to be born into some kind of new perspective and to become familiar with the principle of life itself, going deeper than habits and customs. Everything already said about the creative power of values upon a "spirit" that is not completely crushed, carried away, or exhausted by the "mentality" of the times—everything we said about *ressourcement*,

---

[1] W. James (*L'expérience religieuse* [Eng., *The Varieties of Religious Experience*], Fr. trans., 2nd ed. [Paris, 1908], p. 69), where James refers to Francis W. Newman, *The Soul: Its Sorrows and Its Aspirations*, 3rd ed. (1852), pp. 89f. James is only interested in this distinction between the *once-born* and the *twice-born* from his point of view of describing the difference between optimists and pessimists; so his ideas don't help here in the present context. By contrast, B. H. Thompson does apply James in a useful way in his "The Causes of Disruption: The Roots of the 16th Century Reformation—Ecclesiastical and Doctrinal," in *Union of Christendom*, ed. K. Mackenzie (London, 1938), pp. 149–150.

about the "second sense of fidelity"—all that already made clear the need for twice-born persons and described their characteristics.

At the end of his analytical study of documents about the clergy in the diocese of Constance at the end of the Middle Ages,[2] M. A. Braun wondered why so many attempts at reform scattered across the fourteenth and fifteenth centuries had been so ineffective. He gave a number of reasons (already familiar),[3] and then he pointed out that there was a deficit of persons who were intensely invested in a desire for reform, who would give themselves body and soul to make reform their life's work. It wasn't enough to produce all kinds of spiteful remarks or satire about the state of the church and of the clergy. The question was more serious. To do justice to Luther (along with those who eulogize him[4]), Luther took the reform of the church with the utmost seriousness to the point that it became his life's work.

M. A. Braun, in drawing his conclusion (p. 189), uses this phrase which is still significant: "In the responsibilities by which they earned their living, the reformers (of the 15th and 16th centuries) were almost all bound to the structures of the [ecclesiastical] system." Looking at the decrees of the councils of reforming bishops, you can see that generally the issues were points of order and disciplinary details: priests having concubines or playing cards, cathedral canons not participating in liturgical offices, failure to pay taxes to the bishop, and the like. These reformers remained within the categories of the system in which they had been born and had grown up, without really contributing to a renewal of point of view or to a new perspective, without renewing structures by going back to the beginning. The best minds knew this. Gerson said it to the pope in 1404.[5]

As time went on it became clear that no serious reform would come from persons who failed to call into question some elements of the system in which they had grown up (and which held them captive), no matter how well intentioned they might be. These claims are supported by the conclusions that H. Jedin draws in a study of the ideals for bishops in

---

[2] A. Braun, *Der Klerus des Bistums Konstanz im Ausgang des Mittelalters: Vorreformationsgeschichtliches Forschung*, 14 (Munster, 1938).

[3] Here are some examples: chapters [of canons] who paralyzed bishops' initiatives, the uncooperative spirit of the lower clergy disaffected by heavy episcopal taxation, the mixing together of the temporal and the spiritual, the right of patronage, and the nomination to ecclesiastical posts by secular lords.

[4] H. Preuss, *Martin Luther: Der Prophet* (Gütersloh, 1933), p. 173.

[5] Cf. J. Haller, *Papsttum und Kirchenreform*, pp. 12–14; see also texts by Pierre d'Ailly, Gerson, and Dietrich of Munster.

the sixteenth century based on abundant evidence.[5a] Neither re-insisting upon the canons nor the promulgation of new rules, neither programs nor spiritual tracts have ever been enough to unleash a reform. Something other than such "measures" is needed, namely, the commitment of the lives of those who, by giving their very selves and sacrificing themselves, create a new situation.

Erasmus doubted that a council could do much, so long as the personnel already in place had the leading role.[6] He doubted the effectiveness of the reform even of Pope Hadrian VI, his Dutch compatriot, because despite his exalted personal desires and the integrity of his life, this pope seemed to be immersed *in the Roman system,* bound to the very things that Erasmus knew had to be questioned.[7] Such convictions were widespread, so much so that Vivès, after the events of 1527, could write that the captivity of Pope Clement VII might help to bring about a Christian reform. . . .[8] This conviction was deeply felt: on the one hand, a reform of the whole complex was needed, touching the "state of affairs" as well as the system that sustained it; on the other hand, in order to make that happen, new personalities were needed whose minds and characters were not held captive by the system but who were ready for a "second birth."[9]

Prophets: Their Role and Their Character[9a]

In an exceptional way the prophets were men seized one day and transported above themselves, carried out of themselves for the sake of a transcendent mission. This is how someone is born *from above* and a

---

[5a] See H. Jedin: *Das Bischofsideal der katholische Reformation;* documentation amplified by P. Broutin, *L'évêque dans la tradition pastorale du XVIe siècle* (Paris, 1953).

[6] Cf. A. Renaudet, *Etudes érasmiennes,* pp. 283–284.

[7] Ibid., p. 204. (Cf. pp. 285f. below.)

[8] Renaudet, op. cit., p. 284. At the beginning of the 16th century, given the state of affairs in the church, there was no other recourse to be found (cf. ibid., pp. 167–168).

[9] H. Jedin gives the example of Cardinal Bartolomeo Guidiccioni at the time of the reform of the Council of Trent, a man with a sincere intention for reform but who wanted to stay within the structures of a system that seemed to him to be sacrosanct and all-sufficient. Sadly, this reform effort proved to be insufficiently efficacious. Cf. "Concilio e Riforma nel pensiero del Cardinale Bartolomeo Guidiccioni," in *Riv. di Storia della Chiesa in Italia,* 2 (1948), pp. 33–60; cf. pp. 54–60.

[9a] Let me cite some publications on this topic of the prophetic function in the wider sense that have appeared since the first edition of this book: R. Grosche, *Das prophetische*

second time, according to the meaning of the Greek word *anôthen* in John 3:3, 7. How? It comes through the Word of God, from whom people are born a second time, not by blood, not of the flesh, nor of the will of man, but of God (John 1:13; Luke 8:11; 1 Pet 1:23). This explains the formula used so often in the Bible that indicates the birth or the call of a prophet: "The word of God was addressed to . . ."[10]

To be God's prophets in the Judeo-Christian sense does not necessarily mean to reveal the future. Often the prophets speak after the fact or at the same time as some event, and yet they still speak prophetically. That is because they speak for another, that is, in the name of God. To say what? Essentially they are charged to speak God's judgment upon things, to judge things as to their rightness, to put them in perspective according to God's absolute truth.

This means to show how things fit into God's plan for the world— God's design or purpose. The prophets read the "signs of the times," clarifying the meaning of events with respect to their relation to an eschatological fulfillment. The prophets are the salt of the earth, particularly by preventing temporal affairs from becoming useless in relation to the eternal, by forestalling relative things from becoming meaningless in relation to the absolute. "Religious prophets are those who are detached, and thus able to bear witness to the totality of truth over against partial truths, to integral truth over against accommodations."[11] Basically, their function corresponds to the situation of God's people existing in a kind of "in-between" time: they are on the way to the achievement of their vocation by realizing their true interior relation with God. So their function also corresponds to the people's need to be admonished about the twofold temptation to become "Pharisees" or to cut themselves off as a "Synagogue." The prophets are also among the first to be reformers.

The prophet is opposed to the *means* becoming the *end*, opposed to the external form being sought and exalted for itself. Incessantly prophets remind us that external forms take their meaning from a source way beyond themselves. They work toward interpreting the "spirit" that lies beyond every "letter." In doing so, prophets confront the status quo, the

---

Element in der Kirche (1956), reprinted in *Et intra et extra—Theologische Aufsätze* (Dusseldorf, 1958); K. Rahner, *Eléments dynamiques dans l'Eglise* (Paris, 1967); P. Duployé, *La religion de Péguy* (Paris, 1965), pp. 427f.; A. Ulryn, *Actualité de la function prophétique* (Paris: DDB, 1966); *Concilium* (Sept. 1968).

[10] Above all, this is the case with Jeremiah, Ezekiel, Haggai, and Zechariah. Also, cf. Luke 3:2.

[11] E. Mounier, *Esprit* (May 1946), p. 720.

taken-for-granted frame of reference. Quite definitely, no prophet can be welcome in his own country and recognized among his own. Despite all the ways God's transcendence is betrayed, prophets insist upon God's transcendence and upon what pertains to God. They are opposed to any usage or admixture of Christianity with elements that threaten its transcendence, such as politics or idolatry. Experience shows how close these come to polluting Christian life.

Prophets are likewise those who can give the passage of time its true relationship to God. They are ministers of God's purpose unfolding in time. This explains why, on the one hand, they disclose the meaning of events and sometimes proclaim it ahead of time, while, on the other hand, they facilitate the movement of God's plan toward its end or fulfillment. They oppose an already achieved temporal expression being taken as perfect or definitive if, from the perspective of God's plan, it is only a stage. Think of the examples already given of the temple or sacrifice (perfected only in Christ). Prophets always push God's people to growth; they urge the stem to bring forth fruit . . . and urge the sign and the sacrament to press on all the way to their "reality."

This explains why there is always some confrontation between prophecy and formalism or ritualism (things toward which priesthood as a state of life is tempted).[12] The priest is a man of tradition—he is comfortable with things the way they are. A person of mercy, he wants to be at peace. He aligns himself with the fait accompli—the status quo. When the Golden Calf was made [on Sinai], Aaron, "Moses' priestly brother," unable to stop the Jews from making a bull from cast metal, thought that he could redeem the situation through a compromise. In worshiping this calf, they would give worship to Yahweh. But Moses didn't see things that way, and we can easily imagine Elias in Moses' situation . . .[12a]

---

[12] This clash between prophecy and the priesthood is expressed with the greatest clarity in the episode where Amos confronts the priest of Bethel (Amos 7). Without identifying with the excesses of certain Protestant historians of the 1880s or 90s, we can still affirm that conflict often arises between the two functions here and there. Look also at Kierkegaard, *Du droit de mourir pour la vérité*, p. 32, and the last pages of N. Berdyaev, *Spirit and Reality* (London, 1939). However, we should note that Jeremiah and Ezekiel were themselves priests, and that we find some prophets in the sense just given within the priestly hierarchy.

[12a] Cf. Exod 32:5f. For the example of a priest who supported a prophet, cf. the story of the Levite who attached himself to Micah (Judg 17:7f), then who proceeded to attach himself to the Danites (18:14-20); also, the story of the Sadducees who accom-

You can see how the prophet's role is related to that of the reformer. If you take the reformer's role in its deepest sense, it is to insist that the *end* is the *end*, and that all the rest is *means*; that the source is the source, and all the rest is only an instrument, a stage, or a form of relative importance.

By doing just that, the prophets of the Eternal One confronted and contradicted their times. When the spirit of their times said, "I am going to take that," the prophets said, "No, you can't," or, "You will lose it." When people were convinced of their security, the prophets revealed threats to their security; when the people thought they were lost, the prophets announced their salvation.[13]

It is said about Péguy that "the prophet always sees the opposite of everybody else: he reverses the apparent order of things that is actually false, and rediscovers the real order."[14] In addition, these men who contradict others are often misunderstood and persecuted. They are misunderstood because their prophetic words outpace the received ideas, the given mentality, or the perspective of their time. They are persecuted because they annoy others by disturbing the prevailing order or security. They don't belong to this world.

However, because they are possessed by the absolute demands of truth and of service, overcome by One more powerful than themselves (who seized them and made them his messengers), the prophets are intrepid. They have the independence and the sovereign freedom of those living no longer for themselves. They know that they have nothing to lose. Nothing stops a prophet. Awakened from within, a prophet has the invincible force of conscience—like the conscience of Nathan coming before David after Uriah's assassination and telling him: "You are the man"; like the conscience of Elijah before Ahab to blame him for Naboth's murder; like the conscience of John the Baptist telling Herod: "You have no right to take your brother's wife"; like the conscience of St. Ambrose

---

modated themselves to the Roman occupation . . . Outside the Bible, there is the case of the Persian cleric, recounted by Gobineau in his *Trois ans en Asie*, part II, ch. 2 (Paris: Grasset, vol. II, pp. 31–50).

[13] Jeremiah is a particular example of this. Cf. Jer 12:7-12 (his oracle proclaimed during the years of peace portending false security); 34:1-7 (his oracle given at the beginning of the siege of Jerusalem); 31 (his oracle given after the defeat). This was Jeremiah's vocation: cf. 1:10.

[14] A. Rousseaux, *Le prophète Péguy*, vol. I, p. 119. There are many elements for a phenomenology of prophecy in Péguy and in the powerful analysis of his interpreter here.

refusing the Emperor Theodosius permission to enter his cathedral after the massacre of Thessalonica; like the conscience of the Patriarch of Moscow, Philip, in resisting Ivan the Terrible . . . Such persons could not hold back from speaking. It was the same for the apostles, and for Paul after the Road to Damascus. "If these were silent, the stones would shout out . . . (Luke 19:40). We must obey God rather than any human authority . . ." (Acts 5:29).

Yet none of this prevents prophets from feeling their weakness painfully. They have a cruel awareness of their solitude, and sometimes they are tempted to want to return and mix with others, because they are neither better nor stronger than others. They are tempted to be discouraged[15] and to give up.[16] Moses was not always the powerful man sculpted by Michelangelo; sometimes he was the discouraged man described by Vigny. But the prophet is paradoxical to a certain degree, and every truly faithful believer has something of this. What is impossible to humans is possible for God. The power of God is accomplished in weakness. "*Cum infirmor, tunc potens sum*—whenever I am weak, then I am strong" (2 Cor 12:10).[17]

Prophecy in the Church

The church of antiquity understood itself essentially as operating under the power of the Holy Spirit and filled with the Spirit's gifts. One of the ways the Spirit's action became evident was through prophecy. It pertains to a theology of the Holy Spirit to show the profound connection between prophecy and the Third Person of the Trinity. It is a fact that, since Pentecost, the Spirit's coming has been linked to prophetic activity (Acts 2:17) and that very early the Fathers characterized the Holy Spirit as the one who has spoken through the prophets.[18] The grace of prophecy is one of the affirmations that the church of antiquity most frequently makes about itself.

---

[15] Thus Elijah (1 Kgs 19), Jeremiah (20:14), Jonah (4).

[16] So Moses (Exod 3:11; 4:17), Jeremiah (1; 9:1; 20:9-18), Jonah.

[17] Cf. Matt 19:20; Luke 18:27; (Cf. 1 Cor 1:18).

[18] Cf. P. Nautin, *Je crois à l'Esprit Saint* . . ., p. 52. St. Justin, *1st Apology*, 6, 13, calls the Holy Spirit the *Pneuma prophetikon*.

Let's not speak here about the Didache or about Montanism. The latter almost managed to cast suspicion on the prophetic charism. It is even more remarkable to see St. Irenaeus attribute this prophetic gift to the faithful.[19] Attacking Montanism at its beginnings, Meliton of Sardis did not deny but rather affirmed prophetic grace for the church.[20] It was simply impossible to miss the fact that since its origins the church had received this eminent form of the Holy Spirit's action within itself. In the apostolic writings prophecy was presented as the first of the social charisms.[21] A text like the description of Polycarp's martyrdom, which gave the holy bishop the title of "apostolic and prophetic teacher" (XVI, 2), sounds very close to the Acts and the epistles of Paul. Prophecy was part of the original personality of the church. As the church is the temple of the Holy Spirit, it was normal that the Holy Spirit should prophesy within it.[22] Even before Irenaeus, St. Justin said that the charism of prophecy had passed from the Jews to Christians.[23] Even while fighting against Montanism, Catholic writers affirmed the permanent character of this charism as a continuous gift that will not cease before the Parousia.[24]

Within this prophetic charism that provides penetrating understanding of God's word and God's plan, we need to recognize a further content that also proclaims the future. If this future prophetic insight is not always clear or expressly stated, at least it constitutes a presentiment (intuitive foresight) like that which Polycarp had about his martyrdom. This element of the anticipation of events played an important role in the church of the first three centuries; there are a great many instances of this. This prophetic insight does not disappear from the church, as

---

[19] *Adv. Haereses* V, 6, 1, cited by Eusebius, *Ecclesiastical History*, V, 7, 6; II, 32, 4; III, 11, 9; *Demonstr.*, 99. See also the anti-Montanist referred to by Eusebius in *Eccl. Hist.*, V, 17. Cf. G. Bardy, *La théologie de l'Eglise de saint Clément de Rome à saint Irénée*, pp. 132–133. Concerning the early church's esteem for the gift of prophecy and the prophecy of the first centuries, cf. H. Weinel, *Die Wirkungen des Geites und der Geister in nachapostolischen Zeitalter bis auf Irenäus*, 1899; D. van den Eynde, *Les normes de l'enseignement* . . . (Gembloux and Paris, 1933), pp. 77f.; A. Ehrhardt, *The Apostolic Succession* (London, 1953), pp. 83–106.

[20] Cf. Bardy, op. cit., p. 130.

[21] 1 Cor 12:28; 14:5, 39; Rom 12:6; Eph 2:20 (cf. 3:5).

[22] Cf. *Pseudo-Barnabas*, XVI, 9.

[23] Justin, *Dialogue* 82, 1; Irenaeus, *Against Heresies* II, 32, 4; cf. Bardy, op. cit., pp. 133, 151.

[24] Cf. Bardy, op. cit., p. 151.

can be seen in the life of the Curé of Ars, that of Don Bosco, and in many other cases.

The earliest centuries, because of their prevailing mentality, gave great attention to visions, revelations, and presentiments. From the beginning, even before Montanism, the church discerned about such extraordinary things by applying spiritual criteria that were both gospel-based and realistic.[25] The church would not surrender this attitude. The church would not stop having within her those who were enlightened or seers . . . Nonetheless, she would always rank above all the other gifts of the Spirit those linked to faith and charity. St. Anthony of the Desert was an example of that when he said that we should desire not so much to know the future but rather the inner light that gives insight and discernment.[26]

Prophecy as a permanent charism in the church has many aspects, but they are all related to the knowledge of things that are less than evident. So the word *prophecy* has a wider meaning of the kind that St. Thomas spoke about when he wrote: "All the gifts related to knowledge can be grouped under the name of prophecy."[27] Distinctions are necessary here. It seems to me that the following nuances or applications make sense. Prophecy means (1) a specially insightful knowledge about things pertaining to God, (2) a knowledge or mission related to the execution of God's plan, and (3) the prediction of the future, to which Cardinal Journet adds what he calls "the natural analogs of prophecy."[28]

1. *Specially Insightful Knowledge about the Things of God*

This kind of insight is special because it acts under the movement of the Holy Spirit. This raises questions of discernment that I will not take up here. This is clearly the meaning of the word *prophecy* in the New Testament when it pertains to the church, whether in Acts (2:17-18) or in St. Paul; it signifies an inspired speech.[29]

---

[25] Cf. H. Bacht, "Die prophetische Inspiration in der kirchlichen Reflexion der vormontanistischen Zeit," in *Theol. Quartalsch.* and *Scholastik* (printed together, 1944), pp. 1–18.

[26] St. Athanasius, *Life of Saint Anthony*, no. 34 (PG 26:893).

[27] *Summa Theologiae*, IIa-IIae, q. 171, prologue. See also for this wider meaning q. 174, art. 6, and his *Commentary on Matthew*, ch. 7, lesson 2.

[28] *Nova et Vetera* (1942), p. 73, n. 4, making reference to St. Thomas, *Sum. Theol.*, IIa-IIae, q. 172, art. 1.

[29] Cf. Rom 12:6; 1 Cor 12:10, 28; 13:9; 14:1, 6, 24; cf. Rev 19:10. Sometimes this sort of speech takes the form of a special action within the assembly: Acts 19:8; 21:9; 1 Cor

Similar to this is prophecy in the church. It is rooted in a gift from God and is a function by which the church understands and teaches things that come from God. Some authors consider this function of prophecy, along with priesthood and governing, to be one of the three missions or competencies of the church. All three are rooted in the three functions of Christ as king, priest, and prophet. With the help of explanations and clarifications that I count on contributing some day, I adopt this way of thinking myself. It strikes me as corresponding to a whole ensemble of data from the Bible and from tradition, as well as allowing for a harmonious explanation (rarely done well) of everything to do with witness and teaching in the church. In this wider but precise sense, Vatican II conceived the prophetic function as pertaining to the church and even to the people of God in an ongoing way. The council used the structure of these three offices, as we know. After being applied to God's people in the old covenant, these offices passed over and were assumed by Christ—and were passed on by him to his church: prophecy, royalty, and priesthood.

Prophecy exists both among the whole people, who are touched by the Holy Spirit's charisms, and among the hierarchical ministers through the grace of the Holy Spirit. Look especially at the passage of *Lumen Gentium* 12, speaking of "the holy people of God," that explains: "[it] shares also in Christ's prophetic office: it spreads abroad a living witness to him, especially by a life of faith and love . . . the whole body of the faithful who have received an anointing which comes from the Holy One (see 1 Jn 2:20 and 27) cannot be mistaken in belief . . .," etc.[29a]

Within this wider sense of prophecy there is a kind of reduplication, not of function exactly (which has only one object and one end), but rather of the characteristics of the word that is uttered, according to the situation and the vocation of the one who speaks it in the church, as well as according to the type of assistance given by the Holy Spirit. So there is *ex officio* teaching that is connected to a pastoral responsibility, and

---

11:4; 14:3, 31. The "prophets" are thus persons performing functions that correspond to this action within the church: Acts 13:1; 15:32; 21:10; 1 Cor 12:28; 14:29.

[29a] See also the decree *Presbyterorum Ordinis* 2 (citing Rev 19:10); H. Schürmann, "Les charismes spirituels," in *L'Eglise de Vatican II*, ed. G. Baraúna, *Unam Sanctam* 51b (Paris, 1966), pp. 541–574; I. de la Potterie and S. Lyonnet, *La vie selon l'Esprit: condition du chrétien*, *Unam Sanctam* 55 (Paris, 1965). The text of 1 John cited by Vatican II is the same text used by Erasmus in the very same sense in his commentary on the psalm *Quare fremuerunt*.

then there is *ex spiritu* teaching that is an inspiration freely and spontaneously given.

A churchman may be called a "prophet" simply because he has a charge to teach, that is, the competence of the magisterium along with the charisms that go with it. The gift of prophecy then covers the whole domain of the hierarchical function of overseeing doctrines, from dogmatic definitions all the way to the church's conduct in matters of spiritual life and morality. Père Clérissac and Cardinal Journet describe prophecy in this way, without making this the exclusive description.[30] That seems right.

Prophecy can be applied to any penetration into the things of God, whether intellectual or spiritual, through the wisdom of scholars or the wisdom of saints. This is not contrary to what we said above, but it is broader. Père Clérissac agreed.[31] In this way, it seems to me, Newman speaks of a prophetic tradition that is distinct from the episcopal tradition.[32] By that he means the ensemble or chain of explanations, interpretations, and expressions that doctors and spiritual writers have given to the faith, even in liturgies and devotions.

According to this meaning, where the prophetic quality is verified (above all as a competence in knowing religious objects), the deep religiosity of the person is important, as is his or her way of treating of the things of God. So Pascal, who insisted upon the necessary dispositions in the person, wrote: "To prophesy is to speak about God not based on proofs from outside, but based on an inner and immediate feeling."[33]

At present, the words prophecy, prophet, and prophetic are very much in favor; and this is normal. In my writing in 1946 I used these words a lot. However, based on the observation of Bishop Terrier (whose criticisms I accept), I cut back on this usage in favor of a stricter application of terms. I had begun, as a way of justifying my preliminary text, to make

---

[30] H. Clérissac, *Le mystère de l'Eglise*, in his chapter on the gift of prophecy in the church; C. Journet, *L'Eglise du Verbe incarné*, vol. I, p. 147.

[31] Ibid., and especially his *La mission de sainte Jeanne* (Lyons, 1941), p. 15.

[32] Cf. *The Via Media*, vol. I., lesson 10, note 11: this little paragraph of a page and a half is just about the only one on the "prophetical office" that is the subtitle of the first volume. See J. Guitton's resumé in French: *La philosophie de Newman: Essai sur l'idée de développement* (Paris, 1933), pp. 47–48. In this context, it is interesting that a 12th-century author, Rupert of Deutz, thought that there was an example of prophecy in the understanding that God gives us of the words that we pronounce in liturgical prayer: *De divinis officiis*, prol. (PL 170:12).

[33] *Pensées*, fr. 732.

note of the use of these words by my contemporaries. But I stopped doing that because you can find the terms everywhere today, often used improperly. One of the most widespread misuses is the one that we saw noted by Pascal. Pascal rejects the definition of prophecy as a way of speaking about God and the things of God in the abstract; he insists upon prophecy as knowledge which you know about personally or about which you can say something. To prophesy should mean to speak of a living reality that you know personally. Likes seers (one of the names for prophets in the Old Testament), like witnesses—they are people who have had contact, who have had an experience about which they share their amazement. Prophets are *twice-born*.

This was the same sense of prophecy that Abbé Rétif had when speaking of the "catechist-prophet."[34] This sort of witness merits to be called prophetic, first of all, because it involves a quality of understanding the things of God produced by the Holy Spirit. But in addition, it is prophetic with respect to the transcendence of God's mystery; it fulfills one of the properties of prophecy, which is to speak of distant things (that are also powerfully active and even imminent . . .). Finally, this meaning corresponds exactly to the character of a prophet—a person seized by God and conquered by One stronger than oneself, who transmits a message from beyond, who is captivated by this message and cannot hold back from speaking . . . In a great number of cases we give the title "prophetic" today to any witness characterized by courage or a sense of the intrepid. We find here something of the spirit of our times which, as we know, is less interested in the content and the truth of statements than in their tone—their accent. This use of the word, then, without being false, remains vague.

Concerning the different ways that something can be called "prophetic," the tradition does not give the greatest weight to fearlessness (intrepidity). Rather, the tradition values the contemplation of invisible things—heavenly things. St. Bernard shows this in commenting on St. Paul's phrase: "We know only in part, and we prophesy only in part" (1 Cor 13:9). To "prophesy only in part" for Bernard means to consider not what can be seen but what cannot be seen; to walk in the spirit, to live by faith, to seek what is on high, not what is on the earth; to forget what is behind us and reach toward what is ahead . . . Both St. Bernard

---

[34] Title of an article published in *Prêtres diocésains* (Nov. 1948), pp. 568–575, and reprinted in *Catéchisme et Mission ouvrière: Du catéchisme au catéchuménat: Simples réflexions pastorales, Rencontres*, 31 (Paris, 1950).

and the monastic tradition[35] suggest that contemplative knowledge has an eschatological orientation, like the mission of the prophets who preceded Christ. It means passing through the present life while reaching out toward the Day of the Lord, toward the principle that was given us in Jesus Christ as a beginning and that will work its way through time and whose fulfillment we still await.

The two operations of prophecy that I previously distinguished are in no way opposed. Ecclesiology needs to distinguish between the *ex officio* and the *ex spiritu* (not doing so would be catastrophic). But here more than ever we need to "distinguish in order to unite." Nothing would be more false than to separate or oppose the operations of the magisterium (with their hierarchical charisms) and the more or less inspired personal activities of the faithful. The two work together, each in its own order, to keep the Christian understanding of God in the church faithful and living, to help it progress and make sense. This is nothing more than to achieve the great program that St. Irenaeus expressed in these unforgettable terms:

> That in which we have faith is a firm system directed to the salvation of [human beings]; and, since it has been received by the church, we guard it. Constantly [the church] has its youth renewed by the Spirit of God, as if it were some precious deposit in an excellent vessel; and it causes the vessel containing it also to be rejuvenated. There is where we find communion in Christ, that is, in the Holy Spirit, the pledge of our incorruptibility, the foundation of our faith and the ladder that allows us to climb toward God. For it has been said: In the church, God has placed apostles, prophets, and doctors and all the other means through which the Spirit works; in all of which none have any part who do not conform to the church. . . . [The nonconforming] defraud themselves of life by their wicked opinion and most wretched behavior.[36]

This is why Cardinal Suhard, addressing the role of the priest as "prophet," happily linked together his function of teaching (the ministry of the word) and his character as witness to truth, which ought to provide him not only with a prophetic function but also a prophetic accent.[37]

---

[35] St. Bernard, *Sermo de diversis*, sermon 37, no. 6 (PL 183:642); Dom J. Leclercq, *La vie parfaite: Points de vue sur l'état religieux* (Paris, 1948), pp. 57f.

[36] *Against Heresies*, III, 24, 1 (PG 7:166; Harvey II, 131); trans. in Bardy, op. cit., p. 195.

[37] His pastoral letter of 1949, "Le prêtre dans la Cité," pp. 30f.

2. *A Knowledge or Mission Related to Executing God's Plan*

The Bible and above all the Old Testament (most of it) gives us an understanding of what God has done and what God wants to be for us, the understanding of God as the source of grace. Since all knowledge of God must be in some way distant and prophetic so long as we don't see as we are seen, then every knowledge or mission relative to the development of God's proposal of grace likewise has some element of the prophetic. When God's purpose will be fulfilled, when God will be "all in all," then prophecy will cease (1 Cor 13:8). We should recall here what has been said about God's plan as development and about the way in which we still need to await its fulfillment in the church, as well as about the way the development of the world has implications for the church.

Everything is at the service of God's plan: [human] sanctity, secular activities, even sin. However, certain activities are more particularly sustained by God so as to make us see everything in terms of serving God's plan and promoting its development. In this sense we can talk about a permanent charism of prophecy in the church.[38] This perspective also helps us to contextualize the mission of reformers when they face the temptation that risks turning the church into a "Synagogue." Everything said above about that topic fits here. This is one way in which the activities of reformers and prophets are related.

In this respect the prophetic function aims to reveal the meaning of time and of the initiatives and movements that arise in history (principally from the point of view of God and God's plan). Churchmen have sometimes failed to fulfill this function. Because of this, a positive understanding of the dynamic nature of time and, above all, a fundamental openness to its development often have been found only among the avant-garde or among reformers working at the frontiers. In certain periods, like that of the Reformation, for example, there has been a

---

[38] This is the meaning, in general, of Père Broutin, *Mysterium Ecclesiae* (Paris, 1947), pp. 81–82: "Two essential notions serve as guides in the study of this powerful mystery: anticipation of the future and the preparation of pathways. . . . [Prophecy] is the collective organization of the aspirations of the divine-human society toward a better state in the future through the advancement of the kingdom of God among redeemed humanity. . . . In the New [Testament], it is a matter of ascending toward the Light through the union of scriptural inspiration and traditional revelation, of continually enlarging catholicity, of linking the church militant with the church triumphant. Prophecy is inherent in the church in its pilgrim status. It represents an earthly stage of the heavenly Jerusalem."

painful lack of "prophets," people who genuinely understand the meaning of the events around them. However, in other ways, the church has
manifested a truly prophetic, even clairvoyant understanding of events,
ideas, and new initiatives, and of the spiritual meaning of ideologies.
The church has often exercised a true charism of discernment of spirits.
That has been the contribution of the saints,[39] and it has been above all,
in an outstanding way, the contribution of the hierarchy as a magisterial
authority.

This has also been the contribution of the Christian faithful, in a way
that is less certain but extraordinarily efficacious. God has used the gifts
of the faithful to manifest to his people the secret destiny of their times,
the meaning of what is going on in the world, clear ideas to guide clear
thinking. In giving a few examples, I risk being rather subjective. However, can't we agree on such names as Ozanam, Lacordaire, de Mun,
Bloy, Péguy, John XXIII, and Cardijn . . . to give as examples only those
who are dead?

This topic would be an interesting study. It would be fascinating to
examine the role that people who have been intensely involved in the
great moments of their century (at least in the modern period) have also
played in the church, both as Catholics and often before becoming Catholics. Such persons more than others, especially if they were somehow
converts, show us the character of the *twice-born*.

We would see then how in the church there is a complementarity
between a principle of continuity or form coming from the hierarchy, on
the one hand, and a principle of movement or unexpectedness, even,
coming from those inspired to act on the frontiers. These latter seem to
possess an impulsive energy which compensates for what they lack in
tradition and security. They're the ones who bring the most to the *life* of
the church. They're the ones who, for the most part, reestablish the
church's relationship with the development of the world. Theirs is a
"prophetic" function which the faithful, born and living in the milieu of
sociological Catholicism, are not as well prepared to exercise.

What we commonly call private revelations also have something to
do with prophecy, as they disclose something of God's plan and further
its realization. God's revelations are effectively related to the direction
that God gives either to an individual soul for his or her personal life or
some important work destined either for an individual or for the whole
church. Revelations are chosen instruments which God continues to use

---

[39] C. Journet, *L'Eglise du Verbe incarné*, vol. I, p. 148, insists on this point.

to direct his people and communicate his will. They don't contribute anything objectively new to the dogmatic structure of the church, but they have great importance for the way God guides the life of the church, especially with respect to worship, spirituality, and new foundations. For St. Thomas, all of that is linked to the spirit of prophecy.[40]

Again, we see the prophetic spirit manifested in the recognition of visitations by the Lord—a major case of the interpretation of the signs of the times and of events from God's point of view. (This has nothing to do with Adventism.[41]) The prophetic character of the church is linked to the habitual attention that the church pays to waiting for the Lord's return.[42] We live between his first coming, when the children of Israel acclaimed him with Hosannas because a spirit of prophecy had fallen upon them,[43] and the last coming, which will put an end to history. In the meantime, there are other comings and visitations of the Lord to admonish and to bestow grace. To interpret events from God's point of view, to understand that God is waiting at the door, to recognize that it is God who raps—all that is to exercise prophetic grace.

3. *Predicting the Future: "Natural Analogs of Prophecy"*

This question of prediction is not directly to the point of my topic here. However, there is a certain kind of secular prophecy that looks a lot like a minor manifestation of religious prophecy.

Predictions or so-called predictions are easy to find in the pages of history. Most often, they are political or politico-religious in perspective. St. Augustine gave a lot of attention to predictions of the future—something common in antiquity.[44] Döllinger, who studied a lot of prophecies in the Christian epoch,[45] was very negative about them. On the other

---

[40] *Summa Theologiae*, IIa-IIae, q. 171, art. 6; and cf. *Quaestio disputata de Veritate*, q. 12, art. 2, corpus.

[41] The French Adventist movement has taken for its magazine the lovely title *Les Signes des temps—The Signs of the Times* (and so risks bringing discredit to the idea).

[42] This is the sense of Pastor A. Antomarchi in his *L'Eglise prophétique* (Dieulefit, s.d., 1935).

[43] Cf. R. Guardini, *Le Seigneur—The Lord* (in French trans., vol. II, p. 9).

[44] Cf. J. Guitton, *Le temps et l'éternité chez Plotin et saint Augustin* (Paris, 1933), pp. 217f., 270f.

[45] I. von Döllinger, *Der Weissagunsglaube und das Prophetentum in der christlichen Zeit* (1871). I read the English translation: *Prophecies and the Prophetic Spirit in the Christian Era: An Historical Essay* (London: 1873).

hand, in the lives of many saints there are examples of an intuition of things hidden or to come that seem unquestionable. And what person has never personally experienced some kind of presentiment or intuition of the future?

Someone is called a prophet when he or she has foreseen some sequence of events with impressive precision. M. A. Rousseaux points out texts of Péguy (especially in the last chapters of his book *Prophète Péguy*) that are prophetic in this way. But you can also find similar prophetic texts by Alexis de Tocqueville, Proudhon, or Jacques Bainville. In reality, what we have here is a capacity to link events together, coupled with realism and clear vision and contextual analysis. Rousseaux affirms this with respect to Péguy. He shows how his prophetic spirit emerges from some precise, concrete fact and then perceives, by way of this analysis, some eternal reality and its implications. Rousseaux says: "[Péguy] saw this, as the prophets saw things, not by some kind of extraordinary warning concerning the temporal events that would come to be, but by a deep vision of eternal things, from which every temporal event flows."[46]

This explanation can't be given to all prophetic predictions, particularly those of salvation history. Prophets of the type I am describing here discern a future hidden in the dynamic energy of events or in the potency of things, exception made for the unpredictable way that human freedom can impact upon otherwise predictable possibilities. The prophets of salvation history announce a future that depends entirely upon God's plan and that is equally knitted together from individual acts where human liberty has a decisive role.

Predictions in secular prophecy, based on the analysis of situations, additionally take on a kind of messianic fervor in Marxism, where they represent the very meaning of history. We know that Berdyaev read into Russian Communism a kind of transposition of religious attitudes. Unquestionably, Marxism had vitality and energy. It gave an explanation to history and, above all, it claimed to give a practical orientation to things by referring them to an end term—to a "truth" about things which analogically becomes a kind of secular eschatology. By that very fact, Marxism had a kind of "prophetic" content and function.[47]

So I want to make a place for this secular prophetic spirit which shares something with religious prophecy. Further, there is a certain kind of

---

[46] *Le Prophète Péguy*, vol. II, p. 254; cf. pp. 208, 282, 305, 340.

[47] Cf. H.-C. Desroches, "Du marxisme comme humanisme prophétique" in *Economie et Humanisme* (May–June 1946), pp. 236–257.

prophetic value to poetry. Can I base my claim on the authority of St. Paul? He once called a pagan poet a prophet (Titus 1:12). However, there are more appropriate examples that seem quite clear.[47a] Poets possess what priests often lack, namely, a sensibility for relating earthly things to the invisible. Poets have the gift of deep feeling and of making the secret harmonies of things apparent; they perceive dimensions that are inaccessible to others. In short, poets possess in some way an understanding of what is hidden to ordinary eyes, and they reveal its meaning. That is what makes them prophets. Poets have within them something of the divine. The Latin language spoke of both poets and prophets as *vates* [inspired ones].

This gift is an ability to discover the inner order of things, to discover the nature of what has been created. It is linked to the role of the theologian who, beginning with the word of God, has the responsibility to reconstruct meaning by looking at the order of divine wisdom. When poetry succeeds in investing beauty with profound insight, it becomes much like prayer, sharing both magnificent resources and the dangerous influence of the unconscious. Also, when poetry succeeds in giving to some historical or theological theme striking expression, harmony, amplitude, and a feeling of the definitive and the unforgettable, it expresses an almost shocking power: it provides breath for the word and—once more—creates prophetic echoes.

The Reform Spirit and Prophecy

The prophetic function is an enduring feature of the church. Predicting the future or intuiting what is hidden are not the most essential parts of it. They are rather signs to convince the doubtful, while prophecy, as St. Paul says, is given for the sake of the faithful (1 Cor 15:22). Prophecy essentially means knowing the things of God and understanding God's will. For both of these activities the biblical prophets are the primary examples of those whose intuitions are divinely assured. But reformers, if they are truly from God, are moved in this way by the Spirit, and their function is related to that of the prophets. This function, as we have seen, is to judge their times and the things that exist in time in the light of truths seen in relation to the Absolute and in relation to the end term toward which they are directed.

[47a] Look, for example, at M. Maeterlinck's letter to Léon Bloy, cited by Raïssa Maritain, *Les grandes amitiés*, vol. I, p. 151.

However, between the prophecy of the reformers, which is often compromised by errors or mistakes, and the prophecy of the biblical prophets there are radical differences that have to be kept in mind. One is particularly important, because it deals with the condition of the very norm for prophecy in the church.

The Situation of Prophecy within the Church

The prophecy of the biblical prophets is *structural* for the people of God, forming them and situating them in a relation of service to the "Economy" that leads to Jesus Christ, who is the Universal Cause of salvation for all people. The prophecy of the prophetic spirit in the church takes place within the structures of the church's life. It presupposes this ecclesial structure and is only exercised within the limitations of this structure. As St. Paul says, we should only "prophesy in proportion to faith."[48] St. Thomas clearly distinguished between these two domains of structure and life. He wrote: "The prophets of old had been sent so as to teach the faith and reform moral behavior . . . but today, the faith has already been established; however, prophecy, whose objective is to reform morals, does not cease, nor will it cease."[49]

When considering prophecy under its aspect as revelation or the knowledge of the things of God, or under its aspect of service to God's plan, we must remember that God's work took on its essential form in the revelation made to the prophets and to the apostles in the Bible—all of it centered upon Jesus Christ. The mystery of Christ, confessed of old by Cephas, is the cornerstone of everything. That is why no one speaking through the Spirit of God can curse Jesus (1 Cor 12:3) and why giving witness to Jesus Christ can only be done in a spirit of prophecy.[50] That also explains why the prophetic inclination of Joachim of Flora, announcing an Age of the Holy Spirit following the Age of the Son, had something profoundly anti-Christian about it. We can only be astonished that the Roman Church was not more severe toward it.

Any prophetic spirit looking for new revelation or for substantial additions to revelation or trying to change the revelation given to the apostles is not the prophetic spirit of the church. There is no "freedom of spirit" (either with a capital S or a small s) with respect to revelation,

---

[48] Rom 12:6. The Protestant *Bible du Centenaire* translates this as "*Sans s'écarter de la foi*—without straying from the faith."

[49] *Commentary on Matthew*, XI.

[50] Rev 19:10; 22:9; cf. 1 Cor 12:3.

because the Spirit of the new covenant is the Spirit of Jesus Christ and the Spirit of Pentecost. The only valid prophecy in the church is in the service of the church's apostolicity. Once again we have here the distinction between structure and life. On one hand, there are the apostles and their apostolicity; on the other hand, there is the apostolate marked by zeal and by the service of God. In a similar way, there are the prophets linked to divine revelation, and there is the prophetic spirit corresponding to God's guidance in the order of faith and worship of the people whom he has established. In both cases, the first elements are "structural," and the second are "structured" in order to guide the life of the church correctly.[51]

The Perils of Prophetic Activity

The prophets of salvation history have integrity. In every case they have the guarantee of divine inspiration in the strongest sense of the word. However, prophets of a lesser kind, called "prophets" by analogy in comparison to the role and character of the biblical prophets, even if they bring to the church extraordinary and providential service, can also be the occasion for problems.

Let's not talk about those falsely inspired—there is nothing more dangerous for the church than they. Visionaries who believe they have a divine mission can be the source of great catastrophes. Such people, if they act out of their own personal weakness, will be the only ones (along with their followers) to suffer from their lack of realism. However, if they are invested with power, they can become one of those destructive fanatics, which world history, alas, knows so well. For example, an author recently drew a parallel between Hitler and Ravaillac [who murdered King Henry IV of France in 1610].[52] Unleashing the offensive of May 10,

---

[51] Along with Père Clérissac and Cardinal Journet, I admitted above to applying the term prophecy to the functioning of the magisterium, matching it with its proper charism. This belongs to the *life* of the church, since it is an exercise in obedience to a revelation *already given*. Therefore, it adds nothing objective to the constitution of the church's structure. In this book, if we speak elsewhere of this pertaining to the church's structure, it is as part of its hierarchical constitution and of its interpretation of the dogmatic deposit that structures the church. There is no contradiction here.

[52] Dolf Sternberger, "Toleranz als Leidenschaft für die Wahrheit," in *Die Wandlung* (Heidelberg, 1943), pp. 231–250.

1940, Hitler announced that he was going to settle the destiny of Germany for a thousand years. Later, Rosenberg [Hitler's administrator for Russia]—mediocre, woolly minded, and without genius—stated that people would understand and appreciate what he wanted to do in Russia only after a hundred years.

It's great to be a prophet, but only if one really is one. There is something intoxicating about feeling that you have left your mark on history, that what you have lived, experienced, and dreamed is a kind of prediction of the world's future, and that your personal destiny coincides with the destiny of history itself . . . But this is dangerous stuff, especially if it is not true. Above all, if the "prophet" is impatient and cannot await the unfolding of events with the quiet certitude of the seed anticipating the fruit it will bear, but rather tries to force things to bring about his dream . . . [he can do great harm].

Genuine religious prophets (just as the others) cannot avoid having the feeling of exultation at having been chosen, inspired, and given a mission. This is how they come to be so intrepid in their hope and their action. But if they are genuinely sent from God, they experience as well an even deeper feeling of their own nothingness and their inability to trust themselves.

Every "prophet" has the feeling that there is work to be done. There is a mission to accomplish. There is a personal discovery, turned into an imperative that takes over the prophet's life. Seized by their goal and by their sense of the absolute, "prophets" may be unable to recognize the relative nature of the means and the forms they use, even though they should be recognized for what they are. With a consciousness awakened by personal conversion, solitary by vocation, prophets risk becoming isolated. Intrepid and possessed, they deliver their message bluntly, absolutely, even violently—without concern to balance or harmonize what they say with other elements which are in their own way true.

The prophets of the Old Testament spoke out against the formalism of worship in terms so absolute that they seemed to condemn every external form of worship; they spoke against kings in such fashion that they might be interpreted as condemning the office of king itself. St. Peter Damian, for example, railed against dialectics using language so violent that he sounded like Luther. St. Francis of Assisi wanted to apply the rule of the Gospel and of poverty *sine glossa*, without compromise, without seeking balance, without making any distinctions.[53] Prophets don't

---

[53] There is an element of intransigence and radicalism in St. Francis. With respect to his ideal of poverty, his rule of 1221 contrasts with the tendency of Brother Elias

compromise. For them, the formula is the *Enten-Eller* (either-or) of Kierkegaard. Solitary and obsessed, the prophet risks giving his message an exclusive, unilateral thrust; risks upsetting things in the establishment without seeing how such things are needed for stability or for social balance. Reacting against the group, indeed against the established order, the prophet, depending upon the situation, can stir up revolt. The "prophet" is the person above all who has a vocation. If the sign of a vocation is that one is unable not to act, that one would rather die, then the "prophet" is forced to pursue his work despite everything. How could he keep silent, even if he is commanded to do so? There is something dizzying in the problems of conscience posed by people like Joan of Arc or Savonarola . . .

Later on in this work I will affirm once again the obligation that weighs on the church to move beyond static ecclesiastical structures and to open itself to prophetic voices. I will point out the duty that weighs upon both creative spirits and reactionaries to look for integration in unity, not to become intransigent in the face of established forms so as to become an anti-conformity that can itself be a kind of Pharisaism. If progress is dialectical, if the "thesis" has to face up to the shock and the questions posed by the "antithesis," it is equally true that the antithesis can only be a principle of progress when it stops fixating upon its dynamic of anti-conformity. The professionalism of newly inspired initiatives is no better than the professionalism of the establishment, and it is a lot more dangerous. Mounier wrote about this, speaking of the link and the comings-and-goings between the avant-garde and the Army,[54] a passage that I will cite later on (cf. part 2, second condition).

Why St. Augustine Was a Source of Encouragement for Reformers

To bring to a close this necessary but overly sketchy chapter about prophecy in the church and about reformers as "prophets," let me add a remark that is at once historical and theological.

What I said so far can help us understand the reasons for and the meaning of a fact that appears to be a constant feature of the history of

---

(O. Englebert, *Vie de saint François d'Assise*, pp. 280f.), especially in his ideal of simplicity and his reaction to studies and books (pp. 305–306).

[54] "Le peuple chrétien et ses avant-gardes," in *Témoignage chrétien* (Feb. 25, 1949).

the Western Church. Its reform movements generally are inspired by an Augustinian spirit. I noticed this even before reading Harnack's observation that "the long chain of Catholic reformers, from Agobard [of Lyons] and Claudio of Turin in the 9th century down to the Jansenists of the seventeenth and eighteenth centuries has been Augustinian. If in many respects the Council of Trent can be called a Reform Council, if its dogmas about sin, penance and grace were formulated there in a deeper and more interior fashion than the theology of the fourteenth and fifteenth centuries would have led one to expect, this is due to the always effective influence of Augustine."[54bis] I can add to the names evoked by Harnack those of St. Peter Damian, St. Gregory VII, St. Catherine of Siena, Luther, Pascal, and also certain members of the "spiritual" movement that arose in the thirteenth century and continued down to the Renaissance. The prophetic spirit of the "spirituals" was responsible in part for the hope and enthusiasm of the Renaissance. Yet perhaps a certain absence of Augustinianism was also one of the weaknesses of the Counter-Reformation and the theology that it produced.

These remarks point to a fact whose explanation is clear. The Augustinian synthesis can be described as "a metaphysics of conversion" (E. Gilson). For my part, I call it a dialectic of conversion, seeking always to situate *genuine* reality by leading it from the outside to the inside, from external aspects to the internal reality that they symbolize. Augustine, influenced by Marius Victorinus (the extent of his influence is still being discussed), made a distinction between things *quae vere sunt* [that really exist] and things *quae solum sunt* [that merely are].

Using this distinction, Augustine rediscovered a profoundly biblical perspective. In this light, the Old Testament as a whole is a "sacrament" of things to come. In a similar way, the thought of St. John, by comparison with the Old Testament, is expressed by the words *true* or *in truth*.[55] In Augustine's mind there is a parallel between these philosophical and

---

[54bis] *L'essence du christianisme*—*The Essence of Christianity*, French trans. (Paris, 1902), p. 275.

[55] The true light (1:9), worship in truth (4:23), the true bread from heaven (6:32), truly free (8:36), sanctified in truth (17:17). Cf. A. Dubarle in *La Maison-Dieu*, no. 5, p. 94. For this idea of "truth" in the liturgical, sacramental, and theological tradition of the early church, cf. H. de Lubac, *Corpus mysticum* (Paris, 1944), ch. 9. [Eng. trans., *Corpus Mysticum: The Eucharist and the Church in the Middle Ages*, trans. Gemma Simmonds (Notre Dame, IN: University of Notre Dame Press, 2007).] Cf. Pascal, *Pensées*, section 10.

biblical expressions and the distinction noted even before him[56] between the external sacramental sign and the interior reality of grace that is the objective of the sacrament.[57] All of Augustine's ecclesiology, which finds its way into St. Thomas's *Summa Theologiae*, arises from this insight.

The church as *communio sacramentorum*, the church of the sacraments and of hierarchical powers, is completely oriented to the church as *communio sanctorum*, the union of love in the body of Christ. Even Augustine's way of defining worship, sacrifice, and priesthood[58] is derived from the consequences of this point of view and is clearly linked with the development of revelation that I outlined above. The entire mystery of the church, as well as the ensemble of God's gifts, is drawn into a movement of interiorization. The liturgy, the sacraments, and the whole church need to find their truth and their reality in the faithful themselves, in their spiritual life, and in the faith and charity of the human soul.

You can see how every reform spirit can easily take inspiration from Augustinianism, since the spirit of reform lives by insisting that the end surpasses all means, that the meaning of things is more important than their external expression, and—in a more general way—by a distinction between something in its present condition and this same thing according to the way God wants it to be from his eternal perspective.

That is why Péguy (even though he once wrote that he would exchange all of St. Augustine for one word of Joan of Arc) is still fundamentally Augustinian. From this point of view essential to Augustinianism, one only needs to add the historical dimension—the sense of development—to complete the sources for the reform spirit by affirming the need to go beyond stagnant or outdated structures. This is why reformers find support not only in Augustine himself but also in Augustinians like Newman.

You can also understand how Augustinianism seems to promote dangerous or near-heterodox positions within the church. As a doctrine

---

[56] By Irenaeus, Tertullian, and Cyprian: cf. H. Koch in *Theologische Literaturzeitung* (1932), col. 200.

[57] On this point, see D. Zahringer, *Das kirchliche Priestertum nach dem heiligen Augustinus* (Paderborn, 1932), pp. 77f., 87; H.-M. Féret, "Sacramentum, res, dans la langue théologique de saint Augustin," *Revue des Sciences philosophiques et théologiques* 29 (1940), pp. 218–243; and above all H. de Lubac, op. cit.

[58] Cf. the incomparable text of *The City of God*, Book X, chs. 5 and 6; cf. ch. 2 above, pp. 120f.

linked to an interior experience naturally open to a prophetic attitude, the Augustinian tendency is characterized by ambivalence. This ambivalence was completely resolved for Augustine and his Catholic disciples by their orthodox understanding. But it can also be resolved in a less Catholic sense because of excessive and isolationist thinking, as happened with Luther, the Jansenists, and many others both before and after them.[59] This explains of course why some misgivings or at least some disquiet and suspicion lingers in the church's respect for Augustine, since this great doctor's thought has been adopted by some disciples who are more zealous than balanced. Fifteen centuries have shown us the possible dangers involved. Yet the Augustinian yeast remains an irrevocable and precious element of the Catholic heritage.

Schematic Table Summarizing These Points

I will try to give a clear outline of the different meanings of the word prophecy and of related terms in the following table:

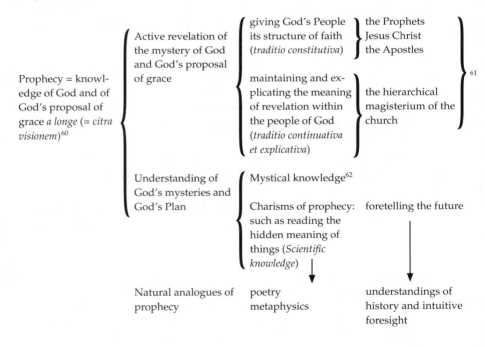

---

[59] I give some examples of this in parts 2 and 3 of this book. A very interesting example of this ambivalence of the meaning of Augustinian texts and themes in ecclesiology,

meriting further study, is given in the work of the General of the Augustinians, Agostino de Favaroni; cf. on this point the study by Turrecremata in *Mansi*, vol. XXX, col. 980f.

[60] Attributed to the Holy Spirit "who speaks through the prophets." It belongs to a theology of the Holy Spirit to explain this attribution and the serious reasons for it, insofar as it is possible.

[61] This prophetic action touches the different ministries linked to what is called *active revelation*; it calls into question the charism of inspiration at the level of the *traditio constitutiva*; the charism of assistance at the level of the *traditio continuativa et explicativa*: this latter charism extending in certain decisive cases all the way to infallibility (which is itself a charism, first, of the church, and then, of the pope; cf. Denzinger, n. 1839).

There is order and continuity in these different prophetic ministries which fill up all of time until we will fully possess the *reality* of what God reveals to us here below. There is the revelation of promise in the Old Testament (itself preceded and contextualized by the traces or fragments of "revelation" that can be found in the non-Judeo-Christian religions and in the philosophers . . .). Then there is the perfect Revelation of Jesus Christ and of his apostles, the revelation that all previous revelation refers to and which the church, in its turn, conserves, lives, and explains (John 16:13). The New Testament contains a prophetic book par excellence, the Apocalypse or Book of Revelation. This book realizes to the maximum the role of prophecy, namely, to make known the meaning of the temporal from the perspective of the eternal. Not that it *predicts* precise events or that one can find exact events that correspond to its particular texts (the tendency of millennialism). It provides the overall meaning of what happens in time from the point of view of the eternal and of the final consummation of all things, on which in fact this last book of the Bible concludes.

[62] What we normally call mystical knowledge obviously has a "prophetic" value, if what we mean by prophecy includes all knowledge of God *a longe*, that is, this side of the full vision of the Divine Reality itself. But we can also note here the prophetic character of everything that the patristic tradition called "mystical": the reading of the Holy Scriptures, the sacramental life, and spiritual experience. In a remarkable article ("Mystique," in *La Vie Spirituelle Supplément* [May 1949], pp. 3–23) Père Louis Bouyer has shown that "mystical" in the vocabulary of the ancients signifies something related to the consummation of the world, basically belonging to the hidden foundation of God's plan—that is, related to the "mystery" of Christ (St. Paul). However, according to the Fathers, everything that can be so qualified then refers to the Christ of the economy [of salvation], and not to a heavenly reality that would be inaccessible in God's positive economy of salvation. We enter into relation with and we have experience of what is given (and foreseen) in the economy—it is that which we affirm and develop. There is a rigorous link between the principle (Christ born of Mary and what he does), the development (what takes place in the time of the church), and the consummation of all things. Christ is really the Alpha and the Omega (Rev 1:8; 21:6; 22:13).

PART TWO

Conditions for Authentic Reform Without Schism

The Problem

The Possibility of Deviations in Any Reform Movement

We know the point of view of the Dean of Blangermont speaking to the country priest of Bernanos: "God preserve us from reformers!" (p. 83). The dialogue continues as follows:

> "Dean, many saints have been reformers."
> "God preserve us from saints as well!"

Clearly that's a bit much. If you want, replace "saints" with "prophets." In any case, it is clear that any effort for reform is going to be dangerous, as will be any prophetic effort. That sort of dynamic always contains the risk of divisions or schism, along with the promise of authentic and fruitful renewal. Examined at its initial impulse, the dynamic of reform is ambivalent, and capable of the worst as well as the best. History is full of examples to illustrate this point. That is why I was led in the first part of this study to review facts that illustrate heresy as well as orthodoxy. Tertullian's thought had potential both for a powerful synthesis of Catholic thought as well as for a schismatic deviation. After the fact, knowing that he became a Montanist, it is easy to find in his early works some elements that point to his later mistakes; however, these elements also could have developed in a perfectly healthy and Catholic direction for the benefit of the church.

By contrast, it is not difficult to find in the writings of St. Cyprian some elements which could easily have made him into another Tertullian, for example, his appeal to *ratio* (reason) in treating the question of the rule of faith and of tradition.[1] This explains why the Donatists claimed St. Cyprian as one of their own. Their ecclesiology is close to his; and

---

[1] See on this point D. Van den Eynde, *Les norms de l'enseignement chrétien dans la littérature patristique des trois premiers siècles* (Gembloux and Paris, 1933), pp. 246–251.

yet St. Augustine was right to emphasize the profound difference of attitude between them and the martyr bishop Cyprian with respect to the requirements for Catholic communion.

The case of the Franciscan reform has often been invoked as an example, as I will do here. Clearly, at the beginning Francis was part of a movement of evangelical life and poverty to which the *Humiliati* and the Poor Catholics (that is, the reconciled Waldenses) also belonged. The ambivalence—even the ambiguity—of the goals of this evangelism were such that the word used to designate the adherents of the evangelical movements that were more or less heretical became the proper name of the thirteenth-century penitent women who fled from the world to lead a life consecrated to God: the Beguines. In his *Life of St. Dominic* (ch. 1), Lacordaire wrote: "How small is the difference between the way great men think and the way public nuisances think. If Peter Waldo had had a bit more virtue and genius, he might have been a St. Dominic or a St. Francis of Assisi. But he gave in to a temptation that has spoiled people of great intelligence throughout history. He thought that it was impossible to save the church through the church . . ."

The intellectualism of St. Anselm and even more the intellectual renewal undertaken by St. Albert and St. Thomas in the thirteenth century were full of dangerous potential. What has been called "Christian rationalism" in their case was potentially a source of serious mistakes, and it was only able to contribute positively and to avoid adulterating Christianity because these great geniuses were also saints whose thought ultimately advanced the development of Christianity. (See below, n. 200.) In this regard, Père Sertillanges said the following: "There was progress here, as always; but the progress of institutions, like the progress of living beings, does not happen without risk; if a wrong turn is taken, then the innovation has to be called a deviation . . ."[2]

We could say as much about people like Luther, Lamennais, Renan, or others as well. These great figures[3] undertook initiatives that, because

---

[2] *Saint Thomas d'Aquin (Les grands coeurs)*, p. 8.

[3] "Great figures" because: "*Nullus potest haeresim struere nisi qui ardentis ingenii est, et habet dona naturae, quae a Deo artifice sunt creata. Talis fuit Valentinus, talis Marcion, quos doctissimos legimus. Talis Bardesanes, cuius etiam philosophi admirantur ingenium*—Nobody can create a heresy except someone of a certain genius, having natural gifts that come from God's creating hand. Such was Valentinus, also Marcion—both very learned persons. Such was Bardesan also, whose intelligence even the philosophers admired" (St. Jerome, *On Hosea*, bk. II, ch. 10, v. 1 [PL 25:902]). Similar words from Augustine: "*Non putetis, fratres, quia potuerint fieri haeres per aliquas parvas animas. Non*

of their dynamic power and their reformist thinking, could have produced a magnificent renewal in the church. Knowing what became of them, it is easy enough to see the beginning of their failures in their first efforts.

Following a very enlightening course given by M. Gilson, I studied the first sermon of Luther (1512) which is printed at the beginning of the Weimar edition of his works (if it really is by Luther). The essential quality of Luther's thought and of his exclusive spirit is already sketched out in this piece. But there are also possibilities here for enlightenment and action in the church which could have been very fruitful. We find here the idea that the purity needed to restore the church depends essentially upon a return to the word of God in its purity. We can't say that this is false; indeed it is both true and profound. But the essence of Lutheran thought is already there in a preliminary state. Still Catholic, and stated in a way that parallels much other orthodox thinking, it represents already a virtual Lutheran teaching on its way to further development.

It would be enough to make the systematic affirmation that the church is pure *only* because of the word and to identify its purity exclusively with *Scriptura sola* (scripture alone) . . . However, knowing what follows, if we examine Luther's teaching at its beginnings, it would be a mistake to see in these beginnings only the later deviation. The first insight had the potential to be either good or bad. It was dangerous, perhaps better, ambivalent. What are the conditions that guide such ambivalence to a Catholic understanding or, by contrast, to a definitively erroneous and false understanding: this is the question to which the present part of my study wishes to give a response.

In any case, we can find in Catholic authors like the humanist Wessel Gansfort theological positions which are fully as demanding as Luther's own most personal statements. This helps to explain, perhaps, (as Möhler remarks) why Catholic theologians hesitated and temporized when confronted with Luther.[4] After all, there are hardly any elements of the Lutheran Reformation which could not be found already (at least as

---

fecerunt haereses nisi magni homines—Brothers, don't think that heresies come from small-minded people. Only great men can create a heresy" (*Enarr. in Ps. 126*, n. 5 [PL 37:1652]). See also Augustine's treatment of the *montes* [mountains] that are not such "*qui suscipiunt pacem populo*—as to sustain peace for the people" (*Tract. in Evang. Joan.*, I, 3 [PL 35:1380]).

[4] From a passage so far unpublished in French, from his *Symbolique*, in J.-A. Möhler, *Die Einheit der Kirche*, ed. Geiselmann (Vienna, 1940), p. 98.

isolated statements) among the theologians or reformers of the fifteenth century, stated with an ambivalence full of various possibilities. Unfortunately the Reformation chose to adopt and employ the least Catholic among them. Denifle, who knew this period well, has noted that the demarcation line in the fifteenth century between authentic reform and a disquieting reform close to schism was very tenuous.[5]

It would be easy to illustrate the same point with the case of England, in an area that is less theological than canonical. Anglican historians have sometimes pointed out traits in the life of the medieval *Ecclesia anglicana* that appear to be claims of independence, from which they draw the conclusion that this church had never been fully "Roman," but had an "Anglican" tendency in the sixteenth-century sense. Today anyone really well informed would consider this interpretation false, because they now see the Middle Ages and the pre-Reformation period in a better light.

In fact, few countries were as "Roman" as medieval England. The truth of the matter is that an ambiguous state of affairs developed by which the church became too involved in temporal things, and by that very fact, the king was overly tempted to intervene in ecclesiastical affairs.[6] Such a state of affairs made for deviant possibilities, and history gave them every chance to develop. These ambiguous potentialities developed especially at the end of the fifteenth and at the beginning of the sixteenth century, but they had existed all through the Middle Ages. The theory that there were "reformers before the Reformation," such as a "Protestant" Francis of Assisi, etc. (something we will look at later on), makes clear enough in its way the ambivalent character of the most interesting spiritual movements in the centuries before the Reformation.

I noted above as a fact of history the deep sympathy between the Augustinian spirit and the reform movements. It is also a fact of history that certain Augustinian themes, including some of his most essential and greatest texts, have encouraged extremely dangerous positions, even clearly heretical ones, right down to the Reformation and even after it. These are authentic texts stating the insights of Augustine, and they genuinely represent his deep and Catholic views. But they have fed into the heretical thinking of people like Berengarius of Tours and Ratramnus. It was authentic texts of Augustine, ambiguous in themselves, that led

---

[5] *Luther und Luthertum in der ersten Entwicklung*, vol. II, 1909, p. 58.

[6] Among others, F. M. Powicke, *The Reformation in England* (Oxford, 1941), explains these factors clearly.

Gotteschalc to his predestinarian ideas and that led Wycliffe and Hus to create an unacceptable ecclesiology—one pregnant with the ideas of the reformers.[7]

The reformers themselves appealed to St. Augustine. They were wrong to do so, sometimes, as in the case of Calvin with respect to the Eucharist. However, with more cogency, Luther began his *Disputatio contra theologiam scholasticam* of 1517 by refusing to admit that Augustine had exaggerated or been unilateral in his Antipelagianism. Abbé A. Humbert has pointed out clearly how Luther's foundational ideas drew upon the *De spiritu et littera* of St. Augustine. Clearly Augustine, who represents a Catholic genius of prodigious potentiality at the beginning of the medieval West, transmitted to thinkers creative ideas whose possibilities were diverse—that is to say, polyvalent.

The Ambivalence of "Seeds"

Let's take another example from the recent past closer to us. All the wayward thinking of Lamennais is already there in the master who gathered around himself at La Chesnaie, among others, Montalembert, de Coux, Lacordaire, Falloux, de Salinis, Rohrbacher, Blanc, Gerbet—that is, the majority of the [French] Catholic elite of the nineteenth century to whom we owe in different ways many of the initiatives from which we profit even today. Lamennais inspired Père Dechamps, the future archbishop of Malines, who signed a series of articles for the *Journal des Flandres* in 1830 as "A.-V. D., disciple of La Mennais." Likewise he inspired Le Sage ten Broek, a convert from Protestantism, who had to wake up Dutch Catholics from their stagnation after three centuries of oppression. Lamennais possessed magnificent prophetic possibilities for renewal.[7a]

Along with a genius for style, Lamennais also had a genius for historical insight. He recognized before others did (and in this he was a *prophet*) the new conditions in which the church found itself following the French Revolution and in which it had to work. Despite all his exaggerations

---

[7] See, e.g., P. De Vooght, "La part de saint Augustin dans le '*de Ecclesia*' de Jean Hus," *Recherches de Théologie ancienne et médiévale*, XIII (1946), pp. 304–336. There are many other cases as well, e.g., that of John, the Abbot of Trastevere, and his *De schismate*, published by Dom Wilmart, and that of Agostino de Favaroni, etc.

[7a] See P.-J.-J. Vrijmoed, *Lamennais avant sa défection et la Néerlande catholique* (Paris, 1930); L. Le Guillou, *L'évolution de la pensée religieuse de F. Lamennais* (Paris, 1966).

and mistakes, he might have become a genuine principle of renewal in the French church; he might have brought to fruition, at least in part, the reform program about which he had dreamed, along with his brother Jean-Marie, the saintly founder of the Brothers of Christian Instruction of Ploermel.

In reality, there is no vital thinking which isn't also dangerous. All seeds in nature are at once both exuberant and fruitful. To cultivate a garden means as much getting rid of useless seeds and inappropriate shoots as nurturing the useful ones. There are no active seeds that are not mixed in with germs as well. Fecundity implies multiple possibilities as well as risks. The only way of killing the germs and avoiding the risks is to pasteurize everything. But in killing the germs, we kill the fecundity as well.

Certain proposals for "tutiorism" (taking the safer path at any cost) unfortunately involve measures of control that are practically the same as sterilization. We might obtain tranquility and a peaceful conformity (at least apparently) by police measures, but at the same time we risk destroying any taste for initiative and any possibilities for creative activity. It has often been noted that some sort of freedom is necessary for the intellectual life. By contrast, there is no more certain means of destroying all thinking than by imposing conformity by demanding that people just parrot what others say without fully understanding.[8] These ideas are

---

[8] See the remarks of Msgr. Amann on the Modernist crisis in *Revue des Sciences religieuses* (1930), p. 636; and Msgr. B. de Solanges, "La crise moderniste et les études ecclésiastiques," *Revue apologétique* (July 1930), pp. 5–30.

Newman quite correctly wrote: "A man of ideas hopes that his ideas are true, believes that they are useful, desires that they will be discussed, but is ready to give them up if they are judged wrong or dangerous. He would not dare to risk entering into controversy if he knew that a supreme sovereign authority is watching every word he says and shows either disapproval or consent for every word he says. In that case, he would be fighting, like the Persians, under the scourge of the whip, and we could truthfully say that his freedom of intelligence had died under the lash . . . Why were the medieval schools so vigorous? Because they were left free to explore, because the disputants didn't feel a bit in their mouth to restrain every word they said. Only after a certain time, if a dispute became dangerous and one of the disputants became obstinate, would Rome intervene" (cited in P. Thureau-Dangin, *Newman catholique d'après des documents nouveaux*, 3rd ed. [Paris, 1912], pp. 16–17). Cf. J. Guitton, *La philosophie de Newman* (Paris, 1933), pp. 170–171.

Finally, let me introduce this appropriate phrase of Leo XIII: "You have to give scholars time to think and to make mistakes" (quoted by Msgr. Keppler, *Vraie et fausse réforme*, trans. by C. Bègue [Fribourg, 1903], p. 31).

not transposable to the order of religion, because we have to admit the "conformity" of faith in the realm of dogma properly so called—a conformity for which the magisterium is the guardian and a guarantee.

But this comparison to natural seeds is somehow not enough. Nature knows what it is doing. Someone who plants an acorn will get an oak tree and not a plum tree. Yet in the spiritual realm there is less certainty. We have to take into account not only the unpredictable freedom of personal initiatives but also the power and ambivalence of original thinking. Insofar as new thinking does not foretell exactly what it will bring forth, it is understandable to wonder what it will express and produce. Certainly this is why the church, which does not appreciate surprises and whose responsibilities are too heavy to allow the faithful to follow approaches that might lead to impasses or errors, so often takes a skeptical attitude toward novelties, no matter how interesting they may appear to be. The church likes things defined, things that manifest clearly what they imply and that don't hold surprises. Above all, Rome, which has the principal responsibility for the Catholic communion and thus a responsibility to "test spirits," is reticent about whatever is new. Perhaps this is one of the reasons why Rome has long shown so much hesitation with respect to "ecumenism."

Yet the Holy Spirit is at work within ecumenism, which has the potential for a great future. But it must be recognized that the name itself doesn't specify clearly what it contains and what it might yield. (I wrote this before the Instruction of the Holy Office, dated December 20, 1949, and published February 28, 1950. It is now clear, I think, that John XXIII and the Second Vatican Council brought about a new situation for ecumenism, fully open to the future.)

Möhler's Distinction:
Gegensatz *(Contrast) and* Widerspruch *(Contradiction)*

In order to further the study of this ambivalence of reactive and dynamic elements, an overall perspective on development and progress in the church would be needed. There are interesting and illuminating insights in Möhler's distinction between *Gegensatz* and *Widerspruch*— ideas that Cardinal Journet has felicitously rendered by the words *contrast* and *contradiction*.[9] According to Möhler, it is normal for the church

[9] For this distinction, see Möhler, *L'unité dans l'Eglise* (*Unam Sanctam* 2 [Paris, 1938]), § 47; J. R. Geiselmann, *Johann Adam Möhler, Die Einheit der Kirche und die*

to contain a multiplicity of elements and so to have diverse points of view and contrasts (*Gegensätze*) because the church is made up of finite realities. These contrasts are healthy and are an aspect of life and of progress. In the end, all progress is dialectical and takes place through a process of surpassing what went before, under pressure from elements that prove unsatisfactory and that call for improvement.

That is the role of the reactive and dynamic factors, of the potentialities, *within the church.*[10] If this yeast—this internal pressure—was eliminated, the very moving force of development would be nullified. However, as Möhler says, there is the danger that what are *contrasts* might become *contradictions.* If these reactive and dynamic elements destroy the communion of the whole, if they become selfishly isolated and, refusing to acknowledge their links with others and with the whole tradition, they make themselves into autonomous principles, then they turn into heresy and break the unity of the church.[11]

The *Widerspruch* (contradiction) is a *Gegensatz* (contrast) that has fallen out of the unity of the whole and developed for its own sake. This is what effectively happens in heresy or schism: the ambivalence that is inherent in the dynamic potentialities (potential elements of progress) is tragically carried in a direction that is wrong and definitively unacceptable.

What I have sketched here in these several pages on the ambivalence of *seeds* in the order of thought seems to correspond to a difficulty raised by Cardinal Journet with respect to an idea that I expressed in *Chrétiens désunis.* Cardinal Journet presents my position like this:

> Concerned to be as courteous and benevolent as possible, the author sometimes seems to distinguish two moments within the spiritual attitude that is at the source of dissident positions, for example, at the beginning of Luther's or Calvin's break. There is, first, the extremely

---

Wiedervereinigung der Konfessionen (Vienna, 1940), pp. 47f., 55, n. 1, and especially 137–166. This latter study goes into this question the most deeply. — C. Journet, *L'Eglise du Verbe incarné,* vol. I (Paris, 1941), p. 59.

[10] Geiselmann clearly shows that by his distinction between the *Gegensätze* (contrasts within and essential to the church) and the *Widersprüche* (extrinsic and accidental contradictions), Möhler distanced himself both from Schelling (who succeeded his professor, Drey) and from Hegel. Möhler was able to avoid making development depend upon oppositions extrinsic to the church (heresies).

[11] See my treatment, "L'hérésie, déchirement de l'unité," in the 1st ed. of *Esquisses du mystère de l'Eglise* (*Unam Sanctam,* 8 [Paris, 1941]), pp. 149–165; Geiselmann, op. cit., pp. 49f.

vivid perception of an authentically Christian truth: the gratuity of justification for Luther or the transcendence of divine holiness for Calvin. Then there is a second stage which consists in detaching this truth, pulling it out of the organic complex of the revealed deposit of faith in which it has been given to us, so as to let it live separately, and consequently to falsify its meaning. From this point of view, one might say that "at the beginning of the great secessions there is generally an authentic spiritual feeling and, in so far as it is positive and pure, it is also authentically Catholic"; or one might also say that Lutheranism is true "as a spiritual attitude," but that the error that precisely constitutes Lutheranism comes from the fact that "Luther, only taking into account his own experience with its violent, personal characteristics, projects it into an abstract and universal theological doctrine"; or again, that "what is true in Lutheran religious experience is missing in the Catholic Church and demands, by its very nature, to be re-integrated."[12]

And Journet criticizes this position in the following way:

> For my part, it seems more exact to consider the original intuition, the "seminal reason," from which Lutheranism arises as something indivisible that can't be broken down into two aspects—one concerning an authentically Christian truth and the other blocking out with this truth the errors that spoil it. I think that the primitive Lutheran intuition about justification was intrinsically wrong in itself, from the fact that it associated inseparably gratuity and the forensic nature of justification; that the fundamental Barthian intuition is false in itself, from the fact that it associates inseparably the transcendence and the non-communicability of divine holiness. The root idea of Lutheranism, of Calvinism, of Barthianism, etc., seems to me to be a doubtlessly complex but nonetheless singular concept: *the unique idea and a unique experience* of the truth *that is deformed*, not as the juxtaposition of two ideas or two experiences, one true and the other false.[13]

This is not exactly how I see things, at least in Luther's case. It seems to me that there is from the beginning an insight whose richness includes

---

[12] Cf. C. Journet, *L'Eglise du Verbe incarné*, vol. I, p. 56.

[13] Cf. C. Journet, op. cit., pp. 56–57. I could more easily concede what Journet says about Barth, whose original intuition (which itself contains a venerable part of the truth) was taken *ab ovo* [hatched from the egg] from a tradition that had already deviated from the initial positions of the Protestant Reformers.

some ambiguity, and that this ambiguity exists not only with Luther before his break with the church but also to some degree with Augustine and the Augustinian tradition. Insofar as such an ambivalent insight or affirmation is held within the church's communion, it benefits from the regulation of the whole and is complemented by different values within the whole. By contrast, there is a moment which is interesting to observe for those who want to grasp it but also (more important) for whoever is called to live it and not to lose it.[14] This is the moment where communion risks becoming broken because the idea goes wrong, and where the idea goes wrong because the communion is already at the breaking point. The ambivalence of the original perception or, if you like, of the *seed* (Cardinal Journet speaks of the "seminal reason") then develops in a sense which very quickly becomes heretical.

When the reactive and dynamic (or, if you like, the antithetical and anticonformist) elements had been expressed in an excessive way and, even more, when such elements had evolved into "contradictions" and were at the point of turning into erroneous doctrine, it is evident that the church reacted defensively. If the church failed to react, it would only be because the church was dead or moribund or lethargic. Its reaction usually translates into condemnations and sometimes into the solemn formulation of a doctrine that seems endangered. But there are two things to fear in this case.

Two Types of One-Sidedness

First, there is the possibility that this formulation, made in reaction to an error characterized by unilateralism, should itself become unilateral in its expression. Next, there is the possibility that the condemnation might include in its condemnation of the erroneous reactive element the seeds of truth as well, whose original ambivalence unfortunately became deviant. Let me briefly explain these two points.

In an extremely rich study that has great significance,[15] Père de Lubac has shown how the spiritualism of Berengarius of Tours, in treating the

---

[14] Père T. Chifflot made this effort to understand Luther in an article that is full of ideas for those who really want to understand where Luther came from: "Luther et l'Evangile: La tentation du Publicain," in *La Vie Intellectuelle* (March 1948), pp. 6f. (I also go into this in my part 3 [not included in this translation].)

[15] Henri de Lubac, *Corpus mysticum: L'eucharistie et l'Eglise au moyen âge*, 2nd ed. (Paris, 1949), *passim* and also pp. 255f. [Eng. trans., *Corpus Mysticum: The Eucharist*

sacrament of the Eucharist (leading to a misunderstanding of the reality of the presence of Christ), had led Catholic theologians to insist on the "real presence." This brought them to change in important ways the economy of the theology of the Eucharist with respect to ecclesiology. It is possible to think, and I am more and more inclined to do so, that this change was not completely for the better.

What happened in the eleventh and twelfth centuries on this point became greatly amplified in the theology of the Counter-Reformation. Under the appearance of being an irenic theology about the whole reality of the Eucharist, it became in reality a polemic theology giving emphasis to controversial points (or points misunderstood by the Protestants) to the practical exclusion of other points of view. The Protestants, for their part, often added to the unilateralism of their fundamental options new one-sided positions motivated by their desire to oppose and distinguish themselves from the Roman Church even more. This is how Calvin came to drop the episcopate and how several regions in Germany also did the same in reaction to the Interim of Augsburg and to the pacifying politics of Melanchthon.

There is, however, a radical difference between heretical unilateralism, on the one hand, and the unilateralism that orthodox theology may develop in reaction to heresy, on the other. (I am responding here to another critique of my *Chrétiens désunis*, made in *Revue thomiste* [1938], pp. 386f.) The unilateralism of heresy affects elements in the apostolic deposit that touch upon the structure or the very existence of true affirmations. For example, the unilateralism of Berengarius touched upon the positions bearing upon the substantial presence of Christ in the Eucharist. The unilateralism of the theology that, in reacting to Berengarius, lost something of an ancient sacramental or "mystical" meaning of the Eucharist did not touch any of the affirmations which concern the substance of the deposit of faith, but only certain dimensions (in depth and scope) of the understanding that the Fathers and the ancient theological and monastic tradition had formulated about it. The loss in the two cases is not on the same level. Canon Draguet remarks that the statements of the magisterium on the question of development or dogmatic progress

---

and the Church in the Middle Ages, trans. Gemma Simmonds (Notre Dame, IN: University of Notre Dame Press, 2007)]. See also F. Holböck, *Der eucharistische und der mystiche Leib Christi in ihren Beziehungen zueinander nach der Lehre der Frühscholastik* (Rome, 1941).

always insist on the aspect of immutability.[16] He explains and justifies this fact (in which there is a certain unilateralism) with the following consideration: "Of the two aspects of dogma, the aspect of immutability is the only one to possess a vital significance for the church"; what he means by *"vital* significance" is its structural and existential importance.

This remark clarifies things. You can easily see how any unilateralism that affirms development and change, while satisfying historians, might turn into heresy; while a unilateralism in the sense of immutability, while giving historians some difficulties, saves a principle of existence and structure for the church. It is easy and perhaps profitable to consider in the light of this idea other facts that we encounter in the domain of theology. For example, on the subject of ecumenism or the place of the laity in the church, these same things could apply. Further, I said in the preface of this book that Catholic theology has been interested in the *structure* of the Church up until now, and very little interested in its *life . . .*

The second danger that I pointed out is situated at the level of the *bene esse* (the better well-being) of doctrine, not the *esse* (being) of dogma itself. My point is this: the condemnation of an error should not cast a shadow over what is valuable in its insights, despite proposals that unfortunately have turned into an erroneous unilateralism. A condemnation should not damage the development of these insights or of these demands with respect to what is true about them. The first consequence of an error is to change the concrete circumstances of doctrinal work—to change the sense or rather the meaning of words (what they *evoke*, rather than what they *say*), the "problematic," that is, the very context of the questions. In certain respects, thought loses the supple freedom that a kind of *innocence* had formerly given it. History seems to show that, after a condemnation, it becomes difficult to speak of certain things. Even some authentic things become shadowed by the suspicion that strikes at the very roots from which errors have emerged, and yet, despite some unfortunate mistakes, many elements remain perfectly viable and fecund.

Of course, there is no general rule, and the church has long practiced the legal principle of *abusus non tollit usum* (an abuse does not take away the right use of a thing). We saw above (p. 177) that Montanism did not impede Catholic teachers from claiming the charism of prophecy for the church and its faithful. However, after Arianism, the text of John 14:28, "the Father is greater than I," concerning the relation of the eternal Son to the Father, was no longer accepted to mean what the Antenicene

---

[16] Cf. *Apologétique* (Paris, 1937), pp. 1169 and 1177.

Fathers (and certain ones of the generation of Nicaea) meant by it (without becoming unorthodox).[17] The definition of Nicaea brought a certain discredit to the ancient Christian prayer which gave glory to the Father *through the Son* and the Holy Spirit (in conformity with the order of the "economy"), rather than to the Father, to the Son, and to the Holy Spirit.[18] The lay preachers and the "apostolic" sects of the twelfth and thirteenth centuries, especially the Waldensians, discredited lay preaching and led the church to place certain limitations upon lay preaching.[19] The way in which the Hussites and the Utraquists of Bohemia demanded communion under both species in the fifteenth century, linking this practice to the reality of the communion, brought Rome to harden its position on this point in such a way as to bring about grave consequences.[20] After the errors of the Reformation concerning the priesthood of the faithful (errors that touched the structure of the church), people talked less in theology about the common priesthood of all Christians.[21]

We saw above that the possibilities for self-criticism in the church practically dried up following the excessive criticisms of Luther and the attacks of Voltaire. As a witness of the events in question, Massoulié noted that after the quarrel about pure love and quietism, which was largely a stupid quarrel, people hardly dared to speak about "peace of soul," etc.[22] A bit later, some excesses and serious mistakes in the liturgical demands of the Jansenists brought into discredit for a time any calls for liturgical change (when there were interesting possibilities) . . . This list could be much longer, and I could find other examples in the history of the Reformation, the initiatives of national churches or in Episcopalian ecclesiology, the question of Modernism and even Le Sillon, etc.

---

[17] Cf. C. H. Turner, *Catholic and Apostolic*, pp. 130–131.

[18] On this topic, see J. Jungmann, *Die Stellung Christi im liturgischen Gebet* (Munster, 1925), and J. Lebreton in *Revue des Sciences religieuses* (1924), pp, 5f., 97f.; *Revue de l'Histoire ecclésiastique* (1924), pp. 5f.; B. Botte, *Cours et Conférences: Semaines liturgiques*, vol. 6 (1928), pp. 107f.; etc.

[19] Cf. L. Spätling, *De Apostolicis, Pseudoapostolis, Apostolinis* (Munich, 1947), esp. p. 109.

[20] Cf. G. Constant, *Concession à l'Allemagne de la communion sous les deux espèces* (Paris, 1923), vol. I, p. 5.— In 1452, at the coronation of the emperor in Rome, the traditional rite of communion under the two species was suppressed (J. Hashagen, *Staat und Kirche vor der Reformation*, p. 513).

[21] See the remark of P. Galtier, *Revue d'ascétique et de mystique* (1923), pp. 6–7.

[22] Cited by F. Florand in his preface to the *Méditations* of Massoulié (Paris, 1934), p. 93.

A certain discounting of motives or values that are in themselves valid, but that appear to some to be compromised by their similarity to ideas that are wrong, proceeds from a desire for safety, which is understandable but has to be kept in its place. For disguised as prudence, faithfulness, or wisdom, this desire for safety can lead to a veritable timidity, a prejudice toward restricting what ought to be a wholehearted passion for the truth and for everything that the church carries within itself that has a potential for growth and for fullness of life. The church ought to be Catholic and missionary not only on the level of pastoral ministry but also on the level of ideas and truth.

In this respect, we can appreciate this profound thought of Emile Mersch (who died too soon): "Truth and error are not separated by an intermediate zone which is neither the one nor the other, a zone which it would be prudent to avoid. Truth and error touch on the same line: the truth goes all the way to the beginning of error, excluding it of course; but to stop too soon, even if the motive is to distance oneself from error, would be to fall into error. It would mean calling false that which is still true."[23]

There are two possible attitudes, each one justified according to its function in the church. One is the attitude of the pastor who ought to and wants to assure peace and security for his flock. For that, he wants to maintain a zone of safety between his people and error; he avoids any risks. This is why, at least in the modern period, we hear the phrase "theologians who are *sure*"; they have been given preference over the others. But the duty to go further remains, and there is a function in the church that corresponds to that. For those who exercise it, there is no zone of security (no sort of *no man's land*) between orthodox positions and errors.

Such a zone of security may appear to be good, because it allows us to keep the enemy at a distance. But those who fight for the church at its frontiers, to the degree that they are apostolic and missionary, find themselves "in contact," on the front line, face-to-face. They find themselves *with the obligation to hold firm* on this slim line which makes the difference between being inside or outside the church. If they go too far, they have fallen into error; but if they fail to move, they have not gone far enough. They have not allowed truth to reach the full extent of its expression.

---

[23] Emile Mersch, S.J., *La théologie du Corps mystique* (Brussels and Paris, 1944), vol. 1, p. 93. [Eng. trans., *The Theology of the Mystical Body*, trans. Cyril Vollert (St. Louis: Herder, 1951)].

Under the appearance of faithful service, we can risk being insufficient in our service. This precisely is the prophetic line, the line of the church on the march, the church at its frontiers. This line includes a sort of ambivalence (unavoidable) because it is the line of contact in the division between authentic cultural progress and a loss of perspective. It imposes on those whose vocation is to take dangerous positions in the avant-garde a role that is genuinely dangerous. Anyone who has been at war, carrying in himself the whole weight of his country, discovers that there is nothing between his body and the enemy. He places himself, in a precarious service, at the front line of his country . . .

This explains why it is of immense interest to discover the conditions for a reform that either has a chance to be realized *inside the church* or, on the contrary, to lead to disruption. How can somebody risk either remaining in the church or going beyond that line and leaving the church, even if he finds himself on the front line? How can somebody be, if necessary, in the avant-garde without becoming a renegade? In sum, what are the conditions for reform without schism?

It seems to me that these conditions can be reduced to four principal ones. However, in his review of the first edition, Louis Bouyer correctly observed that there ought to be a fifth: good sense. I am willing to accept that observation.

FIRST CONDITION

The Primacy of Charity
and of Pastoral Concerns

The Prophetic Initiative Should Not Develop into a System

The reform spirit lives off prophecy. The reformer, even if he is not a prophet in the strict sense of the word, shares the character of prophets. He is a "twice born" person, aware of his mission, captivated by his idea. For these reasons he is usually disposed to be solitary, opposed to the given state of affairs, and does not feel himself fully at home in the concrete church. Think of Savonarola confronted with Alexander VI, or in our day, someone like the novelist Bernanos. As I said, the prophet is not concerned with the balance or the harmony of his message; he is more likely inclined to overstate it in an absolute way. Likewise he is tempted to fall into unilateralism, that is, to see only one aspect of things. If he tries to systematize or even formulate his conviction, he tends to fall into a unitraditionalism—an insistence on one point of view. Without going as far as Luther, who is an extreme example, we can use the examples of the intolerant spirit of Peter Damian or even St. Bernard, as well as the tendency of St. Francis to reduce everything to a single theme (poverty). Great reformers generally are simplifiers.[24] This can be a strength but also a danger. As has been said, heresies arise "from deductions pursued in one direction only, beginning with a principle of tradition or of science

---

[24] Cf. Jean Guitton, "L'Evangile captif," *Jeunesse de l'Eglise* (cahier 10), p. 102.

isolated from everything else, exalted as absolute truth; from this, one reasons out conclusions that are incompatible with the synthetic order of religion and with traditional teaching."[25]

The intuition of the "prophet" needs to develop, but not in an abstract fashion or into a system. The prophetic intuition should not become in itself and for itself a tradition or a school. It risks turning into a sect. It should not become in itself and for itself a corpus, but should rather become incorporated into the existing body of the church. The prophetic perception certainly has to develop, but it shouldn't develop for its own sake; it needs a development within the church, within the existing life of the concrete church. It should not result in an ecclesial novelty, but rather should *renew* the church as an existing reality. The church preexists the reform effort, and therefore it is not the object of discovery, retrieval, or creation.

Möhler, who had a vivid appreciation for the concrete reality of the church, a son's confidence and lively concern for all the church's needs,[26] based his criticism of heresy upon these same points (rooting himself in the spirit of the Fathers).[27] "Heresy is generally the tendency to explain Christianity in terms of ideas, without taking care to draw upon the life of the Christian community and everything that belongs to that life."[28] Instead of taking Christianity as something *given* in the church, as an *existing reality* that needs to be assimilated, the heretic considers the church as a rational *object* constructed by the intelligence. For the heretic, critical analysis and constructive ideas come first. For the faithful, acceptance of what is given and of the life *within* the Christian reality at the heart of the church is first, and reasoning can only come second. The faithful express themselves with great freedom, but *within the church* and

---

[25] Alfred Loisy, *L'Evangile et l'Eglise*, p. 143 (3rd ed., p. 187). On this theme of heresy-ecclesial alienation, cf. *Chrétiens désunis* (1937), pp. 49f., 311f.

[26] These are traits that are noteworthy in all of his writings, both historical and theological. Cf. also *Gesammelte Aktenstücke und Briefe*, ed. S. Lösch, vol. I, pp. 292f., 373f. (a letter to his brother), 484–485; and Minon in *Ephem. théol. lovan* (1939), pp. 351–352.

[27] See especially *L'Unité dans l'Eglise*, § 18f., and M.-J. Congar, "L'esprit des Pères d'après Möhler," *La Vie Spirituelle, Supplément* (April 1938), pp. 1–25, reprinted in *Esquisses du mystère de l'Eglise*, 1st ed., pp. 129–148; and "L'hérésie, déchirerment de l'unité," in *L'Eglise est une: Hommage à Möhler* (Paris, 1939), pp. 255–269, reprinted in *Esquisses*, pp. 149–165.

[28] *L'Unité dans l'Eglise* (*Unam Sanctam*, 2), trans. A. de Lilienfeld, § 18, p. 57.

according to the spirit of the church. For the heretic, the church is some-thing to rediscover or reconstruct;[29] for the faithful, the church exists concretely, calling the faithful to serve it, nourish it, and work within it.

So for the reformer who wants to remain in harmony with the Catholic communion, the church has to remain a *given*, not only intellectually but also existentially. The reformer can never step outside the church to judge it, but can only remain committed *within* its existing conditions, espe-cially if there is need for some dimension of reform. Every reform that is the fruit of pure deduction, like any system elaborated purely by mental reflection, even if the deduction and the construction are drawn from dogmatic sources, will almost infallibly lead to something that will betray the concrete reality of the church and that the church will reject. We will meet examples of this kind of initiative later on in this study (particularly with respect to the fourth condition). But even now, I can give the example here of Saint-Cyran and the Jansenists, without failing to recognize the religious grandeur of their enterprise.[29a]

We have already seen, following Denifle, that in the disquiet of the fifteenth century, there was only a thin line between authentic reform and reforms that upset everything. Denifle remarked that what kept authentic reform within healthy limits was a sense of the church. He put it this way: to have a sense of the church is to never forget the family household, never become a stranger to the church, never critique the church *from outside*, like someone who could kiss his family good-bye and go his own way without ever worrying about them again.[30] This idea is similar to what Lacordaire said about Peter Waldo, in contrast to St. Dominic and St. Francis: "[Waldo] believed that it was impossible to save the church *through the church*." No better way to express the obligation

---

[29] "Christianity has to be sought and discovered—this was the preoccupation of influential academics. But that would suppose that Christianity might be lost bit by bit, or even that it might disappear after a certain period of time, which implies the necessity of searching for and rediscovering it. This again is in contradiction to the church's principles, which profess that the true doctrine is always present in the church and can never fail. The heretic, instead of doing what a true Catholic would do, that is, instead of wondering what the church teaches and what it has always taught, wonders instead what ideas can be called Christian. The heretic thus trans-forms the Catholic norm, which is the determination of its teaching based on history, into a tendency that is purely speculative" (*L'Unité dans l'Eglise*, op. cit., § 18, p. 58).

[29a] See H. de Lubac, *Méditation sur l'Eglise*, p. 188.

[30] *Luther und Luthertum*, vol. II (1909), p. 58.

upon the reformer not to operate on an idea of the church that he creates for himself, but rather always to take the existing church as a concrete reality. St. Augustine emphasized this, in opposition to the Donatists, by insisting on the need to maintain communion with imperfect brothers and sisters inside an imperfect church.

This is not easy to do, since what needs to be reformed in one or another of its aspects is precisely the concrete church itself. At one and the same time, we have to accept the church and yet not accept it *as such*. If you don't accept it, you will have something other than the church (unless you fail completely at initiating something or other) and will not be reforming the church as such. But then if you accept the church as it is, you won't change anything and you will not manage to reform it. What is needed is not to change the church but rather something within it. We don't need to create *another church*; what we need to some degree is a church that is *other* . . . That is the problem behind this entire book, and I have already given the ideal solution in speaking of a double fidelity: either superficial or profound. The concrete aspect of this problem is what I am currently addressing. We are looking for a kind of phenomenology of behaviors needed for *profound* fidelity. Concretely, what are the attitudes that maintain the communion of the church by way of this fidelity? The first condition appears to me to be to insist upon a certain primacy of charity and of pastoral concern.

Successful Reforms Were Motivated by Pastoral Concern

While calling into question some element within the church, we can't call the church into question. We can seek to purify the church but not to make an ideology out of "purity." While beginning with a "return to the sources" that implies an activity of intelligent reflection, we cannot afford to end up with an abstract program that lacks roots in the ground of tradition or lacks living energy. We cannot afford to deviate from tradition, led away purely by intellectual creativity. We know that intelligence guides us and that rules, even if they come from elsewhere, need to be judged intelligently. We will see later (fourth condition) that good theology, nourished by sources and above all by good ecclesiology, is one of the most effective guarantees of a faithful reform effort. But I will show that intellectual effort without charity easily leads to failing to recognize the concrete reality and the given quality of the church. By contrast, reforms that have succeeded within the church are those which have been made with concern for the concrete need of souls, in a pastoral perspective, aiming for holiness.

The model for reforms of this kind can be found in the actions of St. Bernard or of St. Francis of Assisi. When we compare Francis's letters,[31] for example, his "Letter to All the Authorities," with Luther's appeal "To the Christian Nobility of the German Nation," we can see the difference between a reform aiming at holiness and a reform aiming at criticism. We could look at the letter of St. Nicholas of Flue to the people of Bern[32] or the letters of Savonarola to the Christian princes—the Emperor, the French king, and the King and Queen of Spain.[33] The contrast is easy to see and the analysis has already been done[34] between Luther, on the one side, and the Catholic saints who were reformers, on the other side. These latter, consenting to the church's authority, sought to exert themselves and perfect themselves, to engage and perfect others in the Christian faith, and to better the church through the church.

"Every true and lasting reform (*jede wahre und dauernde Reform*)," wrote Pius XI, "in the last analysis had its point of departure in holiness, in persons who were inflamed and impelled by the love of God and neighbor. Generous, ready to listen to every call from God and to respond immediately within themselves, and yet sure of themselves because sure of their vocation, they grew to become true lights and sources of renewal for their time. By contrast, where the zeal of the reformer (*der Reformeifer*) did not arise from personal purity, but was the expression and the outburst of passion, it was a source of disturbance rather than illumination, destructive rather than constructive, and more than once the source of

---

[31] Cf. J. Joergensen, *Saint François d'Assise*, see ch. 2, pp. 398f. *L'Epistola ad populorum rectores* is considered of dubious authenticity by Boehmer, *Analekten zur Geschichte des Franciscus von Assisi* (1904), pp. 70–71.

[32] Letter of Dec. 4, 1482. Cf. Charles Journet, *Saint Nicolas de Flue*, 2nd ed., pp. 83f. and 138–139 (text).

[33] See the text (with a theological commentary by Père Hurtaud) in *Revue Thomiste* (1900).

[34] See in particular K. Germanus, *Reformatorenbilder: Historische Vorträge über katholische Reformatoren und Martin Luther* (Freiburg im Breisgau, 1883). In his manner of treating Luther, the author (who in reality is H. Grisar) follows the traces of Döllinger and Janssen. Over against the Protestant reformer, he places the luminous figures of St. Gregory the Great (1st conference), Canisius (4th conference), St. Charles Borromeo (5th conference), St. Vincent De Paul (6th conference), and finally all the saints of the century of the Counter-Reform, 1540–1640 (7th and 8th conferences). The ensemble of these studies addresses the sense of the present paragraph.

distortions more damaging than the evils to which they claimed to bring a remedy."[35]

A certain lack of the concrete meaning of the church and, more precisely, of its apostolic and pastoral meaning is notable among several reformers who finally left the church. Renan, Döllinger, and Loisy, for example, were predominantly intellectual rather than priestly—something perhaps linked to their vocation as professors, but they also manifested a lack of pastoral preoccupation and a kind of fear concerning the apostolic calling.[36]

---

[35] Pope Pius XI, Encyclical *Mit brennender Sorge* (March 14, 1937), *Acta Apostolicae Sedis* (1937), p. 154. — "If, instead of resting in the heart, purity rises to the head, it creates sectarians and heretics" (Jacques Maritain, *Humanisme intégral*, p. 265).

In the article, "Reformkatholizismus," *Die Religion in Geschichte und Gegenwart*, vol. IV, Fr. Heiler makes profound and correct remarks in this same sense: "The reform efforts (of Modernism) like the earlier ones of Enlightenment theology and of the Old Catholics, were, in part, too rational and too doctrinal; they did not spring from the religious center of the Catholic Church, from Christological mysticism, and from a thirst for holiness. The very controversial work of Bishop Keppler, *Wahre und falsche Reform* (1903), had in fact put its finger in a wound of the Catholic Reform . . . Without doubt history teaches us this, that the Roman Church cannot be reformed through movements that are governed by rational-critical tendencies, like the Enlightenment, the Old Catholics, and Reform Catholicism. A new situation can only come about from a fundamentally religious grasp and affirmation of the ideal of full and entire catholicity and, finally, from the Catholic ideal of holiness. What Newman said in his Anglican period regarding the Oxford Movement applies to all reform movements in the Roman Church: 'If we are holy, all will go well' " (col. 1800–1801).

[36] For Renan, cf. the episode with M. Gottofrey in *Souvenirs d'enfance et de jeunesse*, p. 260. For Döllinger, cf. G. Goyau, *L'Allemagne religieuse: le Catholicisme*, vol. II, p. 87, and vol. IV, pp. 245–246; F. Mourret, *Le Concile du Vatican d'après des documents inédits* (Paris, 1919), pp. 74f.; Döllinger said that he became a priest only in order to be a theologian.

As to Loisy, people who knew him told me things of the same kind, which show up here and there (e.g., in Rivière, Guitton) and can be read into his *Mémoires* (see, e.g., vol. I, pp. 82, 134). It was in thinking of Loisy that Père Portal, speaking to young priests who were headed for graduate studies in religion, counseled them always to stay involved in some pastoral ministry. (Cf. H. Hemmer, *M. Portal, prêtre de la mission* [Paris, 1948], p. 110.) Likewise see the testimony of Bishop Chevrot in E. Poulat, *Histoire dogmatique et critique de la crise moderniste* (Paris, 1962), vol. I, p. 315 note and pp. 314–315. Père Lévie (*Sous les yeux de l'incroyant* [Brussels and Paris, 1944], pp. 180–203) brings up Loisy's concern for his personal freedom, his tendency to isolate himself and, at the same time, to put himself forward, plus his rigid idea of intellectual sincerity that failed to understand the church's pastoral point of view. Finally, despite everything else, Loisy had little piety and almost no realistic idea of spiritual

By contrast, apostolic and pastoral concern puts us at the heart of the concrete church, making thinking and planning fruitful in terms of practical measures that can avoid the fantasies, the excesses, or the unilateralism of personal enthusiasms, as well as avoid a fixation on one single aspect or one single case. This same pastoral concern is manifest also in the realism of points of view tending toward balance or equilibrium. These are measures that spontaneously develop both an orientation toward real life with respect to common everyday needs and a sense of responsibility and of the concrete consequences for the options taken. Intellectuals, religious persons who do not have a concrete apostolic mission or who have one that does not involve direct pastoral care, can easily be more daring and original than priests charged with pastoral responsibilities. There will surely be a difference between the initiatives of the former and the latter, experienced by both with a certain discomfort.[37]

Origen speaks in a different way than St. Irenaeus, who is a bishop; and Tertullian in a way different than St. Cyprian . . . As M. Pontet remarks,[38] St. Augustine speaks differently in his speculative treatises, especially on polemical issues, than in his sermons. In the sermons he no longer has the same edge that we find in his speculative statements:

---

things. Loisy was fervent in his way: he wanted to serve the church (*Mémoires*, vol. I, pp. 363–364), he was a parish priest for two years, and he scrupulously carried out his mandate of teaching religion at the Dominican Sisters of Neuilly; and, in contrast to Döllinger, he would have accepted a small diocese (Monaco). But this pastoral element remained exterior to his thinking, which itself stayed completely critical and cerebral.

Someone like Günther also lacked a sense of the church and of its life: cf. E. Winter, *Der geistige Entwicklung Anton Günthers und seiner Schule* (Paderborn, 1931), p. 16. — By contrast, a profound sense of the meaning of the church (cf. *supra*, n. 26) saved Möhler from developing in an unhealthy direction, which his earliest thinking might have suggested as possible.

[37] Allow me to point out an article of mine in *Prêtres diocésains* (Feb. 1949), pp. 81–97: "Sur deux aspects du travail apostolique: le prêtre chef de peuple et apôtre," reprinted in *Sacerdoce et Laïcat* (Paris, 1962), pp. 207–226.

[38] M. Pontet, *L'exégèse de saint Augustin prédicateur* (Paris, 1946), pp. 511f. (cited in this same sense by Rottmaner). — People say that Zwingli as a preacher and pastor spoke of the sacraments more positively than Zwingli as a systematic theologian and polemicist. Also Luther spoke in a more Catholic way about faith and works when he was speaking from a pastoral point of view (cf. H. Grisar, *Martin Luther*, French trans., P. Mazoyer [Paris, 1930], p. 96; O. Scheel, *Die Anschauungen Augustins über Christi Person und Werk* (Leipzig, 1901), p. 391.

"Unknown to himself, his audience influences him and puts him on a more balanced path." Don't we say with a bit of humor that in theology we should be Predestinarians and in pastoral care Pelagians? . . . One of the reasons scholasticism developed a greater and greater subtlety was that it had become essentially the activity of religious and of university professors. The genuine prophetic spirit needs the pastoral.

In what we call the Counter-Reformation, we find two rather different things. On the one hand, there is first an enormous effort addressed to apologetics and theology in the wake of the challenge of the Reformation; on the other hand, there is a second great effort to bring about pastoral and religious renewal aiming at holiness. This second effort, which began well before the break with Luther, continued during and after the Council of Trent. It nourished the genuine reform of the church and prepared the spiritual flowering of the seventeenth century in France. However, when we look at the genuine reform initiatives of Olier or of St. Vincent de Paul, we see that their source is not to be found in a critical point of view or in an idea, but rather in their pastoral and missionary experience. M. Olier's experience came from Cévennes, the area of Nantes and Brittany,[39] while Vincent de Paul's experience, shaped by different areas of the Gondi region (Folleville in Picardy, Châtillon, etc.), extended across the whole of France. Blessed John of Avila, whose reforming ideas seem remarkable even today,[40] would have preferred to go as a missionary to evangelize America, and he had actually done missionary work in Andalucia and Extremadura.

Pastoral ministry is a great teacher of what is true. I am not alone in remarking that Protestant pastors are often distant from us in their way of thinking, but very near in their practice of personal religious life and pastoral ministry. Others, who were inclined to liberalism during their university days, returned to doctrinal orthodoxy to the degree they felt in their ministry the need to give souls genuine nourishment. Everything great and fertile in the Barthian position came from this question that Karl Barth asked himself as a young pastor: *what* should I preach and *how* should I preach to the faithful on Sunday?[41]

---

[39] This is true, even though his vocation to be a reformer of the clergy was due to the influence of holy souls like Marie Rousseau and Blessed Agnes of Langeac.

[40] See the very interesting article of André Duval, "Quelques idées du Bx. Jean d'Avila sur le ministère pastoral et la formation du clergé," *La Vie Spirituelle, Supplément* (Aug. 1948), pp. 121–153.

[41] Cf. the beautiful passage of Karl Barth, *Parole de Dieu et parole humaine* (Paris, 1933), pp. 128–129.

I have already compared Lammenais and Lacordaire, and I will come back to them again. Both are geniuses, both pioneers and creative spirits, the first more in the order of intellectual insights, the second more in the order of living religious movements. After the condemnation of their journal, *L'Avenir*, Lammenais clung to his ideas and quickly broke completely with the church. Lacordaire accepted the church such as it was. In December 1833, Lammenais finalized in his heart a definitive rupture with the church, while at the beginning of 1834, Lacordaire began the conferences of the *Collège Stanislaus*, the seed of his Conferences of Notre Dame which themselves became the germ of so many fruitful outcomes. Lacordaire follows a pastoral and apostolic trajectory, taking the path of reform through holiness and conversion. Instinctively, he first of all practices the rule set down by Möhler: "The Christian shouldn't try to perfect Christianity, but rather desire to perfect himself in Christianity."[42] Between Lammenais and Lacordaire there is the same difference that exists between a systematic mentality adopted toward and against all others (that becomes hardened by the opposition that it encounters), on the one hand, and a concrete priestly point of view that is docile to

---

[42] *L'Unité dans l'Eglise*, § 39, op. cit., p. 123. Compare this with what Cardinal Nicholas of Cusa said as the papal legate of Pope Nicholas V to the emperor, when he was sent to promote church reform: "It doesn't pertain to men to change religion; rather, it is religion's job to change men" (cited by L. Pastor, *Histoire des papes*, vol. II, 3rd ed. [1907], p. 100). Also see the texts cited by H. Jedin, *Katholische Reformation oder Gegenreformation* (Lucerne, 1946), pp. 25–26; these are texts that refer to the Council of Basel or to the Fifth Lateran Council. — Compare this with Damasus Winzen, who contrasts the secular category of "revolution" with the Christian category of "penitence" (*Catholica* [1932], p. 108). Finally, to fill out this dossier, note these lovely words of Fénelon (*Lettres sur l'autorité de l'Eglise*, letters 3 and 7: *Oeuvres*, ed. Didot, vol. I [1850], pp. 225 and 233): "If you are serious about reform, don't begin from outside with a bitter and haughty criticism, as the Protestants did . . . Rather turn yourself around . . . The more you reform yourselves, the less you will desire to reform the church . . ." "Humble and peaceful souls, who live in contemplation and love, always remain 'small' in their own eyes and opposed to conflict; they are not inclined to raise problems with their pastors . . . Their manner has nothing of bitterness, prickliness, or condescension about it. They never undertake a reform that is dry, critical and haughty, that would shatter unity and that would support the husband who abandons his wife . . . They never say that the church was mistaken through the centuries on the meaning of the Scriptures and never say that they have no fear of being mistaken in explaining the sacred text in a way contrary to the church of antiquity . . ."

What I said above, 1st part, ch. 2 [at the end], allows me to point out what is simply too "moralistic" in these texts which remain quite lovely nonetheless.

authority and looks for possibilities to introduce the most good possible, on the other hand.[43]

At about the same time, a reform movement more or less succeeded in the Anglican Church, namely, the Oxford movement. As Milner-White has written, this was the only reform movement that did not stone its prophets . . . It was a reform led by intellectuals, but from the pastoral point of view, looking at the concrete life of the church. An Anglican contemporary of Newman explained Newman's *secession* with an explanation similar to my own. Newman lacked, he said, the experience of a parish priest, the experience of having had a concrete church present and familiar to his thinking. He was only an *author* addressing the very special audience of the university.[44]

As I will say again in my conclusion, the great good fortune of contemporary reforming tendencies is that they have been born out of the concrete experience of the church, out of the needs of pastoral life and above all of the Christian apostolate. The Young Christian Workers, which is one of the purest of these movements and which has been a stimulus for all the others, is altogether apostolic and pastoral. Our present experience of a successful reform is extremely clarifying. Vatican II has not betrayed these principles. It has been at once both a pastoral council and a council of reform.

Reforms That Tried to Create a System Turned Out Badly

By contrast, reforms that did not succeed (by that I mean those that more or less left the church and so failed to be reforms *of the church*) all had in common the characteristic of having given into the spirit of a "system" and to intellectual stubbornness. It's not that they didn't begin with pastoral and apostolic concerns. Indeed, they drew the best of their energies precisely from that. Many different causes played into the incontestable success of the Reformation at the beginning, and certain of these are due more to the flesh than to the spirit. Nonetheless, it had

---

[43] In leaving La Chênaie never to return, in a remarkable letter of Dec. 11, 1832, addressed to Lammenais, Lacordaire said: "Perhaps your opinions are better and deeper than mine. Considering your natural superiority to me, perhaps I ought to be convinced. However, reasoning is not all there is in a person . . ." (in T. Foisset, *Vie du R. P. Lacordaire* [Paris, 1870], col. I, p. 227.

[44] Mozley, "The Recent Schism," in *The Christian Remembrancer* (Jan. 1846), cited in C. Smyth, *The Art of Preaching: A Practical Survey of Preaching in the Church of England, 747–1939* (London, 1940), p. 222.

an irrepressible spiritual impulse turned toward the people, which corresponded to their thirst to hear the proclamation of Jesus Christ and his Gospel. Luther had gained an audience that the humanists would never have because he brought them a response to their spiritual needs.[45]

Further, the success of the first humanism, which was Christian in inspiration, came from the response it brought to these same needs. By contrast, what was insufficient and even disquieting within it came from a kind of detachment from the concrete life of the church, from its sacramental and pastoral life, as Lortz has remarked about Erasmus.[46] Before Luther, the spiritual movements with their ideal of poverty, and after Luther, Jansenism, owed their relative success to the same factor. But it seems to me that in these great currents of reform, the defects always come, in good part, from the spirit of creating an alternative "system."

We should wonder about what separates a Catholic reformer from a sectarian reformer in his preaching about the ideal of poverty—a St. Bernard from an Arnauld of Brescia, a St. Francis or a St. Dominic from some of the apostolic Waldensians or Fraticelli. Both are opposed to riches and in favor of a poor life for the clergy. We can't just say that the Catholic saints alone practiced poverty and that the others only talked about it . . . Isn't the difference rather that the Arnaldistes, the apostolic sects and the Waldensians, instead of making poverty simply a practical ideal in Christianity, tried to make Christianity itself a universal law, a theory, a system? St. Francis is for poverty, but he never held that possessing property was evil, even for churchmen. He is against studies for his brothers, who should respect their name as "Friars Minor," but he never condemned learning and he esteemed university professors. In this regard, might not the Catholic distinction between precepts and councils, so poorly understood and even denounced by Protestants, be the conceptual instrument that allows us to find an orthodox solution when faced with a sectarian position on the question of poverty and property, or even of marriage and continence?[47] This is a distinction

---

[45] Cf. L. Febvre, "Une question mal posée: les origins de la Réforme française et le problème général des causes de la Réforme," in *Revue historique* CLXI (May 1929), pp. 1–73; H. Dannenbauer, *Luther als religiöser Volksschrifteller, 1517–1520: Ein Beitrag zu der Frage nach den Ursachen der Reformation* (Tubingen, 1930).

[46] Although he does not do full justice to Erasmus in my view, still, cf. Lortz, *Die Reformation als religiöses Anliegen heute* (Trier, 1948), p. 80.

[47] For the questions of poverty and property, cf. Gonnard, *Histoire des doctrines économiques* (ed. 1941), p. 30. For the whole question raised here, cf. Möhler in Vermeil, op. cit., p. 349. Heretics create a system: Marcion forbade marriage, Montanus opposed

which appears to be nothing more than fussy scholasticism, something Léon Bloy, as an excessively outspoken prophet and poor man, (wrongly) called Pharisaism. However, it is a distinction that allows us to avoid the spirit of the "system" and to give expression to a concretely Christian and pastoral point of view, thanks to which the practice of poverty can find practical expression without turning into a denial of the right to property . . .

The case of the Jansenists is even more enlightening. Jansenism was, of course, a religious movement that drew from its Augustinianism its serious tone and generous spiritual energies with a capacity to nourish an authentic reform initiative. But it was spoiled by the spirit of several of its founders or leaders because of the spirit of an alternative "system." This spirit of the system for Jansen himself trumped fidelity to the thinking of the concrete church—the Church of 1640—by a literal fidelity to a text from the past written by St. Augustine.[48] It was this spirit of a system which led astray the spiritual thinking of Saint-Cyran (first simply Christian in character and then increasingly harsh) into Jansenism.[49] Doubtless there are few examples better than his that exemplify the danger of a "prophet" who directly undertakes a reform, makes his own message a program, and turns his prophetic intuition into a system.

This spirit of "system" finally triumphed in Arnauld's work and, because of him, turned the movement into a sect. This case, unmercifully and perhaps too systematically analyzed by Bremond, is remarkably instructive.[50] The *piety* of Port Royal and of Arnauld himself ("if indeed we can discover in him even a shadow of an interior life," Bremond remarks with severity) is Catholic in its concrete lived reality. So also did the *piety* of Martin Luther remain Catholic in great measure. At Port Royal, for the most part people went to communion frequently. However, what was Catholic in this piety becomes devoured in Arnauld's hands by the system of the theologian (doctor). Turned into a system by Arnauld, Port Royal became a sect. This happened to the degree that, needled by controversy, the spirit of the system overtook the spontaneous lived piety of the group.

---

any remarriage; some forbade the use of worldly goods, others admitted it in an unrestrained fashion. The church considers all these goods as good and legitimate but teaches that there is a more perfect way, and has organizations for living the evangelical counsels.

[48] A. de Meyer, *Les premières controverses jansénistes*, pp. 475–478.

[49] On this point, see Bremond, *Histoire littéraire du sentiment religieux*, vol. IV, pp. 148f.

[50] Op. cit., vol. IV, pp. 281f.

"The third generation allowed itself to be permeated to the marrow of its bones with the very dogmas that preceding generations had accepted, but without realizing the implications. They had preached against frequent Communion and yet went to communion twice a week. More logically, in the eighteenth century Jansenists didn't dare even approach the sacraments . . ."[51] How well M. Olier summed up the situation, remarking during a bitter controversy among opposing *doctors* that they destroyed "the heart of charity that makes the Church live" and that can lead penitent souls away from quarreling. "That is nothing but debating . . .," he said.

St. Vincent de Paul reacted in the same way. He thought Jansenism was only a prideful intellectual game.[52] Looking on the Modernist crisis from the outside, Péguy comes to practically the same conclusion.[53] Wrongly, I think, he did not take the intellectual problems of Modernism very seriously. For him they were the residue, the "bottom of the barrel," something secondary. But more seriously, he thought all of that could never have come about if there had not first been a "Modernism of charity," and by that he meant this lack of pastoral realism and depth, this facile complacency found in bourgeois attitudes and social life, following which nineteenth-century Catholicism lost the hearts of the people and became "a kind of superior religion for the superior classes of society, of the nation, a miserable sort of distinguished religion for people recognized as distinguished . . ."

That being the case, the first option that will orient a prophetic spirit toward the creation either of a renewal in the church or of a novelty outside the church would be this decision: either to adopt the practical attitude that takes its point of departure from the reality of the church and aims to serve its development in charity, or to adopt an intellectual and critical attitude that takes its point of departure from a representation of ideas and develops into a system that seeks to reform the existing reality under the influence of this system.

In looking at the evolution of Renan and Newman, who took contrary options but who were exact contemporaries, we can see that Renan went off in the direction of the development of an intellectual abstraction, while Newman applied himself to the development of a concrete reality.[54]

---

[51] Op. cit., p. 304.

[52] Cf. J. Calvet, *La littérature religieuse de François de Sales à Fénelon*, p. 122.

[53] *Notre Jeunesse* (*Oeuvres complètes*, ed. NRF, IV), pp. 169–170.

[54] Cf. J. Guitton, *La pensée moderne et le catholicisme: Parallèles—Renan et Newman* (Aix, 1938); *La philosophie de Newman* (Paris, 1933), pp. 136f.

When he was a seminarian at Issy, Renan wrote: "Truth, truth, are you not the God that I am searching for?" Here he gives us an example of that kind of ambivalent attitude I have spoken about. We can easily find in this youthful expression the seed of his later apostasy, even though what he wrote could have a perfectly Catholic sense and find its equivalent in great masters like Augustine (or even my own notebooks). However, ultimately, the problem is to know if, at the point of departure, someone accepts the concrete reality of the church as normative (while not rejecting the possibility of an infidelity or of a miscarriage of justice by the church itself) or if they make their own thinking an infallible criterion. The schismatic reformer is someone who, having made his principle for truth not the reality of the church but his own ideas and his own judgment, takes for his motto: "Remain as you are, and judge everything by your own thinking." This was, in its pure state, the case of Lammenais as well as the case of Alfred Loisy.[55]

Isn't this the same thing as "making an idol of the truth," according to Pascal's profound formulation (frag. 582)?

This brings us to the question of the essential status of reform in the church and of the judgment to be made about what we call purely and simply "the Reformation." That topic is enormous and so important that I have put it off for special treatment in the third part of this book. [As noted before, the third part is not included in this translation.]

---

[55] Cf. M.-J. Lagrange, *M. Loisy et le Modernisme* (Juvisy, 1932).

SECOND CONDITION

Remain in Communion with the Whole Church

At first glance my treatment of this second condition may appear to do little more than reaffirm the problem under investigation. Staying in communion, that is precisely what is in question.

Nonetheless, there is a positive development here, a clarification about the idea of communion. It is the element of connection with the whole, the idea that, to avoid going off track in carrying out a prophetic mission or a reform activity, you need to stay in living contact with the whole body of the church.

The Whole Truth Is Grasped Only in Communion with the Whole Church

Some important insights in the thought of Möhler help to ground, build, and develop this idea. This has already been pointed out.[56] Möhler's key idea is that vital faith, just like vital human experience, depends upon the action of the Holy Spirit within us. Moreover, the Holy Spirit is the Spirit of love and fraternal communion whose task is not, strictly speaking, to clarify this or that particular matter. The Spirit's work is to enliven and actualize the Body of Christ. Further, the conditions for the Spirit's gifts (we might even say for the Spirit's work) are

---

[56] Cf. *supra*, n. 27. Cf. also Geiselmann's book (cited in [part 2] n. 9), as well as the contributions of Chaillet and De Montcheuil in the collection *L'Eglise est une: Hommage à Möhler* (Paris, 1939).

essentially communal. The Spirit operates within the mutual love of the faithful as a Spirit of love and fraternal communion. True faith does not exist without fraternal communion.

What gives rise to the church, as Möhler says, is the fact that "no one can live a Christian life or be at home in their religion without the influence of the community of the faithful enlightened by the Holy Spirit."[57] Möhler was delighted to point out that the apostles only received the Holy Spirit when they were "gathered in the same place, with one heart, forming a single gathering of brothers."[58] He drew out the implications of this idea, using a formula that shows how great minds always have a touch of poetry: "As part of an organic whole, believers are shielded from deception only when thinking and desiring in accordance with the mind and the heart of all."[59]

Only through communion with the whole body, which itself is subject to the guidance of the magisterium, can someone grasp a truth in its totality. It is clearly impossible that individual persons might know and profess the whole truth by themselves. Someone might have perceived this or that element of the truth, but not some other. Someone might have been struck by one aspect, but not see all the implications and consequences of what he or she discovered and began to promote. Yet what they do not know by themselves, they can know through others. When we are in communion with the whole body, we have the benefit of corrections, clarifications, and the fullness that the whole body offers us effortlessly, simply in virtue and under the influence of being in communion. Because of the unity of the body, what others have, but I do not, also belongs to me and works to my benefit. What I can neither understand nor achieve, nor even formulate or hold explicitly by myself, I can subscribe to in the whole body with which I am in communion. St. Augustine says that every Christian speaks all languages by being in union with the church that speaks them all.[60] The fullness of truth is only found in the whole body. Further, in communion with the whole body,

---

[57] *L'Unité dans l'Eglise*, § 6 (French trans. by A. de Lilienfeld), p. 18; cf. § 27. — Möhler's point of view corresponds exactly to the ancient meaning of the word "Catholic," according to which the Catholic is essentially someone who belongs to the unique church that extends throughout the whole world; Père Galtier recently interpreted Irenaeus's "*ab his qui sunt undique*" in this same way (*Revue hist. ecclés.*, 44 [1949], pp. 411–428).

[58] *Symbolique*, § 37 (trans. Lachat), vol. II, p. 9.

[59] Ibid., p. 11.

[60] *Sermo 267*, no. 4 (PL 38:1231); *Ennar. in Ps. 147*, no. 19 (PL 37:1929).

persons have a grasp of the truth that is superior to what they might formulate personally by themselves. We could easily interpret Ephesians 3:18-19 in this sense.

Two days before dying, Luther wrote these lines (the last writing we have from him) in which this same idea is suggested in a remarkable way: "Nobody can understand Virgil's *Bucolics* without being a pastor for five years; nobody can understand his *Georgics* without being a laborer for five years; nobody can understand what Cicero wrote in his *Letters* without being involved in running a country for twenty years. Let nobody think that they grasp the Holy Scriptures as they should, if they have not governed the churches for a hundred years with Elijah and Elisha, with John the Baptist, Christ and the Apostles . . ."[61] How right that is, and how much Luther, who was speaking against sacramentaries, would have profited by following his own idea more closely. How can one man, even a great religious genius, completely rethink Christianity all by himself? Impossible. You cannot taste and understand the Scriptures as you should, you cannot grasp the truth precisely and especially in its fullness (one affects the other), unless you are the contemporary, the disciple, the companion of Jesus Christ, the prophets, and the apostles—that is, unless you are in communion with the one, holy, catholic, and *apostolic* church.

To tell the truth, the church itself can neither define itself adequately nor give an explicit account at any given moment of everything it carries within itself. It "defines" *what it is not* clearly enough, just as we ourselves know better what we don't want and what we oppose better than what we are and what we hold. The church condemns formulas that don't appear to respect or convey its conviction about whether to think or to hold one thing or another. But it still feels unable to furnish at any given moment an adequate positive expression of what it is and of everything it carries within itself. I used to think this was one of the reasons why the church refused to be represented at important ecumenical conferences.[62] In any case, let us take note of this: for the church itself, complete truth is to be found only in total communion. No exterior form or particular formula either exhausts or expresses adequately the way it lives and thinks.

---

[61] Feb. 16, 1546: *Briefwechsel*, ed. Enders, vol. XVII; ed. Kawerau and Flemming (Leipzig, 1920), p. 60. Also *Dr. M. Luthers Briefe*, ed. De Wette, vol. VI (1856), p. 414; cf. Weimar, *Tischreden* 5002; cf. Köstlin-Kawerau, *Martin Luther* (1903), vol. II, p. 621.

[62] *Chrétiens désunis* (1937), pp. 180–181.

As we will see toward the end of this section, there is a matter of major importance here. Because no exterior form or formula produced at any given moment is an adequate expression of Catholic truth, it will always be possible, in the name of communion itself, to seek to go beyond the expressions held at a given moment. When it is a matter of properly dogmatic formulas, this evolution can only mean development by way of clarification. So the progressive or "prophetic" side of serious reflection or of our activities can find its justification in the same reality, ecclesial communion, which is also its norm and its boundary line.

Norm and determined scope are even more necessary when it is not just a question of any kind of Christian, but of a "prophet," that is, of a Christian whose mission is to take initiatives for development, to strive to shape exterior forms according to the inner sense and the fullness toward which they aspire. The prophet's reactions and insights, as we have seen, always run the risk of unilateralism. As long as the prophet remains genuinely in communion with the church, his statements will remain impregnated with the attitudes and the thought of the whole church. Whatever is excessive or one-sided about these claims that might be a source of schism, if isolated from ecclesial communion, will be found repeatedly corrected or open to improvement within the bosom of the church. There, everything will be said and done in communion and thus in contact and in relation with all sorts of complementary and compensating claims. As long as the communion has not been broken, the claims which are made in communion will show the influence of all the other affirmations held by the church. Ambivalence, if there is any, will be resolved positively in the direction of orthodoxy. The prophets' real meaning is modified by the relation they maintain with the full doctrine and the full life of the church. Consequently, not only what they fail to say is not, by that fact, denied, but what they might say insufficiently and imperfectly can and ought to be interpreted in a truly Catholic sense.

This Communion Makes the Difference between Catholic and Schismatic

This is very important, and it complements what I already said about the ambivalence of reactions to the "prophetic" style. It is easy to find historical examples of this normativity of Catholic communion for reforms without schism. The scholar or reformer who, while affirming a particular aspect of truth, clings to the desire not to deny other aspects and to remain in communion with all the others in the church, remains

Catholic. By contrast, the scholar or reformer who insists first on "being himself," in maintaining the special difference of his own initiative, and in denying compensating elements that modify his special insight, risks falling into schism. When St. Ignatius of Loyola published his *Exercises*, which were a novelty at the time, he appended to them "Rules of Orthodoxy," which testified to his concern to keep his initiative in communion with the church.

By contrast, even the most powerful religious experiences and the most deeply felt truths risk becoming heresies if they are not regulated by the faith and the life of the entire *Catholica*. They develop then according to their own logic, in an abstract way that is autonomous and oversimplified. In affirming certain legitimate truths, they deny other truths equally Catholic and soon distort and spoil whatever good they originally had. Nicholas of Cusa reproached the Czech supporters of Holy Communion with the chalice for insisting on their demands (legitimate in themselves) without caring about requirements or conditions for unity.[62a] Further, heresies, as we have seen, are born "from deductions followed only in one direction, springing from a principle of tradition or science isolated from the totality, held up as absolute truth, and to which are linked (by reasoning) conclusions incompatible with the general coherence of religion and of traditional teaching."

In the history of the church there have been so many originally good and Catholic spiritual insights and experiences that have become the source of heresy, precisely because they developed in an isolated and abstract way outside the communion and the control of the *Catholica*.

What is Pelagianism other than ascetical experience (representing human moral feeling) pushed to an absolute dogmatic position, despite the clear opposing position of the universal Catholic faith? Pelagius had an authentically Catholic insight, but it could only have remained such if Pelagius, correcting his own personal experience by Augustine's experience, and remaining genuinely linked to the whole *Catholica*, had not dared to make claims that became seriously heretical when separated from the community of faith and love.

Take another example, that of the most authentic and Catholic theology you might find, that of St. Augustine. If you were to sever its vital connection with the life of the universal church, to isolate it from that life and allow it to develop in the abstract, if you were to articulate its

---

[62a] *Epist. II,* "De usu communionis ad Bohemos," *Opera* (ed. Basel, 1565), p. 832: "*potius cligentes obscindi ab ecclesia aquam a renovatione desistere.*"

conclusions in a one-sided way, failing to relate and submit them to the totality of the church's life, you would end up with Jansenism. In a way, the orthodox statements of the year 415 found in Augustine's writings, although materially the same, were no longer orthodox in the writings of Jansenius in 1652. These fully Augustinian ideas were orthodox in Augustine's thought because they were regulated not by Augustine himself, considering himself as his criterion or goal, but by the *Catholica*, that is, by the communion that kept them *within* despite themselves. So they had a positive orientation, an intention, and an active impulse to seek for Catholic harmony.

Yet they became heretical in Jansenius, being affirmed for their own sake through an autonomous and abstract logic no longer governed by the living unity of the *Catholica*, but governed by the literal text of Augustine. Further, Augustine, still remaining himself, would have been more in tune in the seventeenth century with the life of the *Catholica* of that time. He would only have compromised his catholicity (while remaining Augustinian) if he refused to be in communion with Ignatius and Molina, in the very bosom of the church. This means that the Augustinianism of Augustine and the Augustinianism of Jansenius, even if they are materially the same in their details, are nonetheless formally different.[63] The concrete challenge for the "prophet" is to be a person of initiative without becoming an "innovator," a reformer, but not a "revolutionary." The norm for the "prophet" will be to do everything he can and must do conscientiously to avoid being disowned or rejected by the church.

For that to happen, certain internal dispositions are decisive. No external means can keep someone with a systematic or rebellious heart in communion. Because my interest here is essentially ecclesiology, I cannot spend much time on this question of inner dispositions. A study that would bring out the psychological and spiritual implications of the sin of schism (such as St. Thomas Aquinas and his commentator Cajetan did)[64]

---

[63] This is a way of responding to the problem that Pascal posed so polemically in these words: "So you admire the Molinist mechanisms which bring about amazing reversals in the church, so that what is Catholic in the Fathers becomes heretical in M. Arnauld, and what was heretical in the Semipelagians becomes orthodox in the writings of the Jesuits; then the ancient teaching of St. Augustine becomes an unacceptable novelty, and yet the new inventions which [the Jesuits] construct day after day are supposed to be taken as the church's ancient faith . . . It is not the *ideas* of M. Arnauld that are heretical, it is only his *person* . . ." (Ending of the *Third Provincial Letter*).

[64] *Summa Theologiae*, IIa–IIae, art. 39, ad 1.

could become the topic of special research. Following St. Thomas, Cajetan identified the essential element of an attitude of communion not with conformity in doctrine and worship, or even with submission to one central authority, but with a particular way of living the Christian life. What is at stake is a way of leading Christian life, says Cajetan, *ut pars* [*as a part of the whole*]. This means the feeling of not being alone, of being part of one single body, leading one single life, pursuing one single enterprise with all other Catholics. It means not considering yourself to be the "whole," not acting or thinking as if your own issues are self-sufficient. Rather, it means living without losing contact with others, without disengaging from the group of which you are a part, clinging to your insertion in the concrete church (something already described above); it means linking your own thinking and actions in some way to a virtual presence of all the other faithful of the whole church. Möhler's formula for this is wonderful: "thinking and desiring with the spirit and heart of all."

This deeply rooted attitude of communion, whose formal rupture is the sin of schism, is made real and brought to the fullness of ecclesial communion through a living relationship with the hierarchy that comes from the apostles. The church is a body organized and structured apostolically. There is "Catholic communion" only in communion with the apostles, in fidelity to their preaching and to the communal life governed by the sacraments and the prayers they celebrated (Acts 2:42). The church is those who are with the apostles, and we can even say that the apostles are those who are with Peter,[65] expressing in this way the profound norm of Catholic communion linked to the apostolicity of the church. Here the Holy Spirit's interior governance, bestowed upon believing hearts on the day of Pentecost (replacing the Mosaic Law, whose promulgation the Jewish feast of Pentecost celebrated), prompts the faithful from within toward unanimity in communion and puts within them an inclination and an instinct to measure their lives by the guidance of the apostolic magisterium.

Communion will always mean not something servile or mechanical, but a living relation to the apostolic authority given by the Lord to structure his church, both at the local and the universal level. By this very fact, communion means a kind of submission that is neither servile nor mechanical, but enthusiastic, loving, and simple, like the acquiescence of children. The Catholic Church has always seen pride and self-centeredness in the perpetrators of schism or heresy. Theologically speaking, just making a material mistake does not suffice to constitute the sins

[65] Mark 1:36; Luke 8:45 (cf. 5:1-11).

of schism or heresy. There needs to be obstinacy, that is, arrogance in clinging to one's ideas. Bishops love docility, not because they hold authority and like to exercise it, even less because it makes the demands of administration easier, but because docility, according to St. Cyprian's expression, favors the sacrament of unity. Bishops want this because they are fathers, doctors, and pastors.

We are going to see how the periphery of the church has to ratify its initiatives through the agency of hierarchical structures—this is extremely important, but not sufficient. Someone like Waldo was able to come with his companions to the Roman Synod of 1179 to seek approval. We can only wonder if he came there with a serious intention of being docile to the synod, when we see with what ease his little group fell into heresy as soon as he was condemned. The break took place in 1184. If, as it seems, the Waldensian treatise (fragments of which A. Dondaine rediscovered)[66] goes back to the beginning of that movement, anterior to its condemnation and its break from Rome, then Waldo and his companions had been disposed, from the beginning, to pursue their own line of thinking, even if they should be condemned and rejected by the church.[67] They responded to the prohibition to preach, ordered by the Archbishop of Lyons, by invoking Mark 16:15 and Acts 5:29: "We must obey God rather than any human authority," a principle that is at once sacrosanct and difficult to apply.[67a] In responding to the church's question for all innovators, "Where was the church in your relationship to Christ?" they claimed to be *themselves* the church, and in so discerning, had already separated themselves from the Catholic Church.[68] Such is the recurring, tragic story of so many great minds who believed they could be faithful to the truth only by clinging to *their own* interpretation, rather than to the sense of the church.

Sentire cum Ecclesia

The sense of the church—*Sentire cum Ecclesia*: this slightly vague formula still has a strong power of attraction. We can feel that it has profound meaning. It cannot be reduced to simple obedience to the demands

---

[66] A. Dondaine, O.P., "Aux origines du Valdéisme: Une profession de foi de Valdès" in *Archivum Fratrum Praedicatorum*, XVI (1946), pp. 191–235.

[67] Ibid., pp. 223, 235.

[67a] Cf. H. Grundmann, *Religiöse Bewegungen im Mittelalter* (Munich, 1935), p. 92. Cf. Bernard Prim, cited on p. 94, n. 42, ibid.; but he himself rejoined and lived within the Catholic communion.

[68] Cf. A. Dondaine, op. cit., pp. 207, 233.

of authority, no more than the very word church can mean exclusively the hierarchy, cut off from the body of the faithful. To interpret it exclusively in this sense, as Abbé Doerner has done recently,[69] is to grasp only one aspect of the reality, and in a defensive way. It is not impossible to imagine a different perspective; and church history seems to offer cases where a genuine *Sentire cum Ecclesia* did not easily fit into the formula of sheer material obedience (superficial fidelity), something that lacks the plenitude of Catholic fidelity. Above all, that kind of interpretation treats the Body of Christ only as a huge administrative apparatus, where everything is determined from on high and where the members, required only to obey, don't seem to be really alive themselves. In fact, the whole church lives from the truth and in the truth—and under conditions which respect completely the prerogatives of the hierarchy, as we will see. St. Ignatius, from whom this formula comes, did not write *Sentire cum Ecclesia*, a formula that would orientate the mind toward conformity to external rules, but he wrote *Sentire vere in Ecclesia militante* [Have a sense of the church bravely acting in the world], which restores to the faithful of the church their part in the life of the body.[70]

I don't intend to develop here a complete theology about the hierarchy's role and of the relation of the faithful to the hierarchy with respect to ecclesial unity in communion. Remaining with the topic at hand, I will consider only the most characteristic aspect of the relation between the initiative of a reformer and the hierarchy, when the reformer desires to remain in communion with the whole. A fitting title for this paragraph might be *"The Periphery and the Center"* or somewhat less poetically, as we will see, *"Structure and Life."*

The Center and the Periphery

Often enough, it is not the hierarchy that takes the initiative. This is not because taking initiatives is foreign to it. For example, the encyclical *Pascendi* rightly enough claimed for the central hierarchical powers the

---

[69] A. Doerner, *Sentire cum Ecclesia: Ein dringender Aufruf und Weckruf an Priester* (M. Gladbach, 1941 [*pro manuscripto*]).

[70] Translation by R. Roothaan—in the original Spanish: "*el sentido verdadero en la Iglesia militante.*" Cf. W. Sierp, S.J., "Recte sentire in ecclesia: Erklärung der Ueberschrift der Kirchlichkeitsregeln," in *Zeitsch. f. Aszese und Mystik*, XVI (1941), pp. 31–36. See also P. Leturia, "Sentido verdadero en la Iglesia militante," *Gregorianum* 23 (1942), pp. 137–168; however, the criticism of Erasmus in this text is disputed by other historians.

honor of not only serving a conservative function but of promoting progress in the church as well.[71] History gives us more than one example in which a reforming initiative came from the central powers. The case of the Gregorian Reform is not the best example perhaps, because the reform movement had already been initiated (particularly in Lorraine), and further, Gregory VII as a reformer was essentially the monk Hildebrand, who became Archdeacon of the Church of Rome and then Pope.[72] The real context for the Gregorian Reform is monastic. In this case a prophetic vocation conceived in the cloister was put to work under the papal tiara. But there are other examples.

The First Crusade, despite some aspect of "awakening," was not really a reform movement; yet we can still point to the important figure of Innocent III. Aware of the many needs of the church and especially its need for good doctrinal preaching, Innocent III was literally on the look-out for new initiatives, even unexpected ones, so as to take advantage of them and encourage them.[73] For this reason, we might say with Luchaire that Innocent III, without personally taking new initiatives, was really the leader of the reform movement at the beginning of the 13th century.[74] We can also mention the forceful missionary initiatives of Gregory XVI, Benedict XV, and Pius XI. Benedict XV and Pius XI installed indigenous clergy and bishops [in mission lands] despite the reluctance of many missionaries. There is also the example of the eucharistic and liturgical decrees of Pius X, even though the liturgical renewal had been inaugurated by Dom Guéranger sixty years earlier.[74a] As Msgr. Dubourg, the Archbishop of Besançon, stated in opening the noteworthy *Congrès des Oeuvres* of 1946 in his episcopal see: "Initiatives can come about in the church from the supreme authority as well as from the most

---

[71] Denzinger, no. 2095, where it is a question of explaining dogmatic development. On the same point, cf. Franzelin, *De divina Traditione et Scriptura*, thes. XXV (Rome, 1882), 3rd ed., pp. 294f., which underlines that the hierarchical magisterium is not only *custos* but also *doctor*, and does not confine itself to merely repudiating or approving the progress made by scholars.

[72] Cf. G. Bardy, "Saint Grégoire VII et la réforme canoniale au XIe siècle," in *Studi Gregoriani* (Rome, 1947), vol. I, pp. 47–64.

[73] Cf. P. Mandonnet, *Saint Dominique: L'Idée, l'homme et l'oeuvre*, with further notes and critical additions by M. H. Vicaire and R. Ladner (Paris, 1938), vol. II, pp. 40f.

[74] Cf. A. Luchaire, *Innocent III, le Concile de Latran et la réforme de l'Eglise* (Paris, 1908); A. Fliche, "Innocent III et la réforme de l'Eglise," *Rev. hist. ecclés.* 44 (1949), pp. 87–152.

[74a] Cf. O. Rousseau, *Histoire du Mouvement liturgique*; R. Aubert, *Pie IX*, pp. 473f.

humble of Christians . . ."[75] However, most of the time, initiatives do not come from the center but from the periphery—from below rather than from above.

The church, like any living thing, is marked by both continuity and progress—progress *within* continuity. The church is in continuity in every part of itself and in progress in every part as well. However, in the church, as in all living beings of a higher order, functions tend to be specialized in such a way that there are parts of the church which are more characteristically organs of development and other parts that are more organs of continuity. On the whole, initiatives or novelties come especially from the periphery of the church, from its frontiers. The central organs fulfill most of all the function of assuring unity and continuity. They exercise par excellence the charisms that guarantee apostolicity, and they provide the criteria for life in the church as one and apostolic.

If we refer to the distinction already explained between *structure* and *life* in the church, the central organs of the church (more exactly, the hierarchy) have the responsibility for ecclesial continuity with its foundation and principles, the responsibility to preserve the form or essential structure of the church. With respect to all the movements of ecclesial life that continue to abound within it, coming sometimes from above, sometimes from below, the first mission of the hierarchy is to oversee what these movements accomplish or to bring them into the structural framework of the church. The hierarchy's concern is to see that they develop in a manner consistent with the framework, just as the fixtures of a house have to fit into its overall plan, or just as the living muscles and activities of a person fit onto the framework of its skeleton and basic activities.

As the guardian of the church's structure and of its continuity with its apostolic origins, the hierarchy is also the guardian of the church's communion across boundaries in the whole vast scope of the living church. So by this very function, the hierarchy is oriented toward overseeing new movements with a view to harmonizing them with the life of the whole church. "Bishops prefer to confirm more than to baptize,"

---

[75] The Acts of the Congress (*Paroisse, Chrétienté communautaire et missionnaire*), p. 8. Cf. Pius XII's speech to the Congress of the Lay Apostolate in Rome, Oct. 1951: ". . . welcoming with an open heart [the initiatives] that may be proposed by [the laity] and, as opportunity allows, approving them broadly. In decisive battles, sometimes the best initiatives come from the front lines. Church history gives us many examples of this" (*Doc. Cathol.* [1951], col. 1052; *AAS*, 1951, p. 789).

we say with a smile. After all, that is their proper function. Cardinal Suhard, in speaking of the different aspects of the life of the church that are due to grassroots initiatives (often by the laity), put this well in saying: "Authority sanctions more often than it creates."[76]

Consider, for example, the twofold response that Christians must make to something like Communism. This twofold response has aptly been described as a movement of opposition[77] (because Christianity has to maintain the purity of its principles) and a movement of efficacious action fighting for social justice. It is clear that even if the whole church and all of its parts ought to practice both of these movements, there will be a certain distribution of roles depending upon the part one plays in the church. It will be more the hierarchy's role to express opposition for the sake of maintaining clear principles (even though the hierarchy is conscious of the demands of justice), and more the role of committed militant Catholics on the frontiers of the social order to bear witness and to fight for social justice. Something similar is the case for a great number of other problems.[78]

Initiatives often start at the periphery. They say that history develops at its margins and that's right. The margin is closer to the periphery than to the center. Further, the center, with its vocation to oversee *structure*, prefers something *defined* to something that is searching and striving for expression. Yet a spiritual organism is more likely to *grow* out of the elements searching and striving for expression. It has often been noted: "In this Catholic Church that is so vigorously hierarchical, not one single religious order has ever been created by the central power. All such initiatives come from the periphery. They are the creation of the simple faithful, pious laypeople, like Francis the Draper of Assisi, or Ignatius the captain of Charles V, or Angela of Merici, or Ceccolella [St. Frances of Rome], a Roman widow . . ."[79] It has also been observed that thinkers, creators in the world of ideas, are hardly ever at home in the church of

---

[76] Address to students, April 7, 1946, in *Doc. Cathol.* 7 (July 1946), col. 676.

[77] Père L. Beirnaert in *Etudes* (Dec. 1945), esp. pp. 299–300.

[78] If I may make such a comparison here, I would point out that the law of evolution also applies to politicians: When they begin their careers at the periphery of the political world, they are revolutionaries and progressives; but they become conservatives and moderates when they themselves come to power.

[79] P. Charles, *La robe sans couture* (Bruges, 1923), p. 136. Cf. H. Urs von Balthasar, *Der Laie und der Ordenstand* (Einsiedeln, 1948), p. 25; (French trans. by E. Bernimont, *Laïcat et plein apostolat* [Liège and Paris, 1949], pp. 39f.).

Rome, but rather in the churches of the periphery.[80] Similar remarks have been made concerning the reform of the canons in the eleventh century and of the reform of religious orders in the fifteenth century. In the eleventh century, said Mandonnet, "the implementation of the reform seemed to me very sporadic—and it was, in effect. The founding of the canons, as a reform of the clergy, was not produced in a single initiative, nor was it sustained simply by a decision of the central power. On the contrary, it appeared here and there thanks to individual initiatives stimulated by the preaching of ardent reformers like St. Peter Damian."[81] With respect to the reform of religious orders in the fifteenth century, little of that initiative came from the popes, even though the popes had several times promulgated reform measures. But the popes also hindered these movements and, in the period from the Conciliarism movement [fifteenth century] to the Council of Trent, the energy for this reform did not come from the popes any more than the original initiative had.[82] The reforms at the end of the fifteenth and at the beginning of the sixteenth century, sketched by the historian M. A. Renaudet in his *Préréforme et Humanisme*, owed nothing to the Holy See nor, generally, to the hierarchy . . .

History also teaches us that reforms undertaken uniquely from on high, without widespread participation of those at the bottom (on the periphery and at the popular level), have little effectiveness. This was so much a part of the consciousness of medieval churchmen that they turned it into a maxim. Even the most authoritarian medieval popes, Innocent III or Boniface VIII, constantly invoked this maxim, borrowed from Roman law but reinterpreted with a communitarian and collegial meaning: *Quod omnes tangit, ab omnibus tractari debet* (Whatever affects everyone ought to be examined [treated] by everyone).[83] They decided that the support of the community for doing something had to be sought

---

[80] Newman, *Apologia*, English ed., p. 265; French trans. (Paris, 1939), p. 300.

[81] Mandonnet, op. cit., vol. II, p. 150. On the reform of religious orders in the 15th century: "The religious reformation was at first the work of isolated individuals, then taken up by governments and by the hierarchy, and then finally adopted by the papacy and by a Council as well; however, it did not take long to overflow the boundaries of a monastery, a religious order, a province or a country." Cf. also Imbart de la Tour, *Les origines de la Réforme* (Paris, 1909), vol. II, p. 522; J. Lortz, *Die Reformation als religiöses Anliegen heute*, pp. 185–186.

[82] Cf., e.g., J. Hashagen, *Staat und Kirche vor der Reformation* (Essen, 1931), pp. 351f., 365–369.

[83] See my treatment of this motto in *Rev. hist. de Droit français et étranger* (1958), pp. 210–259.

through consultation and free discussion. This idea changed in the fifteenth century, but that change should not nullify the deep truth here. *Counsel, council*—they passed easily from one word to the other, simply because they are so closely related.

This explains why the Middle Ages regularly linked the idea of reform to the idea of a council. For example, it was in order to obtain broader and more positive support for his reforms that Gregory VII convoked the councils that he held annually in Rome during Lent, calling together representatives of all of Christendom: bishops, abbots, clergy and "great numbers of the laity."[84] In the thirteenth, fourteenth, and fifteenth centuries, people looked to a council for reform measures. Reform-minded writings, like Humbert of Romans's *Opus tripartitum* or William Durandus's *De modo generalis concilii celebrandi et corruptelis de Ecclesia reformandis*, as well as many others, were written on the occasion of convening councils. The thinking that links church reform and councils was still strong enough in the middle of the sixteenth century to dissuade Paul III and Julius III from seeking reform by means of a pontifical commission, even an expanded one meeting in Rome. This same type of thinking led Paul IV to hope for a council similar to the reform councils that followed in the line of the Lateran Council of 1215.[85]

This link between church reform and the synodal principle makes sense. It clearly expresses something fundamental. It is a question of linking together an initiative from the base to the action of the authorities, linking support from the bottom to the leadership of the organization. An assembly, whatever form it may take—chapter, synod, council, congress, palavers—is a place of dialogue where a common will can form and be asserted, and where authorities can respond to the living consensus of the whole body.

Need for Support from the Base

In fact, this consent is necessary. A reform effort strictly from on high would not get very far. If I may use the categories of Bergson here, I would say that a reform is brought about not only by external force but

---

[84] Cf. A. Fliche, *La Réforme grégorienne*, vol. II, *Grégoire VII* (Louvain, 1925), pp. 207 and n. 1.

[85] On this point, see A. Hauck, "Die Rezeption und Umbildung der allgemeinen Synode im Mittelalter," in *Histor. Vierteljahrsch.* X (1907), pp. 465–482. The *council-reform* connection (see above, p. 20) is evident in Luther's *Von den Konziliis und Kirchen*, e.g., Weimar, vol. 50, pp. 488, 491f., 514.

by interior desire. There needs to be an interior impulse (*élan*) that a decree from on high hasn't the power to awaken.

Take for example the experience of Benedict XII (1334–1342), when his authoritarian rigidity met with hardly anything other than resistance and bad will. We see the same thing, in another way, when the reform proposal does not reach sufficiently outside the narrow and closed circles of the center, as was the case with the reform efforts of the humanists. The councils themselves were often ineffective in their reforms because they only mobilized bishops and theologians. What would have been the legacy of the Lateran Council of 1215 if it had not met with a current of spiritual reform strong enough to make its decrees a vital part of the wider church? Many of the large number of councils and decrees at the end of the fifteenth and at the beginning of the sixteenth century lacked the support of a reform spirit among the clergy and the laity.[86] Even the Council of Trent would not have had the effectiveness it finally had if its decrees had not been reinforced by spiritual currents (sometimes started before the council, sometimes after), as Blessed John of Avila remarked some years after its opening.[87]

The reform of the Brothers of the Common Life, which pursued a spiritual ideal, the return to an interior spiritual life (central to every reform), failed to really catch on with the Christian people. Although it was a spiritual movement and was authentically reformist, in reaching out to the laity it remained confined to the middle class and did not touch the common people at all (the Caliban without whom there is no Catholic renaissance). Further, this movement rapidly peaked in its spiritual energy, and in place of nourishing a broad apostolic movement, it remained exclusively on the level of the spiritual life. Then, for many (cf. Jean Mombaert), it became a method and a formula for meditation. "Doubtless the weakness of the reform of the canons in the fifteenth century was to remain at a moralizing and devotional level, failing to touch questions about outdated structures, and failing to respond with its individualistic piety (even the *Imitation*) to the communitarian aspirations that ultimately decide the fate of peoples. Aside from improving morality, it did not reach the ontological ground of grace."[88]

---

[86] Cf. Imbart de la Tour, *Les origines de la Réforme*, vol. II, pp. 526–538.

[87] Cf. A. Duval, op. cit., p. 153.

[88] M.-D. Chenu, "Réformes de structure en chrétienté," in *Economie et Humanisme* (March–April 1946), p. 91. Cf. L. Febvre, "Une question mal posée: Les origines de la Réforme française," in *Revue historique* (1929), p. 45.

It was one of Luther's instinctive insights to understand that reform by means of the "head" alone would not be effective. "The Church," he wrote in 1518, "needs reform, and this is not the task of one single person, the Sovereign Pontiff, or of a certain number of cardinals, as the last council gave us proof, but *the task of the entire world*, and even of God . . ."[89] The Lutheran Reformation really touched the common people by what was best and worst within it. The best was its spiritual and evangelical element; the worst was its appeal to the princes, to their greed, and to their nationalism. Unfortunately the appeal to the laity, of the kind that we see throughout the Middle Ages and flowing into Luther's appeal to the Christian nobility of the German nation, was not without flaws and did not respect the prerogatives of the spiritual power.[90] Möhler, with his great sense of the concrete life of the church, had understood this point very well, and he responded to the reformist initiatives stirring around him by saying that the starting point for reform has to be priestly formation that aims at good ministry and the education of popular religiosity.[91]

Need for Approval from the Central Powers of the Church

But even if the majority of reform initiatives come from the periphery, and if reforms have no chance of succeeding unless they resonate with wide apostolic movements, they can only lead to a reform *of the church* and reform *in the church*, rather than a break, if they are taken up and incorporated *by the church* into its unity. This means, concretely, the agreement and approval of the central authorities, that is, the consecration

---

[89] *Resolutiones disputationum de indulgentiarum virtute*, conclusion 89, Weimar, vol. I, p. 627.

[90] Cf. the documentation given by J. Hashagen, *Staat und Kirche vor der Reformation* (Essen, 1931). The final result of Luther's appeal to the laity would be the transfer to the secular princes of the *jus reformandi exercitium religionis . . .*; this transfer was formally codified in the Peace of Westphalia (1648), art. V, § 30 (in Mirbt, *Quellen zur Geschichte des Papsttums*, no. 521). This is the origin of the "national churches" that are based on the principle "*Cujus est regio, ejus est de religione dispositio*—it belongs to the ruler of a region to determine its religion." On this, cf. the report of O. Klopp to the Fifth International Congress of Catholic Intellectuals, Munich, 1900 (*Akten*, Munich, 1901), p. 313; "Der Name Reformation," also published as "Was ist Reformation?" in *Hist.-polit. Blätter*, CXXIX (1902), pp. 632–648.

[91] Cf. E. Vermeil, *J. A. Möhler* (1913), pp. 319, 352–353, 359, 368f., 382f.; cf. also pp. 385, 386f., etc. Cf. above, pp. 159–160.

conferred on prophecy by apostolicity. The center gives to the initiatives of the periphery the approval and the blessing of unity.

For a movement born of the needs of a given moment or from the vital impulse of the people to remain on track, it needs both the freedom to develop and the approval of the authorities. In welcoming it, the authorities test it, direct it, keep it within limits, and correct it. For a movement, especially a reform movement, to become truly an ecclesial movement, a reform *of the church*, and not deviant or schismatic, it has to be inserted within the established lines of the church's structure. For that to happen, the reform movement has to be welcomed and ratified by the central authority according to its understanding of the church's need for unity, catholicity, and continuity. The reform movement needs to be adopted by the church, synchronized to the life of the entire ecclesial assembly, and integrated within its ecclesial life. As Cardinal Suhard said in speaking to students, "Your liberty is in no way compromised; your initiatives are a source of progress for the church. But there is one condition: you need to be intimately united to the church through the hierarchy. You will do that by your obedience."[92]

There are numerous examples, both positive and negative, that bear this out. Tertullian felt that it would have been enough for the Bishop of Rome to decide in favor of Montanism for the churches of Asia and Phrygia to be reconciled with him.[93] There we observe, in addition to a certain primacy acknowledged for the Church of Rome, a proper appreciation for the conditions under which a prophetic movement develops *in the church*. Msgr. Battifol remarked in conversation that, had the theology of Origen met with an intervention of the Apostolic See regulating it, setting limits and showing it respect, as Augustinianism had the chance to experience, it would have had an influence in theology comparable to the Augustinian tradition. In the early church, the election of bishops by the people or by the local clergy, which represented an initiative of the periphery and a grassroots movement, still had to be ratified by the Metropolitan bishop or by the Bishop of Rome acting as Metropolitan.[94]

From this we can see how the dynamics of communion have implications for the area of church law. Further, this is not the only case in which church law managed to integrate an initiative from social life. Such

---

[92] Suhard, op. cit., in *Doc. Cathol.* 7 (July 1946), col. 676. (See n. 76 above.)
[93] Cf. P. Battifol, *Cathedra Petri—Unam Sanctam* 4 (Paris, 1938), p. 34.
[94] Ibid., p. 44.

procedures as the election of a pope "by inspiration" or the approval of religious orders give examples of ecclesiastical law taking responsibility for essentially charismatic (*Pneumatological*—Spirit-inspired) initiatives and drawing them into the unity of the church's social life and organization . . .

I stressed above that the initiative for religious foundations came from the periphery. But we also need to observe that, to become truly "Catholic" and to be incorporated within the church, they had to receive the approval of the central authority. This is why we see them all make a pilgrimage to Rome and to the Holy See, as Irenaeus pointed out early on. The center is where all the faithful from the whole horizon of the Christian world come together.[95] The reform of the canons in the eleventh century, as noted above, was brought to completion by the support and blessing that it received from the papacy of Gregory VII.[96] In the last third of the twelfth and first years of the thirteenth century, we see, one by one, Peter Ferdinand, John de Matha, the leaders of the Lombards, Durandus of Huesca and Bernard Prim, other itinerant preachers, the Humiliati, the Waldensians, the Poor Catholics, and finally Francis of Assisi and Dominic Guzman all come to Rome seeking approval for their reforming initiatives.[97]

The Holy See made their initiatives its own, and so made them Catholic. It gave them standing and position in the church, often with astounding boldness and generosity. Innocent III did not want to cut them off but, on the contrary, to welcome everything worthwhile and useful in these spiritual movements.[98] Even more examples could be

---

[95] Irenaeus, *Adv. Haer.*, III, 3, 2 (PG 7:848–849): "*Ad hanc Ecclesiam propter potiorem principalitatem necesse est omnem convenire Ecclesiam, hoc est eos qui sunt undique fideles*— Every church needs to come to this church because of its superior claim to leadership—this is the case for the faithful everywhere."

[96] Mandonnet, Vicaire, Ladner, op. cit., vol. II, p. 150.

[97] Ibid., vol. I, pp. 161f.; vol. II, pp. 36f.

[98] Cf. A. Luchaire, *Innocent III, le Concile de Latran et la réforme de l'Eglise*, p. 164 (references are given there); H. Grundmann, *Religiöse Bewegungen im Mittelalter* (Berlin, 1935), pp. 70–72, 87, 100 n. 55, 114 n. 59, 115 n. 90, 129. Also cf. Mandonnet-Vicaire-Ladner, vol. II, p. 304 n. 26, on the concession of the right to preach granted by Innocent III to the Waldensians or to others who were often reconciled just the day before. The Holy See's welcome of these spiritual movements was magnanimous, as was Urban II's welcome to Robert d'Arbrissel (Mandonnet, op. cit., vol. II, p. 34 n. 103); so also was Innocent III's welcome to the Waldensian *Humiliati* on their way to reconciliation, to Bernard Prim, etc. (Mandonnet, ibid., pp. 43f.). The hierarchy, especially the papacy, had also been very easy on Joachim of Flora and the movement he inspired.

given. The creation of Young Christian Workers constitutes a characteristic example in our day of a prophetic initiative from the periphery, the work of a suburban pastor in Brussels who was sent to Rome with a letter from his archbishop. There he encountered a pope with a prophetic spirit, a blessing which gave to the new movement the character of an activity of the church itself and made it the prototype of the reformist initiatives of Catholic Action. This was a magnificent initiative, full of promise for pastoral evolution—a prophetic work arising from the double prophetic charism of the periphery and the center. Even the hierarchy is prophetic and knows better than to stifle the Spirit.[99]

It is necessary here to dispense with some faulty ideas. First, an over-simplification of the philosophy of Bergson might conceive of ecclesiastical structure as representing a spirit that is *exhausted, frozen*, or *hardened*. Or second, like historians of preceding generations, someone might adopt the Protestant prejudice that *opposes* spirit to form, inspiration to authority, prophecy to power. But all that is wrong: there is only one same Spirit that enlivens and guides the church both at its center and in its periphery, both in its leaders and in the whole ecclesial body. The Spirit of Christ enlivens the church as a whole and also each part, according to what each is and the role it plays within the whole, for the benefit of the church's progress toward wholeness in unity. Thanks to the Spirit, "the whole body, joined and knit together by every ligament with which it is equipped, as each part is working properly, promotes the body's growth in building itself up in love" (Eph 4:16).

---

[99] After approving the *Humiliati* and granting them the right to preach moral exhortations, Innocent III defended them against the skepticism of the local bishops when he wrote: "*Prohibemus autem ne quis episcopus contra praescriptam formam impediat hujusmodi fratres verbum exhortationis proponere, cum secundum Apostolum non sit spiritus extinguendus*—I forbid any bishop to impede these brothers, in opposition to my decree, from preaching a word of exhortation, since the apostle warns us not to extinguish the Spirit" (cited in Mandonnet, op. cit., vol. II, p. 44, n. 161).

Ozanam was only twenty when he went to Msgr. de Quélen, then Archbishop of Paris, to explain what he considered to be the new essentials for Christian preaching as he saw it. Ozanam suggested to the conservative archbishop the name of a priest who had been part of the team that produced *l'Avenir*, Lacordaire, and the archbishop in fact appointed him to be the Preacher of Notre-Dame Cathedral.

In the present day, there is the *Mission de Paris*. At the time of its creation, Père Godin said of the bishops: "They are the brakes; we are the engine; both are necessary . . ." (P. Glorieux, *Un homme providentiel: L'Abbé Godin*, p. 317). However, the hierarchy—the Archbishop of Paris—permitted the *Mission de Paris* (following the *Mission de France*), supported it, and in reality made its continuation possible.

"Pneumatological" and "Prophetic" Functioning of the Hierarchy

The same Spirit enlivens the whole body to become the Body of Christ, to live and evolve in the unity of love; it enlivens the centers of the body to be centers possessing the love pertaining to leadership, and enlivens the church's ligaments to carry out their role of joining things together in a spirit of love, for the benefit of the growth and the adaptation of the whole body into unity. This explains why for the reformer or the "prophet" obedience to the Spirit often means transcending the accepted forms and being critical of anything that replaces growth with its antecedents or replaces the end by means. That still does not mean doing away with formal structures or hierarchical authorities. For in fact these structures, far from being outside the Spirit's movement, are at its service and express the Spirit's action insofar as this action concerns the whole body and finds its fulfillment in unity.

It is the same Spirit who lives in us, who enlivens the church and who assures unity to all its activities, for the benefit of the whole body, by enlivening the persons whose function it is to be guardians and guarantors of unity, centers and ligaments in the ecclesial body. This means that the Spirit brings about the life and unity of the body by making each person serve this vital ecclesial unity according to the function which he or she must exercise for the good of all. The Spirit brings about in each one the contribution appropriate for the service of the whole. In the whole body, which is the believing and loving church (of which the bishops are also a part, as faithful members), the Spirit stirs up the sense of the faith and zeal for good actions in the name of God. The Spirit places a charism of truth, of unity, and of apostolicity in the hierarchy, who act in service of the church's unity.[100]

So in our obedience to the Spirit, there is a kind of inherent tension, that is, an exchange or a relationship between two equally necessary poles. Ecclesial obedience attains its fullness only by including both poles and filling up the gap between them.

The two poles are initiatives on the periphery and the benediction from the center. Borrowing from some lovely pages of G. Goyau,[101] I will call these the *Orbis* (world) and the *Urbs* (city), without however failing to acknowledge the partial centers which are not *the* universal center of

---

[100] Worthwhile for this topic: M.-B. Schwalm, "L'inspiration intérieure et le gouvernement des âmes," *Revue thomiste* VI (1898), pp. 315–353 (esp. pp. 345f.); "Le respect de l'Eglise pour l'action intime de Dieu dans les âmes," ibid., pp. 707–738.

[101] At the conclusion of *Romée*, by N. Maurice-Denis Boulet. [By ancient tradition, the *Urbs* is Rome and the *Orbis* is the church spread out across the world.]

the church, but exercise a function analogous to it. The concrete life of the Church represents a perpetual exchange between the *Urbs* and the *Orbis*. The *Orbis* constantly brings to the *Urbs* its hopes, its problems, and its requests. The *Urbs* constantly remains concerned about the whole universe.[102] The *Orbis* brings its initiative to the *Urbs*, and the *Urbs* provides it limits and regulations. The *Orbis* brings to the *Urbs* the voices of the world that are multiple and impetuous, sometimes even violent and discordant; and the *Urbs* reiterates for the *Orbis* the apostolic voice of unity. The grace of the center is to harmonize the voice of the parts with the voice of the whole, not only across space (catholicity-unity), but across time (apostolicity-unity). It thus ensures that in a body which is immense and whose parts are all active participants, all nevertheless "are in agreement, without divisions among them, but united in the same mind and the same purpose" (1 Cor 1:10).[103]

Application of These Principles to Religious Orders (Troeltsch)

The preceding points explain how movements of renewal can become movements *in the church* and sources of renewal *of the church* without becoming sects.

Ever since Max Weber and especially since Ernst Troeltsch,[104] we generally distinguish between two types of religious groups: the "church"

---

[102] The *sollicitudo omnium Ecclesiarum*—the concern for the good of all the churches on the part of the Church of Rome—has been an historical fact from the beginning, and has great ecclesiological value. Many texts and examples illustrate this.

[103] For a fully developed theology about the relation of the center to the periphery, it would be necessary to discuss (among other things) the missionary function of the center. There again would be found the sort of tension or dialectic already noted concerning *Urbs* and *Orbis*. If *Orbis* amplifies the unity which is the norm for the living fullness of *Urbs*, *Urbs* nonetheless brings to completion in *Orbis* whatever fullness is contained in its intimacy and intensity. Both history and theology show us an essentially missionary quality at the center of Catholicism. The center's dynamic is to promote the expansion of the church beyond its existing frontiers.

[104] Max Weber, *Die protestantischen Sekten und der Geist des Kapitalismus*, in *Gesammelte Aufsätze zur Religionssoziologie*, vol. I, 2nd ed. (Tubingen, 1922), pp. 207–236 (this edition is augmented by an article which appeared with the title "Kirchen und Sekten," in *Die christliche Welt* [1906], pp. 558f., 577f.); cf. esp. p. 211 and 221. Weber is interested above all in the economic consequences of the two attitudes.

Ernst Troeltsch, *Die Soziallehren der christlichen Kirchen und Gruppen*, 2nd ed. (Tubingen, 1912), esp. vol. I, pp. 360f. I learned too late of the work of H. Schmidt, *Die Kirche:*

type and the "sect" type. According to Troeltsch, both are linked to the Gospel. However the "sect" type only retains the mandate to be in opposition to the world. Further, sects develop among little groups of people who, on the basis of an inner call, take up an attitude of opposition to the ordinary realities of social life. On the other hand, the "church" type is inclined toward universalism, addresses itself to the masses, and tries to harmonize the Gospel with everyday social reality. This approach shows the essential difference between sect and church.[105]

The church as an institution exists prior to its members and endures after them. The church influences its members by its objective reality, enveloping their lives and making up for their personal deficiencies. The members of the church are born *in the church*, so that she is their mother. The sect is a voluntary community: no one is born in it; people enter it through a personal decision. Everything depends on what the members themselves are personally. Belonging to a sect is not an institutional action but the personal action of the one who joins.[106]

Further, as Ritschl had suggested concerning Pietism, Troeltsch thinks that the gospel impulses that give rise to sects are the same as those which produce religious orders in the church. These orders are only an "ecclesification" [a *churchifying*] of sectarian spirit.[107] In the orders, the attitude of personal choice and flight from the world that creates the sects seeks expression in another way. For this reason, the church, hoping to assimilate a sect like the Waldensians, tried to convert it into religious orders (cf. Durandus and his one hundred Waldensians). There is also the example of the group of Penitents, mostly laity, recruited by St. Francis,

---

Ihre biblische Idee und die Formen ihrer geschichtlichen Erscheinung in ihren Unterschiede von Sekte und Härese (Leipzig, 1884), and so his unusual position is not presented here.

[105] Troeltsch, op. cit., pp. 371f.; Weber, op. cit.; cf. H. Mulert, *Konfessionskunde*, 2nd ed. (Berlin, 1937), p. 10.

[106] This is Weber's formula, developed by Troeltsch. For Weber, the church is a *Gnadenanstalt*: she takes in everybody who comes to her; persons are born into her and she acts upon the individuals who belong; no personal qualification is needed for membership. By contrast, the sect is a *Verein der religiös Qualifizierten*: someone chooses to belong and then pays the price of observing a discipline in order to stay; but the person is then also personally qualified.

[107] Troeltsch, op. cit., esp. pp. 360 and 809f. Cf. F. Parpert, *Das Mönchtum und die Evangelische Kirche* (Munich, 1930), pp. 58f. Luther had already described religious orders as "sects," but that was only to point out that (for him) they were opposed to the unity of the church. He put them in the same category as his other enemies, the Anabaptists.

who were, against his will and causing him unspeakable suffering, reduced to a regular type of religious order. Less tragically, we find something similar in the foundation of the Ursulines and the Sisters of the Visitation. In yet another area, it seems that laypeople devoted to theology go on to become monks, and the church seems anxious to integrate these scholars more closely into her structure by conferring the priesthood upon them.[108]

The view of this Protestant historian is both interesting and on target. However, Troeltsch seems less perceptive to me when he tries to describe the differences that separate sects from religious orders. He remarks upon their diverse ideas of asceticism. In his view, the sects represent the simple asceticism of a faithful Christian life following the Gospel in a literal way and expressing its hostility to the world. On the other hand, he sees in religious orders an asceticism of withdrawal from the world and of transcendence beyond the order of the senses.[109] Troeltsch is mesmerized by an old Protestant formula. He does not see the profound difference between sects and religious orders with respect to their *attitude toward the church*. Because of their attitude toward the church, religious orders depart from a sectarian mentality and become a concrete part of the church.

Christianity is always renewing itself through movements that represent more or less a sort of "revival." The monastic movement in Gaul and Ireland in the sixth century,[110] the eleventh-century reform, the Mendicant movement, the *Devotio Moderna*, the Counter-Reformation with its launching of new congregations, the reform spirit that motivated Lacordaire, that inspired Le Sillon, the Young Christian Workers and Catholic Action—all these are so many different Catholic revival movements. Protestantism also experienced revivals and initiatives of renewal, but it is noteworthy that in claiming to go back to authentic Christianity, these movements in the Protestant world often ended up creating a sect.[111] Troeltsch correctly notes (pp. 809f.) that Catholicism, being at once

---

[108] Dom Basile Steidle, *Die Kirchenväter* (Ratisbon, 1939), p. 60 (cited in H. Urs von Balthasar, *Der Laie und der Ordenstand* [Einsiedeln, 1948], p. 37).

[109] Troeltsch, op. cit., pp. 363, 368f.

[110] On this, look at J. Chevalier, *Essai sur la formation de la nationalité et les réveils religieux aux pays de Galles, des origins à la fin du VIe siècle* (Lyons and Paris, 1923).

[111] For example, Methodism was a sect within Anglicanism, and the Brethren communities a sect within Lutheranism. Cf. Möhler, *Symbolique*, French trans., vol. II, p. 305.

centralized and also broad and flexible, has been able to destroy every sect that tried to come into being alongside it, while in its religious orders it gave a canonical status to the spiritual tendency that is liable to create sects. By contrast, Protestantism, open to new interpretations of the Bible and lacking a hierarchical central authority, offered fertile ground for the emergence of sects.

This needs further analysis. I can only evoke here a theme that takes on greater importance in part 3* of this work. But it is necessary to show how Protestantism, in its desire to give "glory to God alone," has come to see in Christianity nothing but the act *of God* and not the aspect of a *given reality*; so it has emptied out the full meaning of the church, postulating simply Pentecost, but without its ecclesial consequences.[112] Having maintained (and desiring to maintain) only the *prophetic* aspect of the church, Protestantism has lost the sense of hierarchical *apostolicity* of the mission. Therefore it always fails to address and to resolve the problem of integrating prophetic movements into the unity of the church. Misunderstanding the apostolicity of ministry, Protestantism misconstrues the church as an institution, seeing in the church only a community of faithful people. Protestantism also misunderstands the order of ecclesial structure and lacks the institutional organs to bring about the insertion of peripheral movements into the framework of the church.

Returning to the topic of religious revivals and the principle which turns them either into a sect or into a renewal movement in the church, there are some further points. The revival which ends up *in* the church is the one that does not consider itself *the* true Christianity to the exclusion of all others, but simply an effort within Christianity to bring about a more perfect realization of it. The church exists for this. The church preexists such a movement and never ceases to surpass and dominate it. Such a movement consequently is assimilated into the spirit of the church and at no point places itself *outside*, so as to judge or correct the church.

While sects become preoccupied with their own point of view, which they identify with true Christianity, religious orders become preoccupied with the spirit of the church, seeking to be established and to develop

---

* Not included in this translation.

[112] Nothing is more typical of this point than the otherwise marvelous work of J. Ellul, "Signification actuelle de la Réforme," in the collection *Protestantisme français* (Paris, 1945), pp. 137–165.

within an institution accepted as a given. The church, fully aware of its own spirit, can offer religious orders a normative value.

In the religious entities that arose out of the Reformation itself, renewal movements which did not turn into sects were those for which the church was considered a *given* and for which the goal was to revitalize the tradition. So in contemporary Protestantism, the Barthian movement or an initiative like the community of Taizé, and in Anglicanism in the nineteenth century, the Oxford movement, are examples of this. It is noteworthy—and I am not the first to make this remark[113]—that if the revival movements of the sixteenth to the nineteenth centuries generally developed into sects, that is no longer the case today because of the clear revival of the idea of the church.

In a concrete way, religious movements in the Catholic Church are guided and brought to maturity by approval from the centers where the mind of the church finds its natural expression. Revival movements, initially marked by the kind of ambivalence that we have recognized in prophetic initiatives, become movements of the church and a renewal in the church by accepting the guidance of the center. The classic example of this—perhaps the best example—is the Franciscan movement. There were, both in the personality and the initiative of Francis, clear possibilities for sectarian expression.

So once more, God's word is proven true: "Whoever loses his soul saves it, whoever wants to save himself or herself will lose themselves." This sort of handing of the self over to hierarchical direction will mean for a religious movement some sort of loss of control and almost a kind of resignation. St. Francis underwent this trial in an exceptionally vivid fashion. But today, where is the spirit of Francis maintained, if not in the Franciscan Order? The spirit of Waldo no longer exists anywhere in a concrete way; the spirit of Francis exists, and those attracted to it know where to find it. Those who have, like Benedict, the spirit of religion and praise know where to go to live that charism. Those who, like the Madames Bigard, feel called to assist the indigenous clergy will rediscover the spirit of these two women in the Work of St. Peter the Apostle that they founded. This is how the institution protects inspiration, how law protects life, in the Body of Christ which is the church. The prophetic

---

[113] Cf., e.g., C. T. Craig, "Report on the Study of the Church," in *The Nature of the Church: A Report of the American Theological Committee of Faith and Order* (Chicago, 1945), p. 22.

spirit finds a body for itself and, in animating this body, it is conserved within it.

Being Connected to the Community

I want to add another consideration here, namely, the benefit that belonging to a community brings to the Christian who participates in a reformist movement. Both history and contemporary experience show how apostolic and reform movements are connected to a desire for community and to the building of teamwork in a spirit of brotherhood. This is a norm both for human life as well as for the Gospel. Père Mandonnet makes this desire for community one of the characteristic traits of the early thirteenth century, a period rich in reform initiatives.[114] In our time, the thirst for community and teamwork is noteworthy in all of today's "missionary" initiatives and efforts at pastoral renewal. Sharing everything in common is called for by the Gospel itself; and in the ecclesiastical tradition, the words "apostolic life" and "evangelical life" still imply poverty and common life.[115] But there are other reasons for the common endeavor characteristic of a reform movement.

The first reason is effectiveness. One single person is too weak to change the situation or to carry off projects by himself or herself. The reform of the clergy by founding seminaries in the spirit of the Council of Trent was able to succeed only because of the founding of religious congregations of priests. Cardinal Lorraine in Rheims and Cardinal de Joyeuse in Rouen both failed to reform their clergy by themselves. On the other hand, M. Bourdoise, Pères Condren and Bérulle, Monsieur Olier and Vincent de Paul, all founded congregations of priests for seminary teaching and succeeded.

At a deeper level, assessing the real missionary challenges and the true needs for reform in the church is more effective when done in a group. Moreover, in the church, especially living in the spirit of charity which I discussed earlier, a genuine reform spirit requires loyalty, single-

---

[114] P. Mandonnet, "Les origines de l '*Ordo de Poenitentia*,'" in *IVe Congrès scientifique internat. des catholiques* (Fribourg, 1898), p. 183f. (reprinted in *Saint Dominique* [Paris, 1938], vol. II, pp. 295f.)

[115] Cf. J. Leclercq, *La vie parfaite: Points de vue sur l'essence de l'état religieux* (Turnhout and Paris, 1948), pp. 82f.; cf. M. Vicaire, *L'imitation des Apôtres* (Paris, 1963).

mindedness and transparency, which succeed and are more expressive when people stimulate and help one another in a fraternal way. In accord with the demands of charity, which is the heart of the church, the more someone is committed to critical work for reform, the more someone ought to refocus on the fraternal life of the church just as it is.

We have already seen that, according to Lortz, Erasmus failed to live and think sufficiently in tune with the currents and the context of the church's sacramental life. Further, he overintellectualized his idea of the church and so became a critic who was, if not dangerous, at least troubling.[116] Common fraternal life, by its very nature as well as in its many different expressions, provides mutual control, correction, and complementary perspectives which ought to assure a spirit of communion in the whole. Our brothers and sisters around us become a kind of virtual representation of the whole church. Often their objections, expressions of surprise, and corrections are precisely those that we would encounter in the wider Catholic community. So concretely, through contact with them in our exchanges on the local scene, we can experience the beneficial influence of the ecclesial community in simplifying, rectifying, and purifying our ideas.

Even more important, one person often can provide us the benefit of putting our personal ideas in the perspective of the whole body. We call such a person a spiritual director, counselor, or older brother (or sister), it doesn't matter. Such a person can be the means for us of avoiding the pitfalls of isolation. He or she bears witness *to the others* and, more explicitly, to the church and its tradition. We often think of the benefit of this direction or advice only from the point of view of personal spiritual interest. We have failed to point out the ecclesiological significance. In this respect, the advice of a director or, more simply, the fraternal guidance of another person can be the means of attuning the movement of one person to that of the whole church, of guiding the truth of a particular spiritual feeling toward the wholeness of Catholic truth.

The "director" can be someone who, in a way, makes the virtual presence of the whole church real. He or she ought to be someone living within the church, knowing its doctrine, its history, the writings of its spiritual masters, and the lives of the saints, so as to be able to guide, encourage, and correct another individual soul in the name of the tradition. In the internal forum, the director represents the tradition for this

---

[116] J. Lortz, *Die Reformation als religiöses Anliegen heute* (Trier, 1948), p. 80.

person, that is, the integration of the church's teaching, the totality of what it has received, understood, lived, and expressed through time and through space. The director is there to help the individual take advantage of everything that the Catholic Church has taught and experienced. This explains why St. Teresa of Avila preferred a theologian as her director rather than a holy man who was nothing more than holy.[117]

Communion Justifies the Possibility for a Breakthrough

As noted above, a prophetic movement finds in the idea of communion with the whole church both the standard for its orthodoxy and the justification for its desire to transcend the actual state of church practice, should that be necessary. This point is extremely important. This follows from the very possibility of there being a prophetic movement *in the church*. For if people were always required to conform themselves to the actual state of theological thinking, church practice, spirituality, and administration in the church, there would never be adaptation, reform, or progress. We would never have had religious orders, frequent Communion, devotion to the Sacred Heart, the *Summa Theologiae*, Catholic Action, missionary renewal, the new translation of the Psalter,[118] or any of the other moments of church renewal with which history is filled. From one end to the other, church history presents us with examples that transcend the received thinking of a given moment. That is, history shows us the perpetual exercise of prophecy that, as we've seen, is the work of the hierarchy as well as of the periphery. However, the innovations described here are taken for granted today; they no longer seem to us to be daring initiatives. They become almost

---

[117] Cf. M.-J. Savignol, *Sainte Thérèse de Jésus et l'Ordre de Saint-Dominique* (Toulouse, 1931), pp. 291–292. St. John of the Cross is also, for his part, very hard on directors who don't know the doctrine of spirituality; cf. *Montée du Carmel*, vol. II, ch. 16.

In this context it would certainly be interesting to look again at the way the scholastic theologians and Saint Thomas developed the theme of the "*clavis scientiae*—the key of knowledge."

[118] As to criticisms made against the new Psalter, I myself heard the Holy Father [Pius XII] and a person high in the Roman Curia say in 1946: "If, when something is changed, such criticism is leveled, it becomes hard to reform anything . . . Sometimes people accuse the church of being behind the times, even reactionary, but in reality the church is for progress and needs to seek progress . . ."

like a sacred tradition. As an example, a young Catholic painter was complaining that no one was giving contemporary artists work to do in the church. A priest countered: "Modern painters are impossible—if only we had a Puvis de Chavannes!" To which the young artist replied, "When he was alive, how many churches was Puvis de Chavannes asked to work on?"

The problem with every reform initiative is how to transcend not only actual existing forms but also those that are officially approved. This touches not only behaviors but also ways of thinking (exception made for what is properly considered dogma). At issue is the freedom to adapt and make progress in the development of thought. An example would be the pursuit of biblical research beyond the barriers erected at a certain moment, for reasons which were given at the time by the Biblical Commission of the Holy Office (as in the case of the verse about the "three witnesses").[119] Another example is the pursuit of engagement and dialogue between Christianity and the modern world that advances beyond the barrier established by Proposition 80 of the Syllabus.[120] Or again, how we can develop a liturgical reform that transcends not only certain present-day usages but also, for example, texts grounded in an outmoded situation or a passé state of affairs. These are all examples of realities in the church, realities that can be met on a daily basis. But if one had *never* transcended *any* disciplinary norm, Catholics would have been obliged from the time of Galileo to 1822 to hold that the earth is the center of the universe and that it doesn't move . . .[121]

We can aim to transcend the presently given limits precisely in the name of a more genuine communion and a more Catholic truth. Fidelity can go beyond a kind of superficial fidelity, a two-dimensional affair, to achieve fidelity in depth, contextualizing the literal expression of Catholic principles and articulating their appropriate contemporary development.

---

[119] *Decree of the Holy Office* of Jan. 13, 1897; cf. Mirbt, *Quellen zur Geschichte des Papsttums*, n. 636. The text cannot be found in Denziger or in the *Enchiridion Biblicum*.

[120] The condemned proposition reads as follows: "*Romanus Pontifex potest ac debet cum progressu, cum liberalismo et cum recenti civilitate sese reconciliare et componere*—The Roman Pontiff can and ought to be reconciled with and accommodate to progress, liberalism and recent social change," in Denziger, 1780. See below under the Fourth Condition (p. 301 and n. 213).

[121] The text of Galileo's condemnation is in Mirbt, op. cit., n. 515. In the 17th century, Galileo's condemnation was considered parallel to the condemnation of Aristotle's philosophy in the 13th century; cf. J. de Launoy, *Dict. Théol. Cath.*, vol. IX, col. 3.

The church sometimes expresses in its condemnations or solemn repudiations a sure articulation of what her principles *are not*. In this respect, an anathema condemning a heresy with a penalty is something that will not be revisited. *Positive* expressions about doctrine or morals, however, leave room for reconsideration or for a broader realization of the principle realized in their articulation. Condemnations that are not about pure ideas but about historical movements have a character that is in part practical *and cannot be understood outside their historical context.* These will be susceptible to some kind of revision, as the church's central powers themselves show us, even as they remain judges of when this may be opportune.[122] In certain cases, like that of the decrees of the Biblical Commission, texts are edited in such fashion as to leave possibilities open for research that will integrate new conclusions.

Further, what is the meaning of "positive theology," if not an effort to enrich theological thinking with the contributions of the whole Christian tradition? This eventually leads to a reformulation of currently held positions, in the name of a broader and more Catholic communion with the larger and deeper tradition. In summary, it is an effort to rediscover, as far as possible, the purity and the fullness of the theological principle by grasping it in its totality and by seeing the developments and the expressions it has provoked. History is, for every reform movement, marvelous as an educator and an aid, for history acquaints us with the principle in other contexts, forms, and developments than those in which we see it empirically realized. The "prophet," as a man of action, has a sense of history and loves to be schooled by her.

Within groups more or less close to the *Reformkatholizismus* (a German Catholic reform movement that insufficiently guarded against Modernist tendencies), they spoke sometimes about *Zukunftkirche*, a church situated in the future that will have improved the state of the church and reformed itself . . . Some people have abused this idea and turned it into a dangerous formula. All things considered, however, the notion does value the idea of *church* upon which reform initiatives are grafted and into which they are integrated. However, if this should presuppose a disparate development of a fallible church (one even that has failed), a critical

---

[122] So a series of liberating decrees from the Congregation of Propaganda progressively: (1) declared civil ceremonies in Korea and Japan (of Shinto origin) in honor of the emperor to be licit (Decree of May 26, 1936), (2) suppressed the oath concerning the Chinese Rites (Dec. 8, 1939), and (3) suppressed the oath concerning the Malabar Rites (April 9, 1940).

type of reform, a purely symbolic relation between the ecclesiastical structures and the principle of the church—presuppositions that were generally those of Modernism—then the notion of *Zukunftkirche* can only be unhealthy. But, on the contrary, if this presupposes the proper understanding of development, of the form and continuity of the church, of the conditions for a true reform, and of the proper relation of ecclesiastical structures to the principle, then the idea of *Zukunftkirche* can serve to express the tendency toward a state of things where the principle of Catholicism is being achieved in a fuller way, more in conformity with its own deep tradition and better adapted to the needs of the time.

The real problem will always be how to move toward a renewed state of affairs while keeping continuity with the present church. Undoubtedly one of the dangers of the idea of a *Zukunftkirche*, or even with the notion of a *Papa angelicus* [an angelic Pope],[123] is that an imaginary and more or less illusory future ideal becomes an alibi for avoiding true Christian fidelity and for allowing the humble but existentially real conditions of church life in the present to be forgotten. This links us back to considerations we developed earlier.

In searching for communion with a richer tradition, it is necessary not to lose communion with the actual concrete church, which remains the norm for everything. When Saint-Cyran wrote, for example, that "to judge the spirit of the church fairly and even its true doctrine, it is not enough to see what is commonly practiced or one of the opinions of the modern schools, but it is necessary . . . to go back to the purest sources of the most universal tradition,"[124] he articulated essentially what we have just explained. But he didn't stop there. With the Jansenist taste for going back to the past, he left out, both in his thinking and his practice, a consideration of the necessity to keep a living relation and a real obedience to the actual church.

---

[123] The idea of a *Papa angelicus* (an ideal pope completely freed from earthly constraints) was launched by Joachim of Flora and later by Arnaud de Villeneuve. The idea was rather widespread in the late Middle Ages; cf. Baethgen, *Der Engelpapst* (Halle, 1933), who gives bibliography for the topic.

From an ecumenical motive, Lord Halifax occasionally, and F. Heiler very often, called for the coming of a *"Papa angelicus"* . . . Cf. a book that is at once the latest and the best book of F. Heiler, *Altkirchliche Autonomie und päpstlicher Zentralismus* (Munich, 1941); on the *"Papa angelicus,"* see pp. 287f., 386f. (bibliography). Cf. my review of this book in *Revue des Sciences philosophiques et théologiques* (1947), pp. 276f.

[124] *Mémoires* by Lancelot, cited in Bremond, *Histoire litt. du sent. religieux*, vol. IV, p. 150.

That was the drama of Jansenism that Pascal lived: "After Rome had spoken and was thought to have condemned the truth of what they wrote, and their books (which said the opposite of what was claimed) were condemned, I had to cry out as loudly as possible that they had been censured unjustly and that the word was being violently smothered; until a pope who would listen to both parties and who would examine the past should see that justice be done. And so good popes will still find the church in discord . . . If my letters are condemned in Rome, what I condemn in my letters has been condemned in heaven. *Ad tuum, Domine Jesu, tribunal appello*—Lord Jesus, I appeal to your tribunal." [125]

When Pascal adopted this word of St. Bernard as a kind of motto for Port Royal,[126] the ambivalence of the prophetic movement brought him close to a spirit of schism. Pascal's attitude, as sublime and prophetic as it was, was not entirely pure. The Christian tradition has always respected a conscience that is certain of itself. It has always admitted that some souls, even without a hierarchical mission but prompted by the Holy Spirit, could *reprimand* the hierarchy and even the pope.[127] However, consciences just as prophetic, just as mortally wounded, but holier and more humble, as well as more faithful, speak differently than that. If you want examples, read the letter of St. Columban to Boniface IV,[128] St. Bernard's *De consideratione*, the *Dialogue* and *Letters* of St. Catherine of Siena, those of St. Bridget to Gregory XI, and, closer to us, the report of the chaplains of the lycée to Msgr. de Quélen,[129] edited by Lacordaire. Even closer to our day, there was the report of Père Lebbe to Msgr. Reynaud, his bishop in China, in 1917, followed by a heartbreaking

---

[125] Brunschvig, frag. 920.

[126] Cf. E. Jovy, "D'où vient l'*Ad tuum, Domine Jesu, tribunal appello* de Pascal?: Pascal et Saint Bernard, 1657," in *Etudes pascaliennes*, III (Paris, 1928), pp. 54–87 (first edited and published in 1916); also J. de Blic, "Note sur l'*Ad tuum, Domine Jesu, tribunal appello*," in *Arch. de Philosophie*, I (1923), pp. 301f. We find something comparable in Savonarola's last sermon of March 18, 1498: "When the highest authorities [of the church?] fail, and they become a harmful influence on the church, one has to take refuge in Christ and say to him, 'You are my superior, you are my pastor, you are my pope . . .,'" etc.

[127] See the texts and references in J. Leclercq, *Jean de Paris et l'ecclésiologie du XIIIe siècle* (Paris, 1942), pp. 129, 155, n. 7.

[128] PL 80:274f.

[129] The text is in T. Foisset, *Vie du R. P. Lacordaire* (Paris, 1870), vol. I, pp. 86–92. See also Lacordaire's letter of Oct. 31, 1834, to Msgr. de Quélen about the accusations made against him as lecturer at the Lycée Stanilaus, op. cit., pp. 569–575.

postscript.[130] There you can see the language of a prophetic conscience, captivated by its mission or its truth but maintaining total submission and communion with the church just as it is.

I said earlier that one of the fundamental errors of Jansenism was to take its inspiration from the texts of St. Augustine without maintaining sufficient docility toward the concrete life of the contemporary church. Here again there is a dynamic of tension. To the tension already examined between the periphery and the center, there is here the added tension between an appeal to a broader and more ancient tradition, on the one hand, and the requirements for communion with the church of the present, on the other hand; between fidelity to insights of unquestionable authenticity and submission to the living church.

The Responsibility of the Center to Listen to the Periphery

This need for the reformer to be submissive has a counterpart in the church's obligation (especially of those who hold centralized authority) to be attentive to the appeals that are addressed to them. St. Bernard did not hesitate to write to Pope Eugenius III with respect to the pope's failure to pay attention to appeals made to Rome: "How long are you going to refuse to listen to the complaints of the whole world?"[131] If heresy or sects represent a one-sided development of an initiative that has lost its way, and if they are obliged to listen closely to the call to unity and to obey its demands, a comparable duty is imposed on the authority to listen to new voices that it is not accustomed to hearing. If there is a sin on the part of the reformist movement in refusing or misunderstanding the demands for unity, there would be a parallel sin for the institution to misconstrue or stifle prophetic impulses. Besides, since real vital impulses are irrepressible, if they cannot find a sufficient outlet, won't they have to create an alternative expression elsewhere? When liturgy is excessively rigid, "paraliturgies" come into being that are never the right solution for the problem of adapting worship to human needs.

However, these two related obligations are not on the same level. The obligation of the periphery to seek an ecclesial status and receive the

---

[130] Part of the text is in L. Levaux, *L'Orient et nous* (Louvain, 1932), pp. 92–99; and the complete text in L. Levaux, *Le Père Lebbe, apôtre de la Chine moderne* (Brussels and Paris, 1948), pp. 195–209.

[131] *De consideratione,* I, 3, ch. 2, no. 7 (PL 182:762).

blessing of the center corresponds to what is imposed upon a vital movement so that it will become part of the life of the church and rooted within
its ecclesiastical structure. If you do not build on the same frame, you
are not part of the same house . . . The question here is, to be or not to
be. If the center does not respond to the initiatives and demands of the
periphery when the sap is bubbling in a tree having growing pains, still
the existence of the church is not in question here. The only risk is the
church not achieving its fullness. This is serious, very serious, but it
doesn't call into question the very foundations of the church.

We ought to be glad that the church's hierarchical powers have a
strong desire to be open to the appeals of the periphery, in dialogue with
the *Orbis*. But here as elsewhere, the question is not just moral or spiritual; there are technical implications. To be realistic, the solution presupposes the implementation of appropriate means.

First of all, should there not be, alongside the central power, in the
midst of the top administration of the church, a substantial representation of all the elements of the *Orbis*, of all the tendencies of the periphery?
This point, which I had tentatively raised before,[132] seems so important
to me that I don't hesitate to bring it up here again. I insist all the more
in seeing that the tendency of the world at large has influenced a certain
decentralization in the church, symbolized by the Consistory of Cardinals
of February 18, 1946, showing the desire for a representation of the universality of peoples in this supreme advisory council.[133] I see the same
hopefulness in developments which have followed since then and in the
new things that have emerged from Vatican II.

In no way does this call into question the administrative centralization
of the church, even though many do consider it excessive. Historically,
centralization has been a necessity and a good thing. Introduced by the
salutary measures taken by the Gregorian Reform, centralization has
permitted the church since then to be confident of its independence with
respect to secular rulers and especially with respect to the nomination of
bishops. This centralization led to an important and lasting progress in
the propriety of clerical morality and in the seriousness of ecclesiastical
life. However, in order that the *Urbs* be genuinely open to the voices of

---

[132] *Chrétiens désunis* (1937), p. 132.

[133] Cf. on this point the allocution to the Sacred College of Dec. 24, 1945, in which
the Holy Father explained the significance of his decision (*Doc. Cathol.* of Jan. 20,
1946); and Y. Congar, "Rhythmes de l'Eglise et du monde," *La Vie Intellectuelle* (April
1946).

the *Orbis*, it is indispensable that the administrative organs that serve
the central power of church represent the immense diversity of the
church and the broad trends of the world. This is pertinent, of course,
for the spiritual and Christian world but also for the cultural world.
Consequently these administrative organs, in welcoming global initiatives (both Christian and non-Christian) and thus living the problems
of the world along with it, can then truly represent within the central
See of the church the desires, the problems, the initiatives, and the hopes
of a humanity in development.

But we need to see development beyond a merely "diplomatic representation," going beyond simply personnel who are international by
origin but still purely Roman by mentality; there needs to be at the heart
of the Church a *representation of the problems*.[134] Being out of touch, even
a little, with living contact at the base or at the periphery is always dangerous for those in charge. Contemporary examples can be given both
from political parties as well as from the church. There is also the case
of the French Court at the end of the Ancien Régime, or the case of the
French episcopate in 1791 on the question of resistance to the Civil Constitution of the Clergy.[135]

Taking and developing a great idea of Msgr. Constantini, Dom Pierre
Célestin Lou recently showed the need for an effective representation of
the Chinese cultural world at the center of the Catholic world. China is
the oldest human civilization in existence and it represents 450 million
people.[136] He wrote, "The results of this effort would infinitely outweigh
all the trouble it would involve. It would give to the church (mother of
all the churches) the ability to be not only the spiritual capital of the
Christian world, but to become as well the cultural and moral capital of
the universe."

---

[134] Rightly or wrongly, a great number of those who work at the church's frontiers
in the intellectual life or in the apostolate feel that the church's highest administration
is sometimes out of touch spiritually with the problems of thought and of pastoral
life in which the local churches are involved. A great number of good pastoral workers in Catholic ministry do not conceal that, although they find understanding *at the
very top*, they don't find enough at the staff level. Cf. an article discussing this (testi-
monials are legion) in *Esprit* (Aug.–Sept. 1946), p. 270; in *Revue Nouvelle* (May 5, 1952),
pp. 511 and 518–19.

[135] Cf. Latreille, *L'Eglise catholique et la Révolution* (1947), vol. I, pp. 101–102.

[136] P. C. Lou, *Souvenirs et pensées* (Paris, 1945), pp. 145–153, citing a conference by
Msgr. Constantini that appeared in *Osservatore Romano* on Jan. 25, 1940.

What we are talking about here is not, properly speaking, decentralization, but rather the question of avoiding the danger of isolation. In a text written with reference to the Modernist Crisis that is still valid, W. Foerster developed this thought with depth and realism.[137] It shows how a certain kind of recruiting of personnel for the central administration leads in reality to "not reinforcing papal power, but simply isolating it." In fact, if personnel are chosen only from men of a certain type, generally conservative and safe, reinforcing only the static dimension in the notions of fidelity and tradition—that is, choosing people who don't cause problems, are not the source of surprises, and don't take any risks—then evidently the institution ends up placing a barrier of isolation between the periphery and the center, making the center a sort of "party." Such an agency would meet some of the needs of the institution, such as security and moderation, but it would fail to respond to other needs, equally sacred, of a body always anxious to adapt and to make progress in the world. Many ideas or hopes of those in the church—above all, among the most dynamic elements of the church—would never be heard in that case.

The problem is serious enough that I feel permitted—even obliged—to raise it, respectfully, but frankly. Further, in reediting today [1968] this book written in 1950 after the council of Good Pope John XXIII, I can only salute, with gratitude, the beginning of a transformation whose importance the future will reveal. This transformation is seen not only in episcopal collegiality, the Synod of Bishops, and the internationalization of the Roman Curia, but also in the central instruments of contact with "others," such as the five secretariats created at Rome alongside the classic dicasteries: the Secretariat for Christian Unity, the Secretariat for non-Christian religions, and the Secretariats for nonbelievers, for the laity, and for justice and peace in the world. These are organs of information, dialogue, and action that correspond to the need to receive ideas from others and to truly be a church for the world.

---

[137] *Autorité et Liberté*, French trans. (Lausanne, 1920), pp. 138–148.

THIRD CONDITION:

Having Patience with Delays

In any reform movement, impatience threatens to ruin everything and to make an ambivalent initial inspiration evolve in a sectarian direction. In a passage worthy of status as a classic,[138] Newman offered some reflections about this that Jean Guitton has taken and aptly applied to Newman himself.[139] The innovator, whose reform turns into schism, lacks patience. He does not respect the slowness either of God or of the church, or the delays that come into everyone's life. He moves with a kind of inflexible and exasperated logic toward "all or nothing" solutions, in which viable possibilities are rejected along with problems. For a while, he insists that the church should satisfy his demands immediately, or otherwise he will leave. The heretical innovator doesn't know how to

---

[138] *Apologia pro Vita Sua*, French trans. (Paris, 1939), pp. 294–295.

[139] J. Guitton, *La pensée moderne et le catholicisme: Parallèles—Renan et Newman* (Aix, 1933), pp. 167f.; and *Justification du temps* (Paris, 1941), p. 93: "Those who want to be at the cutting edge of the moment fall into an excess of haste, which comes from investing the present with a significance that it cannot really bear . . . The strategy of 'leaving things for tomorrow,' of which laziness is only a kind of deformity, is so wise. Justice has never found any other means of making peace under precarious circumstances than that of splitting up the trial into many distinct parts, of expecting interruptions, of making provision for appeals, not only so as to exhaust the parties involved, but to impose time for waiting—just as tragedy imposes waiting. Delay is the victory of the weak; and just as, generally speaking, the weak are just, delay is a saving grace. This is what the violent cannot bear. Of course, all these aspects of delay can very easily become degraded. Delay becomes lateness, waiting becomes laziness and resignation . . ."

wait for an idea to mature; rather, he launches his idea, immediately and inflexibly pushing it to its consequences. In so doing, such people not only risk failing to achieve the change they seek, but they spoil for others the possibilities for change that might have come about. So many times impatience or excessiveness has seriously harmed causes in the church which of themselves were perfectly appropriate. For example, in the history of granting Communion under both species in Bohemia, the impatience of the *Utraquists* and their exaggerations made a favorable outcome more difficult.

The Nature of Patience and Its Role

If the spirit of reform is going to remain *in the church*, then it must have patience. By that I mean a lot more than the lapse of time or an attitude of temporizing. What is needed is a spiritual and mental disposition that understands the meaning and necessity of delays. This is a kind of humility and spiritual flexibility that is conscious of imperfections and even of deadly compromises. Jean Guitton thought that he could characterize the Catholic and Protestant attitudes toward reform respectively by, on the one hand, a *sense of fullness* and, on the other hand, a *search for purity*.[140] This seems right to me with respect to a phenomenology of behavior. There remains something more to explain, however, and perhaps the third part of this book will contribute some valuable reflections along these lines. [The third part is not included in this edition.]

I can willingly accept that the Catholic Church and the Reformation, with respect to the content of their claims, represent a wisdom perspective, on the one hand, and a voluntarist or personalist-existential idea of God on the other. They are opposed temperamentally, with respect to how their believers receive or find their religion. On the one hand, it is a religion of life in its fullness, and on the other hand, a religion seeking for purity. In this way, Protestantism is more intellectual than Catholicism. An idea can be pure, but reality and life cannot be. So it is clear that this condition of patience is connected to the first of the conditions sketched above—the submission of the intellectual and systematic point of view to the pastoral.

---

[140] J. Guitton, *Difficultés de croire* (Paris, 1948), pp. 230f. I find the same idea in J. Hessen, *Luther in katholischer Sicht* (Bonn, 1946), pp. 39f., or in *Platonismus und Prophetismus* (Munich, 1939), p. 178.

"The mind moves quickly." The mind can easily and quickly understand something in a dialectical way, grasp a difference, an opposition, or a logical consequence. However, to appreciate the full depth of a reality, it takes a lot of time and of life experience. Without doubt, this fullness of meaning can never be grasped by the mind alone, much less "defined." (Dogmatic "definitions" are generally negative in form.) By contrast, the fullness of meaning can be lived and embraced only in the life of communion to which this study is dedicated.

Heresy comes in large part from a purely intellectual grasp of something—a grasp too impatient to wait for life to develop and for the gradual learning that comes from experience. It is easy for the mind to grasp a straightforward truth. However, it is equally true that an idea *develops* only over time, with respect to aspects other than those grasped by dialectics alone. This fuller kind of development demands experience, lived and nourished by human sensibility, by contact with the questions and conditions of life itself. This shows us the immense difference between a truth grasped only by the mind in a dialectical fashion and a truth maturing in solitude or in faithful service, a truth carried for a long time in one's heart, nourished by one's life. Too quick a formulation of an idea that would be the fruit of dialectical intelligence alone produces results that are dry and superficial.[141]

Everything that involves life experience, at least here below, presupposes delays which cannot be sidetracked or avoided. Only what's done in cooperation with the nature of time itself can conquer time. Sometimes we are tempted to wonder why, after the discovery of something like aviation, for example, we could not have more rapidly deduced and applied the principles of aerodynamics. It seems that a sufficiently bright mind would have been able from the start to develop the consequences that in fact it took a lot of precious time to explore . . . But that is only fantasy. Time and experience were necessary, as well as systematic trials that led only to dead ends. In fact, it was the obstacles that occurred that opened up new approaches.

---

[141] This holds true not just for the ideologues of the sects but ultimately as well for the reaction of orthodox scholars. For example, too quick a reaction of a purely intellectual and dialectical kind, when faced with the spirituality of a Luther or a Gregory Palamas, runs the risk of overlooking profound issues, while producing an illusory clarity and an easy victory. We also know the expression of W. G. Ward, who wished he could receive a new papal bull every morning at breakfast time, along with his *Times*. (Cf. P. Thureau-Dangin, *La renaissance catholique en Angleterre*, 3rd ed., vol. II, p. 323.) What the English call "breakfast dogma" has little spiritual depth.

This is even truer in life, where moral decisions represent an even more decisive factor. Even supposing that a "prophet" might have seen and predicted before others something that the passage of time would finally prove true, it still would have been imprudent to follow him. In order for certain decisions or changes to be put into place, the passage of time must reveal facts, leading to possibilities whose uncertain value is impossible to foresee. Take an example. Many Catholics in the last third of the nineteenth century and the first quarter of the twentieth thought that the Holy See should have given up all its temporal possessions. When the Treaty of the Lateran was signed in 1927, they felt a genuine liberation. But could one have foreseen in 1870 what might be the consequences for the Holy See of losing its sovereignty? Of course, in the nineteenth century many Catholics had predicted that a church disengaged from all temporal involvements would have a greater impact on the world. The future showed that they were right. But there were others, not lacking in insight, who prophesied that the loss of temporal power would be the ruin of the church.[142] In fact, their point of view turned out to be wrong. But they legitimately asked if the independence of the Holy See might not be seriously threatened, and it is understandable how the ecclesiastical authorities refused to immediately follow prophets who foretold a new freedom based upon the absence of any earthly guarantees.

Basically any reform is in some way a foretaste of the eschatological kingdom and its justice and purity. On the one hand, this is so because reforms have an aspect of judgment and condemnation bearing upon history and its insufficiencies (a theme upon which Berdyaev insisted). On the other hand, reforms have a positive tendency aiming to bring about a state of affairs which comes closer to perfection and purity. Revolutions and reforms are a sort of partial anticipation of the Apocalypse and of eschatology. Reformers always have a tendency not only to initiate things but also to rush their development. They not only want to clean up the field; they want to free it of every weed. The Gospel parable of the wheat and the weeds, however, teaches us to respect the period of waiting until the harvest for the growth of the seeds. It teaches us not to anticipate the harvest with impatient efforts to clean things up,

---

[142] See what Frederick II thought, for example (*Corresp. de Voltaire*, July 9, 1777). Many saw temporal power as a condition for the freedom of the Holy See in 19th-century Europe; for example, Döllinger (in the preface of the French trans. of *L'Eglise et les Eglises*).

lest "in gathering the weeds you would uproot the wheat along with them" (Matt 13:29).

The Boastful Spirit of the Reformers

History gives us many examples of impatient reformers. Luther was an impatient reformer. It wasn't that he didn't feel he had been patient—too patient even. (He blamed himself for waiting too long before rebelling against the pope.)[143] We can even find in Luther certain conciliatory and conservative traits.[144] But what happened during those ten years while Luther organized his thinking ("*infrenavi tamen cogitationes meas ultra decennium*—I harnessed my thoughts for more than ten years . . .")? Patience or impatience is not so much a question of the passage of time as the question of a certain spiritual quality in our attitude. Beyond putting up with delays, patience means a certain spiritual docility, a mistrust of self, holding back when tempted by simple, abrupt solutions or by extremes of "all or nothing." It was above all that kind of patience that Luther lacked. Few "prophets" ended in so distinctly one-sided a position as he, or unleashed so much violence in opposition to a tradition (which was, after all, the tradition of holy church!).

If the comparison were not so distasteful, I would evoke a resemblance in this respect between Luther as a reformer and the "prophet" of National Socialism, Adolf Hitler.[145] They were alike in their way of being subjectively convinced, of claiming things, of criticizing their adversaries, of mocking them, of questioning their integrity; they were also alike by a similar kind of pride (which had a certain grandiosity of style), by an interior passion which was pitiless to all opposition. They were similar in their taste for getting to the bottom of questions, solving them in a radical way without delay; they were similar in their kind of violent rebellion, going so far as to use sarcasm and cynicism against everything "conventional," against everything that might be satisfied with half measures or nuances, and against whatever (to preserve its own interests) would refuse to raise questions or to do justice to the uprising of people who had been oppressed for too long.

---

[143] *Rationis Latomianae confutatio*, 1521. Weimar, vol. VIII, p. 45.

[144] Cf. H. Preuss, *Martin Luther: Der Prophet*, pp. 188f.

[145] I am transcribing here a note I took during the war, one day when I had the occasion to hear a speech by Hitler at the same time that I was reading *The Appeal to the Nobility* and the *Treatise on the Free Serf*.

The haste of the impatient reformer can be seen as well in a spirit of improvisation that tends toward oversimplification and imprecision in doctrinal formulations. Of course, a genius is precocious, but still . . . Calvin was twenty-seven when he completed his *Institutes*, and his fundamental studies had been in law, not theology. Michael Servetus was not yet twenty when he published *De trinitatis erroribus*. This century was keen on novelty and change . . . The hasty quality of work done too quickly is something that strikes me frequently in the texts of the sixteenth-century reformers, sometimes even in certain "creedal writings" of the Reformation. In my view such a judgment is so serious that I have to give some examples in order to explain myself.

Unquestionably, Luther had a kind of theological genius, but he allowed himself to be guided and finally ruined by polemic. He allowed himself to be pushed into becoming the founder of a church and into rethinking the meaning of Christianity all by himself. The fatal logic of his position was this: he had to reinvent Christianity not *with* the whole church and *within* it—(and yet he had said: "Let nobody think that they grasp the holy scriptures as they ought . . ., etc." [cf. above, p. 231])—but *against* the church and *against the integrity of its tradition.* From this position, he made enormous approximations, bold generalizations in his affirmations, and he did this concerning points as essential and decisive as the church, the priesthood, the Mass, and even the doctrine of the Trinity.[146] His theology of the church, whose diverse claims he changed and modified according to the needs of his anti-Roman or anti-sectarian polemics (and, on the whole, going in a direction progressively more traditional)[147] never again found a balance that was satisfactory and perfectly coherent.

But how could the reformer deny the sacramental priesthood (from the time of his *Appeal to the Nobility*) in opposition to the unanimous

---

[146] Cf. J. Lortz, *Die Reformation in Deutschland*, 2nd ed., vol. I, pp. 394f. As to the doctrine of the Trinity, I am thinking of his rejection of the canon *Firmiter* of the Fourth Lateran Council (Denziger 428); cf. Luther's *Theses* in support of Georg Major, Dec. 12, 1544 (Weimar, 39/2, pp. 287f.). Luther said that he didn't see why we couldn't say "*essentia genuit essentiam*—essence has begotten essence" and content oneself with affirming that the Deity was "*dreierlei*—threefold." That borders on Modalism and won from Zwingli the reproach of Luther's being like a sow trampling on a flower bed.

[147] On this point, see (among others) O. Piper, "Vom kirchlichen Wollen der deutchen Reformation," in the excellent collection *Luther in ökumenischer Sicht* (Stuttgart, 1929), pp. 93–110.

tradition of the church (with the exception perhaps of Tertullian, who had become a Montanist)? To give an objective example, how had Luther been able (unless by some sort of congenital incapacity well analyzed by J. Lortz)[148] to say that the doctrine which he had found in the church was the doctrine of justification by works, and that before him the church had interpreted the text of Romans 1:17 in the sense of the justice by which God is just when he judges us? In fact, Denifle has shown how the whole patristic and theological tradition (except perhaps Abelard and Peter of Corbeil to some degree) understood this text to be about the justice which God gives to us through mercy.[149]

If Luther was violent—judged so by his contemporaries, even by his friends and admitted by himself as well[150]—Melanchthon was a peaceful man. However, the "creedal" texts that Melanchthon edited show a distressing haste, a flaw inherent in the reform spirit of a "professor." When we read the *Augsburg Confession*, which is a moderate text, we are struck by the vagueness and the lack of clarity of several parts—for example, what it says about Communion under both species (art. 22), the Mass (art. 24), and religious vows (art. 27). According to the *Apology of the Confession*, Catholic teaching would have held that someone earned pardon for sin through works (the chapter on justification). But above all, how could it have presented as the current Catholic teaching (art. 24) —which the *Apology* rejected—the crazy raving in which the pseudoepigraphical writing of Albert *seemed* to hold that Christ had made satisfaction for original sin and for actual sins committed prior to his coming, while the Mass made satisfaction for actual sins committed since Calvary . . .[151] The schism with the Roman Church was encouraged on the basis of such reasoning as this!

---

[148] *Die Reformation als religiöses Anliegen heute*, pp. 134f.

[149] Cf. H. Denifle, *Die abendländischen Schriftausleger bis Luther über Justitia Dei (Rm 1:17) und Justificatio* (Mainz: 1905). — Cf. J. Lortz, *Die Reformation in Deutschland*, vol. I, p. 398; vol. II, p. 177; and *Die Reformation als religiöses Anliegen heute*, pp. 126f.

[150] Cf. H. Koll, "Luthers Urteile über sich selbst," in *Gesam. Aufsätze*, vol. I, pp. 381–419; cf. p. 383, n. 4, and p. 409, n. 3f. Luther judged that without his naturally violent tendency, he would not have been able to accomplish what he did. That is true, but for the evil he did, as well as for the good . . .

[151] On this question, see the studies done by N. Paulus, G. Dummermuth, A. Vacant, J. Kramp and E. C. Messenger. These authors support the conclusion just stated. However, might there be in some more recent (and less valuable) works one or two texts that would have suggested this misunderstanding? According to R. Desreumaux, "Une réputation surfaite? Josse Clichtove, 1472–1543," in *Mélanges de Science relig.*

Was there not a similar superficiality in the haste with which Zwingli simply suppressed the Offertory of the Mass and everything else that referred to an act of offering; or the haste with which Calvin dealt with such ecclesial realities as the sacrament of confirmation, the episcopate, and the apostolic succession of the ministry, whose apostolic origin could be shown with so much important evidence?[152]

Anglican texts are often more nuanced. Very early on, the Anglicans learned to make distinctions that remained unknown among the continental Protestants almost to the present. Yet there is still some impatience and haste in the way that Cranmer expressed ideas in his writings (and more or less inoculated his church with them)—ideas that he had become newly aware of under the successive influence of Bucer, then Bullinger, then Laski . . . Is there not, for example, something less than serious in the way that the twenty-eighth of the thirty-nine articles speaks about transubstantiation?

On the whole, one advantage that the Anglicans had over the continental Protestants was a better knowledge and a deeper respect for the Fathers and for Tradition. Nonetheless, even they established their critical position too quickly, before taking advantage of a better understanding of the texts from antiquity available to them and of the clearer light that these might bring to the question of Christian ministry and traditional orders.[152a] The reformers often threw out the evidence of this tradition from the Fathers and the liturgy with little consideration.[153] In a general

---

(1949), pp. 253–276, this strange idea was implied in the *Antilutherus* of Clichtove (book II, ch. 15, § 6). This needs to be looked at more carefully. Nonetheless, on the whole, the reformers' teaching on the sacraments showed Bellarmine to be right in judging "*de haereticorum levitate in re sacramentaria*—the superficiality of the heretics in treating the sacraments" (Preface to "Controv. de Sacramentis," *Controv.*, vol. III, p. 5).

[152] On these points, cf., respectively, R. Paquier, "Liturgie de baptême et de confirmation," *Eglise et Liturgie*, vol. VII (Lausanne, 1936), pp. 9f.; J. Pannier, *Calvin et l'épiscopat* (Strasbourg and Paris, 1927); R. Paquier, "La succession apostolique," *Eglise et Liturgie*, vol. VIII (Lausanne, 1937), p. 40.

[152a] See G. Dix for this topic: *The Apostolic Ministry*, ed. K. E. Kirk (London, 1946), pp. 289–90, 301.

[153] On their failure to grasp the church's liturgical tradition, there are some characteristic words concerning Melanchton in E. W. Zeeden, *Martin Luther und die Reformation im Urteil des deutschen Luthertums*, vol. I (Freiburg, 1950), p. 33. Cf. H. Chirat, *L'assemblée chrétienne à l'âge apostolique* (Paris, 1949), pp. 267–268.

Fr. Francis Dvornik has correctly observed that the reformers (especially those on the continent) particularly lacked any understanding of oriental Christianity and its

way, they knew very little about the Eastern Church, which they could not have imagined to hold papal sympathies, and yet whose agreement with the pope on the points that have just been mentioned as examples ought to have held them back from laying waste the church's patrimony in the three areas of dogma, liturgy, and forms of ministry.

A bit of respect for tradition, and so also a bit of patience (in the sense that the word is used here), would have made them less passionately negative with respect to the papal office itself. It's not just me, a priest and Roman Catholic theologian, who says this; Anglicans, historians, and noted theologians say the same. "The doctrinal services that the papacy had rendered to the whole of Christendom from the second to the sixth century, no less than the political and religious services that it gave to the whole of the West from the seventh and eighth centuries (by way of the Gregorian reform of the eleventh century and also by resistance to the Turks) would have sufficed to suggest that the papacy was fundamentally too valuable an institution to be sacrificed because of the Borgia or Medici popes. The ease with which the reformers, almost from the beginning, eliminated the papacy even as a possibility shows how deep was their radical ignorance both of the New Testament doctrine on the 'universal' church as an inherent part of the Gospel, and their ignorance of the link between the human-divine social order and the *here-and-now* of history . . ."[154]

The continuation of this very dense passage shows the extent to which the reformers were unaware of the real conditions for the unity and visibility of the church, such as recent biblical studies and the ecumenical movement have brought contemporary Protestants to understand them. At issue is a great deal more than a question of ecclesiology. On a number of decisive points, Protestants today are discovering the Christian and

---

tradition. Such an understanding would have spared them from making so many hasty and disastrous claims about the sacraments, the episcopacy, devotion to the Virgin Mary, etc. Luther identified himself with the tradition of the oriental church in opposing the papacy, but in fact he never penetrated its deepest meaning; cf. E. Benz, "Beziehungen zwischen den deutschen Reformationskirchen und den orthodoxen kirchen von der Reformation bis zum 19. Jahrhundert," in *Orthodoxie und Evangelisches Christentum*, Studienheft no. 1 (Witten, 1949), pp. 20–21. In the *Apology for the Augsburg Confession* (XXIV, 78, 83, 88, 93), Melanchton is wrong in appealing to the Orthodox Church to support the non-sacrificial character of the Eucharist.

[154] *Catholicity: A Study in the Conflict of Christian Traditions in the West* [a report presented to the Archbishop of Canterbury at his request, by fourteen noted Anglican theologians] (Westminster, 1947), p. 36.

biblical character of the elements of Catholicism that the reformers often let go so cheaply in their anger. For our part, we are discovering the Christian character of some of their basic demands. As a result, on both sides, the patience of [ecumenical] work carried out in love and prayer is moving us toward rebuilding the ruins that the impatience of revolt and polemics piled up in the vineyard of God.

The Link between Impatience and an Intellectual and Dialectical Point of View

In this sad outcome there is the product of something more than impatience. At the least, there is also here the consequence of that attitude related to impatience that I have described as dialectical and critical intelligence pursuing its train of thought without reference to what is *already given* in traditional teaching and in the life of the church. This surely applies to the reformers, but I also wonder to what degree they were in some way continuing the obsession of the scholastics to construct theses on very partial documentation without being aware of its limited character. My critique, however, envisages a much more profound deficiency to which I will return.

Christianity, I repeat, is a *reality*. It was given to us as a life to be received and practiced and not simply as a text to be consulted. As a transmitted, lived reality, Christianity completely transcends what we are able to say about it. Take, for example, religious life, profoundly misunderstood by the reformers of the sixteenth century. The unanimous tradition of the East and the West considers religious life as profoundly linked to Christianity itself. However, if you take only the viewpoint of critical intelligence and of texts alone (a viewpoint which seems to have been the controlling perspective for Protestantism), then religious life is difficult to justify and, doubtless, even to understand. If religious life, with its vows of obedience, chastity, and poverty, pertains to the heart of Christianity, this is less because of what texts say about it than because of its profound link with the life of Jesus, his mother, and the apostles. These are things that the church inherited from them and that it *hands over* and *transmits* more than it *explains*.

In their haste to rebel against the church and their impatience to find fault in order to justify their rebellion, the reformers failed to understand that these kinds of Christian realities are *handed over* more than *proclaimed*. Among these Christian realities are the sacraments, the lives of the saints, and the church itself. In this case, this seems to be a sign of an impatience typical of intellectuals, which the Protestant reformers were indeed.

We are forced to think that any reform invoking history and a more exact critical awareness of facts and of texts risks always being precarious and partial. Such a reform depends upon *a certain limited* awareness of facts and of history that pertains to one person or, at most, to one group of people, linked to a particular moment of time and to a certain development of documentation and research. Without question, people would speak differently today about the Mass, about monasticism, and about priesthood, etc., than they did in the sixteenth century. And if the Lutherans could rewrite their "creedal writings," they would express them differently. Some among them have let this be known.[155] Once again, one of the tasks of the ecumenical movement is to rework those things that the impatience and narrowness of superficiality disrupted, calling for greater patience, and the purity and fullness of a deeper fidelity.

The same thing could easily be said about Lamennais, whom Newman accused of lacking patience. Likewise, the same could be said about reform programs marked by haste and idiosyncrasy, which treat complicated, delicate, and profound issues superficially, crossing them out with the stroke of a pen without allowing time to see the consequences of such a dismantling. I am thinking here of the reform projects of some German theologians at the beginning of the nineteenth century[156] or of certain Modernists and representatives of *Reformkatholizismus*[157]—projects unfortunately still being pursued to the present day.[158]

---

[155] It is profitable to read the courageous texts of Superintendant W. Staehlin (cf. the journal *Documente*, 1947, fasc. 2) or those of Pastor R. Paquier, "Des théologies confessionelles à une théologie oecuménique," *Verbum Caro* 155 (1948), pp. 3–15. See also R. Baumann, *Des Petrus Bekenntnis und Schlüssel* (Stuttgart, 1950).

[156] There are numerous examples given in E. Vermeil, *J. A. Möhler et l'école catholique de Tubingue* (Paris, 1913). Cf. below, pp. 299f.

[157] See the works by Mensching and Mulert, cited above, p. 36.

This also makes me think of the Aglipay Schism in the Philippines, which was a miserable, hasty echo of rationalism, evolutionism, and comparative criticism from the end of the 19th century (today out of fashion); cf. M. Boonen, "Le schism aglipayen," in *Obstacles à l'apostolat* (reviewed in the *VIIe Semaine de Missiologie* [Louvain, 1929], pp. 104–130).

[158] For example, recently Msgr. Carlos Duarte da Costa, then the bishop of Botucatu, Brazil, called for the following, in a haphazard fashion: a return to primitive Christianity; separation from Rome; adoration of God and of Christ alone to the exclusion of veneration of Mary and the saints; priestly ordination for laypersons who would continue in their professions; study of the Bible; abolition of auricular confession; recognition of only the four sacraments of baptism, holy orders, Eucharist (Communion), and marriage; aid to liberate the masses from ignorance and superstition; and the establishment of a Brazilian national church with the guarantee of freedom

Blocked by the Church, the Impatient Reformer Appears to Be Persecuted

Obviously, impatient reformers see themselves "blocked" by the church, and not only by those aspects that we earlier called the "Synagogue" or "Pharisaism," but more by the aspect of an authority conscious of its responsibilities for guarding the unity of the body. In this way, as Newman remarks,[159] the innovator appears to be a misunderstood and persecuted creative genius, while the authority condemning him appears backward and tyrannical. Remember what we said above (p. 37) concerning the prestige that a heretic or someone persecuted enjoys in the contemporary world. The fame that someone gets from publicly taking a nonconformist position is likely to go to his head and to lead the immoderate reformer to the edge of rebellion.

Jerome de Hangest, from a family with which Calvin was close in his youth, said that one of the things that encouraged people to embrace the Reformation was the *gloria sitis* [the fame of being connected to the famous].[160] On the other hand, it seems that a lot of people owed their influence in higher circles—and sometimes their career—to their reassuring character, adopting (sometimes with surprising skill) an attitude that supported or justified the "state of affairs" . . . There is no movement of reaction, reform, or initiative that does not have at the beginning some truth—sometimes a lot of truth. Unfortunately, someone taking initiatives or undertaking reform with impatience compromises the true with the false; by trying to hurry up growth, he ends up slowing down its development. By contrast, the prophet who respects delays and who has the courage to practice not only *aggredi* (confrontation) but also *sustinere* (tenacity) has a much greater chance of success for his message. There is a profound truth in this maxim taken from the Vulgate: "*Vir*

---

of conscience for everyone (cf. *Service oecum. de presse et d'information*, No. 33, Sept. 1945). This is a mixture of some acceptable ideas, some that are just about disastrous, and some formal errors. Msgr. Duarte da Costa was excommunicated on July 6, 1945.

[159] Op. cit., pp. 294–295: "This act of authority will pass to future generations as an example of tyrannical intervention against private judgment. They will have forced the reformer to keep quiet; they will have obeyed a lowly inclination to corruption and error. Finally, this act of authority will be considered even more unfavorable if the sovereign power lacks prudence or reflection in its proceedings . . ." Cf. St. Thomas, *Commen. In Rom.*, ch. 5, lectio 6, about the prestige of those who hold heterodox ideas.

[160] Cited in L. Febvre, "Une question mal posée," in *Rev. Histor.* (1929), p. 48.

obediens loquetur victoriam—The one who is obedient will have the last word." [161]

The Church Is Against Ultimatums and the Via Facti *

The church does not like to be ordered to do things, much less to find itself faced with a fait accompli. The church is a hierarchical institution whose structure is much more than useful and practical; it reflects and carries a mystery within itself. [162] The church realizes that reform initiatives are often peripheral, but it wants to control them and, after testing them, to give them its approbation. It is understandable that the hierarchy should wish to protect the rights that alone allow it to exercise its heavy burden of responsibility. The church wants to maintain the freedom and initiative of its own decisions. That is why the church avoids taking orders. The story of Lamennais and the *L'Avenir* affair are enlightening in this respect. This also explains why the church dislikes the *via facti* [confronting a fait accompli], as Cardinal Bertram recalled in communicating to the German episcopacy the directives of the Congregation of Rites with respect to a number of hasty liturgical innovations. [163] This much is certain: the church does not like the *via facti*. However, it is worth explaining the meaning and the implications of this dislike more fully. Otherwise we might risk attributing to the church (here, the hierarchy) a position which is really not its own, thus putting it in contradiction to itself.

In actuality, there is a *via facti* which the church rejects and another which it cannot reject. Take for instance the Emperor Charles V who, in 1548, on his own authority conceded the use of the chalice to the laity until a decision of a council of the church should intervene on this point. [164] At least this attenuating circumstance should be noted, namely, that this granting of the chalice, requested for a long time by the Czechs,

---

* *Via facti* refers to changes introduced into a legal system by those subject to the law without the permission of the authorities (by contrast with *via juris*). The law often lags behind circumstances, and changes in the law occur as a result of catching up with what is already going on.

[161] Prov 21:28. The original text reads: "The one who listens will always be able to speak" (Crampon trans.).

[162] Cf. *supra*, pp. 99f.

[163] From his letter of Jan. 15, 1943. The text is found in *La Maison-Dieu* 7 (1946), p. 107; *Les questions liturg. et paroiss.* (Apr. 1946), p. 105; *La Pensée catholique* 7 (1948), pp. 72f.

[164] Cf. G. Constant, *Concession à l'Allemagne de la communion sous les deux espèces*, vol. I (Paris, 1923), pp. 35f.

had already been requested by the emperor since 1537, under alarming conditions, as a means of holding people back from going over to Lutheranism (and also of bringing Lutherans back). Things were urgent, and yet Rome, doing nothing genuinely constructive, only granted the chalice in 1564, grudgingly and with restrictions, only to take back its concession soon thereafter . . .

But if there is a sort of *via facti* that has to be rejected, isn't there also a legitimate one? I mean *legitimate* in the strong sense of the word, that is, fundamentally in conformity with the spirit of the legislator and of the law. It is well known that church law, much more than most modern law, gives an important place to custom. A great number of things which are highly regarded in the church were introduced by a *via facti* that became first custom, then law. It would be surprising to make a list of all of them. Among them, there are certain things which today are controlled by the most meticulous and strict legal norms.

Here are some examples: the replacement of leavened bread with unleavened in the eucharistic celebration beginning in the eighth century, the introduction of the *"traditio instrumentorum*—the handing over of [symbolic] objects" in the ordination rites beginning in the ninth century (under the influence of Germanic ritual books), Communion under only one species,[165] the obligation of saying the Breviary for clerics (and even the formulation of the Breviary itself), the impediment of disparity of cult for matrimony, and, finally, the liturgy as a whole in which, for seven to ten centuries, there was very great variety. Church authority finally intervened in order to maintain fundamental unity and the major symbols of unity in the liturgy.[166]

In this year of 1950, there is a Year of Jubilee. Everybody knows that the jubilees are proclaimed by the pope, but do they know that they were created by a sort of *via facti*? At the approach of the year 1300, most of the faithful in the West felt that in a year that marked the centenary of Christ's birth, people should have been able to gain a very extensive indulgence in Rome. Boniface VIII, aware of this, looked into the matter and came to the conclusion that there was no document governing this. Yet the people's conviction persisted. From the first days of the year 1300, Rome was invaded by crowds of pilgrims, and the pope was under pressure to establish by law something that the *vox populi* had called for.

---

[165] Communion under both species as the ordinary practice disappeared in the 13th and 14th centuries without any official decision rendered to bring it about.

[166] Cf. F. Cabrol, "Initiatives individuelles dans la liturgie et Magistère de l'Eglise," *Questions liturg. et paroiss.* (June 1927), pp. 129–152.

The Bull establishing the indulgence (note the date) was promulgated on February 22, 1300.[167]

It is clear that the *via facti* brings about custom in some way, and that custom, in some fashion, brings about law. (We also distinguish between *consuetudo facti* [a custom in fact] and *consuetudo juris* [a custom in law].) Canon 25 of the present Code [1917] specifies that the consent of the legislator (which can be either general, anticipated, or tacit) is the actual source of the legal force of a custom. This clarification is invaluable, and further it seems to be in accord with our categories. We have only to remember what we said about *structure and life* and about *the center and the periphery* in order to explain how a *via facti* creates custom and custom creates law, and in what sense, nonetheless, the legal force of all of this still comes from above in a hierarchical fashion.

Clearly something does come from below, that is, the faithful have a role in the creation of law and in this sense determine its subject matter, because they provide that.[168] "The people take the initiative by desiring, in so far as they can, to introduce a law and then to tacitly solicit the consent of the authorities."[169] However, only in this way, by giving at least tacit or general and anticipated consent, does authority give to an initiative that arises from the life of the people the full value of law and the recognition of legitimacy. Thus the people's initiative achieves the quality of something that happens not only *in the church* but which is also *of the church* and linked to its structure.

Under these conditions, we can see how the *via facti* is *normal* in one way. This also allows us to recognize that many important and fruitful things (as well as others more dubious) have come about in the church by way of facing up to the spontaneous emergence of grassroots creativity (*via facti*). This includes all the examples I gave above touching the relation between center and periphery. A great many renewal initiatives, even those of which the hierarchy is justly proud (for, without the hierarchy, the initiators would have "run in vain" [Gal 2:2]), had their start

---

[167] Cf. A. Boudinhon, "Le jubilé," in *Le canoniste contemporain*, XXIII (1910), pp. 79f. (making use of the study by P. A. De Santi, S.J., "Bonifacio VIII e l'anno secolare 1300," in *Civiltà cattolica*, Jan. 6, 1900). See again J. Lecler, S.J., "Boniface VIII et le jubilé de 1300," *Etudes* 264 (Feb. 1950), pp. 145–157.

[168] Cf. W. Bertrams, S.J., "Die Eigennatur des Kirchenrechts," *Gregorianum* 26 (1946), pp. 527–563; cf. pp. 560f.

[169] Suarez, *De legibus*, bk. VII, ch. 12, no. 1 (*Opera* VI, 181). R. Wehrlé's commentary on canon 28 of the Code (*Custom in Canon Law* [Paris, 1928], p. 412) shows how well this text of Suarez sums up practice, intention, and the rule of the church.

in this way.[170] There would be no such thing as renewal unless someone began to change something, to do something other than what is usually done, to do things differently than what regulations prescribe, for the sake of seeking a more profound truth and a deeper tradition.

The Church's Via Facti *vs. the Wrong and Revolutionary* Via Facti

But we need to be more precise. What is the criterion for judging between a good and a bad *via facti*? The preceding paragraphs allow us to differentiate two forms of *via facti* that have a very different spirit and so a very different meaning for the church, despite their similarities (an ambivalence present from the start). For we have to pay attention to a remarkable characteristic of church law, in particular, that it integrates elements of moral intentionality. From a moral and canonical point of view, schism and heresy presuppose obstinacy. Initiatives of a *via facti* type that might seem at the start analogous must be judged in an analogous fashion. That is because they could be (or not) completely and substantially good and, because of this, be found to be in an incomparably more favorable position.

There is, however, a *via facti* that usurps the place of authority and in fact deprives it of its right to govern and decide by imposing a new rule without taking care to harmonize it with the existing order. Moreover, it is determined to pursue its own way even if it should be repudiated. This is the *via facti* of revolution, characteristic of rebellious forces. In the church, this can only be described as pre-schismatic. Along these lines, an initiative arising from life experience aims effectively to impose itself and force its positions on the church's structure, instead of allowing itself to be governed by the church and to evolve within the church.

But there is also a *via facti* that does not usurp the place of authority. It does not undermine the church's structure, but rather acts in and for ecclesial life by opening up creative or adaptive possibilities that the authorities do not disavow. This kind of *via facti* does not represent a revolutionary substitution of one rule by another. Rather it admits the existing law, even respecting in general the letter of the law. Yet this kind of *via facti* still undertakes some creative or adaptive initiative, proposing in this way a trial run, an experiment, that it then submits to the hierar-

---

[170] For example, what Abbé Remilleux of happy memory did for the eucharistic celebration at Saint-Alban in Lyons; cf. H.-C. Chéry, *Communauté paroissiale et liturgie: Notre-Dame de Saint-Alban* (Paris, 1947), pp. 45f.

chy's evaluation. Isn't this how religious orders get founded, and almost everything else that happens in the church?

Here again the link is clear between a reform initiative of a schismatic type and a completely intellectual and abstract agenda. By contrast, the pastoral point of view leads to moderate adaptations which do not turn the structure upside down, whereas purely abstract and critical intellectual research easily leads to innovations, substituting one law for another. This explains why pastoral authority does not repress some transgressions, even though it does not easily give them complete authorization.[171] The church is broad-minded with respect to what is done *per modum actus* (with respect to individual occasions), but it doesn't like it when someone develops a "theory" about innovation. The church is less alarmed about a precedent in activities than by a juridical precedent. Very liberal about what arises from the church's life, authorities quickly become alarmed about anything that calls its basic structure into question.

A final point has to be made before leaving this topic of the *via facti*. It would be a serious mistake to support a *via facti* of the revolutionary type: that would turn upside down the structure of the church, which is hierarchical. But it would also be a mistake—a less serious one (for this would be a mistake about an element of the church's life, and not its structure)—not to pay attention to the role played by the grassroots, the periphery, in the development and the modification of concrete decisions for the life of the church. Further, that would also be a misunderstanding about the whole order of *initiatives*.

For example, when Père Lebbe opposed a provision of French law in the French protectorate in China that was an abuse and even a mistake, his bishop, Msgr. Reynaud, replied to him as follows: "Since it was Rome that accepted or requested it, it is also up to Rome to relinquish it when

---

[171] I could cite a great number of cases where different hierarchical authorities (the Holy See, bishops, nuncios) have responded to proposals by saying: "Go ahead and do it, but these are things that you shouldn't ask about, because we would be obliged to respond negatively from the standpoint of the law." Don't forget either the advice that St. Francis de Sales gave to Jeanne de Chantal: "My solicitor says that one is mistaken to go to Rome for unimportant matters, and the cardinals say the same. They say that there are some things that don't require authorization, because you are free to do them or not. However, when someone seeks authorization, these things are considered in a different way. The pope is happy enough to let custom authorize several things that he could not authorize himself because of the consequences" (Letter of Aug. 21, 1621, *Oeuvres complètes*, vol. XX, no. 1821, p. 136).

it sees fit. *Our job is only to await Rome's instructions,* without prejudging anything."[172] This reply was correct, except for the small phrase that I have italicized in the text. It was correct in affirming the competence of authority in an area where it properly exercises responsibility. But it was insufficient (and to that degree false) in failing to recognize the creative role of the base or the periphery with respect to even those determinations which are decided exclusively by the authority. It does not give enough space for the dialogue between *Orbis* and *Urbs* that we spoke about earlier. Rather, it gives support to a way of seeing things that skirts around the role of the faithful and of the on-site minister to the exclusive benefit of the hierarchy. This ends up sacrificing something that belongs to the life and to the truth of the structure. It is a way of dealing with problems posed by life experience *only* by the most literal application of existing jurisprudence, leaving no place for the creation of a jurisprudence better adapted to the facts. It seems to me that this tendency arises from the same kind of insufficient consideration for concrete reality. Ultimately it rejects a very real function of the base and of the periphery, namely, that of cooperating *from its own perspective* with the hierarchy in the church's development. For there is development, simply because there is life.

So the reformer is once again forced to deal with the reality of tensions. Error, here as elsewhere, is closely linked to oversimplification. (The case of the intemperate reformer is, in a way, a lot simpler.) Error consists in trying to suppress one of the poles of the tension. Someone who eventually will succeed at reform has to do two things at once: both take initiatives and also avoid an unhealthy *via facti*, both open avenues for development and also pay attention to the requirements for unity and continuity, for which the hierarchy is at once the interpreter and the guardian. This requires a twofold fidelity to which the reformer has to be wholly and loyally committed, causing him or her to live with emotional strain and inner turmoil, until the day when the novelty is assimilated into unity and then appears to be an authentic development of the church's principles. At that point the reformer will experience the intense joy of a consecration of the "spirit" by the "mission."[173]

[172] Cited in L. Levaux, *Le Père Lebbe, apôtre de la Chine moderne* (Brussels and Paris, 1948), p. 192.

[173] I am using here the categories and language of H. Clérissac in ch. 7 of his *Mystère de l'Eglise*.

The Tension that Results for the Faithful Reformer

Reformers run the risk of being impatient because they feel that time is running out and that the *via facti* in question is not about them but about other souls, about real events, and about the way the world is moving. When *Quadragesimo Anno* appeared in 1931, Père Rutten, who was one of the founding spirits of the Catholic social movement, told me: "We have been waiting for forty years for this encyclical." Prophets feel as acutely as a kind of suffering what they see as missed opportunities and as the weakness of measures adopted too late (and sometimes in the wrong way). Their impatience has to be seen in relation to an official lethargy that tends to put everything off too long.

It is the job of the faithful who have some spirit of "prophecy" to sound the alarm and to wake up their leaders, to speak prophetically to authorities, to tell the truth, and not to let the hierarchy live in a gilded illusory world of disastrous routine or false security. Let me repeat what Gregory VII said (according to Yves of Chartres) to those who resisted his reforms and the novelty of his way of exercising pontifical authority. By the way, this phrase comes from the Christian Africa of antiquity (Tertullian, Cyprian, Augustine): "Christ didn't say, 'I am custom,' but 'I am truth.' No matter how old or widespread a custom may be, it has to give way to the truth . . ."[173a] This same phrase, repeated by Urban II and expressed in the *Decretals* of Gratian,[174] has been invoked more than once by reformers in the past.[174a] We can reflect upon it here as well.

The true prophet, the prophet according to the Spirit that gives life to the church, finds a way to do what must be done and to be listened to. For there is a certain tone that does not deceive and that the church can discern as authentic. When you read, for example, Père Lebbe's report or some similar texts cited above (cf. p. 260), you see how the "spirit" speaks to the "mission" in the Catholic Church.

It is clear that every "prophet" ought to be ready to face opposition, if not persecution, or at least resistance. This also is part of "patience."

[173a] A study of this text with full documentation by G. B. Ladner can be found in *Studi Gregoriani*, vol. V (Rome, 1956), pp. 225–235.

[174] Urban II to the Count of Flanders on Dec. 2, 1092 (PL 151:356); Gratian, Dist. VIII, ch. 5 in Friedberg I, 15. Cf. *infra, Conclusion*, n. 4 and p. 312.

[174a] So said Hervé de Bourgdieu (cf. G. Morin, "Une critique en liturgie au XIIe siècle: Le traité inédit d'Hervé de Bourgdieu, De correctione quarundam lectionum," in *Revue Bénédictine* 24 [1907], pp. 36–51); and William Durandus at the beginning of the 14th century (*De modo generalis concilii celebrandi*, part II, preface, [Paris ed., 1571], p. 48).

Nobody gives birth without pain. A number of saints have found themselves in prison, even in the cells of the Holy Office; for example, Blessed John of Avila,[175] Cardinal Morone, St. John of the Cross, St. Ignatius Loyola, St. Joseph Calasanzus, St. Grignon de Montfort, and a lot of others . . . At a minimum, they had to be tested by the church, as St. Francis was subjected to the scrutiny of Cardinal John.[176] Many people who have proposed something new or unaccustomed met, at least at the beginning, the opposition of those who wanted to hear only what they were used to hearing. We saw this above with respect to the twofold plan of Catholic fidelity. Such persons remained patient and submissive, faithful on the whole both to their own spirit and to their church. Their difficulties finally stopped, and their work remains. By being more patient, reformers are ultimately more effective.

Responsibility of Church Leaders Not to Be Too Patient

History, which is a great teacher of the truth, condemns impatient reformers. History also teaches us about the responsibility incurred by the overly patient and sluggish attitude of some authorities at times of great catastrophe. In speaking of the reform movement in Bohemia, which would lead through John Hus to the sect of Bohemian Brethren, Bareille wrote: "It was the right and duty of the church, through the intermediary of the pope and the bishops, to set about [reforming abuses] with authority, and the church was far from refusing to do so. But rather than leaving to those who by right had the job of fulfilling this mission

---

[175] A. Duval, *art. cit.*, p. 124; and C. M. Abad, "El processo de la Inquisición contra el Beato Juan de Avila: Estudio critico a la luz de documentos desconocidos," in *Miscellanea Comillas*, 6 (1946), pp. 95–167.

I want to cite these words of Billot responding to a friend who was indignant about how he had been treated: "You can escape criticism by saying nothing and doing nothing. That is not my case. But I don't want to turn these violent actions into a drama. Am I worthy of a saint's reward? I still have not been accused of heresy, as St. Basil was before Pope Damasus; nor condemned as a heretic and then deposed, as St. Cyril was by a council of forty bishops. Nor have I been pursued on the charge of sorcery, as St. Athanasius was; nor for bad morals, as St. John Chrysostom was; nor solemnly condemned and deposed by the tribunal of the Holy Office, as St. Joseph of Calasanz was, and he died in disgrace at Rome at the age of 92." (H. Le Floch, *Le cardinal Billot, lumière de la théologie* [Paris, 1947], p. 125). — Yet you can feel some bitterness and stubbornness in this text; they would have talked like that at Port Royal. This shows us how delicately one must treat the point that I am making here, especially in applying it to oneself, no matter how historically accurate the account.

[176] J. Joergensen, *Saint François d'Assise*, pp. 124–132.

and accomplishing it through an attentive examination of what was wrong, through a search for appropriate means and the progressive and firm application of the most appropriate remedies; instead restless, impatient and fearful minds, lacking both mandates and authority, undertook to reform the church from the beginning of the fifteenth century."[177] All that is exactly, ideally (idyllically) true. But what had those who acted *by right* actually done?

When we study the history of the reform efforts that took shape after the Council of Vienne (1311), we are struck by the fact that it had been profoundly unsatisfactory from the start. Here we are looking back on one of the great tragedies of history, where the turn of events ultimately makes a catastrophe inevitable. The Council of Vienne had done something, but too little; and it had failed to address its reform activity *in capite* (at the head of the church), that is, with the reform of the Curia. From the time of Durand de Mende down to the Memorandum of the Cardinals in 1537 and the calls for reform by Charles V, the body of the church unanimously cried out for such a reform.[178] A real despair took hold of the best among the faithful when they discovered that so necessary a reform had not been seriously undertaken.

From the fourteenth and fifteenth centuries, there was a growing feeling that the church was lost if it would not reform itself, and that a reform was impossible precisely because the head refused to cooperate.[179] The Christian people went into a panic and, faced with leaders who seemed powerless or reticent, they looked for chance outcomes which (ecclesiologically speaking) are really impasses. At the Council of Basel, Cardinal Aleman (later beatified) spoke in favor of the legitimacy of the initiatives of the lower clergy, in a sense favorable to conciliarism, because of the failure at the head of the church.[180] In the middle of the fifteenth century,

---

[177] See the entry *Bohèmes (les frères)* in *Dict. de Théologie catholique*, vol. II, col. 931.

[178] Cf. J. Lecler, "La réforme de l'Eglise au temps de Philippe le Bel," *Etudes* (July 5, 1935), pp. 5–20; cf. pp. 19–20.

[179] Cf. some testimonies to this in Döllinger, *Prophecies and the Prophetic Spirit in the Christian Era* (London, 1873), pp. 69f. It was this feeling of despair, lived under the insoluble problem of multiple popes, that led to the conciliar movement. Cf. Fliche-Martin, *Hist. de l'Eglise*, vol. XIV/2, p. 888, n. 5 and p. 883; H. Jedin, *Histoire du Concile de Trente*, vol. I. Note that at this time there was an analogous situation among temporal rulers, who had also promised *reformatio* to their subjects and were not keeping their promise.

[180] Cited by J. Lecler, S.J., "Les théories démocratiques au Moyen-Age," *Etudes* (Oct. 20, 1935), p. 186. — Cf. what Möhler wrote (*Unité dans l'Eglise*, concl., trans. by A. de Lilienfeld, p 231): "In the first part of the 15th century, certain reformers tried to drag

there appeared the famous *Reformation des Kaisers Siegmund*, which had a wide influence. Faced with the timidity of the papacy and its ineptitude for reform, the princes felt called to take responsibility for reform. They appealed to the old theory holding that in the case of the failure of one side of the Christian body, one should turn to the other (here the secular branch) to ensure that the church is reformed,[181] if necessary without the cooperation of the ecclesiastical branch and even contrary to it.[182] A whole theory of *epikeia* (judicial prudence) was developed then, according to which in the case of the failure of the leaders, anyone, a *minima vetula* (a little old lady), could call for a council and undertake to reform the church. This is how they arrived at the abyss and how catastrophe came about.

Luther was certainly an impatient reformer. But he had begun like so many others by calling for a reform council. His initiatives at the beginning met with broad support because he responded to a widespread desire: "*Quis initio non favebat Luthero?*—Who was not in favor of Luther at the beginning?" wrote Erasmus in 1522.[183] Erasmus himself had the feeling that the attempts for reform at that point had been insufficient[184] and, like many others, he did not see any further recourse . . . In such an environment, Luther's outburst can be understood, even if not excused. In 1539 Luther wrote: "Because the pope has refused to call a council and does not want to reform the church, we have no other recourse than to search for a reform by going to our Lord Jesus Christ."[185] And in 1528 already, he wrote: "People have long called for a council so that the church could be reformed by it. However, I feel like I have created a council and also achieved such a reform as to make papist ears ring."[186]

---

the church from within toward the necessary changes. People mocked these attempts. From then on, reformers began to work from the outside."

[181] Cf. J. Hashagen, *Staat und Kirche vor der Reformation* (Essen, 1931), p. 310; on the practice of this principle, pp. 433f.; on the application made of it in the Reformation of the 16th century, p. 438.

[182] Denifle-Weiss, *Luther und Luthertum*, vol. II (Mainz, 1909), pp. 56–57.

[183] Cited by Renaudet, *Etudes erasmiennes*, pp. 198, 298. For example, this was the case for Emser, Murner, Cochleus—future opponents of Luther; cf. E. Isserloh, *Die Eucharistie in der Darstellung des Johannes Eck* (Munster, 1950), p. 14.

[184] Cf. what Erasmus wrote concerning Hadrian VI; Renaudet, pp. 204, 246. Cf. pp. 167–168.

[185] *Von den Konziliis und Kirchen*, Weimar, L, p. 512.

[186] *Von der Priesterehe des würdigen Herrn Lic. St. Klingebeil*, Weimar, vol. XXVI, p. 530; cited by Preuss, op. cit., p. 234. In 1519, Luther began to doubt the efficacy of a council for church reform because such a council would not be "free": *Operationes in Psalmos* (Psalm 10:12), Weimar, vol. V, p. 345.

Alas, for five hundred years people in the church had been calling for a reform council. There had been only some partial reforms, patching up the existing system, dealing with questions of observance or organization. The popes at the end of the fifteenth century had been conscious of the need for reforms, and they deserve credit for that.[187] But when we take stock of their efforts, it is clear that nothing that they had done had gone beyond a draft or planning stage.[188] They had reformed the "apostolic calendar," modified the observance of poverty in the mendicant orders, legislated about the election of abbots and the residences of bishops . . . "Questions about clothes and shoes," said Luther;[189] and Erasmus thought much the same.[190] When the Council of Trent opened on December 13, 1545, with little hurry and without much desire for renewal among many of its members,[191] Luther had no more than two months left to live.

---

[187] Cf. L. Celier, "Alexandre VI et la réforme de l'Eglise," in *Mélanges de l'Ecole française de Rome*, XXVII (1907), pp. 65–124. Some excellent historical studies have traced the continuity between the reform current at the end of the Middle Ages and that which was already active before Luther's uprising and that resulted in the Council of Trent and the Catholic Reformation of the 16th century. Cf. C. von Höfler, "Die romanische Welt und ihr Verhältnis zu den Reformideen des Mittelalters," *Sitzungsber. der Wiener Ak., phil.-hist. Kl.*, XCI (1878), pp. 257–538); H. Jedin, articles on the reform of the cardinals and of the religious orders, respectively, in *Römische Quartalschrift*, XLIII (1935), pp. 87f., and XLIV (1936), pp. 231f.; P. Brezzi, *Le riforme cattoliche dei secoli XV e XVI* (Rome, 1945); K. A. Fink, "Papsttum und Kirchenreform nach dem Grossen Schisma," in *Theolog. Quartalsch.* 126 (1946), pp. 110–122 (pontificate of Martin V); A. Cistellini, *Figure della riforma pretridentina* (Brescia, 1948). — Various studies are cited in *Katholische Reformation oder Gegenreformation?* (Lucerne, 1946) by H. Jedin, who outlined the history of this idea of an ongoing Catholic reform movement begun before Luther.

[188] According to Imbart de la Tour, there was only a plan to reorganize the Curia under Sixtus IV, and a commission and a draft of a papal bull under Alexander VI (*Origines de la Réforme*, vol. II, pp. 527–528). This is also what emerges from the research of L. Celier, cited above, and of his study on "L'idée de réforme à la cour pontificale du Concile de Bâle au Concile de Constance," in *Rev. des Questions hist.*, LXXXVI (1909), pp. 418–435.

[189] *Genesisvorlesungen* (1544–1545), Weimar, XLIV, p. 171.

[190] Cf. Renaudet, op. cit., p. 204.

[191] This was especially true of the papacy, along with a group that didn't want the question of the reform of the Curia to be raised. This was evident all through the 14th and 15th centuries (cf. above, pp. 171 and 285, and J. Haller, *Papsttum und Kirchenreform* [Berlin, 1903]), and it was the case all through the Council of Trent as well. Nevertheless the whole of Christendom was demanding reform *in capite*: the emperor was insisting upon it, as well as the commission named by Paul III in its report of

Everything possible has been said to excuse the popes of the fifteenth and sixteenth centuries. This is not the place to put them on trial or to evaluate the importance of their excuses. Catholic historians—people like Pastor and Baudrillart—have pleaded extenuating circumstances for them: the popes of the fifteenth century felt pressed for time. They had to strengthen the church's internal constitution, shaken by the great schism and by conciliarist theories, to warn about danger from the Turks, to verify the independence of the Holy See by way of strengthening the pontifical state, and to both welcome and moderate humanism and the renaissance of the arts . . . There is a lot of truth in all that. But what significance can attenuating circumstances have when the popes did nothing decisive to avert tragedy? All that cannot and ought not distract from the salutary lesson to be learned from the facts.

Those responsible for the administration of an organization don't like things to be called into question. Novelty always looks dangerous to them and reformers inopportune, indeed troublesome. In fact, the impatience of reformers often enough risks spoiling everything. The impatience of reformers doesn't take account of the delays needed for transformation to take place, not mechanically or from the outside, but arising from the deep energies of a founding principle so that the organism will not self-destruct. Popular wisdom, however, knows that the *best* can be the *enemy of the good*. The church is decidedly in favor of the *good*, and only welcomes the *better* if it builds up more than it risks breaking down. We will come back to the question of the motivations of those who temporize (a serious question), and we will try to understand them. But it is also necessary to understand the impatience of those who find themselves committed on the front lines, where the church is in contact with a terribly demanding world. They have the feeling that time is running out, and that it is not they who are in advance of their time, but their time that is in advance of the church . . .

1537. But Rome incessantly sought to avoid bringing up the question, and finally Pius IV closed the council down for the same reason (cf. G. Constant, *Concession à l'Allemagne de la communion sous les deux espèces*, vol. I [Paris, 1923], pp. 461f.). The same reaction came to light at the First Vatican Council, as Cardinal Pitra frankly admitted (cf. F. Mourret, *Le Concile du Vatican d'après des documents inédits* [Paris, 1919], pp. 216f.). Such a constant reaction can only be explained by the fear—very much alive in Rome—that such reform-minded proposals might express or push forward viewpoints that attack the structure ("monarchical" structure, some would say) of the church.

These prophets on the front line must feel the truth of the prophetic message of Hezekiah to Isaiah, saying: "Children have come to the birth, and there is no strength to bring them forth."[192] We can only insist that reformers not be too impatient if we ask the overseers of the tradition not to be too patient! We must ask the overseers to be aware of the pressure of the people's demands, which threaten to explode some day because they have been held in check for too long. We must ask them to confront their inclination to delay things with the people's feeling of urgency about needs, with an understanding of the signs of the times; to not easily lend their support to lies, to mediocrity, or to routine practices that scandalize the faithful. St. Paul's warning, "Fathers, do not provoke your children to anger" (Eph 6:4), is addressed to everyone who has received, on whatever account, the responsibility and name of "fathers."

---

[192] 2 Kgs 19:3; Isa 37:2; cf. Isa 26:17-18.

FOURTH CONDITION

Genuine Renewal through a Return to the Principle of Tradition (Not through the Forced Introduction of Some "Novelty")

Two Kinds of Adaptation: As Development and as Innovation

There are only two possible ways of bringing about renewal or updating.[193] You can either make the new element that you want to put forward normative, or you can take as normative the existing reality that needs

---

[193] I was pleased to find this same idea expressed so well by J. Guitton, *La pensée moderne et le catholicisme*, vol. III: *La pensée de M. Loisy* (Aix, 1936), pp. 57–59. His text is so close to mine—even though I arrived at this idea by another route, namely, reflection on the problem of ecumenism—that I cannot fail to cite his text:

"There are two, and only two, methods for achieving a combination of the tradition with the present, of what is old with what is new, of truth with conscience . . . The first method consists in focusing first and above all on the tradition (which is, in the final analysis, the history of truth's identity) so as to grasp it correctly and to understand it well, both as to its formulation as well as to its spirit. Even more precisely: we need to understand the truth in the spirit of its formulas, and then to consider the thinking of the world where one is living, that we call the present-day world. The goal is to know that world also, under all its aspects, both as to the letter as well as the spirit. Finally, you need to discern what there is in this thinking of the world that is in conformity with the tradition, and what is contrary to its spirit, so as to affirm the first and reject the second as tainted.

The second method consists in focusing first and above all upon the thinking of the present, borrowing its language, being nurtured by its principles, and becoming steeped in its spirit. Then you turn to the tradition to reject everything that seems to

to be updated or renewed. In either case, it means bringing an existing reality together with a new element that you want to emphasize in order to achieve some kind of unity.

For example, this could mean joining Catholic doctrine with an idea brought to light by human effort, or it could mean linking the liturgy inherited from past centuries to certain new forms called for by present needs, or it could mean uniting Catholicism with the inculturation (*mentalité indigène*) needed for a new Christendom. In these different cases, you can devote your energies principally to the new element that remains external, at least for the moment; or you can focus on the reality of the church that you seek to update. Depending on whether you choose the first or the second option, you will end up with either a mechanical updating in danger of becoming both a "novelty" and a schismatic reform, on the one hand, or a genuine "renewal" (a true "development") that is a reform *in* and *of* the church, on the other hand—a reform without schism.

Another way to say this is to make reference to the category of the "twice born" explained above. The second birth of the "prophet" or of the reformer has to take place *in the church*. Whatever the source of the motivating shock that brings about an urge for change (usually it comes from the world that is not part of the church), when we seek principles and criteria at the stage of integration, we must study Catholic Tradition and not turn to masters foreign to the Tradition. (That was the case for both the Liberalism that the church condemned and for Modernism.) In fact, what Modernism took as a principle (which it inherited from the eighteenth century) was not so much *development*, but rather the "perfect-

---

be contrary to contemporary thinking and you adapt what remains . . . In the first case, you arrive at either a confirmation of the tradition and its approach that imparts a new appreciation for its riches—or you arrive at an unforeseen expression that adds precision to a traditional approach . . . In the second case, you come away with an expression of the tradition in which the tradition would not recognize itself. For if the expression is novel, its novelty indicates an alteration and not just a precision . . .

The first method is that of so-called orthodox reformers . . . The second is that of heterodox reformers that we would justly call innovators . . ."

After having already planned this section, I received a lot of insight about how to express it more precisely from the fine work of W. Foerster, "La vraie et fausse adaptation," published in *Autorité et Liberté*, French trans. (Lausanne, 1920), pp. 179f. Because of the great similarity between some of Foerster's ideas and some basic ideas in my *Chrétiens désunis* (1937), I need to point out that I only read *Autorité et Liberté* in the winter of 1945–1946.

ibility of Christianity," that is, its progressive transformation thanks to accretions from outside its given nature. That is something totally different from development.

This same difference of attitude can easily be applied, as I have already done, to the different orientation that exists between a non-Catholic ecumenism and a Catholic ecumenism.[194] Up to this point, non-Catholic ecumenism has generally taken its point of departure from the *diversity* of Christian confessions as a given and has sought to find unity within that context. However, I gladly recognize that more and more non-Catholic ecumenism has been open to the search for one authentic unity, in particular at the world conference at New Delhi in the fall of 1961. For its part, a Catholic ecumenism cannot forget that the church of Christ and of the apostles *exists*. Therefore, the point of departure for Catholic ecumenism is this existing church, and its goal is to strengthen within the church the sources of catholicity that it seeks to integrate and to respect all their legitimate differences.

On the one hand, a reunited church risks being thought of as a kind of concordat or a juxtaposition of the various churches now actually divided. On the other hand, this reunited church would really have the fullness of unity, and it would signify a *development* with respect to the Catholic Church considered in its present state. (In this case, the Catholic Church would be a church that has become *other*.) Nonetheless, this development would be that *of the Catholic Church*—and in this sense it would not be *another* church, that is, an ecclesial body other than the Catholic Church, the Church of Christ and of the apostles. To clarify what I mean, I borrow a simile from St. Augustine:[195] Catholicity is like the branches of a great tree receiving life from the unity of its trunk; catholicity is not like a mound of cut branches scattered in a pile around the trunk of the tree.

Adaptation as Development Comes About through Ressourcement

A Catholic reform movement therefore will be obliged to begin with a return to the fundamental principles of Catholicism. It will be necessary first of all to consult the tradition and to become immersed in it. It should be clear here that "tradition" does not mean "routine," no more than it means something "in the past." Of course, tradition has an aspect of

---

[194] *Chrétiens désunis* (1937), *passim*, but particularly pp. 125–126, 143f., and 180.
[195] St. Augustine, *Sermo* 46, ch. 8, no. 18 (PL 38:280–281).

what is in the past; in one way, it is the treasury of texts and realities that come from the church's past. But it is much more than that. Tradition is essentially the continuity of development arising from the initial gift of the church, and it integrates into unity all the forms that this development has taken and that it actually manifests. Tradition is the presence of the *principle* in all the stages of its development. It is therefore sources (Scripture, the events of the primitive church),[196] the thought of the Fathers, the faith and the prayer of the whole church (liturgy), the authentic investigations of the church's doctors and spiritual masters, the development of piety and of doctrine, and, finally, the thinking and the development of the actual church. That means today's church, perpetually seeking to express its faith, its praise, its contemplation and its apostolate—all under the guidance of the magisterium.

Some elements coming from the church's past are strictly normative: the Sacred Scriptures, dogmatic definitions, doctrine unanimously embraced, something that is an element of life for the universal church. There are other realities like the liturgy or like doctrinal expressions that are so full of ecclesial meaning and so much shaped by the life of the church that, without demanding as rigorous a conformity, they nonetheless represent for Catholics an exceptionally authoritative norm. There are also a great number of doctrinal expressions, historical experiences, and particular contributions of different moments or different aspects of the tradition. It should be clear that what is true remains true, despite the flow of time.

A "return to the tradition" does not necessarily mean binding today's Catholic to the literal acceptance of a contingent expression of Christian thought or life from some moment in the past (however venerable it might be as a part of the concrete fabric of the church). Such an expression is not identified with the essential structure of the church and in fact remains (in its material expression) something *outdated* and belongs to the past. The encyclical *Mediator Dei* (no. 59 f.) clearly made a distinction between the process of going back to the sources in antiquity and a kind of textual archaeology. (It makes an explicit allusion in this sense to the program of the Jansenists in Pistoia [*Mediator Dei*, no. 64].)

---

[196] In the great movements of reform, there has always been an aspect of returning to the sources of the truth in the primitive apostolic church. For the Gregorian Reform and the reform of the canons that continued in its impulse, cf. above, p. 166, n. 82. For the mendicant movement and the "apostolic" currents, as well as for the 16th-century reforms, this point is clear enough. It would also be easy to develop this idea with respect to present-day reform initiatives.

Returning to tradition means absolute respect for ecclesial expressions that are permanent and always viable, and a critical and intelligent respect for transitional forms, in a spirit of loyal respect and affection for all the forms. It means earnestly studying the very sources of Catholicism. It means being penetrated by the spirit of the church—going beyond what the church said with respect to a particular problem in the past—penetrated by the spirit that inspired the church's response, by what the church thinks at its deepest, by what it has said and wishes to say through us with respect to the problems of the present time. To return to principles, to "go back to the sources," as we say now, means to rethink the situation in which we find ourselves in the light and in the spirit of everything that the integrity of the tradition teaches us about the meaning of the church.

Here again we are dealing with the idea of *ressourcement* that we met before when treating the two levels of fidelity. It is at the heart of our question. *Revertimini ad fontes* (return to the sources) was St. Pius X's motto for the liturgy. In fact, it was in the liturgical movement that the present return to the sources made its first discoveries, before becoming a patristic and a biblical movement. Already the first efforts of this return to the sources have shown much promise. In this threefold return to liturgical, biblical, and patristic sources, the movement of *ressourcement* has found its true character. It is something altogether different from a simple return to the past, from a "restoration" of the sort that characterized the Protestant reforms of the sixteenth century or Jansenism. It asks today's questions of the ancient texts but also something more, and more central.

Ressourcement consists in a recentering on Christ and on the paschal mystery. This is why a liturgical renewal is always so fruitful for a reform movement returning to the sources. This is why the work of St. Pius X and of Pope Pius XI (guided by their respective mottos, *Instaurare omnia in Christo* [to restore all things in Christ] and *Pax Christi in regno Christi* [the Peace of Christ in the kingdom of Christ]) has had a real impact for reform. This also shows us how this kind of reform, even if it requires theological work (something always indispensable), will never find that sufficient. Reform is a renewal of life, I say it once again. Without the commitment of a corresponding life, a reform effort, even profiting from an intellectual return to the sources and a recentering, will not arrive at the necessary spirit of evangelization or at the fullness of authenticity and efficacy. Perhaps this was the dimension that Erasmus's attempts at reform, although sometimes so interesting, ultimately lacked.

This does not in the least diminish the necessity for theological research. There would be nothing more dangerous than to work at reforming something in the life of the church without being grounded upon a very solid ecclesiology, that is, a theology about the *structure* of the church. Indeed this distinction between *structure* and *life* clears up a whole lot of points. A great number of heresies in ecclesiology came from an unwarranted slipping from the area of life to that of structure; and the majority of dangerous and daring positions have been taken because people created theories about the life of the church without having first considered the data concerning its structure. In this respect once again, a liturgical renewal offers an exceptionally favorable base or framework for a reform movement. Not only does it tend to give primacy to the pastoral and to link a recentering on Christ to a return to original sources, but by its very nature it is also completely trustworthy theologically, guaranteeing that the renewal of the church's life will take place with respect for the dogmatic, sacramental, and hierarchical structure of the church. The facts bear witness to this.

The point of departure and the ruling principle for every healthy reform movement will be a return to the sources of the very principles of the tradition, to guide both the evangelization of life and the quality of theological thinking. That is the foundation and the light needed for the prophet's work in the church: "Only a deep understanding of the tradition can guide us to discern what is useful in what the modern world offers, and to choose that with assurance and adapt it with tact."[197] In this way, the Catholic principle guides conscience and reflection in order to allow them to achieve the twofold task of discernment and assimilation.

This discernment puts into effect St. Paul's magnificent program: "Do not quench the Spirit. Do not despise the words of the prophets, but test everything; hold fast to what is good; abstain from every form of evil" (1 Thess 5:19-20). This is precisely right, because in order for an adaptation not to be mechanical or purely exterior, but rather to represent a development of Christian principle, the Christian principle must both guide and assimilate the new element. It can do this only by discerning the aspects or parts of the new element which are appropriate for expressing the principle's growth. Assimilation always means to some degree a loss of what is assimilated. Successful adaptation shouldn't be an *external* novelty that penetrates Christianity and perpetuates itself within her, but it should be Christianity which profits from an element or form judged to be apt for genuinely Christian expression or growth.

---

[197] Foerster, op. cit., p. 183.

Some examples will help to make this clearer. If St. Thomas was able to bring about what has been called (inaccurately, by the way) the only Modernist program that ever succeeded in the church by introducing Aristotle into theology without violating either Catholic dogma or the spirit of evangelization, that is unquestionably because of the profound understanding that he had of the tradition, which came from his docility and his equally intense reflection. Likewise, if Abbé Mercier at the beginning of the scholastic revival was able to sketch out at least some kind of synthesis between theology and modern psychology (according to his gifts and despite lots of opposition), this is because of his primary and fundamental fidelity, his concentration upon what he considered essential, and his recollection (which one of his biographers considered the typical expression of his soul).[198]

The problem of adaptation is a classic and crucial problem for the missions. What we have described finds its fullest application there. The real question is how to nourish the development of catholicity, that is, to achieve its reality in the fullness or universality of unity. You can see how a hasty, external, or mechanical adaptation might try to amalgamate pagan elements (or at least new elements) directly with Catholic elements, that is, with forms belonging to Catholicism, both effectively taken out of context. But the church's mission, transmitting grace as the responsibility of its catholicity, should live and assimilate the new element *in the church* in such a fashion as to create, not a sort of Chinese or Hindu enclave within Latin Catholicism, but a genuine development of catholicity. This means the nurturing or the reality of the *Una Catholica* lived out according to this particular dimension of humanity represented by the Chinese or the Hindu world.[199]

I think in a similar way about reforms in the liturgy. Sooner or later, there will be adaptations that will constitute true liturgical creations. More than in any other area, a liturgical adaptation or liturgical renewal demands a return to the deepest tradition, for it touches upon an infinitely

---

[198] J. Guitton in *Trois serviteurs de l'unité chrétienne: Le Père Portal, Lord Halifax, le cardinal Mercier* (Paris, 1937), pp. 74–77.

[199] What is said here could also be applied to the question of the Chinese Rites. Perhaps the Jesuit missionaries tried to make too hasty and mechanical an adaptation. In any case, their Roman censors certainly stayed only on the level of a mechanical fidelity to the letter of the law, lacking perspective and depth. Dom Pierre-Célestin Lou remarks with a lot of truth in his enticing *Souvenirs et Pensées* (p. 106): "Instead of wasting time discussing the Chinese Rites, wouldn't it have been more fruitful to acquaint the Chinese with the incomparable Catholic liturgy of the dead?"

profound reality connected with the church's most interior life—at the very soul of Catholic principle. Such a return to principle can be brought about only by way of profound research in biblical, patristic, pastoral, and apostolic tradition. This is a very pure and contemplative approach that succeeds only through a new intensification of love of God and of people. As Msgr. Ancel appropriately said with respect to adaptations in religious poverty, "to adapt yourself, you have to be fervent"; you have to live intensely the spirituality of the principle so as to reconstruct the new forms that it calls forth according to its true spirit. Calling existing forms into question, if that must be done, should proceed not from a weakening but from a strengthening of fidelity. Without that, instead of adaptations, you end up with mitigations that will only be sterile.[200] As I will soon say, the success of such a program can only be the work of an entire people and of an entire generation, not of one man or one team.

To tell the truth, all the big problems facing contemporary Catholicism are such that solving them with quick and mechanical adaptations would lead to catastrophe. Such problems require a lifelong effort and the collaboration of all the people for a long time. As examples, to list only a few, there are the problems of the synthesis of Christianity and liberalism (inescapable and already begun), an updated conception of the role of humanity in the universe and in evolution, and (on a more practical level) the search for a meaningful religious life.

The history of attempts at mechanical adaptations (what I call *innovative adaptations* as opposed to *developmental adaptations*) is also instructive. It gives precise examples of all the aspects of faulty reformism that we have already met: the use of a purely rational process, individualistic stubbornness in the conviction of being right even in opposition to the common tradition of the church, spiritual impatience, and, finally, the absence of deep research into the sources and their principles, as well as a completely cerebral elaboration of an artificial program foreign to the entire concrete living tradition of the church. Without question, you can find in every period (even into the High Middle Ages)[201] examples of

---

[200] Msgr. Ancel, "Des adaptations de la pauvreté," *La Vie Spirituelle—Supplément* (May 15, 1948), pp. 44f. Cf. Harnack's remark from a historical perspective (*Dogmengeschichte*, vol. III, p. 213, n. 1) that only religious personalities possessing a strong faith had been able to assimilate and fuse Christianity with elements that had been considered contrary to it: for example, Neoplatonic mysticism. Cf. also above, pp. 199f.

[201] A simple example: Under St. Bernard, Cîteaux sought to reform things—to return to the authentic and the pure. Nothing could be more praiseworthy. They did this by

such attempts at reform. The most characteristic in Christian antiquity was that of Marcion, whose similarity to the Protestant reform of the sixteenth century would be interesting to explore.

But it is above all in the modern period—a rationalist, individualistic period eager for originality—that we find examples of this kind of reform. In the eighteenth century, the philosophy of Wolff and Naturalism were sources for this. The program for reforming theological teaching elaborated by Rautenstrauch substituted trendy philosophy (Wolff's Deism)[202] for the church's tradition. What there was of a reform nature in Josephism had a similar inspiration.[203] The whole current of Febronianism-Jansenism, which ended in the Synod of Pistoia, sought to rebuild the church along the lines of a mechanical adaptation to the spirit of the century.[204] This could be traced in the elaboration of the Civil Constitution of the Clergy in France in 1790, with its idea of an elected clergy who were state bureaucrats. The same trends and the same errors were repeated in the nineteenth century, especially in Germany. When you read about reformist projects of certain priests from Württemberg at the beginning of the nineteenth century (a Werkmeister, for example)[205] you are dumbfounded by the superficial, hasty, external character of the recommended changes. If these people had been listened to, we would have suppressed nothing less than the Mass itself in the service of a mechanical adaptation to the

---

moving along the path of devotion and deep fidelity. However, on one point, Citeaux's efforts at reform seem to have taken the wrong path, following abstract principles that were erroneous in the case. This was the reform of the chant. They proceeded from an intellectual analysis, from a priori principles such as the unity of the modes, the incompatibility of authentic and plagal tones, and the limit of not using more than ten notes (because Ps 33:2 says, "*in psalterio decachordo psallam tibi*" [I will make melody to him *with the harp of ten strings*]). They knew they were going against the texts, but in the name of their "ratio" [agenda], they thought that the consent of their Cistercian tradition allowed them unanimity despite the error involved . . . Cf. D. Delalande, *Le Graduel des Prêcheurs* (Paris, 1948), pp. 31–39, and 72, n. 2.

[202] Cf. F. X. Arnold, *Grundsätzliches und Geschichtliches zur Theol. der Seelsorge—Untersuchungen zur Theologie der Seelsorge*, 2 (Freiburg im Breisgau, 1949), pp. 75f.

[203] Cf. E. Winter, *Der Josefinizmus und seine Geschichte: Beitrag zur Geistesgeschichte Oesterreichs, 1740–1848* (Brünn, Munich, Vienna, 1943).

[204] Cf. A.-M. Weiss, O.P., *Le péril religieux*, French trans., 2nd ed. (Paris, 1907), pp. 227f., 238f.

[205] Cf. E. Vermeil, *J.-A. Möhler et l'Ecole catholique de Tubingue: 1815–1840* (Paris, 1913), pp. 301f.; O. Rousseau, *Histoire du mouvement liturgique* (Paris, 1945), p. 70, n. 3. The liturgical reforms inspired by the Aufklärung and summarized by Dom Rousseau (pp. 59f.) are examples of mechanical adaptation.

tastes of their day, which would be foreign to us today. It is wonderful to see how a man like Möhler, who was basically sympathetic with the reform current, was able to separate himself from innovations of the mechanical kind and remain orientated to a genuine renewal from the inside, based upon a revival of scholarship and of priestly spirit.[206]

So strong has been the triumph of the Catholic tradition that we have difficulty imagining what the "liberal" current of a naively rationalist reform movement (superficial and foreign to the living tradition of the church) was like at the beginning of the nineteenth century and in the first years of the twentieth.[207] It seems, however, that the lesson has not been learned by everybody. The contemporary period has again witnessed such programs of modernization for the church to replace the tradition with the mechanical substitution of ideas shaped by hasty and completely cerebral criticism. The examples drawn from Modernism are well known. But closer to our time we have seen the complaints made by Hungarian priests[208] and by the group Jednota (meaning "unity") in Czechoslovakia,[209] the attempts of Msgr. Carlos Duarte da Costa[210] and of Ferdinando Tartaglia[211] . . . Alas, the list goes on.

The story of Lamennais and to a lesser degree of Le Sillon [*The Furrow* —a journal] also shows us the danger of attempts at too mechanical a reconciliation between the church and the modern world. Their project was grandiose. It inspired the most generous element of elite priests and laity for more than a century. Practically speaking, it finally found its fulfillment in the new attitudes adopted by most Catholic countries and by almost all the lay faithful and the young clergy. But that only became possible on the foundation of a profound renewal whose origin and tendencies could somehow be found in a whole series of linked events. These included the Thomistic revival, the renewal in the church stimulated by Modernist activities, and by the condemnation of Modernism in sacred studies and Catholic piety. It also included the liturgical movement with its strong foundation in Christology, sacramentology, and

---

[206] Ibid., pp. 308, 317–318.

[207] Cf. Weiss, op. cit., pp. 227f., 272f. (on the beginnings of Modernism, pp. 298f.).

[208] Cf. Benedict XV's letter to Cardinal Csernoch of Mar. 12, 1919 (see Doerner, *Sentire cum ecclesia* [1941], pp. 64–66).

[209] Cf. N. Hilling in *Archiv für Kathol. Kirchenrecht* (1919–1920), pp. 134–137 (cf. Doerner, loc. cit.).

[210] Cf. above, p. 275, n. 158.

[211] He was the instigator of a "Convegno per la Riforma religiosa" whose sessions were held in a Methodist church in August 1948.

ecclesiology; the generous and very serious effort at social progress; the severe but beneficial lessons of secularism (*laïcisme*); and the serious effort to understand the church's contacts with the problems, the doctrines, and the contributions of the secular world. It involved the church's complete exposure to the life of society, taking part in the pain, the effort, and the hope of people for whom two wars and a resistance movement had been the occasion of profound change, and in the church's magnificent apostolic efforts and its communion and symbiosis with remarkable lay activists . . . All that, and a lot of other factors, along with the directives of the Holy See, the reflection of philosophers—the work of Blondel, Maritain, and Péguy—all that began to allow us to make the necessary discernment so that a spiritual opening to the modern world would avoid becoming a superficial amalgam of diverse elements and instead become a true development of Christianity. Such a Christian development follows what is valuable in the directions that humanity has taken since the Renaissance and since the French Revolution.

For Lamennais, as also for Le Sillon, the principles for addressing ideas such as freedom and democracy (and other ideas that the modern world was very fond of) and assimilating them to Christianity had not been sufficiently reflected upon or penetrated deeply enough in order to provide for the discernment and purifications needed to bring about a truly organic adaptation. Progressives had taken up ideas conceived in another, often hostile, world—ideas still charged with an alien spirit[212]—in order to introduce them into Christianity and (as it were) baptize them. Doubtless the eightieth and last proposition of the *Syllabus* of 1864 (*supra*, n. 120) essentially meant to condemn every adaptation to the modern world in which the church would have changed its own principles so as to adopt other principles.[213] However, reconciling the church with the modern world cannot be done by introducing ideas from this modern world *as such* into the church. Such reconciliation would require deep research through which the permanent principles of Catholicism would take on

---

[212] Typical of Lacordaire's realism, he wrote in 1838: "Too many disparate elements are mixed and crunched together here. A century will not be too long for the difficult task of separating them out, and we will be dead before it is done. But we ought not to complain about that" (*Lettre sur le Saint-Siège*, pp. 73–74). I sketched out some implications of this remark for the idea of freedom in the *Supplément aux Cahiers de la paroisse universitaire* (Dec. 1945), pp. 44f. (reprinted in *Sacerdoce et Laïcat* [Paris, 1962], pp. 447–457).

[213] Cf. the text of Cardinal Régnier, cited by Msgr. Delassus, *Le problème de l'heure présente*, vol. I (Lille and Paris, 1905), p. 327, and the commentary that follows it.

a new development through assimilating the valuable contributions of the world after having "decanted" and purified them as needed.

Other assimilations currently underway,[214] including the reconciliation of Christians which the ecumenical movement has as its goal, pose the same kind of challenge and require the same kind of work.

This kind of return to the depths of the tradition was what the Modernists especially failed to do. In the midst of the Modernist crisis, Foerster warned them about this:

> Modernism is right in feeling that a great many souls who belong to the church are looking for more freedom, for a more universal understanding of salvation, for a more living exegesis of traditions. But where it is mistaken is in the completely temporal way of interpreting this yearning, and in believing that it only has to broaden the church's perspective in order to bring about a reconciliation between modern culture and the church. However, what is really called for is a full-blown resurrection of the great tradition . . . The Modernists are too inclined to consider or judge the church from a point of view outside the tradition.[215]

Modernism was a crisis in the application of the new critical methods to religious knowledge, and it attempted to introduce into Catholicism a philosophy that arose from a modern subjectivist stream. On these two points which were essential to it, Modernism represents a hasty attempt to achieve a mechanical adaptation—an innovative adaptation. But in its critique, Modernism often allowed itself to use improvisations, dangerous hypotheses, disconcerting and frequently precarious reversals of the tradition. But now, where are so many of those new conclusions that we were encouraged to adopt?[216]

---

[214] In particular, the ideas of respect for freedom and for tolerance—one of the major problems facing our generation.

[215] Foerster, op. cit., p. 181.

[216] Accordingly, if the Modernists had succeeded, the "juridical" idea of hierarchical power would have been replaced by a completely "spiritual" concept . . . The positions commonly held by the critics of the 1880s and put forward by the Modernists, with respect to the nature and the constitution of the church, the ideas of hierarchy, unity, episcopacy, etc., are completely outmoded today. See O. Linton, *Das Problem der Urkirche in der neueren Forschung* (Upsala, 1932); F.-M. Braun, *Aspects nouveaux du problème de l'Eglise* (Fribourg and Lyons, 1942). The critical evaluation goes on.

In religious philosophy, Modernism transposed or elaborated inter-pretations that represented enormous approximations, interpretations that it often drew from the most questionable philosophies. By doing so, it threatened to compromise a genuine *development* in Catholic thought concerning meaning from the subject's point of view: this is the great discovery of modern thought. From this point of view, following Pascal, Newman, and Blondel, apologetics and contemporary Catholic thought are in the process of discerning a fruitful new approach to the truth.

A mechanical sort of adaptation can be the work of a single person; it can be the work of a single mind—of the mind alone. If, in order to reform the Breviary, it sufficed only to substitute one text for another without seeking to adapt a prayer form arising from the deep tradition of the church, then the project of Quignonez (1535) would have long ago sufficed. If, in order to reconcile the church with the age in which it lives, nothing more was needed than a mechanical adaptation of modern political ideas, then the ardent spirit of Lamennais would have been perfectly capable of achieving that. As to the application of critical sci-ences to the Bible and to the history of dogma, the sharp flexible mind of Loisy would perhaps have sufficed to achieve the task. At most, these men would have had to call upon the team that they had formed around them, a small group of others similarly concerned.

However, on the contrary, a genuine development of the tradition with all that implies—of a return to deep sources, of discernment and purification, of balance and of a full spiritual communion and comple-mentarity—all that transcends the possibilities of one person or even of one team. It has to be the work of at least a generation. Better, it has to be the work of a whole people (of the whole body of the church—clergy and faithful together). In fact, this kind of development under the impulse of prophetic elements can only be accomplished in communion with the whole church.

What we said before about patience and delays fully applies here as well. There is need for waiting so that the process of discernment can operate, so that organic assimilation and development can be expressed. "Assimilation is not a mechanical operation that can be accomplished overnight. In proposing it as a simple, easy operation, these impatient reformers demonstrate to what degree they are strangers to the essential spirit of the church." [217] They are also strangers to the meaning of history

---

[217] Foerster, op. cit., p. 183.

and the meaning of living reality. If the intellectual life were only an accumulation of facts, then a dictionary and some work are all that would be needed. But if the question is how really to appropriate an idea, that is, a new illumination, a spiritual seed, then time is needed. There is need for opportunities, for time for maturation, clarification, and fruitfulness. Someone who in the course of a year has acquired three or four ideas which are genuine spiritual principles has not wasted his time.

But what we are dealing with here is not even strictly intellectual work. We are dealing with religious truths and with a development of the principle of Christianity in the communion of the church. These are all things which require an infinitely greater commitment than mental exercise. However, one mind can plant the seed for such a development. This is even truer when we consider different spiritual families and different intellectual vocations of a prophetic type. Unquestionably, Newman's intellectual work was of this kind. He planted within Catholicism seeds of discernment, assimilation, and development which are still awaiting their full outcome.

The Church Needs to Live in Contact with Its Deepest Tradition

At the end of this section, we should note a parallel responsibility. While reformers are obliged to question the tradition of the church with docility, the pastors of the church have a parallel obligation. By church here I mean not only the whole body of the faithful, but particularly the hierarchy and, in general, what the medieval theologians called the *majores* (the bishops).

As we have seen, the central offices of the church have the special role of moderating and protecting the church. The hierarchy is the guardian and interpreter of the tradition. It confirms and it condemns. Its first instinct, faced with a prophetic initiative, is to pull back (or at least to be reserved) and sometimes even to refuse or disown it. In the process of discernment and purification, by way of returning to the depth of principles, this moment of checkmate or even of condemnation plays an important role that can be positive, despite appearances. For this precisely is what forces a return to the sources. It obliges the reformer not to be satisfied with a mechanical adaptation or a simple introduction of some new element.

Foerster wrote wisely in the middle of the Modernist crisis: "It is from this point of view that we have to judge the attitude and the historic role of the head of the church (often criticized). By putting conservative piety back at the center of the Christian life, resituating the church once again on the soil of primitive dogma and insisting on this for the interior life, the Pope is actually clearing the way for a future assimilation of useful aspects of modern culture. For genuine assimilation is not a mechanical exercise that can be accomplished overnight . . . ."[218]

This observation also holds for the attitude of the Catholic Church and of the Holy See with respect to ecumenism. Their attitude appeared harsh, and it did effectively have its severe side. The encyclical *Mortalium Animos* of 1928 expressed a blunt refusal of non-Catholic ecumenism, and perhaps some of its formulas no longer do justice to the ecumenical movement as it is today.[219] However, if the ecumenical movement has become purified, doesn't it owe something to the intransigent and doctrinally firm attitude of the Catholic Church in making that happen? I wrote in 1937 that the Catholic Church had its own way of serving the cause of ecumenism, which was to be itself and to assert itself as being the one, apostolic church. I added that by refusing to enter the ecumenical movement, it had done for ecumenism with respect to what is most serious more than the participating Christian groups, and that the present evolution of this movement owes much to the Catholic Church.[220]

Coming to know ecumenism better has only confirmed my judgment about this. It is evident that the Catholic Church, faced with the optimistic, hasty ecumenism of the 1920s that was tempted by apparent reconciliation, obliged ecumenism to make a serious and patient return to basic principles because of its refusal. This was an unavoidable step if the reunion was to be something other than syncretism or a mechanical alliance. For that, a bit of goodwill and a few conferences would have been enough. But what was really needed was integration in the sense of a tradition grasped at its deepest level and the development of the genuine and abundant catholicity of the one church.

However, this good aspect of a preliminary reaction of refusal when faced with novelties does not reduce the church's overwhelming duty to keep itself deeply in contact with its tradition. This means contact not

---

[218] Ibid.

[219] Cf. the remarks of Dr. W. H. Van de Pol, *Het christelijk Dilemma Katholieke Kerk-Reformatie* (Roermond, 1948), p. 364, about the first part of this encyclical.

[220] *Chrétiens désunis*, p. 171.

only on the surface and according to the letter of the law but also in depth and according to the reality of the progressive change that gives this tradition its full meaning. This is why I pointed out at the beginning of this study that the church, like Christianity itself, starts with a seed and moves to its fullness by way of development.

Just as there is a mechanical adaptation that can become nothing more than a "novelty" ending in rupture, there can also be a mechanical fidelity. There can be reactions that fail to honor the life of the very structure that they aim to preserve, and that do not respond to the structure's needs for life. There can be a purely orthodox mechanical amalgamation: *The Book of Concord* (1580) is an example of that. There can be a mechanical return to the Fathers: the Jansenists made that mistake. There can be a purely mechanical fidelity to St. Thomas—such a danger has not always been imaginary. In short, as I said above, we risk in the church becoming like the "Synagogue" with respect to the gifts committed to our fidelity when we aren't running the risk of becoming "Pharisees."

There should be some more sensitive way of addressing, not mistakes that remain mistakes, but legitimate requests for adaptation or openness. In such a stance, the impulse to return to the deepest principles would not become a mechanical attachment to some *outdated* expression of the tradition, or an unfeeling fidelity to principle that lacks understanding and openness to vital initiatives (even the smallest initiative and the tiniest risk). For where there is life, there is always both initiative and risk. "It is because they lack a skeleton that certain animals must surround themselves with shells."[221]

Certainly there are completely erroneous initiatives that merit nothing more than condemnation and, as far as possible, oblivion. But there are also errors that conceal a spark of truth and that are combinations of doctrinal error and doctrinal truth. With respect to such initiatives, simply condemning them would not be adequate in view of the possibility of a more perfect truth. Then such a condemnation would also have about it the qualities of hastiness (perhaps necessary at a given moment), of automatic reflex, or of too immediate a response without the possibility of assimilation.[222] That cannot be what governs a church about which

---

[221] E. Mersch, *La théologie du Corps mystique*, vol. II (Paris-Brussels, 1944), p. 97. This is like the theme of Claudel's magnificent poem, *Légende de Prâkriti*.

[222] See G. Thils, *Théologie des réalités terrestres*, vol. I: *Préludes* (Desclée, 1946), p. 115.

St. Irenaeus says that the Spirit of God ceaselessly remains and acts within her, rejuvenating the deposit confided to her, and even the structure into which the deposit has been entrusted.[223]

---

[223] This kind of contraction by the church, turning in on itself, has a further meaning within the general rhythm of its historical life. The church is preparing for a movement of expansion or mission. We see this in the 13th century, following Innocent III; in the 16th and 17th centuries, following the Council of Trent; and finally in the 19th century, when a magnificent missionary expansion and a flowering of pastoral work and holiness followed upon the church's self-preoccupation. Look at what historians say: J. Madaule, in the "Introduction" to Toynbee's *Le Monde et l'Occident* (Desclée de Brouwer, 1953), p. 39.

CONCLUSION

Perspectives on the Attitude to Take toward Concrete Reform Initiatives

By way of conclusion, I would like to examine the different attitudes that we can adopt in concrete cases when faced with the phenomenon of reform. First, I will examine the spirit of reform in general, then the reform movement at the time of my writing (1950), according to the description that I gave in my introduction. In this way, the book's conclusion, following our long intermediate journey of research, will come back to its original questions enriched by what we have learned about the *reasons* for what we know. This is one of the benefits of *science*—the science of the theologian as well as of other researchers.

A. About the Élan and Spirit of Reform in General

I pose two questions here, corresponding to the two possible options facing us. The second option is pertinent only if the first has been affirmed in favor of the spirit of reform. First, then, there is the question of accepting or refusing reform. If the response is positive, then there follows the concrete question concerning the relation between the faithful and the instigators of schism.

1) *For or Against the Idea of Reform*

The facts show that often, when faced with rather shallow questions or reform initiatives, the attitude of the church (the *third* sense of church that was distinguished above, that is, the hierarchical leaders) has been first of all to refuse them. There are exceptions, of course: we have seen the remarkable example of Innocent III (above, p. 238), and we are currently living out an even more sensational example with the *aggiornamento* of John XXIII and the council. But when the church is confronted with novelty, it is inclined first and foremost to distance itself and to turn in upon itself. As if leaving to the future the need to respond to its present challenges, the church focuses in upon itself and refuses to consider anything other than what it has always found familiar.

There are profound reasons for this that generally have both dogmatic and pastoral dimensions. First of all, the church wants to insist on the purity and integrity of its principles. It happens sometimes that churchmen in responsible positions block initiatives in the name of what are simply their habitual thought patterns or received ideas. It is also possible that in some cases of conflict, the essential element can only be protected by defending nonessential and peripheral elements that are historically linked to it. [There are examples of this kind in Part 3 (not included here).] It is a shame that this is so, even though we have explained why it is. However, above all, we need to recognize the seriousness of what is involved. Before all else, the church has to safeguard its very being as well as the integrity of its principles. *Depositum custodire*— "Guard what has been entrusted to you" (1 Tim 6:20).

Adapting the church to the needs of a changing world, responding to the expressed desires of the faithful, making real improvements in theology or in pastoral practice—these are all desirable things to do. But all of them have to do with the *living practice* of the church (its *bene esse*—its *well-being*). Yet the primary concern of church leaders is with the *esse* (the *essential being*)—the basic structure—of the church.

The church's turning in on itself in defense of its principles is resolved rather quickly, by the way, in a positive fashion. On the one hand, as we saw (part 2, fourth condition), this kind of situation represents at one and the same time not only a difficulty but also a condition ultimately favorable for authentic growth, adaptation or reform leading to true development. On the other hand, as history shows, the church's contraction or drawing in on itself has to be understood in the context of the rhythm of its overall historical existence. Often such a position represents a preparation for a subsequent movement of expansion or mission. You can see this in the thirteenth century, following Innocent III; in the sixteenth and seventeenth centuries, following the Council of Trent; in the nineteenth century, where flourishing pastoral activity and new expressions of holiness came after a period of self-preoccupation on the church's part. Finally, the greater openness of Catholicism following the First World War certainly profited from the restorative initiatives undertaken by Pius IX, Leo XIII, and St. Pius X. In the end, the life of the church benefits from the strengthening of the church's structure.

Pastoral concerns are equally decisive. Such concerns arise from experience, which teaches us to envisage consequences and evaluate them. For example, the critical reform spirit of the fifteenth century shook the confidence and undermined the meaning of the church for many people.[1] Likewise, for the bulk of the Christian population who were unprepared to follow subtle distinctions, certain innovations in the liturgy that were too radical became an opening for the introduction of heresy in the sixteenth century.[2]

In that century we meet for the first time the idea that the culture of the Catholic population is able either to encourage or to render practically impossible attitudes and activities that are themselves positive, according to the case in question. Pastoral experience (as well as human experience as such) teaches us to be cautious about the temptation to novelty—beware of the forbidden fruit.[3] In Christianity, "error" is essentially a novelty. Experience also shows us that a highly refined ideal of some uncommon nature can camouflage either a temptation to pride or an evasion of responsibilities . . . All these objections have some weight. Ecclesiastical superiors are right to take them into consideration.

It is not impossible that less Catholic attitudes also weigh upon the pure dogmatic or pastoral motives that I have mentioned. My objective and frank perspective impels me to review this area of hidden motives that are not so much linked to Catholicism as such, but rather to the "Catholic world," the milieu or the mentality in which people are guided by fixed ideas. It concerns the habit of clinging to what has been familiar and maintaining consistency, more than protecting a dogmatic principle linked to Catholic tradition.

---

[1] Cf. Denifle-Weiss, *Luther und Luthertum*, vol. II (Mainz, 1909), pp. 61, 65f., 79–81.

[2] Cf. A. Duval, "Le Concile de Trente et le culte eucharistique," in *Studia Eucharistica* (Antwerp, 1946), pp. 379–413.

[3] A.-M. Weiss, *Le péril religieux*, 2nd ed. (Paris, 1906), pp. 221 and 223. Weiss cites 1 Tim 6:20 (*Devitans profanas vocum novitales*, vulgate; the Greek has *kenophonias*, meaning empty or vain words), and Prov 9:17 ("Stolen water is sweet, and bread eaten in secret is [more] pleasant").

I have pointed out how an imperfect but stable order is often worth more than change. However, we remember the impressive declarations of St. Cyprian, St. Augustine, Pope Nicholas I, and St. Gregory VII: "When you have custom without truth, all you have is the antiquity of error"; "The Lord never said: 'I am the custom, but I am the truth.' "[4] In a more general way that is also more visceral, Catholics and churchmen (especially) are brought up and trained for *literal* obedience.[5] This is a powerful dynamic, and it deeply affects their submissiveness to everything that is a *given* in the church, by which the essential imperatives of the structure are expressed. But sometimes this instinct leads to excess, the excess of imagining that there is only one virtue, obedience, just as there is only one sin, the sin of the flesh.

This perspective habituates priests and faithful alike to a kind of passivity (lack of initiative), especially where there is a need for someone to get a grip on the possibilities for real vitality.[6] At the extreme, this leads to imagining that religion is only something prefabricated, completely determined from on high, excluding personal decisions of conscience. So the *Sentire cum Ecclesia* becomes nothing more than a mechanical docility that complies with meticulous and exhaustive regulations and leaves no margin for personal decisions or adaptation.[7] We

---

[4] "*Consuetudo sine veritate vetustas erroris est.*" St. Cyprian, Ep. LXXIV, 9, 2. "*Si consuetudinem fortassis opponas, advertendum est quod Dominus dicit: Ego sum veritas et vita. Non dixit: Ego sum consuetudo, sed veritas. Et certe, ut beati Cypriani utamur sententia, quaelibet consuetudo, quantumvis vetusta, quantumvis vulgata, veritati omnino est postponenda et usus qui veritati est contrarius abolendus.*" C. 5, D. VIII (Friedberg, I, 14; cf. canons 3 to 9 [Friedberg, col. 14–15], where several texts of St. Augustine, St. Cyprian, and Nicholas I are cited.) To track the use of this idea, cf. R. Wehrlé, *La coutume dans le Droit canonique* (Paris, 1928), pp. 81–82, 85–86.

[5] See an interesting analysis of this kind of formation and of this attitude from the point of view of apostolic contact with the world in A. Rabut, "Pour une psychologie religieuse moderne," *La Vie Spirituelle—Supplément* (Aug. 1949), pp. 123–136.

[6] There are interesting and important remarks on this point in M. de la Bedoyère, *Christianity in the Marketplace*, French trans. by E. Dethise, *Le Christianisme sur la place publique* (Bruxelles, 1947). Beginning in Oct. 1932, Colonel Roullet made excellent observations along these lines in articles in *La Vie Intellectuelle*, later published as a booklet, *Les catholiques dans la vie publique* (cf. pp. 43f.).

[7] This is the position of the book by A. Doerner, *Sentire cum Ecclesia: Ein Dringender Aufruf und Weckruf an Priester* (Munich: Gladbach, 1941). This huge work which attacks everything new in contemporary German Catholic life (as well as things ancient and traditional) contains some good things. But its fundamental position identifies *Sentire cum Ecclesia* with immobility, with the most literal obedience to every law, with devotion to laws for the sake of laws, with the "ready-made" solution and decisions from

saw above (part 2, third condition) how this is a mutilation and practically a caricature of a genuine *Sentire cum Ecclesia* or of an authentic meaning of tradition. It becomes a banal fidelity in which the spirit of Catholicism is respected in only a superficial way.

In my view, this also represents a certain spineless quality that manifests, if not fear, at least very little confidence in the power of the truth and its principles. Without going into the zoological aspects, there is surely a profound spiritual truth in the maxim of E. Mersch: "Because they lack a backbone, certain animals have to be enveloped in a shell."[8] In attitudes of defensiveness that above all avoid risk (and so also avoid what is new, if not vitality itself), there is a feeling of weakness and sometimes even of fear. It is because we are not sure of ourselves that we can feel eclipsed culturally and dynamically by a world that we know in only a distant way. Fright makes us put up barriers. Innocent III, Leo XIII, and Pius XI, by contrast, were open and took initiative because they dominated their time through their intelligence and strong personalities. It is more than chance that a timid and defensive Christianity becomes a religion for women and children, a religion afraid of adult men (who themselves have no interest in it). Further, it is not due to chance either that under a rigorous authority of strict regulations, the clergy tend to seek the security of what is familiar and to prefer canonical formulas, the "ready-made."

This attitude of the clergy as a kind of opposition to initiative is encouraged and at the same time legitimated by the estrangement of the church from the real world. This is due both to a lack of experience and to a lack of formation in considering the state of society realistically. I have to clarify here, because, in one sense, priests are among the most realistic and best informed persons. A parish priest knows his people not only as to their moral and religious life but as to their human situation and their social behavior as well. However, sometimes (and this was especially true some years ago) I meet priests who know too little about history, about technology and society; or who, if they have some idea of these things, draw practically no practical conclusions from what they know.

It seems like any clear and conscientious analysis of the real state of the pastoral field has always led to some reformist conclusions. That is

---

on high by way of authority. For these reasons, it is disappointing and really too simplistic. The Bishop of Trier refused to give it his *imprimatur*.

[8] *Théologie du Corps mystique*, vol. II (Brussels and Paris, 1944), p. 97. Cf. Newman, *Essay on the Development of Christian Doctrine*, ch. 5, section 4, § 5 (p. 188).

the result of linking an understanding of the human situation, sociology, and the technical aspects of ministry or spirituality with the genuine needs of the Christian world. What is needed here is not knowledge of what never changes but knowledge of what represents eternal spiritual truths along with concrete human situations. What is needed is an understanding of the linked historical and sociological realities that describe the moral and religious *situation* of real human beings today. If we look around ourselves, we see that churchmen who are eventually open to reform are also open to a real consideration of historical and social conditions, whereas churchmen who are a priori opposed to any reform are likewise closed to any consideration of historical and social conditions. It is always possible that an awakening to this historical and social conditioning might arouse in them a more positive attitude than one of pure opposition and condemnation of their own times that are always guilty of the sin of being *modern*, that is, of living in the present, not the past.

Sometimes this strange attitude of escapism really exists. There are people for whom anything that happened after a certain date is ipso facto considered to be a mortal sin and damned. I won't stop to further critique this strange attitude from which very few of us are completely free. We feel that we are not getting what we really should. We are suspicious of the new; we may even feel betrayed. Is this jealousy? Is it the complex of in-laws who are disturbed that the young generation has chances that they never had?[8bis] That's not really important. What is important is to be aware of the attitude and to be ready to be self-critical.

If we wanted to be complete in this rapid review of motives for opposing the movement of reform, especially if we wanted to analyze the French situation completely, a paragraph would be needed about two attitudes adopted by a good number of French Catholics (which are generally linked). I refer to what we call in sociological-political language *"the mentality of the right,"* and what we call in theological language *"integralism."*

Resisting demands for reform, along with misunderstanding them and systematically refusing them, can have grave consequences. The first consequence is to exasperate and practically push out of the church

---

[8bis] Cf. Péguy in *L'Argent*: *"Ces malheureux qui en veulent à leurs élèves de tout, d'être jeunes, d'être nouveaux, d'être frais, d'être candides, d'être debutants, de ne pas être pliés comme eux . . . .* — These unhappy persons who hate their students for everything— for being young, new, fresh, frank, at the beginning of life, not bent as they are bent . . ." (*Oeuvres compl.*, NFR, vol. IV, p. 426).

any reformist inclination. Impatience or a lack of proportion does not mean that someone has no right to be heard. It has often been remarked that this is how some personalities were practically driven out of the church: Erasmus made such a claim about Arius, Tertullian, and Wycliffe, and he wondered if churchmen were trying to drive him out too.[9] In fact, while these are examples of heretics convinced not to give in, the remark serves as well for those whom we have previously considered in a more favorable light. The best we might say is that in these cases the responsibility is mixed.

Look at Waldo who went to Rome to submit his growing movement to the judgment of the Lateran Council (1179). The way he was treated by secondary Roman officials (not Pope Alexander III!) does not suggest that they acted in good conscience. I can't help thinking that things would have gone differently in 1210 if, instead of meeting Walter Mapes, Waldo had met with Innocent III or Cardinal Ugolino. But Waldo was not Francis Bernadone and, alas, he probably came predisposed to hold onto his position, whatever the ecclesiastical authority might decide.[10] It has been suggested that the Czech movement of the fifteenth century, despite serious doctrinal errors, represented the hopes and aspirations of nationalism at the dawn of modern times.[11] I can't help thinking that if these hopes and aspirations had been welcomed and understood by the church, if the use of the chalice had been granted in time, that schisms that have weighed down subsequent history even to our day perhaps could have been avoided . . .

It has been suggested (I am not an authority on this topic) that the "Jansenist" church of Utrecht owed its origin to the Catholics' failure to understand and to their rigidity.[12] It has been suggested that if Döllinger had been invited to Rome to work on the preparation of the First Vatican

---

[9] Cf. Renaudet, *Etudes érasmiennes*, p. 264. Without excusing Erasmus, you can understand the kind of threat that flavors his writings because of his being constantly denounced, threatened, and hunted down wherever he was. The sort of serenity you find in Père Lagrange, Touzard, or Père Sertillanges, for example, presupposes people with exceptional religious depth.

[10] Cf. the study already cited by A. Dondaine in *Archiv. Fratr. Praed.* XV (1946), pp. 220–221.

[11] Cf., for example, F. Dvornik, *National Churches and the Church Universal* (London, 1944), pp. 44–45.

[12] This is the idea of B. A. Van Kleef, "An Outline of the History of the Old Catholic Church," in the collection *Northern Catholicism* (London, 1933), pp. 531f.

Council, perhaps he would have remained Catholic.[13] That seems doubtful, and Döllinger put himself out of consideration for such a thing by his attitude. But I myself heard an English prelate, who knew George Tyrrell quite well, say that Tyrrell might have remained in the church if he had not been pushed to the limit. Again, I cite this opinion without making it my personal judgment, and I add this case to the preceding ones, not for the sake of preparing an indictment against the hierarchy, but in order to show that there is a problem.

The problem is that the hierarchy is not always sufficiently open to valid demands, so that those who take the initiative for them may despair of being heard concerning what they believe to be true. The church fundamentally recognizes there is a problem here. That is why we have often seen the church put up with difficult persons and, in some way, even with their errors, in order to avoid pushing them to the breaking point. Alexander VIII avoided pronouncing a solemn condemnation of the [Gallican] Four Articles of 1682 in order to prevent a schism. The way in which Lamennais was treated at first was marked by similar consideration. The church knows that "if you hit someone's nose, it bleeds."[13bis]

But you can no more ask the church to accept all that than you can ask parents to give in to all the whims of their children so as to keep them from losing their temper. The bad attitude of reformers who have secretly decided to be right, in opposition to the whole church, makes even the most positive attitudes of welcome and understanding useless. Impatience, stubbornness about unilateral demands, a spirit of revolt—these, at a certain point, can only lead to expulsion.[14] It's true that the

---

[13] Cf. F. Mourret, *Le Concile du Vatican*, p. 75. Pius IX himself would have wanted to invite him to the council.

[13bis] Prov 30:33 [*Good News Bible*]. Cf. St. Thomas (*Summa Theol.*, 2a-2ae, q. 43, art. 7, ad 1), citing St. Augustine (*Contra epist. Parmeniani*, bk. III, ch. 2, PL 43:92): "*Quando ex excommunicatione aliquorum imminet periculum schismatis, tunc excommunicationem ferre non pertinet ad veritatem justitiae* — When the danger of schism is the imminent result of the excommunication of some persons, then to excommunicate does not fulfill the completeness of justice."

[14] Thus Luther said in 1523 that if the council about which people were talking were to grant communion under both species, he would refuse that decision and insist on communion under only one species; then he would anathematize those who follow the council in using both species in Eucharistic communion: *Formula missae seu communionis pro ecclesia wittembergensi*, cited in a document of the Council of Trent: *Concil. Trident.*, ed. Goerresgesellschaft, vol. V (1911), p. 870. Cf. also G. Constant, *Concession à Allemagne*, vol. I (1923), p. 31, n. 2; p. 78, n. 1.

structure needs openness to life in order to be ready to receive it. But the living experience needs openness to the structure to accept its regulation. Living experience needs to develop within the structure and according to it: this is an absolute condition for the success of its demands.

The structure needs to be attentive and open to these appeals. Without that, it fails in its role of facilitating the growth of the body. Then the central structure would have to bear the judgment of history for having contributed to depriving the church of its creative energies. The adaptation needed will come either too late or not at all. Reform initiatives that cry out for an authoritative response will either secede from the church or they will become exhausted or wither away somehow in the church. The church will remain itself, but without a (more or less important) part of the living forces that arise from within her. (These are the forces of the periphery, of the frontier, of contact with the culture, of assimilation—these are the "missionary" forces of the church.)

In pages filled with deep meaning (despite some errors that I will point out in the footnotes), Foerster has described how a schismatic reform initiative within the church compromises for a long time some part of the truth (sometimes a very important part) that had been responsible for the church's spiritual energy and perhaps even its mission at the beginning.

He writes:

> The clearest damage that the church carried away from the great schism of the sixteenth century is that it sees itself obligated, since then, to consider religious freedom suspect, even hostile, in Catholic Christianity. As a result, personal conscience, subjective devotion, a mystical tendency, evangelical spontaneity, all of which formerly was part of the *anima catholica* (the Catholic soul) and nourished the spiritual life of the church along with dogmatic theology, have become little by little completely suspect.[15] The fight against schismatic Protestantism has extended even to suspicion about our human faculties, as though they were compromised by the schism—to the point where the word "life" itself has to be denounced as a symptom of Protestant free will. For a great number of zealous Catholics today, it is enough that something be Protestant in order for it no longer to

[15] I transcribe these lines because they are part of Foerster's passage. Perhaps they give a false impression, because they represent only some particular cases. Fundamentally, in general they are false. In fact, the period of the Council of Trent and the years following it were great periods of holiness and mysticism in the church.

be considered Catholic. For them, Catholicism is expressed in the formula: *Christianity with Protestantism subtracted . . .*

All these repercussions of the Reformation ended up creating in modern Catholicism a kind of exaggerated mistrust of the personal element in religion. Instead of assimilating and socializing new liberating tendencies, the church confronted them and ended up rejecting spiritual elements that were formerly part of its concern.

As a result the church more and more lost contact with the mystical element[16] and recruited its leadership exclusively from groups preoccupied with rules and regulations. As a result it contributed to disenchanting a growing number of those seeking personal freedom.[17] Consequently, today the church resembles a mother who can only speak good about one of her sons, while the other—the one who would have had the greatest need for her care—deepens his stubbornness and separates from the church, finding only a lack of understanding there . . .

The first schism that separated the East from the West already put in peril not only the part that was cut off, but the Western Church itself . . . Without this first schism, it is possible to imagine that Protestantism would not have had the occasion to develop, for the church of the Renaissance would have found in the vitality of the Slavic spirit a corrective for its own superficiality. For its part, the Orthodox Church would have found in its contact with the Western Church a corrective for Czarist absolutism—something that would not have failed to have repercussions on Russian political life and spared it some of its social turbulence.[18]

Foerster makes similar claims of equal importance with respect to some of the political attitudes of modern people and their demand for freedom, a demand taken up by masses of the people who left a church linked to political power.[19]

---

[16] See previous note, which applies here.

[17] These lines were written in the middle of the Modernist crisis. This remark, less true now, still has some pertinence at our time. In the following lines, Foerster's own case can be read into what he says.

[18] Foerster, *Autorité et liberté*, pp. 155–158.

[19] Op. cit., pp. 166–169. "In the course of its modern evolution, the church became separated from another element which formerly was part of the Christian patrimony and which was an integral part of the church's life during the Middles Ages. This was political freedom . . . How did it happen that the modern church should renounce this prerogative? The reason is that the social classes, who threw off social and political tyranny, separated themselves at the same time from ecclesiastical tradition; and

Parallel to this loss of creative forces (for which we could give other examples), the church failed or was slow to generously develop its own life. We have already seen that the church accepts initiatives for growth from the contributions of the world around it and gives new dimensions to the Body of Christ. Instead of deep fidelity to the tradition, leading to adaptation/development by way of discernment and assimilation, as we have shown, the church clung to a static fidelity with no concern for the future. Its perspective was anti-innovation.

However, even if you can slow down the progress of human vitality, it is impossible to suppress it. Just as a seed sprouts its stem and the stem makes its way by getting past all the obstacles, so any movement that comes from the depths of humanity will always end up by expressing itself and, if it is worthwhile, by succeeding.

Further, in opposing such a movement, we always risk creating the growth of an *Underground*, as the Anglo-Saxons called the activities of the Resistance in the countries occupied by the Nazis. The transposition of such a phenomenon into the church would be distressing and hateful. But when leaders are too rigid, a danger like that can come to pass. The biographers of John Wesley[20] point out that he really only wanted to be a moral reformer, not even a reformer of the abuses of the church. If the official Anglican Church, instead of refusing to welcome him or instead of victimizing him, had supported him, then he would never have

---

consequently the church thought that it was obliged to rely on the social classes who were adhering to the old state of affairs. The result was a particular situation that is dangerous for the church, namely, that in several regions Catholicism leans for support on reactionary minorities in the areas of economy, politics and social life. This leads people to conclude that the Catholic communion is aligned with outdated forms of social life. The result is that popular opinion continues to impute to the church the severity of anti-populist authorities, while the liberal government ends up having a profound detestation for the church. Isn't this, then, the moment for the ecclesiastical milieu to recognize the essentially Christian character of political freedom? . . .

"The evolution of history has willed that these three ideals: Liberty, Equality, and Fraternity, qualities that developed in the human spirit thanks to centuries of education, should become detached from the trunk of the tradition so as to live an independent life. However, in becoming emancipated from the moderating and educative influence of Christian thought, these ideals came to support either doctrinaire rationalism or political violence, and so to be in league with the lower passions of human nature. And once again the church thought that it had to take an attitude of defensiveness and hostility toward this degenerate offshoot. This justifiable attitude of the church explains the tragic destiny of a man like Lamennais."

[20] Cf., e.g., A. de la Gorce, *Wesley, maître d'un Peuple (1703–1791)* (Paris, 1940).

seceded from the church. If he created a Methodist "church," it is because Wesley couldn't find room for a purely evangelistic ministry in the sclerotic body of the established church.

We can find examples of this problem in the history of the Catholic Church as well. The repression of nationalist and political aspirations in the Papal States under Leo XII, Pius VIII, and Gregory XVI was responsible for the development of the Carbonari. Reflecting on why so many enthusiastic Catholics were drawn to Lamennais, Lacordaire pointed out that at times when the church seems inert by comparison with the world outside, disengaged young adults "look in vain for a place where their zeal and enthusiasm might be understood, tested, and put to work in some Catholic activity. They languish in an isolation of self-preoccupation, and they are lost without being able to do anything for God. It is seriously wrong that so many intelligent young people capable of working for the good should be lost. But we can never block people caught up in a movement that promises them self-fulfillment without paying a price. People for whom no acceptable outlet has been offered will sooner or later meet one another in their unhappy quest, become united in an unhealthy glee, and become upset by their feelings of frustrated enthusiasm and inactivity. One day this disorganized social group will fall upon a church that lacks wisdom figures like a bolt of thunder long held back in the clouds."[21]

This is how some generous people end up "leaving in place," because their progressive hopes have been deceived. They end up feeling more or less strangers and indifferent about a community that they had previously loved deeply and hoped to serve.[22] Magnificent resources are either lost or not put to work; enthusiastic Christians fall back into an indifference that we often complain, with reason, about meeting in the masses of the faithful. This is a waste of energy that is all the more deplorable given the actual situation. Our times are more tragic, our needs more pressing, and we have available this great spirit of enthusiasm among the elite of the Christian people—an enthusiasm whose absence, as we have seen, neutralized the reform proposals of the clergy in the past.

---

[21] *Considérations sur le système de M. de Lamennais*, pp. 28–29, cited by T. Foisset, *Vie du R. P. Lacordaire*, vol. I (Paris, 1970), pp. 81–82. Lacordaire describes exactly the disarray that made him take the road for La Chênaie, cf. Foisset, vol. I, p. 142.

[22] Might not the present crisis of vocations for the diocesan clergy in a great number of areas of France (alas!) be due in part to the feeling that pastoral ministry is out of touch and that the life of the priest is unrealistic?

So a synthesis is needed that engages both enthusiasm and stability, both new demands and the tradition. To the *"Devita profanes vocum novitiates de te* — Avoid profane chatter and contradictions" of 1 Timothy 6:20, there corresponds the *"Spiritum nolite extinguere . . . omnia probate, quod bonum est tenete* — Do not quench the Spirit . . . but test everything; hold fast to what is good" of 1 Thessalonians 5:19-21. But let me borrow from Cardinal Suhard a practical formula for this difficult synthesis that has to be made, at which he succeeded so well. Here is what he said to his priests at the end of the annual retreat in 1946, a decisive year for French church reform:

> One of the real problems at the present time is the *spirit of criticism*. This means two things. "Modern" persons, believing that "the times have changed," insist on—or undertake—reforms. Nothing that happened before their time seems worthwhile in their eyes. They think that we have to clear the ground and move forward. "Old-fashioned" persons are astonished or scandalized by the audacity of their presumption. They point out how dangerous these "critical generations" are. But don't some of them fall for the same excess that they have condemned? To criticize the criticism is still to criticize. Is the defense reflex or the resistance which they adopt as their own posture always more insightful and more charitable than the appetite for novelty that they stigmatize? It is true that it would be naive or simplistic on the part of the innovators to refuse to consider wisdom tempered by the times and to set up their own methods as an absolute, as if the pastoral work of today will not be judged tomorrow for its insufficiencies. But in condemning these initiatives, does one always take account of the intentions, the efforts, the inevitable mistakes, and the hopes for the future? So the solution is not going to be "mutual excommunications." We have to find something more lofty, in a spirit of charity that is both informed and comprehensive. This is what a good number of priests have understood. From their mutual concessions, some real progress has been born: exuberant initiatives have been tempered by prudence, while familiar routines have been opened to trying new things. (*Documentation Catholique* [Oct. 1946], col. 1215–1216)

Among Reformers, the Distinction between the Faithful and the Revolutionaries

In the light of what history has taught us, can we imagine what the differences are between reformers who remained faithful and those who become revolutionary? It would be interesting to understand the reasons why some of those, whose hopes for reform were common in the beginning, went one way and others another way. I will be more precise here about what I said in the second part about the initial ambivalence concerning hopes for reform and about the conditions for a reform without schism.

Let's reexamine the principal examples that history suggests to us: the apostolic or evangelical movements of the Middle Ages, the sixteenth-century reform movements, and the entourage of Lamennais. (I will limit myself to comparing Lamennais with Lacordaire.) As we go about making a systematic account of parallel results that is a bit facile in some ways, let us remember that it would be wrong and unwise to paint the one side white and the other all black. Nonetheless, one side remained Catholic, while the other fractured what is greatest among created things—the communion of the Church . . .

Medieval Apostolic and Evangelical Movements. Unfortunately the individual persons in these movements are not well known to us. Within the great yearning for an "apostolic" or "evangelical" life that followed upon the Gregorian Reform, semi-heretics were often similar to Catholics.[23] They were of course interrogated concerning their faith, but often enough an ordeal was the only procedure used to discern the authenticity of their positions.[24] It seems that the characteristic attitude of the non-Catholics might be reduced to these two traits that a certain Master Vacarius remarked concerning Hugh Speroni (and that Vacarius considered blameworthy). On the one hand, Hugh was too satisfied with his own personal judgment, thinking himself right in opposition to all the others; on the other hand, he thought badly about what was going on in the church and was excessively critical with respect to it.[25]

---

[23] Cf. H. Grundmann, *Religiöse Bewegungen im Mittelalter* (Berlin, 1935—new edition, Hildesheim, 1961).

[24] Thus for the "Apostolics" of Soissons; cf. L. Spätling, *De Apostolicis, Pseudo-apostolis, Apostolinis* (Munich, 1947), p. 55.

[25] Speroni is an isolated figure whose thinking is entirely personal. The only thing he has in common with the "apostolic" current is the rift between spiritual authority and personal holiness. (Spätling considers this point to be the common denominator for all the "apostolic" movements.) We know the positions of Speroni from the exposé and refutation made by a former classmate of his named Vacarius in the *Liber contra multiplices errores*, recently edited by P. Hilarin de Milan (*L'eresia di Ugo Speroni* [Vatican, 1945]). The passages to which I refer are taken from the *Liber*, § XIII (p. 510: "*Sed quia, sicut imprudentium mos est, tu sequeris cor tuum cum sit totum subversum et*

It was the first of these points that struck Spätling in his study of the "apostolic movements" (op. cit., p. 213); we have seen this already in Waldo and his companions as a conviction to make no change, whatever the church should decide (cf. p. 236). Waldo and his companions, from the beginning, were convinced that they were the true church. However, a bit later, groups of Waldensians, recognizing the possibility of satisfying their desire for poverty within the church, came around and became the Poor Catholics. — As to the second point, it becomes clear in comparing the Cathar or Waldensian movements with that of St. Francis. The heterodox movement is striking for its critical and negative tone and for its bitter opposition to the Catholic clergy. By contrast, it is remarkable that in the relatively numerous writings and words that we have from St. Francis, we cannot find any criticism of the state of affairs in the church or of its churchmen. Rather, Francis expressed a deep respect for the priesthood, the sacraments, and the ceremonies of the church, while the "apostolic groups" showed themselves clearly critical of them.[26]

Sixteenth-Century Reforms. The first thing to remember is this. When reform groups form among the humanists within the church at the beginning of the sixteenth century, there is a division among them: some join the Reformation, others choose to remain in the church. So among the disciples of Lefèvre d'Etaples, Gérard Roussel and Josse Clichtoue remain Catholic, while Farel and Louis de Berquin embrace the Reformation. Next, the reform spirit of the Catholic humanists, Erasmus in particular, had many important concerns in common with Luther at the beginning. Their common interest was in evangelical teaching, which was Luther's only real interest: justification by faith, Christian freedom, and a critique of a religion of observances and practices (in which, said

---

ab Ecclesia Dei alienatum, ideo te solum veritatem putas videre . . ."), and § XXVI (p. 556: *"Excecat te cupiditas impugnandi Ecclesiam . . .").*

   [26] Such were the "Apostolics" of Périgord (Spätling, p. 57). Here and there we even find a radical denial of the use of corporal elements (Spätling, p. 74). But there is nothing like that in St. Francis, of course . . . For Francis's respect for priests, cf. his *Testament*, § 3; J. Joergensen, *Saint François d'Assise* (ed. 1927), pp. 52, 227, 266, 328; J. Lortzing, "Franz von Assisi als Reformator," in *Wissenschaft und Weisheit*, IX (1942), pp. 61–70, 126–139; S. Clasen, "Priesterliche Würde und Würdigkeit: Das Verhältnis des hl. Franziskus zum Priestertum der Kirche," ibid., 20 (1957), pp. 43–58; K. Esser, "Die religiösen Bewegungen des Hochmittelalters und Franziskus von Assisi," in *Glaube und Geschichte: Festgabe J. Lortz*, vol. II (Wiesbaden, 1958), pp. 287–313.

Erasmus, the Judaizing that St. Paul battled in the Letter to the Galatians was being revived) . . . Several Erasmus sympathizers had had moments of sympathy for Luther's ideas, and if some went over to the Reformation, others maintained or recovered their Catholic faith, for example, W. Pirckheimer in Germany and Paul Eliaesen in Denmark.

Even closer to Luther, his friend and superior Staupitz had experienced everything needed to embrace the Reformation. He held the strict Augustinian interpretation on grace and predestination, and Luther said that he was the first to light the spark of the Gospel for him.[26bis] Staupitz wanted a renewal of theological studies according to a biblical perspective; he had acted in this direction at Erfurt, cooperated with the foundation of Wittenberg, had Luther made a Doctor, and fostered the beginnings of Luther's reform . . . Yet, in fact, Staupitz did not follow his friend in seceding from the church, and he died at the Benedictine abbey of Salzburg. As for Erasmus, living Catholicism in his own manner and holding back from giving his all to the church,[27] he nonetheless remained Catholic by virtue of a formal opinion whose motives we will soon examine (motives that, if not heroic, at least were not shameful).

What is striking about the reformers who went into schism is their radicalism. Luther himself was violent and irritable. He knew this about himself, but he thought that it was helping his mission and that without it he would not have achieved the work he had to do. That is not only because he would not have dared to do it, but because too moderate an approach, like that of Erasmus, would fail to achieve anything effective.[28] Luther was surely right on the level of events: his violence advanced his work such as he carried it out and conceived it. Erasmus thought that the role to which Luther had been called should have been exercised differently—and this, of course, shows us that Erasmus had another conception of what reform means.[29]

One can imagine, in fact, that if Luther had advanced what was good and Christian in his thinking without the violence, the radicalism, and

---

[26bis] Cf. Scheel, *Dokumente*, nn. 74, 216, 512.

[27] In Erasmus's *Hyperaspistes* there is this disquieting remark: "*Hactenus solus esse volui, nisi quod ab Ecclesia catholica non segregor* — Up till now I have desired to remain solitary, lest I should cut myself off from the Catholic Church" (*Opera omnia*, vol. X, 1257c). I have already pointed out J. Lortz's severe judgment on Erasmus.

[28] Cf. K. Holl, "Luthers Urteile über sich selbst," in *Gesamte Aufsätze*, vol. I, p. 383, n. 4, and p. 409, nn. 3f.: here there are many texts that leave nothing to desire. Luther was angry, but lucid.

[29] Cf. A. Renaudet, *Etudes érasmiennes* (Paris, 1939), p. 345.

the unilateralism that was characteristic of him, he would have served the very cause of reform even better. What is more, he would have gained the support of the emperor and of the whole of Christendom, which desired a reform. However, Luther, convinced that he was inspired, thought his impulsiveness and violence were the work of the Holy Spirit. He needed the violence to excite him and to stir him up. He himself said that he stirred up his courage by evoking the abominations of the papacy.[30] On several occasions, we find him clearly and deliberately strengthening his capacity for violence, reviving hostilities, and accentuating opposition and initiating unpardonable offenses; as, for example, after Augsburg in 1530. Calvin, with a cooler head, did the same thing on several occasions: at Hagenau in 1540, and during the interim period at Augsburg in 1548.

Part of the reformers' radicalism, in virtue of which they were not afraid to break with the church, was the fact that they took very seriously the cause of reform that those who remained faithful did not feel as profoundly. On several occasions, Luther pointed out that he had taken things extremely seriously.[31] From the point of view of his own personal problems, to which what he did and what he thought were so decisively linked, this means that he wasn't able to live in any other way except bringing matters to their maximum intensity and resonance.[32] From the point of view that interests us here, that means he immediately drew the consequences that were the most explosive and the least rectified by the analogy of the faith of the Church. This is just the opposite of what Luther blamed Staupitz for doing—"*frigidulus est et parum vehemens*—a little cold and hardly forceful"[33]—or likewise John Eck:[34] they were able to hold an intellectual position without making it fundamentally a question of life and death and the goal of their action.

This point is certainly very important. In the attitudes that shape revolutionary reformers, on the one hand, there is a kind of intrepid spirit, a certain radicalism in their way of pushing their feelings to the extreme limit of their consequences, whatever happens. On the other hand, docile reformers who remain inside are moderate, mistrust themselves,

---

[30] Cf. Holl, op.cit., p. 395, nn. 4 and 6.

[31] In particular, in the famous preface to volume I of his works in 1545: "*Ego serio rem agebam*" (Scheel, *Dokumente*, p. 187, n. 511).

[32] Cf. Holl, op. cit., p. 388.

[33] From the letter of Feb. 7, 1525, to W. Link, *Briefwechsel*, Weimar, vol. III, p. 437.

[34] Loc. cit., n. 31.

and are concerned to remain in harmony with the faithful and their pastors. This is already clearly evident in the Czech movement in favor of using the chalice: it explains the great difference between Rokycana, the head of the Utraquists and a man of balance, and a Martin of Krčin or the Taborites who, by their radicalism and their rigidity, pushed the movement into schism.[35] This is even clearer in the reformist milieu called Fabrian or Fabrician after the name the "Lutheran" sect would have borne if it had been named after its first leader (as Béda said in 1526). Gérard Roussel, for example, certainly drew back when faced with the consequences of too radical an approach, and also when faced with the effort needed to do something. Things, he thought, were not sufficiently developed.[36]

A dozen years later, Calvin, who had been deeply linked with Roussel and owed a lot to him, blamed him for lacking the courage necessary to turn down a bishopric and to quit the Roman communion.[37] A French partisan of the Reformation made a similar judgment about Lefèvre himself: "He has no courage," he wrote to Oecolampadius; and about Farel, he said, "He is not up to the responsibility of evangelical leadership."[38] Farel, on the contrary, was determined, violent, and aggressive.[39] The distinction between those who left the church and those who remained in submission to it can practically be drawn according to temperamental dispositions.

We see this again, for example, in the reformist group from Lyons where Castellion formed his ideas at the time when the first shocks of the Reformation were being felt.[40] There are those who want to live in

---

[35] Cf. V.-L. Tapié, *Une église tchèque au XVe siècle* (Paris, 1934), pp. 9–14 (Rokycana); 14f. (the Taborites); 55 (Martin of K.).

[36] Cf. his letter of Aug. 24, 1524, to Farel: Herminjard, *Correspondences des Réformateurs*, vol. I, p. 271.

[37] W. Walker, *Jean Calvin*, p. 105, referring to Calvin, *Opera (Corpus Ref.)*, vol. V, pp. 279–312; vol. XXX, p. 127.

[38] "*Nihil habet animi* — He has no soul"; "*Impar est oneri evangelico ferendo* — He is not equal to the burden of proclaiming the Gospel" (cited by J. Pannier, *Recherches sur la formation intellectuelle de Calvin* [Paris, 1931], p. 31). — Note that W. G. Moore, *La Réforme allemande et la littérature française: Recherches sur la notoriété de Luther en France* (Strasburg, 1930), p. 153, protests against the idea that Lefèvre would have been a timid person.

[39] Cf. Walker, op. cit., p. 182 — Michelet described him like this: "Impatient, frank, direct, intrepid among others, he had the admirable heart of the knight without reproach, and a knight's thirst for danger . . ." (cited by Pannier, op.cit., p. 43).

[40] Cf. F. Buisson, *Sébastien Castellion* (Paris, 1891), pp. 77f.

peace. They submit, even though they know in their heart of hearts or comment discretely to others about what has been imposed on them. In this category, to which Calvin gave the name Nicodemites [people who conceal their real beliefs], belonged Marot, who recanted, Nicolas Bourbon, and others. And there are those whose temperament doesn't allow for half measures. It is a question of character, said Buisson (p. 87). Such types need only some excuse for their hearts to rebel—a procession, an image they refuse to reverence, and they are carried away into a relentless chain of resistance and attacks.

The case of Erasmus merits special consideration. He thought Luther was fundamentally right about the principle of Christian freedom and about Paul's theology (in contrast to Judaizing tendencies), but he thought Luther was wrong to insist on these in a revolutionary way, with violence and impatience, destroying good things, above all, peace itself.[41] Luther and his companions did a disservice to the cause of the Gospel by their excessive behavior. Instead of proceeding in a spiritual way, with respect for the hierarchy and with moderation, they wanted to change everything in one stroke, *quasi subito novus mundus condi posset* (as if suddenly a new world could be built).[42] Over and over, Erasmus employs the words *seditiosum, seditiose* (with sedition)[43] to express Luther's approach, which he condemned as insurrection, a revolutionary approach. Convinced that serious reforms were needed, Erasmus did not desire to change anything without the authority of the church, on the one hand, and without respect for continuity, on the other hand.[44]

---

[41] Cf. Renaudet, *Etudes érasmiennes*, pp. 211f., 260, 282, 298, and above all 305f. Renaudet downplays Erasmus's Catholic loyalty to some degree. See the reaction of L. Bouyer, *Autour d'Erasme* (Paris, 1955). This gives a good analysis of the difference in attitude and temperament between Erasmus and Luther in the introduction (pp. 4–34), reprinted in the translation by C. R. Thompson of Erasmus's *Inquisitio de fide* of 1524 (New Haven: Yale University Press, 1950).

[42] The second *Hyperaspistes*, Renaudet, pp. 352–353.

[43] For example: Letter to Zasius of Jan. 4, 1522 (Allen, 1252, 7, vol. V, p. 1); to John Glapion, Apr. 1522 (Allen, 1275, 24, vol. V, p. 48); to Noel Béda, Oct. 2, 1525 (Allen, 1620, 44 and 47, vol. VI, pp. 181–182).

[44] Nothing outside the authority of the church: "Nihil tamen horum mutari volo praeter auctoritatem Ecclesiae. Nec ea mutatis damnat patrum instituta, sed admovet forte pro horum temporum moribus variandum esse remedium . . . cum censeam nihil esse novandum nisi interveniente Ecclesiae auctoritate": To Noel Béda, Oct. 2, 1525 (Allen, 1620, pp. 55f., vol. V, p. 182); cf. Renaudet, op. cit., pp. 256, 283, 298, etc.

Nothing that breaks continuity: cf. Renaudet, pp. 42–43, 169, 171, 174. Cf. the *Hyperaspistes* of 1526: "*Fero igitur hanc Ecclesiam donec videro meliorem*" (Renaudet, p. 260).

Evidently Erasmus did not have the temperament of a martyr; he loved his tranquility. Luther had some reason to accuse him of betraying the cause of the Gospel by failing to have courage and spiritual force; Zwingli treated him as a procrastinator.[45] Erasmus's position was anti-dogmatic and expressed a theological relativism which favored a supple and open posture opposed to any excess.[46] It seems unquestionable that he would willingly have accepted everything and made peace with the church, provided that the most scandalous things could be moderated.[47] However, it seems to me we would diminish the real quality of his attitude and the illuminating value it represents if we reduce it simply to an amiable liberalism in search of peace and quiet. For Erasmus was perfectly aware of the audience he would have had, and of the historic role he would have played, if he had declared himself a Lutheran. His dislike for the act of schism and rebellion was great. It is something very positive that he did not want to be responsible for a break, either directly or indirectly.[48] Although in agreement with Luther on many intellectual positions at the beginning, he did not want to break the unity of the church at any price. This presupposes a rather clairvoyant sense of the church, for not everyone at that time had the feeling that the reform initiative would break the unity of the church in a definitive way—far from it.

---

[45] Renaudet, pp. 258 and 312.

[46] Renaudet, pp. 169f., suggests that we should search for the explanation of his attitude in these terms.

[47] Cf., e.g., Renaudet, pp. 41, 148–150.

[48] "*Si Luthero vel tantulum favissem, nolo jactare quid potuerim in Germania. Sed ego vel decies mortem oppetiero quam ut periculosi disidii sim auctor vel adjutor . . .* — If I have favored Luther even a little, I don't want to contribute to what is going on in Germany. But I will encounter death ten times rather than become the author or the helper of the danger of schism . . .," to Louis Coronel, Apr. 21, 1522 (Allen, 1274, 55f., vol. V, p. 47); "*Epistolis etiam maeditis declaravi mihi nihil umquam foederis fuisse cum ullo Lutherano, sed seditiosum negocium mihi semper displicuisse . . .* — By way of published letters I have made it clear that I have never entered into compact with any Lutheran, but rather that their seditious business has always displeased me . . .," to John Glapion, same date (Allen, 1275, 22f., vol. V, p. 48); "*Possem turbare mundum, si velim; verum citius moriar quam sim futurus auctor novi tumultus . . . Ego semper studui prodesse omnibus, neque quisquam magis abhorret a dissidio* — I could upset the world, if I wanted to, but in truth I would rather die than become the source of new troubles . . . I have always tried to be a positive influence on everyone, and there is no one more abhorrent than a schismatic . . .," to Josse Laurens, July 14, 1522 (Allen, 1292, 83f., vol. V, p. 87). — Cf. Renaudet, pp. 193–194.

There is certainly something unpleasant about Erasmus. He is the intellectual who makes judgments from a perspective of superiority and, by that very fact, places himself outside the object of his judgment. We have seen how Möhler quite correctly makes this very remark about him. Moreover, the judgments that Erasmus made often have something superficial about them and betray only a mediocre appreciation of the church's deep tradition. The scholarly perspective of Erasmus is that of a humanist and a critic, consequently manifesting an attitude that is a bit abrupt. His wisdom is often nothing more than a pragmatic choice aiming to avoid extremism. But yet there is something else as well: he has a sense of the church and a fundamental attachment to its unity. Of the four conditions described in our second part, Erasmus did not exemplify them perfectly, but he did hold onto the essential: namely, the desire to preserve unity, despite a life of communion a bit thin on the mystical dimension; an understanding and respect for the concrete religious life of the faithful;[49] an understanding of delays and patience;[50] and finally, within the limits of a critical humanism that is a bit cerebral and abrupt, the element of *ressourcement*—respect for the tradition.

Lamennais and Lacordaire.[51] Lacordaire is an extraordinary example of a priest who is at once progressive, open to positive reform, and concerned to live within the Catholic communion without the slightest shadow of defect or even indelicacy. We cannot heap abuse upon Lamennais here; Lacordaire did not do that. Rather Lacordaire felt sorry for him, but he saw himself obliged to make a judgment in order to justify quitting Lamennais' project. From the distance of a century later, the clarity and balance of Lacordaire's judgment appear to be even more sensible.

With Lamennais, great talent and even genius reappeared within the French clergy, from whom they had been absent for almost a century. Under the Restoration, he understood that the patronage the church

---

[49] Cf., e.g., his attitude about the question of confession: Renaudet, pp. 42–43, 152, 171, 187.

[50] He wanted to proceed gradually by promoting a new attitude and spiritual outlook; cf. Renaudet, pp. 174, 185.

[51] In this paragraph, I am guided above all by T. Foisset, *Vie du R. P. Lacordaire*, 2 vols. (Paris, 1870). His bibliography is a model of honest research. If we take account of the date of its writing, it is a wonderful example of intellectual courage. — For Lacordaire's attitude at the time of the condemnation of *L'Avenir*, you can read with profit the good article by H.-D. Noble, "Lacordaire et la condamnation de L'Avenir," in *Revue des Jeunes* (Feb. 25, 1927), pp. 410–436.

formerly sought from princes now had to be sought from the people. It was necessary to substitute for the church-prince relationship a church-people relationship: "Everything has to be done by the people" (1828). Nothing more than these few words are needed to understand the extravagance by which Lamennais compromised his vivid understanding of the modern social movement. From one end to the other of what he did, this extravagance was evident, accompanied by a rigidity that made him feel the slightest disagreement as a wound to his pride: "If people reject my theses, I don't see any way to solidly defend religion. Moreover, I asked Rome to examine my book. If the judgment is unfavorable, I have decided to write no more."[52]

Already you can feel here the threat of a tragic outcome as well as a propensity to identify his way of seeing things with the very cause of Catholicism itself. Lamennais was always confident that by himself he was right. It gave him a dry and haughty disdain for all those who did not think as he did, whoever they might be; there are innumerable examples of this.[53] After 1826, Lacordaire said about him: "Should he be alone in the world, it would be an infallible sign for him that he was right."[54]

Lamennais went to Rome with these proud and rigid feelings, and he had only bitter judgments to make about the grand personages of the Roman Curia.[55] With the same rigidity and the same extremism, he burned what he formerly had adored[56] and, rejected by Rome, found in the church only an obstacle to the truth (which became identified with his own personal feelings). Since he identified the truth with himself, in his eyes it was not he who left the church, it was the church that fell away from him: "The old political and ecclesiastical hierarchies together left me behind. They are only two ghosts embracing over a tomb"; "I would like to change our language on one point and substitute the word *Christianity* for the word *Catholicism*, in order to make clearer that I want to have nothing more to do with the hierarchy." Concerning the Roman hierarchy, he said: "After I saw up close the springs that make everything move, such things interest me about as much as what is going on in China at the College for Mandarins."[57]

[52] Letter to Abbé Carron, Nov. 1, 1820, in Foisset, vol. I, p. 112.

[53] Cf. Foisset, I, 203, 533f.

[54] Ibid., I, 140.

[55] For example, see Foisset, I, pp. 203, 207, 223.

[56] Ibid., I, pp. 158f.

[57] These three texts from January to May 1833 are found respectively in Foisset, I, pp. 242, 243, 244.

On August 4, 1833, Lamennais wrote to the Holy Father: "For all kinds of reasons, but especially because it only pertains to the head of the church to judge concerning what can be good and useful, I have resolved to remain for the future, in my writings and in my actions, totally estranged from everything to do with this authority."[58] Thus Lamennais placed himself on the side of schism with respect to this line of demarcation that Deniflé defined as follows (with reference to the reform initiatives of the fifteenth century): Don't become disinterested in the family household; don't let yourself become a stranger there, like someone who writes his family off and goes his own way without having anything further to do with them. (Cf. also below, pp. 358–359, the text by Saint-Exupéry.)

Poor, great Lamennais! He did not leave himself any period for reflection, any margin for a better comprehension of things, at the end of which he might have begun perhaps to perceive the well-founded aspects of the church's position at a deeper level. In this way, he also is an example of a lifeless fidelity. He doesn't look for any deepening of his own ideas through communion with something larger. He doesn't even suspect that he might have to do justice to some aspect of the truth that others hold, that would be complementary, that would clarify and would be salvific for his own proper intuitions. By his approach, Lamennais' spirit was foreign to the conditions for development toward fullness, because he refused any calls to communion. "M. de la Mennais was narrow, incapable of grasping both sides of a reality at the same time, and never able to come back to examine what he had not looked at before," said Lacordaire about him.[59]

Lacordaire saw in this rigidity and this incapacity to communicate with the thinking of others the reason for the striking sterility of Lamennais.[60] This "sterility" is relative, however; since even though Lamennais remained isolated and solitary, some of the ideas he put forth finally ended up in the Christian democracy of a later time, even as soon as 1848. Speaking about this great moment, Lacordaire wrote in his *Testament*: "What would have been needed for Lamennais to be among us at that time? A bit of patience, of silence, of faith, the acceptance of his first fall and, undergirding these holy feelings, a natural fidelity to his friends."[61]

---

[58] Ibid., I, p. 249.

[59] Letter to Foisset of Dec. 23, 1858, in Foisset, I, p. 564; this whole text is worth reading.

[60] Cf. his letter to Mme Swetchine of Mar. 31, 1854, in Foisset, vol. II, p. 306.

[61] Ibid., ch. 11 (ed. 1870), p. 150.

Lacordaire and Lamennais went to Rome in December 1831 with distinctly different attitudes. Lamennais had decided in advance not to change anything in his position. Lacordaire, for his part, aware of that, interiorly separated himself from him. In the painful crisis about *L'Avenir* and its break with the church, in his ultimate break with Lamennais, and then in many circumstances and actions which caused him difficulties, Lacordaire never abandoned an attitude that we can admire, even more to the degree that we understand it. I express it in this way: obedience and acceptance; patience, silence and faith; submission to the concrete conditions for communion; and temperance and moderation.

FIRST, OBEDIENCE AND ACCEPTANCE. How many times Lacordaire had to deal with decisions opposed to his initiatives, often in public. First there was a discreet disavowal, then the condemnation of *L'Avenir*. Following suspicions and accusations made by mediocre people who were slaves of the status quo, his conferences at the Lycée Stanislas were interrupted at the direction of Msgr. de Quélen (Foisset, vol. I, pp. 239 and 568–569, Lacordaire's strong letter of submission). There was the dispersion of the first French Dominicans for whom Lacordaire had prepared a novitiate at Rome—a measure about whose causes (the intervention of Metternich) Lacordaire forced himself to never say a word, so that only after his death was the reason known (Foisset, I, 526–527). He gave up pursuing a reply to the newspaper in Nancy at the request the bishop made of him, even though it was a matter touching the question of freedom and his honor as a Friar Preacher (II, 37). He agreed to put aside the habit for which he had fought so hard in order to preach at Notre-Dame, although he had publicly and clearly maintained his right to wear it (II, 48). The life of Lacordaire had been punctuated by acts of docility that were often very meritorious and whose meaning was the expression of his desire to remain in harmony with the ordinary life of the church in his understanding and respect for its actual situation, he who was at the forefront of the religious movement of his century. Msgr. Affre was right in seeing in this docility "the disposition that is most contrary to the character of innovators."[62]

PATIENCE, SILENCE AND FAITH. There are a great number of texts in Lacordaire's writings that are remarkable in affirming these values, and his behavior wonderfully confirmed what he said. These three words also

---

[62] Cited in Foisset, vol. II, p. 497, n. 1.

come directly from him (*supra* and n. 61). Lacordaire was not afraid of a fight, and he had a maxim that proved true in experience: "I have always believed that the most favorable moments for sowing seeds and planting were times of trouble and tempest."[63] He knew how to confront contradiction forcefully. But if he was "contradicted" by ecclesiastical authority, he stopped and withdrew, not to fall into a prideful silence, but to give himself time. He obeyed a twofold fidelity to himself and to the church[64]— to mature and clarify his own initiatives, and to give others and circumstances the necessary time for truth to do its work. So after the failure of *L'Avenir*, he worked quietly, knowing that some day he would again have the possibility to speak and to act "with the force of those who knew how to be still. Silence is, after speaking, the second great power in the world."[65] He had the conviction that "every man will always have his hour, he only has to wait for it and do nothing contrary to Providence."[66]

We shouldn't read into such a text the rather vulgar idea that it is enough to wait until others recognize we are right. Instead Lacordaire had a deep sense of the meaning of delays; they are needed for the maturation of truth and the working out of Providence. If Lacordaire withdrew and kept quiet after the first conferences at Notre-Dame, it was to give himself time for his thought to mature.[67] But it was also because future results developed while waiting for the seed that has been planted

---

[63] *Lettres à la baronne de Prailly*, Jan. 2, 1849 (Paris, 1885), p. 147. — This idea of being able to achieve good things in a time of turmoil is found again in a letter of Sept. 17, 1848, to M. Cartier on the subject of the attitude adopted by Lacordaire in 1848: Foisset, II, p. 145.

[64] ". . . I respect his thinking, and mine as well," wrote Lacordaire in a letter announcing his break with Lamennais, Dec. 11, 1832: Foisset, I, p. 227.

[65] Letter of Apr. 22, 1832, to Montalembert, ibid., p. 210.

[66] Letter of June 30, 1833, to Montalembert, ibid., p. 291. — In a letter to Foisset of Dec. 23, 1858, where he gives his view of Lamennais, Lacordaire writes: "I tried a thousand times to make him understand that the times were on his side and that he only had to keep silence, that victory was near at hand to win what he had lost. He simply was unable to understand such language. He gave in because of powerlessness, not because of excessive force . . .": Foisset, I, pp. 564–565. Cf. that with this remark of Blondel to Père Laberthonnière (*Correspondence philosophique* [Paris, 1961], p. 203): "They will eventually come back to us, particularly as we will have become wiser, more in control of ourselves and supernaturally peaceful and hard at work."

[67] "I need to age, to let time pass, to write a solid book, to become better. These first ten years of priesthood have been too swift and too agitated. I owe myself a long period of solitude": Foisset, I, p. 383.

to sprout and grow. The essential is to have sown the seeds.[68] But he also respected that Providence has its own plan—a general direction of things—in which each person is in solidarity with others and needs to know how to await the hour appointed by God.[69]

SUBMISSION TO THE CONCRETE CONDITIONS OF COMMUNION. On this point, there are texts and actions that are highly significant. For example, in his farewell letter to Lamennais, Lacordaire wrote: "Perhaps your opinions are more correct and deeper than mine and, considering your natural superiority over me, I ought to be convinced of them. *But reason is not the whole person . . .*"[70] Likewise, in writing to Montalembert, in the remarkable letter where he comments upon the so-called submission of Lamennais: "No amount of talent, no services can compensate the evil that a separation (whatever it might be), an action undertaken outside its being, does to the church. I would prefer to throw myself into the ocean with a millstone around my neck rather than create a community of hopes, ideas, and good works even *alongside the church*" (Foisset, I, 251). From this we can see how Lacordaire with delicacy felt pressed to submit himself spontaneously to the judgment of the Holy Father when he was seriously attacked and under suspicion. This explains as well these rules of practical action which were for him effectively the conclusion to be drawn from the story of Lamennais: moderation in polemics, charity in action, avoid becoming part of a divisive group or separating from others, pursue nothing without the support of the bishops.[71]

FINALLY, TEMPERANCE AND MODERATION. In a man who was so spontaneous and could even be impetuous, we have to admire Lacordaire's sense of possibility and of what is true, even as he avoided extremes: "Time will always be in favor of what is true, just, and moderate and

---

[68] An idea that Lacordaire uses frequently: "My conferences are going well; the seed is sprouting" (Foisset, I, p. 295); "I will wait for another time, and I will do whatever good will be possible then. The present moment is not important; the future is everything" (ibid., II, p. 48, comp. p. 210).

[69] "You and I both have proof that time is needed for anything to happen, that it is enough always to be ready without ever anticipating the hour when Providence will act. What a difference there is between 1834 and 1844 . . . ," Letter to Montalembert of May 15, 1844 (Foisset, II, p. 65). — Cf.: "I believe that a man only sees a small piece of time, while God sees the whole, and the church (inspired by God) conducts itself according to the whole, without seeing it . . . ," Letter to M. de Dumas of Oct. 28, 1833 (ibid., II, p. 104).

[70] Ibid., I, p. 227. Italics are mine.

[71] Ibid., II, p. 100.

what represents solid virtue."[72] Lamennais complained that his young companion in the struggle did not have his own fiery radicalism, and he said about Lacordaire: "He has a sort of strange tendency for the right middle position."[73] For Lacordaire, this temperament seemed linked to the purity of an initiative and to effective forcefulness: "Who are the ones whose memory has remained pure? Only those who were never extremists . . ."; "The *modus in rebus* (way of doing things) is one of the aspects to which I pay the most attention, persuaded that moderation is at once something most rare and something that contains the greatest power."[74]

B. Considering Contemporary Reform (Text from 1950)

1. *Three Motives for Optimism about Contemporary Reforms (in France)*

If I return now in a more concrete way to the present-day currents of reform and renewal with which I began this study, I have to conclude that, judged by the twofold light of theology and history that I have tried to join together, we can be very optimistic about the future of this movement in the church.

I am optimistic because the present reform movement seems completely healthy in its theological orientations. It is possible, at the same time, that some theologians may have followed pathways in their research in which the magisterium has discovered some dangers. But the reformism of the years 1945–1950 did not take its point of departure there. In my view, there is no case where a reform activity began from Modernist theological presuppositions or had anything in common with Modernist positions. The revealed faith, the apostolic tradition, and the hierarchical structure of the church are in no way called into question. If they were in some way or another questioned, that would be by pure inadvertence, by ignorance, without anything of the consciousness or stubbornness characteristic of the schismatic or the heretic. There is nothing "revolutionary" in present day reforms, neither in France nor elsewhere.

Sometimes people think the French are extremely daring. During conferences I gave in Germany, in Austria, in Holland, in Belgium, and in England, I had the pleasure of being able to correct an audience or a

---

[72] Ibid., II, p. 348, for the case of the separation into virtually two distinct Dominican provinces; also very clear in the same way on the same topic: II, pp. 310, 462f.

[73] Cited by Foisset, vol. I, p. 213.

[74] Ibid., II, p. 468.

listener when I was speaking about ideas and apostolic trends in contemporary French Catholicism. For it was clear they were expecting something sensational. However, I told them the simple truth. There is in France neither the Mass in the vernacular, nor laity directing parishes, nor even any "new theology," but only new problems or a new awareness of old problems. People have been trying to address these generously, under the direction and the control of the hierarchy with the dispositions that I will again recall . . . Often enough strangers see France under the symbol of 1789 or 1848 [the years of the French Revolution]; they don't understand how traditional France is and how little inclination there is here toward schismatic attitudes. Yet it must be said that this country has always been a kind of precursor in the realm of ideas, and that what is going on with us today will one day be going on throughout the world. Msgr. Baudrillart one day recounted a story about the disagreeable questioning by a foreign Cardinal[75] returning to this old prejudice: "Well now, what about your little French priests jumping over streams [obstacles]?" Baudrillart replied: "I agree, they do jump over streams, but sometimes they manage to cross great rivers for those whom they lead or who see them in action."

Analyzing the reform spirit of 1946, Père d'Ouince summed up the situation in these two reassuring statements: "[We see] how the hierarchy is inspired to promote the necessary reforms, and [we see] how the reformers are inspired to remain in the church as true sons of the church."[76] It should be noted, as I have pointed out more than once, that an attitude of rejection or lack of understanding on the part of the episcopacy would have been perilous. To give an example, in education, to always deal severely with students and to demand rigorous conformity in every area runs the risk of damaging a great deal. The result will be people without character or people who are rebellious. In an atmosphere of freedom (moderate freedom, intelligently controlled), on the contrary, students' aspirations can be expressed peacefully, without conflict; thus they avoid exaggerations and avoid becoming deaf to authority at the risk of irreparable conflict.

The bishops first, then Rome as well, have learned to welcome and to direct, to listen and to give judgment, in the full consciousness of their pastoral responsibility and with a spirit of personal disinterest. Without doubt, rarely in history has the hierarchy paid more careful attention to

---

[75] "Les aspirations des moins de vingt-cinq ans: La jeunesse ecclésiastique," in *Excelsior* (Nov. 24, 1933).

[76] R. d'Ouince, "Les réformateurs de l'Eglise," in *Etudes* 251 (Nov. 1946), p. 149.

the demands and interests of the periphery. Likewise, we have never seen in the church a reformist movement more respectful of the requirements for communion and for the prerogatives of the central powers. Perhaps never has a reform movement developed with this degree of attachment to and of filial confidence in the church, hoping to be of better service to Christ. Today's reformist movement is much more the result of the church's purity rather than its impurity. The picture of the church today is beautiful and comforting.

But my optimism about the future of the present reform movement has another motive, likewise taken from what we have learned from history and theology. This present-day reform situates itself at the point where the church traditionally is disposed to welcome it—on the pastoral level, where it is apostolic and missionary, and in the order of charity. Certainly thinkers and theologians (among others) are active in the present movement. On the condition that they are submissive and that they become disciples, their participation is a blessing. However, the present reform is clearly the fruit of a deep Christian consciousness coming to grips with human reality and with the apostolic needs of the present. It is not about intellectual or aesthetic exercises, nor is it concerned about some false notion that the church might have mistaken the faith and that it might be necessary to lead it dogmatically back to the Gospel.

Today's reform arises from apostolic concerns and from the desire for an effective witness that priests and laity ask for on one point or another, concerning the renewal of worship, the methods of Christian education, the inclusion of the laity as active members of the church, the formation of the clergy, the apostolic life of parishes, and even perhaps the administrative style of the church. As a result, this great movement of reform within many different sites within the church is less critical than constructive and religious. It possesses *everything* needed to be genuinely a movement of the church, a reform of the church, and one of the most fruitful moments ever given to the church to live.

If this movement knows how to respect the conditions I have attempted to analyze here, I have confidence that the hierarchy's approval and blessing will not be lacking. The Spirit will recognize the Spirit at work.

2. *The Problem of a Divided Spirit among Catholics*

A real and difficult issue still remains. It is very important that we pay attention. Paying attention and recognizing the problem is an indispensable condition for solving it—and goes halfway to finding a solution perhaps. Here is the problem: In France, there won't be a schism in the church; the people adhere to their bishops (according to St. Cyprian's formula), and everybody remains solidly in communion with the Apostolic See of Rome. But merely a glance at the map of world Catholicism raises a question. Isn't there a gap between the intellectual and spiritual perspectives of the different churches of the world? How can these different churches be kept in a communion that is not only about faith, sacraments, and the hierarchical backbone of the church (that is, about church structure), but also genuinely about Christian life and all that it implies about human warmth, reciprocity, and a concrete and active mutual sympathy?

On the one hand, the different local Christendoms have neither the same conditions of life nor the same problems—nor are they positioned at the same point of historical development. Certain areas of Flanders, French Canada, or Holland experience a kind of Christendom that still exists in only some scattered areas of France. Irish Christendom (or Christendoms formed by Irish influence) base their pastoral work upon principles that would not work in France. Finally, we know that the glorious and fervent Spanish Christendom at our threshold regards with uneasiness some of our ways of thinking and acting, while we would not be able to share their way of doing things . . . On the other hand, even inside the same country, the differences that exist between groups, with respect to their way of thinking about Catholic activities and their attitude toward the modern world, threaten sometimes to place them in opposition to one another to such a degree that cordial cooperation is just not possible. Msgr. Gröber, the archbishop of Freiburg-im-Breisgau, began his alarmist memorandum of 1943 by denouncing as dangerous "this notorious polarization within the clergy of the great German nation."[77]

This problem is certainly a deep concern. We owe it to ourselves, at the end of a book that is favorable to a healthy reform movement in the church, at least to sketch a principle for solving the problem.

Whether it is a question of different groups of the faithful within one same Christendom, or different Christendoms within one same church, the way to avoid schism always comes back to the clear formula of Cajetan, namely, to live and act as a part of the whole (*agere ut pars*).

The real communion between Christendoms within the bosom of one same church presupposes that the Catholics of one region do not consider themselves as representing the very norm of Catholicism itself, or abso-

---

[77] Text in *La Pensée catholique*, 7 (1948), p. 64.

lute truth. On the contrary, they need to open themselves to the perspectives of others in such a way as to understand their position and to see how they have resolved for the best the problems of fidelity and Christian responsibility in their given historical conditions.

A genuine and cordial communion between the faithful or between spiritual groups within one same Christendom should suppose that the faithful of these groups are not judgmental and critical one of the other, but rather that they are moved to understand the complementarity of their positions. This, for example, is what *La Vie Intellectuelle* recently invited certain French Catholics to do with respect to the question of the meaning of Holy Scripture today.[78]

It must be said, however, that this double task of trying to understand the motives and the situation of others implies certain concrete conditions. This is a truth which is in no way Marxist, but which Marxists have particularly highlighted, namely, the importance of history, the way history works, and the conditions needed for something to become genuinely effective. In the light of this let me make two points:

1) With respect to the communion among Christendoms, it is necessary that the relations between the parties become more active within the totality of Catholic unity. This unity is, thanks be to God, a reality; but it only seldom operates through reciprocity, through mutual service, and relations between the different local Christendoms, and above all the national ones. In fact this unity is realized rather by a relation of all the parts to the center, which is excellent, and should not be diminished. But we need to see that there would be a great enrichment for Catholic life if mutual recognition, reciprocity, and mutual service became freer among the other parts of the church.[79]

2) With respect to an effective and cordial communion between Catholics or groups of Catholics, the following conditions seem necessary: first, within the limits of the faith (overseen and guarded by the bishops), we should have the possibility of explaining and discussing peacefully (without presuppositions) our various opinions without feeling ourselves under the threat of judgment. This threat for some might be to feel themselves misunderstood or judged old-fashioned, while for others it might mean to know that they are considered suspect or that they

---

[78] The issue of December 1949.

[79] See my article, "Rythmes de l'Eglise et du monde," *La Vie Intellectuelle* (Apr. 1946), pp. 6–22.

might be denounced by someone who, certain that his accusation is secret, will not have to bear any consequences.[80] If everything could take place in the light of day, or at least eventually come to light, the atmosphere in the church would clear like the atmosphere of the dog days of summer after a cooling storm. People's faces would relax; their hearts would open wider. However, in fact, in the conditions of the present (1950), some Catholics can barely manage to get together with others simply to talk as the brothers and sisters that they are.

[80] Look at what L. Bouyer said with respect to theological research: "It is one of the principal roles of a review like this to address opinions and to clarify them by mutual confrontation. The craziness of denunciations that afflict theologians at times is unpleasant and irritating, as are the pointless polemics in which mutually contradictory errors are condemned without seeing the complementarity of the positions; but such interactions of thought should be fruitful. The great glory of the medieval universities was their ability to permit and facilitate such interactions. It is greatly to be desired that the major Catholic periodicals inherit this tradition. Without such exchanges that are both critical and serene, it is not clear how theological thinking can avoid either errors or paralysis": "Où en est la théologie du Corps mystique?" in *Revue des sciences religieuses* 22 (1948), pp. 314–315. You can find in Newman more than one passage saying the same thing. But in the present situation, groups are closed in on themselves, each group with its own publications, like Jews and Samaritans, *non coutuntur* [they don't mix with one another].

AFTERWORD (July 1968)

The events of May–June 1968 (which, by the way, kept the proofs for this revised edition inaccessible at the bottom of a postal sack for two months) have to be mentioned in a few pages here after what has already been written. The Paris uprising of 1968 added to the postconciliar situation of the church the uncertainties of a revolutionary climate and the seeming possibility of a worldwide, permanent state of confrontation. In such a climate, things that yesterday appeared certain and solid suddenly seemed outdated or at least uninteresting.

The council was not responsible for either the current problems or the new attitudes. It is unjust and even stupid to attribute to the council the difficulties that we are having today, or even the disquiet and pain about matters of the faith. However, it is true that the council opened up the church to facing problems and that, even before other institutions, it was aware of the transformations going on in the world. The council began to put structures of co-responsibility into place at every level.[1] It also lifted barriers that had restrained freedom of speech and research. Abuses, to the degree that they exist, do not diminish the genuine goodness of this new openness.

Everything is being called into question at the same time: liturgical rites, the classic formulas for the eucharistic presence, the priestly state and priestly celibacy, the heretofore simplistic interpretation of the Scriptures, and other simplistic (but traditional) interpretations of supernatural realities. The discovery of the contemporary world and of humanity's role in the world have become so dominant as to seem sometimes exclusive. The danger of *horizontalism* is not a fantasy! A generation traumatized

---

[1] Cf. Cardinal Suenens, *La coresponsabilité dans l'Eglise d'aujourd'hui* (Desclée de Brouwer, 1968).

by the war in Algeria, by the American adventure in Vietnam, by a pre-occupation with poverty in the world (kept in misery by the overdeveloped countries), by the revolutionary exemplars of persons like Fidel Castro and Che Guevara are calling into question all the structures of our society with a violence such as we have never seen before. The key word for this year 1968 is "protest." Protest [*contestation* in French] is a beautiful word, according to P.-H. Simon, "more concrete and more personal than its proximate homonym 'refusal' [*récusation* in French]. . . . To protest something is to 'refuse' as a form of witness—*testis* (in Latin)—that is, protest embraces a personal conviction, a vital impulse, in such a way that feeling and reason are not separated . . ."[2] But it is a formidable word also, since it risks conveying the idea that *nothing* is acceptable, and so it is becoming the motto for an era of universal and radical unrest.

This wave of protest has evidently reached the church as well, for the church is not made up of people different from those who (some of them) have set up the barricades and occupied the factories. The spectacular forms this wave of protest has taken, fascinating fodder for journalists, cannot disguise the gravity, even the seriousness, of the movement. I see in the violence and the global character of the protest the sign of people's immense need to participate in the creation of values for more personal communities. This could hardly fail to be of interest for the church of Christ and of the apostles. This critical questioning is being addressed to the church as well. For example, some Christian students in the Eighteenth Arondissement of Paris expressed their concern this way:

> Don't Christians in fact participate directly in a bureaucratic and hierarchical system: the church?
>
> How can we fail to protest against this system also?
>
> Where is the administrative participation of laypeople in the running of their church?
>
> Why is there this law of silence that demands, by a so-called obedience, that we be content to simply grumble against established institutions that we no longer understand?
>
> It is time—high time—to go into action and to become engaged and creative in the life of our church.[3]

---

[2] *Le Monde*, July 24, 1968.

[3] A document published in *La Lettre*, 118–119 (June–July 1968), pp. 40–41.

The protest articulated here shows that there is a new impulse and a new character in the reform movement in the church. Genuine church reform can never accept either chaos or anarchy; that would be contrary both to the charity that is the heart of the church and to the ordered structure that was given to the church by the Lord. But, because the church wants to be, and is, open to the healthy reform spirit that John XXIII named *aggiornamento* (updating), the church is invited today to make a greater effort that ought to begin by a search for clear-sighted courage and creativity. For the *aggiornamento* of the council and the reform spirit that this book has examined is something different than an effort of restoration. On this point, I refuse to accept the opposition made by René Pascal between reform and creativity.[4] I have carefully avoided describing a program of reform, but I have sought in this book to clarify the general conditions of a healthy reform movement. In this same spirit, I would like to contextualize and evaluate the new outbreak of protest.

First, a remark is needed. The present demand for the *right* to protest is inseparable from the *motivation* or the *content* of the protest. As the text just cited makes clear, young people are demanding the right to protest about things whose meaning they no longer understand or things that seem to them to be profoundly linked to social structures they reject. On these two counts, they are protesting about what seems to alienate them from themselves. I don't see any possible solution except in accepting to address the problems raised in this way, safeguarding of course for today and for tomorrow a lively awareness of truths and values that are always valid—and doing all this in a spirit of intentional patience. By intentional patience, I mean the behavior of someone who doesn't rush immediately or quickly to conclusions but who recognizes that delays are needed to bring things to maturity. The person who practices this intentional patience will not confuse it with a procrastinating attitude but will work actively with the protesters in a give-and-take of dialogue, with effective mutual trust, to arrive at and develop a mature solution.

There are certain things that the expression of protest can never do in the church: (1) It can never destroy the bond of charity, or act in such a way, or frame issues, so as to wound the bond of mutual love. It can never agree to destroy Catholic unity and thus impede sharing in the breaking of the eucharistic bread.[5] This is not so simple, if we go beyond

---

[4] "One can wonder if the time for reforms is not close to its end and if, for better or worse, the time for re-creation is not about to begin," *Esprit* (Jan. 1968), p. 112.

[5] The possibility that the church will be split in two is not mere fantasy: either because, within the framework of an externally preserved institutional unity, the

idealistic and vague talk, because neither can we agree to emasculate every serious question posed to the church or to render sterile every effective and concrete commitment, or to water down every public stand taken in the name of Christianity . . .; (2) It can never call into question the hierarchical structure of the church's pastoral life, given to us by the Lord's own institution; (3) It can never deny or question in a hasty, superficial, or irresponsible way the articles of doctrine, for which one rather ought to be willing to give one's life; (4) It can never fix parameters for the "limits of fraternity," excluding those who think differently than we do as bad or hopeless, checking them off as useless and impossible; (5) It cannot admit expressions of protest (it seems to me) within the celebration of the liturgy, as, for example, in the homily. That would create for the assembly an insufferable climate of tension and exasperation. Whatever our reactions may be, others have a right to peace and to respect for their positions. There are always other possibilities for making legitimate expressions of protest.

I will accept an expression of protest if it permits everyone to express themselves effectively and to be heard. The conditions set down for the meeting held at Saints Peter and Paul Church in Lille on June 17, 1968, allowed for exchanges and discussion, and were healthy. I only know about this from the press and from reviews of the event.[6] This is a new form of that "freedom of speech in the church" that so many Catholics before the council were asking for; but it is a genuinely new form, since it is more collective, more spontaneous, and more tied to present circumstances. However, this also carries the danger of being more passionate, and of giving greater weight to what makes the stronger impression, with the possibility that things might not be understood in due proportion. I see another example of healthy and constructive criticism in the intervention of the young people in the work of the World Assembly of the World Council of Churches in Uppsala in July 1968.[7]

---

church might really become a community of the Right and of the Left (a bit like the "High" church and the "Low" church in the Anglican Communion)—or because the division might go even further and end in a formal schism. In any case, we should keep in mind the truth of Harvey Cox's remark (*The Secular City*): "The true ecumenical crisis at this moment is not the one that divides the ecclesial life of Catholics from Protestants, but the one that divides traditionalists from progressives in all the churches." The concelebration of 61 Catholics and Protestants on Pentecost 1968 in Paris is an example of what Cox is talking about.

[6] See *Informations catholiques internationales* no. 315 (July 1, 1968), pp. 38–40.

[7] See *Le Monde* (July 21–22, 1968).

For my part, I believe in the value of peace making as seen in the following consideration. When a question is very complex, it can legitimately be addressed from different perspectives and lead to several different conclusions, none of which can claim to completely satisfy all the data involved. It is necessary to admit the possibility of other options and other conclusions than one's own. This requires adjusting the "margin of fellowship," according to the expression of Jean Guéhenno.[8] It is true that not all the options are of equal weight, either with respect to the issues in question or with respect to the Gospel. Some are more insightful, some more attentive to the future, and some more expressive of Gospel values. But those who think differently also have reasons that are weighty for them, and they have to be welcomed and listened to. This is how we can make progress together toward a more holistic and unanimous expression of the truth.

The strongest and most authentic request, among those made during the protests of May 1968, is certainly the demand for fraternal interactions and for the full participation of everyone in those affairs and activities that concern everyone. This demand brought forth an extraordinary phenomenon of communication: people talked to one another, they listened and questioned, since nobody had a ready-made response. By way of sometimes utopian demands (that people knew were such), there was expressed a desire to live as free human beings, to share, and not to be treated (and not to treat others) as objects, but only as responsible subjects. Clearly this wave of concern cannot stop at the doorsteps of our churches.

It shouldn't stop, either; because co-responsibility and sharing belong to the logic of the fraternal communion that belongs to the church at its most profound, according to its origins in the Gospel. The council opened possibilities for this in many ways. It recognized well before others the transformation of the world—and that itself is significant. That was because in the immense and noble nave of Saint Peter's, the council was a fraternal assembly where people spoke of their feelings, leading to a "consciousness-raising" of the majority and to great insight. It is reasonable to expect, then, that from widespread common sharing there will

---

[8] J. Guéhenno, "La Marge de la fraternité," in *Le Figaro* (Jan. 6, 1951): "Let our thoughts be frank; let us expound them with complete precision. Loyalty demands this. Let us give ourselves heart and soul to doing this. This is the expression of our courage. But, just as we leave a margin on every page that we write for editing, corrections and additions, for the truth that we have as yet only hoped to find, so let us leave a margin around the expression of our ideas—a margin of fellowship."

be a multiplication of similar results and progress in the exercise of co-responsibility in the church at every level.

The first condition for making this happen is information. If we look for serious effort on the part of the faithful, then they must be able to understand what the project is, and where it comes from, and where it is supposed to be going. I know of urban districts in the areas around Paris, for example, where the municipal government has succeeded in considerably enhancing cultural goods (schools, for example) that required serious investments covered by the imposition of excise taxes. This could happen because the reasons for the change were well explained and the advantages shown to be reasonable.

Information is a two-way street, however. Despite making substantial progress, the clergy are still insufficiently conscious of the lives, the ideas, the concerns, and the desires of the faithful. I accuse myself of this, first of all. It's not a question of pretending to be a layman or of losing oneself in sociology or journalism. What is needed is the ability to utter a valid pastoral judgment. This is a fact: the laity still complain about not being listened to and about priests being unwilling to dialogue with them. The priests, for their part, say they were not trained to do that. The nondirective interview [meaning *active listening*] is not necessarily always the answer, but it works and it should have its place. Clearly we will have to create or multiply structures for participation. But this doesn't mean a growth of bureaucracy. Such structures will be effective only if they genuinely express a common will for communication.

Nonetheless, this is the church's tradition. When I was preparing my *Lay People in the Church* (1953, 1964), I made a deep study of the tradition and history of the church. I constantly found there the coexistence of a hierarchical principle along with a communitarian framework in virtue of which all parties were invited to take part in the maturation of decisions by way of councils, discussions, and collegial gatherings (in the broad sense of the word). The Second Vatican Council instigated the institution of the Synod of Bishops, presbyteral councils, and pastoral councils. Almost everywhere—Santiago, Utrecht, Rouen, Colombo (Ceylon), etc.—pastoral synods for *aggiornamento* have been participatory assemblies for the whole people of God. The council has reopened, for the sake of a healthy reform, the chapter on the church's conciliar life. The fundamental articles here are a theology of the church as communion and as fraternity.

In this respect, the church has put itself in rather good shape to address this work of *aggiornamento* in one of the most difficult moments of its history, since it finds itself caught up in a rapidly moving transformation of society, joined to a crisis of civilization assailed by a questioning of everything—or almost everything. The developments in this book may seem too timid or too prudent. However, today and tomorrow—as yesterday—I continue to believe with Lacordaire that "time will always be on the side of what is true, just, moderate, and represents genuine virtue"; "moderation is at once what is most rare and what possesses the greatest power."

July 1968

Appendix I:
Collective Responsibility[1]

There are clearly new features in present-day awareness of the problem of collective responsibility. Certainly the great revolutionary crises and ideological struggles that turned into inexcusable wars, first in Spain (1936–1939) and then in the rest of Europe, have shocked our consciences and stirred into action some processes that had been already somewhat at work. St. Paul says we need heresies to test the integrity of true believers. So, might a certain degree of horror and tragedy in the collective dramas of our times be the conditions for progress in moral thinking and the refinement of our conscience?

While progress has not been made in personal moral sensibilities—for individual insights disappear along with those who have discovered them—still, there may be (and I believe that there is) progress in moral thinking. It is slow and limited, but real. Because people are evil, we still practice torturing those who are accused (and sometimes witnesses too), but we don't admit it. Before, it was different—this was both practiced and admitted. We are hardly better than before with respect to justice or human brotherhood, but our ideas have further evolved and are doubtless more refined. So it is not impossible that contemporary consciousness is becoming aware of a range of concerns that could constitute the area of collective responsibility. I think this is exactly what is taking place.

---

[1] A more complete version of this appendix was published in *La Vie Intellectuelle* (March 1950), pp. 259–284; and (April 1950), pp. 387–407. Look at that text for my attempt to analyze the ideas of guilt, collective responsibility, and sanctions. I only retain here what applies immediately to the subject of this book.

This discovery is linked to a twofold awareness of modern thought: first, a sense of the meaning of history, and second, a more realistic, analytical awareness of social realities. These two insights have guided modern thinkers in interpreting society and in explaining what is going on. The linking of these two facts and their systematic exploitation largely explains the attraction of Marxism for certain people. Undeniably, Marxism has done a lot to develop the new understanding of historical and collective responsibility. We can profit from its valid ideas without becoming enmeshed in its conclusions or its postulates. Further, the foundations for my thinking about collective responsibility go far beyond the terrain of Marxist analysis.

History as a knowledge of the past based on the critical investigation of documents was not invented just recently. For example, with respect to ecclesiastical history, who could claim to surpass those giants of erudition of the seventeenth century? However, as strange as this might seem, it is possible to have vast historical knowledge without having the *sense* of history. That is something more than knowing the past; it means knowing about the movement and development of events and their passage through successive stages. Events are not just dates situated in time and space; they emerge from what went before and they have implications for the future. So history is not just the reconstitution of dead events according to places and dates; it is also the attempt to discover the stages that explain its unfolding or development and to understand genetically how things came about and by way of what causes and decisions.

In this respect, popular revolutions, although not unknown in the past, are still characteristic of the modern period. They have given us an exceptionally vivid sense of history and a new kind of maturity for our interpretation of events. Lacordaire was profound in saying: "The eighteenth century was too young for history; it read history like a child, while we, thanks to the revolutions that gave our age maturity, now read it like adults" (Sixth Conference of Toulouse, 1854). Helped by the great growth of historical research, our contemporaries succeed at understanding their own place in the development of history. We possess not only a detailed understanding of events but also a historically grounded grasp of the stages and the crises of the past, so as to be able to analyze the present in a historical context and to be aware of our own situation and eventually of the role we must play in the ongoing unfolding of history. Consequently many of our contemporaries have discovered a sort of historical dimension of consciousness that is also a kind of prophetic dimension, given that prophets grasp the meaning of their times, open up and foresee developments, and so can explain the meaning of an event. We are henceforth alerted to the antecedents and the consequences of our attitudes, not only at the level of personal moral responsibility but also at the level of historical and social realities. Our consciousness that we are living in history and making history is today not only just the privilege of prophets or would-be prophets, of dictators or would-be dictators (how dangerous this awareness was during the Great War!); this awareness of history is commonly shared among all those who follow the developments of their own century.

This is likewise true with regard to our awareness of the social dimension of humanity and of culture. What modern people have discovered here, however, is not something that they invented. The idea that every person becomes himself/herself only in a social group was lived out and admitted quite consciously in antiquity, in the Middle Ages, and in the France of old. In one sense, it is rather the singularity of the person and individualism, which sometimes becomes anarchy, that is the creation of the modern age. In part by reaction against the modern age, in part under the pressure of new socioeconomic conditions (both new and desperately dysfunctional), the nineteenth century discovered in a new way the social dimension of humanity. More exactly, it created a new kind of analysis using new means.

In creating the word *sociology* in 1839,[2] Auguste Comte did more than propose an artificial structure of new sciences. The word would not have gained respect in that case. Rather, *sociology* represents one of those names that became necessary so as to designate a new reality perceived by the human mind. In a similar way, the word *proletariat* arrived around 1817, and *ecumenism*, around 1919. Socialism (another new word that announces a new perspective) and Marxism gave us categories and points of view to analyze social facts. For example, the nouns *class, class warfare, rising class*, etc., correspond to Marxist-socialist perspectives.

Marxism claims to be the most developed example of a philosophy of history taking on a "prophetic" character by trying to explain the genesis of human events. It fails, I think, by reducing all historical explanations to a single element among them; but then this is not the place for a critique of Marxism. But certainly we can no longer think about this question exactly as we did before the rise of Marxism. In a merciless fashion that admits of no exceptions, Marxist ideas convince us that persons are caught up in history by way of a struggle between opposing forces. In the midst of this struggle, refusing to take sides means playing the game of the conservative or reactionary parties. So even without

---

[2] *Cours de philosophie positive*, Lesson 47.

personally making a choice, people, by reason of their situation and their group identity, make a contribution to collective historical forces that have significance and weight. The argumentation used by the judge to prove that Roubashov in Koestler's novel [*Darkness at Noon*] was a traitor and an agent of reactionary politics gives us a romanticized interpretation of what a Marxist would say on the subject. Such a conversation with a Marxist, by the way, could be well worthwhile.

An expression that has become current in recent years captures well the new point of view taken in ideas about morality. People speak about having a "good" or "bad" conscience (or true or false consciousness). In other words, besides whatever blame might arise according to conventional morality (specified in the examinations of conscience familiar to our parishioners), people are also accountable for the attitudes, behaviors, or omissions that derive from their solidarity with groups that they blindly accept or at least don't disavow. In this way, many among us have been made to feel responsible not only for what we have personally done or failed to do but also for a state of affairs or for events that effectively have a social character. That is why we have also seen in recent years acts of withdrawal in order to express a refusal of solidarity with the state of affairs that someone imagines to be contrary to the truth and integrity of human life. How many bourgeois youth—aristocrats even— and sometimes younger clergy as well have withdrawn from their environment in a way similar to persons gripped by the absolute transcendence of God who, from the beginning of Christianity, have refused to cooperate with a corrupt world. The fact that many of these gestures can be criticized, that sometimes generous people have in this way established a new solidarity with structures that are hardly more authentic than what they left behind, in no way changes the facts and their clear significance. These are examples of a new domain of responsibility previously little explored.

Of course, we have always had the obligation not to participate in injustice or to profit from an injustice that we have committed. Père Conrad, the spiritual director of St. Elizabeth, Princess of Thuringia, directed her not to eat anything or to clothe herself with anything that could possibly be tainted by some suspicion of injustice. The very expression, "good conscience," is imported into the text that tells us this anecdote.[3] Gestures of this kind have occurred throughout Christian history

---

[3] I cited this text in an article on St. Elizabeth in *La Vie Spirituelle* (Jan. 1932), p. 71. I am including some passages here because it is quite remarkable: "Magister Cunradus praecepit ei ne uteretur bonis mariti sui de quibus non haberet sanam conscien-

down to the present. But they remained in the realm of a purely personal choice. They did not express responsibility for a state of affairs or a desire for integrity with respect to our collective solidarity with the group— even when a group has an historical impact.

In this domain now open to a new sense of responsibility, contemporary consciousness weighs events by linking historical and social meaning. Think of how binoculars suddenly allow us to perceive the details of the objects we examine. Here is the domain of what I called historical failings and collective faults. Responsibility falls not so much upon a personal failing of mine as upon a distortion in a state of affairs or upon an historical event caused by forces in which I am implicated. Everyone has to face this in their own life.

Certainly, at this level, this kind of dynamic largely escapes our attention. In truth, except for several thousand individual Germans, no German citizen desired Auschwitz or chose to liquidate entire populations. The young Captain De Mun, who one day in 1871 heard himself described by a communard: "The insurgents—they are you!" had neither chosen nor desired the unjust and oppressive state of affairs against which he would soon decide to fight. Here responsibility is, at most, de-subjectified, if we can use such a word. Responsibility is not grasped at the level of the conscious personal intentions of this or that person, with the exception perhaps of some who are genuine moral monsters. Rather, responsibility is grasped in the wretched outcomes seen in the facts. However, the actual responsible subject is a collectivity, or even an ensemble of collective realities, whose existence and activity call into question a host of factors that are extremely complex.

If we systematized this in a linear fashion, we would discover an idea that is today at the border of the new awareness of historical and collective responsibility (a border that actually belongs to a new way of thinking). The moral qualities, goodness and malice, are no longer situated in the acting subject, but rather in impersonal objective realities. We pass here from a morality of intentions (of integrity of consciences) to a morality

---

tiam, quod ipsa stricte observabat, adeo ut ipsa sedens in latere mariti in mensa abstineret ab omnibus quae de officiis et quaestu officiatorum proveniebant, non utens cibis nisi sciret de reditibus et justis bonis mariti provenisse . . . Qui [Cunradus] etiam inhibuerat ei ne bonis quorumlibet aliorum uteretur, de quorum bonis laesam haberet conscientiam . . ." (*Dicta quatuor ancillarum*, ed. A. Huyskens, p. 813). St. Nicholas of Flue left the world in part to avoid being in solidarity with a sentence that he considered unjust (he was a judge): G. Méautis, *Nicolas de Flue* (Neuchâtel, 1940), pp. 33f.

of results. That means a morality concerned with the causation and the efficacy of actions considered in their materiality as acts with regard to an end which would only be the immanent finality of history—the meaning of the evolution of events.

Evidently dialectical materialism is bound to see things in this way. Its character as materialism consists precisely in the fact that it denies the dimension of an idea or a spirit antecedent to the phenomenon of the world. Thus there is here no morality based on a transcendent law given by some spirit who gave order to the cosmos, but only a morality of *results* evaluated with reference to the world's evolution. One of the difficulties with this position (to say nothing of the metaphysical problem implied by the denial of God) is its failure to give evolution a normative and transcendent character, and to retain only its purely factual character as a "result" of events. As a matter of fact, however, Marxism has frequently been criticized for reintroducing an ethical or evaluative point of view that goes beyond pure facts. Once again, my purpose here is not a critique of Marxism. These few observations were needed to set up the boundary line that I don't want to cross or adopt, namely, that of a morality of "results," de-subjectified and transposed from the domain of intentions to that of effectiveness.

Traditional morality offers resources for thinking through the problem of collective responsibility and social-historical failings that I won't treat here in detail (cf. above, p. 349, n. 1), but that provided an overall orientation.

Properly speaking, guilt is strictly personal. It becomes manifest in individual "objective" expressions of guilt in particular physical persons, that is, imputable to these individuals. I don't like the position in morality that talks about common faults, that is, faults of the community as such. Seen that way, the community is the subject of rights and duties in terms of which individuals have title by being members of the community.[4] This way of treating the individual seems to me to push too far the realism of the social unity. It presupposes an organic unity and solidarity among the members of the group that is quasi-biological. This doubtless works in primitive societies living in the context of small natural groups.

---

[4] According to the reviews, this would be the position of Prof. R. Egenter, "Gemeinschuld oder Strafhaftung," in *Aus der Theologie der Zeit*, a publication of the Catholic Faculty of Munich (Ratisbon, 1948). Egenter argues from the case of Adam. But Adam's case is altogether exceptional, linked to his position as the head of the human race and a positive divine will to offer him grace.

It works better for families than for clans, better for clans than for tribes.[5] But a society is not an entity endowed with its own knowledge and freedom. Responsibility and especially guilt have to be traced to faults of commission or omission performed by physical persons. However, among these persons, some are more directly responsible than others. They, acting as representatives of the group or in the name of a collectivity, involve the ordinary members of the group in some kind of responsibility.

Guilt falls individually on all those whose choice is involved in reprehensible acts. In principle, it is possible to say who is involved and to what degree. Even if that is not possible, this question of principle still doesn't change. Guilt is evidently diverse and of different degrees. It can be attributed first to the individual faults of those who act directly in the crime. Among them, guilt falls first of all and most seriously upon those who ordered the crime, and then less gravely upon those who carried it out. At the level of morality, as at the level of penal or social codes, some of the latter can even be more or less excused. All normal human jurisdictions[6] recognize attenuating circumstances like ignorance, constraint, passion, etc.

Guilt is attributed, in the second degree, to the individual faults of those who encouraged or aided the wrongdoers of the first degree by their moral consent, their financial or political support, or indeed simply their weakness in failing to oppose the crime or its agents and to denounce any solidarity with them. The responsibility to do this (at the level of morality and guilt) is real; it is rooted in social solidarity, but it is different and more serious than simple material solidarity. Material solidarity in itself represents only a fact—people are implicated in the

---

[5] This system of collective responsibility is very clear in Celtic society before Christianity, based on unity through bloodlines: cf. J. Chevalier, *Essai sur la formation de la nationalité et les réveils religieux au pays de Galles des origines à la fin du VIe siècle* (Lyons-Paris, 1923), pp. 115f., 149–150. Christianity eliminated this concept, ibid., p. 366. Cf. also *Journal of Religion* (Jan. 1944), p. 22, the same article shows (p. 21) that in Israel the whole life of the people was dominated by the covenant, the very principle for Israel's existence as *God's* people. Every sin that broke the covenant attacked the link that united Israel to God, and so justified the replacement of election with rejection.

[6] I say "normal" to eliminate military jurisdictions which admit only material facts and take neither intentions nor attenuating circumstances into consideration. Fundamentally the Marxist idea of a morality based on efficacy, which is extended and made concrete in the revolutionary justice of popular tribunals, is linked to the idea of class warfare and to a warlike view of existence.

consequences of a defeat as they are in an epidemic, just as they are included in enjoying the fruits of victory.

That suffices to show that those who are not culpable still have to put up with their share of pain.[7] But that is not a moral quality. In the area of moral responsibility, some kind of solidarity had to have existed requiring at least a minimum of knowledge and power. From the moment people know about an act and can do something about it, they become complicit to some degree in the wrong which they do nothing to forestall. St. Augustine said as much with a clarity that leaves nothing to be desired,[8] and Péguy's Joan of Arc was overwhelmed, in her charity, by the feeling that "accomplice means author: someone who lets things happen is like the one who really does it. It is one reality. It goes together."[9] Regarding the events in Poland in 1863, Père Gratry said that Europe, in letting these events occur without protesting them, was in a state of mortal sin.

Everything depends upon the degree of knowledge and power that each person may have. Clearly in Nazi Germany, someone like Barth or Guardini had other possibilities and so other responsibilities than those who were merely underlings. It must be recognized that in complex situations people often don't have much information, or only slowly and sometimes too late come to understand the exact circumstances that allow them to envisage the consequences. Finally, espousing one or another position may lead a person to support unfortunate causes or other evils . . . And can we even suppose that it is possible to really know what is actually going on or what can be done? How can we oppose a crushing social pressure or a police state? What can we do to avoid solidarity with injustice without falling into greater injustices, to avoid evil (even limited evil) and even great malice? It is not always clear.

---

[7] In this sense, they are deprived of goods they would have enjoyed if those from whom or with whom they ought to have received them had not been justly deprived of them. So the children of a guilty man suffer when his goods have been taken away by confiscation or fines. When these sanctions are undergone because of real solidarity, they do not have a character of *punishment* properly so-called for the non-guilty.

[8] *The City of God*, bk. I, ch. 9 (PL 41:22): ". . . Too often we neglect to instruct or to warn [those who do evil], either because we don't dare to affront them, or because we want to avoid their dislike; because of fear of having troubles and undergoing loss of the temporal goods that our greed still desires or that our weakness dreads to lose . . ." This whole passage defines perfectly complicity because of weakness.

[9] *Le mystère de la charité de Jeanne d'Arc* (*Oeuvres completes poétiques*, Pléiade ed.), p. 57.

Think, for example, of any national war and the acts of violence that accompany it. How can we form a judgment about what to do, after seriously trying to know and understand and asking a dozen reputable, well-informed experts, and still finding ourselves faced with *pro* and *con* opinions that are impossible to resolve? How can we oppose the influence of the military if by doing so we support a political party that we don't approve of? . . . These are only some of the hundreds of questions that could be explored.

Doubtless, responsibility is attenuated by the difficulty of knowing or foreseeing consequences, in this way limiting our ability to do something. Nevertheless, we can always do *something*: help create public opinion, support it, or do something that breaks our solidarity with evil. We can make a symbolic gesture. We can't afford to ignore our guilty conscience too easily. Difficulties do not excuse weakness or laxity. This is where our "examinations of conscience" are generally silent, even though these are areas of real moral responsibility.

This is the perspective for raising the problem of collective responsibility and social-historical failings within the church's historical record—the element that directly concerns us here.

We can imagine the responsibility of Catholics in some of the great tragedies of history from a historical viewpoint. For example, we can wonder what their role was in the schism of the eleventh century and the ruptures of the sixteenth century, or in the massacre of St. Bartholomew's Day . . . The answer comes from a good critical understanding of the facts, from a sufficient and detailed historical method, and finally from wise and penetrating judgment about extremely complex matters. We find this in works like Dvornik's work on Photius or Lortz's study of Luther. Representative of the current self-criticism, the clarification of attitudes, and the growing awareness of the social-historical dimension of humanity, contemporary historical science is more and more engaged in this kind of research. We can expect the outcome of a quieting of passions and a genuine liberation from the poisonous effects of polemic and chauvinism. (Cf. my preface to *Photius* by Dvornik [1950] and my "Luther vu par les catholiques," in *Rev. des Sc. ph. th.* 34 [1950], pp. 507–518, reprinted in *Chrétiens en dialogue* [Paris, 1964], pp. 437–462.)

We can imagine this question from two points of view: *prudential* and *pastoral*. We might wonder if research or admissions like this might risk shaking the confidence of the faithful or encouraging religious indifferentism leading to a sort of neopaganism. Can we really be prudent in sharing with the whole world writings of self-criticism or self-accusation? Is the current interest in this kind of information really healthy?

Let's take this question from a spiritual viewpoint. It seems genuinely important. Either from the consideration of the action of the Holy Spirit within us (which first of all *convicts us of sin*), or from the consideration of the authenticity of our moral and Christian attitudes, this authenticity will never be attained without recognizing and admitting our guilt. Further, there is the consideration of needing to admit our guilt in order to obtain the spiritual fruit of peace and reconciliation. Reconciliation among Christians, which is their special vocation in the twentieth century, is similar to restoration of peace and communion among peoples. People have taken up the problem of the reunion among Christians in one church not only with their minds and with accurate information but also with their hearts and souls, with their prayer (on their knees). They all understand that only a conviction, an acknowledgment and a forgiveness of faults that we've committed against each other in the days of schism, will make it possible for the Spirit of unity to accomplish this work.

Still, from a spiritual point of view, we have to insist again on the seriousness of what is at stake. In several self-critical writings in recent years that have become public, this serious feeling of collective responsibility is not always evident. Rather, there seems to be a kind of iconoclastic glee like that of an adolescent who has discovered that his more adult voice requires him to slay idols and put down his teachers. Others express themselves in such a way as to cause us to doubt their seriousness. Genuine repentance sounds different. Its serious tone keeps it from being a stunt. In a case like that, the conviction and the avowal of repentance lacks seriousness if it is not truly in solidarity with those who are troubled and if the author does not also suffer from the evil that is being denounced. Let me import into the context of the church and into Christian categories a remarkable text by Saint-Exupery which has the power of lines written in blood:

> Since I belong to them, I can never deny my own whatever they do;
> I will never speak against them before others. If it is possible to
> defend them, I will defend them. If they cover me with shame, I will

hide my shame in my heart and keep silence. Whatever I come to think about them, I will never testify against them . . . So I will never break my solidarity even because of a defeat that often will humiliate me. I belong to France. France made the Renoirs, the Pascals, the Pasteurs, the Guillaumets, the Hochedés. It also made those who are hopeless, those who are politicians and tricksters. But it would be too easy for me to claim solidarity with the noble ones and deny all relationship to the others . . . If I accept being humiliated by my household, I can do something about my household. It belongs to me, as I belong to it. But if I refuse its humiliation, my household may be completely destroyed at will, and I will be alone, maybe personally glorious, but more useless than a dead man.[10]

Don't these lines illustrate well those places in the present study where the genuinely Catholic reformer has appeared to us as someone who never despairs of "saving the church through the church," and who will never accept or consider it as other than the family household?

The question of collective responsibility can be addressed from the point of view of ecclesiology, that is, a theology *de Ecclesia*. The distinctions proposed above (first part, ch. 1) seem apt for clearing up the problem, which is not so difficult once we examine it clearly.

As we said, there is a way in which the faithful (including churchmen) make up the church: this is its aspect of community and of a people, a people that ought to be the people of God and that have all the objective means to be so, but who sometimes act, in one or another part of the church, like the people of Mammon, the people of Venus, the people of Jupiter—giving into temptations to money, the flesh, power, and pride. We know that the history of the church is full of failings of this kind, and we can categorize them in useful ways. We have done all that; no need to return. But let's try here to sort out the aspect of collective responsibilities that are incurred.

The church, empirically considered as a people or community, lives according to laws (*positis ponendis*—making necessary distinctions) analogous to those of any other community. In moments of great tragedy, in times of failure where a complex collective responsibility comes into play, there are those responsible in the first degree and those responsible in the second (by way of a solidarity that has not been disavowed, by way of laxity or connivance). In the church more than in other societies, there is a connection between a state of affairs lacking integrity and great

---

[10] *Pilote de guerre* (1942), pp. 209–210.

tragedy. Perhaps we could even say that the tragedies are materially the product of the long maturation of inveterate misdeeds taken for granted as a state of affairs in moral standards. This means pastoral morals above all, including devotions, the quality of preaching or its absence, theological doctrines, etc. In sum, we are talking about what we have recognized both as a genuine area for reform as well as an area of the most ordinary kind of collective responsibility. Let me make this more concrete by rapidly referring to three or four examples drawn from history (and what a history!).

In what is known as the "Eastern Schism," there are evidently faults on both sides. We only have to think of those of the Patriarch Cerularius, which were enormous, or those of Cardinal Humbert, whose rigidity and impatience led him to act beyond the powers he had received from the pope. But it is not at this level that we find the true causes and responsibilities that are the most decisive. To discover those, we have to go back to the slow and complex process by which the East and the West, the two sides of the Christian body, became progressively distanced from one another and ended finally by accepting an "estrangement." The genuine schism is in accepting this. From that it becomes clear not only that the responsibilities for the schism had been collective, not only that churchmen were responsible even before the schism was formally consummated, but that we Christians of the twentieth century continue to commit this schism to the degree that we accept the "estrangement" caused by it and remain in solidarity with attitudes that were responsible for the estrangement.

In this respect, collective responsibility spans the whole of history. Didn't St. Paul say that those who fall after having tasted the word of God crucify the Son of God once again? (Heb 6:6). To be in solidarity with a state of affairs or a system that tends toward evil is to consent to it. Luther said he felt responsible for the deaths of John Hus and of Wycliffe by being part of the papal and monastic system that were the true authors of those deaths. Luther cried out at that time: "John Hus was burned unjustly."[11] Luther judged according to bad doctrinal criteria, but if we abstract from his thinking, his feeling was correct. We have to make better applications of it. We would discover on our hands perhaps some traces of blood that we might have thought long ago washed away. Each time that we accept the "liquidation" of those who don't think as we do, we give consent to St. Bartholomew's Day; when we fail to clearly

---

[11] Sermon of 1529, Weimar, XXIX, pp. 49f.

denounce the use of constraint to force consciences, we cooperate in the use of violent dragoons. Further, note this as well: it is not just a sin of *thinking*—we lend power to a system, we contribute to the system's existence and activities. It may be an indirect and rather distant cooperation but one which is not entirely negative in nature.

Möhler thought that schisms and heresies were the responsibility of earlier generations.[12] How true that is, and how especially true it is in the case of the Protestant Reformation! More than one churchman at that time[13] and more than one Catholic historian today[14] have pointed out the responsibilities of Catholics for the great divisions of the sixteenth century. Vatican II also recognized them (Decree on Ecumenism, no. 3), and Paul VI more than once expressed his desire for mutual forgiveness.

But, it is important to see how these are the responsibilities of more than some several thousand individuals whose actions can be described. Responsibility falls as well upon a state of affairs which endured, without any serious corrective, over three centuries in the three areas of pastoral administration, piety, and theology. For more than two centuries, voices had cried out for the reform of the church "in head and members," the head meaning the Roman Curia with its system of finances and benefices entailed in the nomination for every high office. For an even longer time (representing a continuity that recent research has brought to light and that has impressed me deeply), people living unfortunately on the fringes of orthodoxy and even beyond it cried out against the temporal character of the church, its riches, and the secular power of prelates. This was a state of affairs going back (at least in the thought of the time) to the Donation of Constantine to Pope Sylvester. They were wrong to mix so many different ideas together (some seriously erroneous but some not altogether foolish). But was the church right to refuse to listen (for that is what it did) to this questioning of its temporal involvements that it did not finally let go of until forced to do so by the ravages of history?

---

[12] *Die Einheit in der Kirche*, § 6, according to the two editions that I have; cf. R. Geiselmann, *J. A. Möhler: Die Einheit der Kirche und die Wiedervereinigung der Konfessionen* (Vienna, 1940), p. 49.

[13] Cf. the texts cited above, pp. 77f.

[14] To cite only the most recent, cf. J. Lortz, *Die Reformation in Deutschland, passim; Die Reformation als religiöses Anliegen* (Trier, 1948), pp. 99–105; K. Adam, *Una Sancta in katholischer Sicht* (Dusseldorf, 1948), p. 32 (French trans., *Vers l'unité chrétienne* [Paris, 1949], p. 42). Other references in U. Valeske, *Die Stunde ist da: Zum Gespräch zwischen den Konfessionen* (Stuttgart, 1948), pp. 43, 75.

Everything points to Luther's protests having been occasioned by religion being overwhelmed by practices (cf. pp. 139 and 161). It is not possible here, even in the simplest way, to sketch out a history of devotions as links to the causes of the Reformation. But keep in mind only one little fact. All through the fourteenth and fifteenth centuries, the story was told that St. Francis, on his feast day, came to free from purgatory the souls of those who had worn the habit of his Order or his Third Order.[15] Similar things had been said about the Virgin Mary and other saints. Ecclesiastical authorities knew this was being preached. The Franciscans collectively, and to some degree the entire church, especially the major figures (bishops and theologians), were complicit in tolerating this, if not in propagating the legend. They were also complicit in profiting from it, for they did profit . . . It is but one detail, I know; but we shouldn't too quickly pass over it in saying that it is of little importance, for there are thousands of others just like it, the collective impact of which is undeniable.

There were hundreds, thousands of false relics that provided the livelihood for hundreds of shrines. Just read the list made in 1509 of the relics venerated in the chapel of the Castle of Wittenberg (since that takes us to a high place of the Reformation). The list contains 5,005 small pieces of bone, the majority claiming to come from the great figures of the Bible, but in fact only ten of them at most had the least chance of being authentic.[16] Of course it would be unwise and unjust to reduce religious life at the end of the fifteenth century to these examples, but I am saying there was a system of religious practices that represented on the whole a state of affairs in which the responsibility of the major figures among the clerics was seriously compromised. Luther was not the first to speak about this, but no one wanted to listen because "received ideas" are easier to live with than *"ressourcement"* and critical questioning. "Let's hang onto our prejudices, they will keep us warm."

A comparable incrimination falls upon theologians. Not only those of the two centuries that preceded (and prepared) the Reformation—Père Clérissac called it "scholasticism gone to seed"—but there was also the Semi-Pelagianism of the Nominalists; and then those theologians that

---

[15] Cf., e.g., L. A. Veit, *Volksfrommes Brauchtum und Kirche im deutschen Mittelalter* (Freiburg-im-Bresigau, 1936), pp. 205f.; J. Hashagen, *Staat und Kirche vor der Reformation* (Essen, 1931), p. 14.

[16] Text found in Mirbt, *Quellen zur Geschichte des Papsttums*, n. 411 (indicates sources and studies).

the reformers found defending the fortress of the church. I know the merits and the genius of some of them. In the past I studied rather seriously the work of Thomas de Vio, called Cardinal Cajetan, who presided at the hearing of Luther at Augsburg in 1518. I have read more than one of the treatises of the Catholic apologists of the period. It is astonishing to acknowledge that these men, although they had been capable of refuting and above all condemning Luther by referring to the received doctrines, had absolutely failed to perceive (doubtless had not even tried to perceive) what deep motivation the Augustinian monk had for his protest. Neither Cajetan, despite his kindly manner in 1518, nor Eck who, writing in 1530, listed the errors of Luther in 404 articles like a professor recording the faults in an examination—neither appreciated Luther's motivation.[16bis]

But even today, who among our reputed theologians has really made this kind of effort? Once again, we find ourselves retrospectively in solidarity with those who were responsible for a tragedy whenever we adopt their attitudes. By contrast, four hundred years later we are called to do what people better and greater than ourselves did not succeed in doing. Carried on their shoulders, perhaps we see further than they. In any case we profit from the lessons of history. I believe that one of the meanings of the actual development of theological thinking is to reconsider the work of the generations that preceded us and that in some way had prepared the great schisms of the eleventh and the sixteenth centuries. Profiting from what we can learn from the dissidents, we are called to create in the holy Catholic Church a state of affairs such that, had this existed rather than what had been allowed to take place, the evil of the schism would doubtless not have happened.

I would have willingly said a bit about the Galileo affair. It teaches us so much, even from the point of view of this appendix. It could be a new example of collective responsibility of churchmen and theologians within a state of affairs and an ensemble of received ideas which were, as sometimes happens, false and had not been critiqued in time. So often, those who don't really know are the ones to criticize and condemn those who do know, because the latter have said things that people aren't used to hearing. We could find there once more how much historical faults cost us dearly, because we bear today the excesses of what happened in the "centuries of faith" and in that ecclesiastical guardianship which had

---

[16bis] See, e.g., E. Iserloh, *Die Eucharistie in der Darstellung des Johannes Eck: Ein Beitrag zur vortridentinischen Theologie* (Munster, 1950), pp. 16–17, 57, 350, etc.

once been beneficial, but which became completely anachronistic and abusive. There would be a great deal to say about all that, but the subject matter would be almost infinite. After this example, others would present themselves.[17] What I have rapidly sketched out here is sufficient to give us an understanding of the tragedies (and the states of affairs pregnant with tragedy) at the level of the historical life of the church, where the faithful and churchmen, each in their own measure, bear genuine collective responsibility.

[17] Among other topics: the way in which the church "lost the working class" in the 19th century—a fact that Pius XI considered a major scandal. There is, however, no scandal without responsibility for it. Who would dare to say that Catholics were not responsible here? —Another example: the collective responsibility of Christians for the ideas that for so long treated "witches" with savagery (cf. A. Adam, *Spannungen und Harmonie*, 2nd ed. (Nuremburg, 1948), pp. 90f. The Catholic Middle Ages had no monopoly on savagery, alas!

Appendix II:
Two Types of Fidelity

It strikes me as useful to deepen and clarify this idea that came up several times in the course of my writing (first part, ch. 2, pp. 126, 155f.; second part, fourth condition). So as not to repeat and further extend a text first written in 1946 and added to in 1949, I propose here some summary reflections on this point.

Fundamentally, although utilizing diverse categories, it is always the same deep structure of things that presents a twofold distinction between its essence and the form in which it is realized and expressed. The essence of the thing is stronger than its form. The essence governs the form and so tries to make it match the essence; the essence attracts the form to itself and guides it. That is why we see, on the one hand, that living things tend to transcend their actual forms in order to realize themselves completely and, on the other hand, that the objects of knowledge are related to the mind like living things, wishing to assimilate themselves by means of the intellectual forms they inspire.[1] In the two cases, the essence attracts the form to itself, governs the form, and invites it to match itself to the essence.

There are all sorts of examples and expressions of this tendency of the form transcending itself so as to be an adequate expression of the essence and to achieve its full truth in this way. Clearly one of the best efforts to translate this reality was Augustine's dialectic between *ea quae sunt*

---

[1] Cf. the text of St. Augustine where Truth says: "*Non me in te mutabis, sed tu mutaberis in me* . . . And you do not change me into you [like the food you eat], but you will be changed into me" (*Confessions*, Book VII, ch. 10, no. 16 [PL 32:742]).

365

(things that are) and *ea quae vere sunt* (things that fully exist) (cf. above, pp. 192f.). Augustine discovered the usefulness of this Johannine distinction, taken from the very heart of God's plan. I apply this schema not so much in the sense of a relationship between transitory things and eternity as in the general sense that I have described: the relation of something to its ultimate truth, the relation of a form realizing its essence in a limited way compared to the fullness of being that this essence can bring about. In the case of living realities, or again in the case of objects in their relation to mind, things seek to achieve their full truth. They move toward a completion that transcends forms that are not identical with their essence.

It is important to note, however, that the substance of the plenitude that is sought for is already found given in the principle. This doesn't mean that everything would have been given in an initial definition and that development would be purely a logical unfolding in the manner of Leibniz and his dictum, "*Omne praedicatum inest subjecto*—every predicate exists in the subject." There are beginnings which are truly beginnings; the development of free spiritual beings in an order of things where freedom is at work is not a linear unfolding where at the end you find something unwrapped that had existed from the point of departure wrapped up or hidden.

Despite appearances, I am not concerned here with a general philosophy of development: I am only thinking about the case of Christianity. Christianity is *given* already in its principle. In its case, it is an ultimate, eschatological reality but one that is anticipated by the coming of its principle into time; it has to develop itself to the point that the principle once implanted in time may attain the fullness for which it was destined. That is why, at least in the case of Christianity, it is true to say that, although it is judged by the "truth" of the fullness to which it aspires, yet that fullness is already there in its principle. Thus the concrete forms in which Christianity realizes itself are themselves judged by this "truth," which is found at the beginning and which, by means of the "truth," is found fully at the end. This explains why the return to the sources (*ressourcement*) is the fundamental energy and the supreme guide of Christian development as well as of the continuing amplification of already achieved forms that things require in order to realize their truth.

This is the perspective in which it seems to me that Catholic fidelity can be thought of on two levels and so in two ways. Fidelity to Christian reality can be a fidelity to the present state of things, to forms presently expressing this reality, that is, a fidelity to what is at present achieved.

It can also be a fidelity to its future development or a fidelity to its principle. The two expressions come to the same thing according to an explanation developed by a historian of the church in *L'Avenir du Christianisme* (A. Dufourcq). If Christian history in one of its fundamental aspects is the development of a principle (the realization of its Principle), then it is less the memory of a dead past than the development of its seminal power and its future.[2] A profound, not shallow, fidelity to this dimension of Christianity is at once a fidelity to principle, to the tradition, and to the future, that is, to what Christianity can and ought to become in order to arrive at the truth given at the beginning, in substance, in its principle.

Catholic (= embracing the whole) fidelity will have to embrace the two aspects: a fidelity to the presently realized form, because this is the concrete present form of existence of Christianity, and also a deeper fidelity embracing its future, thus fully respecting its principle or its tradition. Fundamentally, the kind of dialectic implied by this double fidelity is at the heart of this whole book. I hope to have shown that if, between these two types, there is a tension, there can and ought also to be a communication, indeed a continuity and a harmony between them.

In a more general way, this type of dialectic is at the heart of every problem of development or growth, because such a problem always involves an aspect of transcendence. The missionary function of the church in all the domains where it comes into play—intellectual as well as apostolic, as explained in a number of places in this book—presupposes an eventual transcendence of already achieved limits and forms; it can only be fully exercised if the spirit (that is, the principle) re-creates itself according to the needs brought about by new circumstances and

---

[2] Once again, we can't forget the real quality of human freedom. What I called the dialectic between "what is given and what is done with it" or between the already achieved and the still to be done (cf. ch. 1, p. 90) surrounds these two aspects, both of them essential to Christianity and linked to God's purpose: (1) "*Ipse (Christus) est totum Ecclesiae bonum: nec est aliquod majus ipse et alii quam ipse solus* — He (Christ) is the complete good of the church, and Christ and other things [taken together] are not anything greater than he himself alone" (St. Thomas Aquinas, *Comm. In IV Sentences*, d. 49, q. 4, art. 3, ad 4), cf. John 16:14—"He will take what is mine and declare it to you"; (2) God wants the free cooperation of human beings toward the final result of our cooperating with him to fill up "the fullness of him who fills all in all" (Eph 1:23), thus coming "to the measure of the full stature of Christ" (Eph 4:13). A theology of the proper operations of the Holy Spirit would show that the Spirit returns precisely to accomplish this—that what is of God shall be also fully and *freely* from us as well.

that go beyond what has already been achieved and approved at some given moment. I suggested (p. 155) that ecumenical work properly speaking can eventually make sense for the Catholic theologian only by emphasizing truly traditional and Catholic positions, but positions understood more deeply than they generally have been in confessional polemics. It is not a case of abandoning dogmas or simply dreaming of bringing about reconciliation by reducing everything to simple historical misunderstandings. But it does seem that by each of us going back to our sources, we can together manage to grasp the truth more fully than if we remain tied to those historical forms from which the divisions began and oppositions solidified in a spirit of controversy and triumphalism.

We might apply to this question of development, that is, the question of the truth at its deepest, what Leconte de Noüy said in *L'Homme et sa destinée* (Paris, 1948): The "fact," as the "object" of our intelligence, and the meaning that we give to it depend on the scale of the instrument that measures it. So we might take a short scale, that of the present (of the actual life of the church and of the historic forms that are at present expressed there). Gauged by this measure, some things would appear audacious, novelties; some would even seem impossible, and we would be inclined to exclude and condemn them. Too bad for Galileo if he was judged by a jury that used an insufficient instrument, that of the "received ideas" of his period . . . But we could also take another, longer scale, the scale of history. I'm not talking about a distant history that is unforeseeable, but a certain segment of history on the horizon that is in the process of coming into being.

Look at development as it begins to emerge in the present. When you look at new ideas with such an instrument of measurement, you start talking about "looking at the future," "genial foresight," and "prophetic vision." It would be interesting to study the idea of a "precursor" in this context. A precursor is only judged to be such according to the scale of history; judged by too short a scale in the present, he or she looks like nothing more than a utopian dreamer or a dangerous revolutionary. The case of Theodore Hertzl would be exceptionally appropriate. In 1897 he said he would be understood in fifty years; in 1947 the Jewish state in Palestine declared its independence. In 1897 Hertzl would have been considered a utopian dreamer; in 1947 he was a precursor.

Clearly it is difficult to judge the historical significance of an event from our experience in the present. "Prophets" have that role and privilege, but nothing is more miserable than a false prophet; and by playing at being a precursor, you risk being only a utopian or a troublemaker with false doctrines. Nonetheless we have to recognize the reality of development and to manage the margins in which it can be eventually expressed. That is the challenge for fidelity in depth which, in Christianity, means fidelity to the future by fully respecting fidelity to both tradition and principle. Thanks to that fidelity, the church, maintaining continuity with itself, can experience the amplifications and the transcendence by which it realizes its missionary function, its program of catholicity, growth, and adaptation. What St. Paul said to the Thessalonians was not an easy charge: "Do not quench the Spirit. Do not despise the words of prophets, but test everything; hold fast to what is good" (1 Thess 5:19-21).

That presupposes that while conserving the present achievements of the life of the church and a perfect loyalty to the authority that rules it, we remain open to possible transcendence and developments; that we will know how to criticize our "received ideas" in view of a better fidelity to the tradition; that we will not only be people with solutions but also people who can face up to problems; and that we will not turn away from challenges. This is so, not because we lack fidelity, but because we have learned to exercise a more difficult and deeper fidelity.

I judge it useful to complete my considerations here by reproducing some passages of Péguy to which I already made allusion. They are in no way the source of my own ideas on these topics, but they discuss the topic with an unequaled evocative gift and express thoughts similar to my own. They are taken from his introduction to the *Cahiers de la Quinzaine* (March 1, 1904) and printed in the N. R. F. edition of his *Oeuvres completes* (vol. 12, pp. 186–192). Péguy did not write these lines in the perspective of Christianity or thinking about the church's problems. The words "revolutionary," "revolutionary situation," taken in a material sense, could be dangerously false in our context. But this text fits in here because of its fundamental idea, namely, going back to the sources of a deeper tradition.

> What makes full understanding of a traditional situation powerful is that, transposed into the present, it gathers together the meaning of a present initiative (and of today's life) with the full meaning of humanity in the past, a whole experience of life and action, of feeling, of passion, and of history. Facing that, absolutely nothing is

worth a revolutionary reversal, a false turning back, a political, parliamentary, academic, or literary setback. But on the contrary, an inner call, a call to recognize other deeper human powers, a new and deeper probe of ancient, inexhaustible, and common resources is what counts.

Against a traditional context, fully traditional—against a fully traditional context—nothing, absolutely nothing is worth anything except a fully revolutionary situation; that is, not a situation of transfer of authority or an upheaval against authority that is arbitrary and theoretical, but fundamentally an appeal to a deeper tradition. A revolution is the appeal of a less perfect tradition to a more perfect tradition, an appeal from a less profound tradition to a deeper tradition, a search for the deepest sources—in the literal meaning of the word, a search for resources.

It is not only because they are equally powerful, equally strong, because they have greatness of the same order, that a fully revolutionary situation can confront a fully traditional situation. It is not because they have greatness of the same order; it is something deeper; it is because they have a greatness of the same kind, of the same nature. It is because they constitute operations of the same kind, the same operation at different degrees of depth, and as far as possible to us, growing in depth. A revolution is never truly and fully revolutionary and never succeeds as a revolution unless it attacks with a probing stroke, unless it makes rise up and come forth a humanity that is deeper than the traditional humanity that it opposes and attacks. It is not worthwhile unless it brings forth a humanity that is deeper and more traditional than the existing humanity, the current version, the humanity already well known. It is only worthwhile if it brings about that marvelous renewal, that marvelous refreshment of humanity by deepening it, that gives a spirit of euphoria to genuine revolutionary crises in the midst of all their pain, their misery, and their effort. Fundamentally, a revolution is not a real revolution unless it restores the whole tradition, unless it is a complete preservation of an older tradition that is deeper, truer, more ancient and so more eternal . . .

It is necessary that by the depth of its new, deeper resources, the revolution prove that preceding revolutions were insufficiently revolutionary and that the corresponding traditions were insufficiently traditional and full. It is necessary that by a deeper mental, moral, and emotional intuition it vanquishes the tradition by its own clearer tradition. Far from being a superaugmentation, as is generally believed, a revolution is actually an excavation, a deepening, a transcendence in depth . . .

So a revolution is not the contrary of preserving the tradition. It doesn't oppose or attack preservation as an anticonservatism would, as an act that is contrary but with equal power. A revolution is nothing if it is not the introduction of a new plan, if it does not involve a new perspective, a new viewpoint, a whole new sense of life, if it does not introduce a new social, moral, and mental plan. A revolution is not a revolution unless it is entire, global, total, and absolute.

Appendix III:
His Holiness Paul VI Speaks about the Reform of the Church (From the Encyclical *Ecclesiam Suam*, August 6, 1964)

44. It will be for the Council, naturally, to decide what reforms are to be introduced into the Church's legislation and discipline. The post-conciliar committees, or commissions—especially the Commission for the Revision of Canon Law, which has already been set up—will concern themselves with the task of formulating in concrete terms the recommendations of the Ecumenical Synod. It will be your duty, therefore, Venerable Brethren, to indicate to us what decisions are required for purifying and rejuvenating the Church's image. Let us, for our part, give public expression once again to this resolve of ours to do all we can to sponsor this reform. How often in past centuries has the determination to instigate reforms been associated with the holding of ecumenical councils!

46. First we must lay down a few rules to guide us in the work of reform. Obviously, there can be no question of reforming the essential nature of the Church or its basic and necessary structure. To use the word reform in that context would be to misuse it completely. We cannot brand the holy and beloved Church of God with the mark of infidelity. We must consider our membership in it as one of our greatest blessings. It testifies to our spirit "that we are the children of God" (Rom 8:16).

47. In this context, therefore, when we speak about reform we are not concerned to change things, but to preserve all the more resolutely the characteristic features which Christ has impressed on His Church. Or rather, we are concerned to restore to the Church that ideal of perfection and beauty that corresponds to its original image, and that is at the same time consistent with its necessary, normal and legitimate growth from its original, embryonic form into its present structure [as the seed grows into the full-grown tree].

(Cf. www.vatican.va/holy_father/paul_vi/encyclicals)

Index of Names

Albert the Great, St., 56, 91–92, 200, 271
Ambrose, St., 72, 86, 97, 112, 146, 175
Aquinas, St. Thomas, 10, 32, 42, 82, 95, 96, 128, 151, 185, 188, 297
Augustine, St., 11, 42, 73, 121–122, 123, 146, 185, 192f., 203, 218, 226, 233f., 293, 356, 365

Barth, Karl, 207, 222, 356
Bergson, Henri, 135, 143
Bernard, St., 29, 181, 219, 260, 261, 298
Boniface VIII, 29, 241, 278
Bouyer, Louis, 91, 195, 213, 340

Calvin, John, 91, 98, 144, 203, 206, 209, 270, 272, 325–326
Charles V, 277, 285
Chenu, M.-D., 49, 165–167, 243
Clérissac, Humbert, 137, 180, 189, 282, 362
Couturier, Paul, 116f.
Cyprian, St., 60, 199, 236, 283, 312, 338

Denifle, Heinrich, 29, 202, 217, 271, 286, 311, 331
Dominic, St., 20, 51, 63, 152, 200, 217, 225, 246

Erasmus, 32, 139, 149, 154, 162, 172, 286, 315, 323f., 328–329

Foerster, W., 264, 292f., 305, 317–318,
Francis, St., 51, 190, 200, 202, 217, 219, 225, 246, 253, 323

Galileo, 81, 108, 154, 158, 257, 363, 368
Godin and Daniel, (Abbés), 34, 43, 247
Görres, Ida, 14, 28, 33, 144
Gregory VII, 20, 167, 238, 246, 283
Guéranger, Dom, 159, 238
Guitton, Jean, 52, 143, 265–266, 291, 297

Hadrian VI, 31, 32, 77, 106, 172, 286

Ignatius Loyola, St., 152, 233, 237, 240, 284
Innocent III, 14, 20, 238, 241, 246, 307, 310, 313, 315
Irenaeus, St., 177, 182, 230, 246, 307

John XXIII, xi, xii, 2, 29, 184, 205, 264, 310, 343
Journet, Charles, 76, 82, 104, 115, 178, 180, 184, 189, 205–208

374

Index of Subjects

Modernism, 11, 37, 158, 165, 220, 264, 275, 292, 300, 302
Mystici Corporis, 80, 86, 97–98, 111

Orthodox (Church), 79, 110, 273, 318
Oxford Movement, 220, 224, 253

Pharisaism, 133, 135f., 191
prophet(s), prophecy, 172f., 215f., 292

reform (reformism), 13, 16–17, 19f., 117f., 268, 309f.
Reformation, 30, 244, 361
religious orders, 251f.
ressourcement, 39f., 295, 366

sacrifice, 120f., 174, 193
scholasticism, 10, 137, 144, 151, 222, 362

self-criticism, 22, 25, 29, 33, 36f.
sentire cum ecclesia, 236, 312
Spouse (church), 16, 69, 72f., 79, 87, 94, 100
state of affairs, 161f., 169f., 202, 215, 257, 268, 352, 360
Syllabus (of errors), 257, 301
synagogue, 126, 133, 147f., 183

tradition, 294f., 304, 346
"twice-born," 169f., 184, 215, 292
Two Powers, 4

Vatican I, 33, 288
Vatican II, 3, 80–81, 91, 179, 262, 361
via facti, 277f., 280

Young Christian Workers/Students, 21, 43, 224, 247, 251